DR. J. B. ALEXANDER.

The History of Mecklenburg County

North Carolina

from 1740 to 1900

J. B. Alexander, M.D.
Charlotte, North Carolina

HERITAGE BOOKS
2008

HERITAGE BOOKS
AN IMPRINT OF HERITAGE BOOKS, INC.

Books, CDs, and more—Worldwide

For our listing of thousands of titles see our website
at
www.HeritageBooks.com

A Facsimile Reprint
Published 2008 by
HERITAGE BOOKS, INC.
Publishing Division
100 Railroad Ave. #104
Westminster, Maryland 21157

Copyright © 1902 J. B. Alexander, M.D.

Index Copyright © 1996 Heritage Books, Inc.

— Publisher's Notice —
In reprints such as this, it is often not possible to remove blemishes from the original. We feel the contents of this book warrant its reissue despite these blemishes and hope you will agree and read it with pleasure.

International Standard Book Numbers
Paperbound: 978-0-7884-0469-6
Clothbound: 978-0-7884-7511-5

Index to Illustrations.

The Author	*Frontispiece*
Map of the County....................	*Page* 1
Dr. D. T. Caldwell...................	70
Margaret Alexander Lowrie............	135
Samuel J. Lowrie, Esq................	136
Capt. John Walker....................	137
James Davis	139
Dr. Isaac Wilson.....................	149
William Maxwell	152
Dr. Samuel B. Watson.................	156
Robert Davidson Alexander............	159
Adam Brevard Davidson................	164
W. F. Phifer.........................	168
Col. Zeb Morris......................	172
Gen. W. H. Neal......................	175
Brawley Oates	177
Dr. David R. Dunlap..................	178
Rev. W. W. Pharr, D. D...............	180
Dr. W. A. Ardrey.....................	182
Lieut. Gen. D. H. Hill...............	186
Dr. Robert Gibbon....................	190
Maj. Jennings B. Kerr................	195
Gen. Rufus Barringer.................	197
Senator Z. B. Vance..................	209
Hon. James W. Osborne................	231
Rev. A. W. Miller, D. D..............	258
Mecklenburg County Court House.......	376

Index.

Preface ....Page	3
Early Settlement	9
Early Recollections of Charlotte..............	12
May 20, 1775............................	25
Martin's Historical Account of the Declaration of Independence...................	28
Prominent Men who Took an Active Part..	33
The Celebration of May 20, 1775, in the Year 1825	42
A Historical Fact Not Generally Known.......	47
Troops Furnished for the War of 1812-14......	52
Members of General Assembly from 1777 to 1902, Inclusive, and Time of Service..............	58
County Officers and Time of Service..........	61
Rev. Alexander Craighead....................	66
Dr. D. T. Caldwell.........................	71
Lives and Peculiarities of Some of the Signers..	73
Some of the Bar One Hundred Years Ago....	91
President James Knox Polk..................	95
William Davidson	97
Gov. Nathaniel Alexander	98
Maj. Green W. Caldwell.....................	99
The Opinion of the Ladies...................	100
Matthew Wallace and George Wallace.........	101
Adam Alexander	104
Humphrey Hunter	107
Hopewell Church and Graveyard.............	115
The Part Mecklenburg Took in Mexican War...	118
Banks and Banking.........................	119
Some of the Prominent Citizens in the First Half of the Nineteenth Century..................	120
The Champions of the County...............	123
Blind Dick	124
Negroes Before the War Between the States....	125

INDEX.

State Laws Before the War in 1865 .... *Page*	129
Biographical Sketches	131
The Central Hotel..........................	194
The Charlotte Hotel........................	195
Rufus Barringer, of Cabarrus and Mecklenburg..	197
The Great Commoner, Z. B. Vance............	209
Calvin Eli Grier............................	222
Matthew Wallace and Family.................	225
Capt. John Randolph Erwin..................	227
Hon. James W. Osborne.....................	231
Rev. John Hunter...........................	234
The Hunter Family.........................	235
The Descendants of Some of the Famous Men who Fought in the Revolutionary War......	237
Many Men Who Sustained a Splendid Reputation as Ministers of the Gospel in the Various Years of the Nineteenth Century...................	
Rev. John McCamie Wilson, D. D.........	252
Rev. A. W. Miller, D. D.................	258
Two Church Sessions Act as a Unit............	261
Methodists in the County....................	264
Roman Catholic Church.....................	271
The Associate Reformed Presbyterians.........	272
The Lutheran Church.......................	276
The Baptist Denomination...................	277
The Rock Springs Burying Ground............	279
Sugar Creek Church........................	281
Steele Creek Church........................	286
Providence Church	291
Flowers Now and One Hundred Years Ago.....	295
The Old Four-Horse Stage...................	297
Lee Dunlap Kills James Gleason..............	299
Mint Built in 1836.........................	302
The Two Town Pumps......................	303
Public Works in Charlotte Fifty Years Ago....	304
Changes in Mecklenburg in the Last Century....	308
Healthfulness of Mecklenburg................	311

Snow on the 15th of April, 1849..............*Page*	313
Aurora Borealis as Seen in October, 1865.......	314
Stars Fell in the Fall of 1833..................	315
The Passing of an Aerolite From West to East..	316
Earthquake Shocks in 1886.....................	317
Progress	320
Gentlemen and Ladies Before the Civil War.....	323
Patrol in Slavery Times.......................	329
Roster of Confederate Troops..................	333
Reconstruction Times in Mecklenburg	361
Last Chapter of Mecklenburg History.........	370
Appendix	385

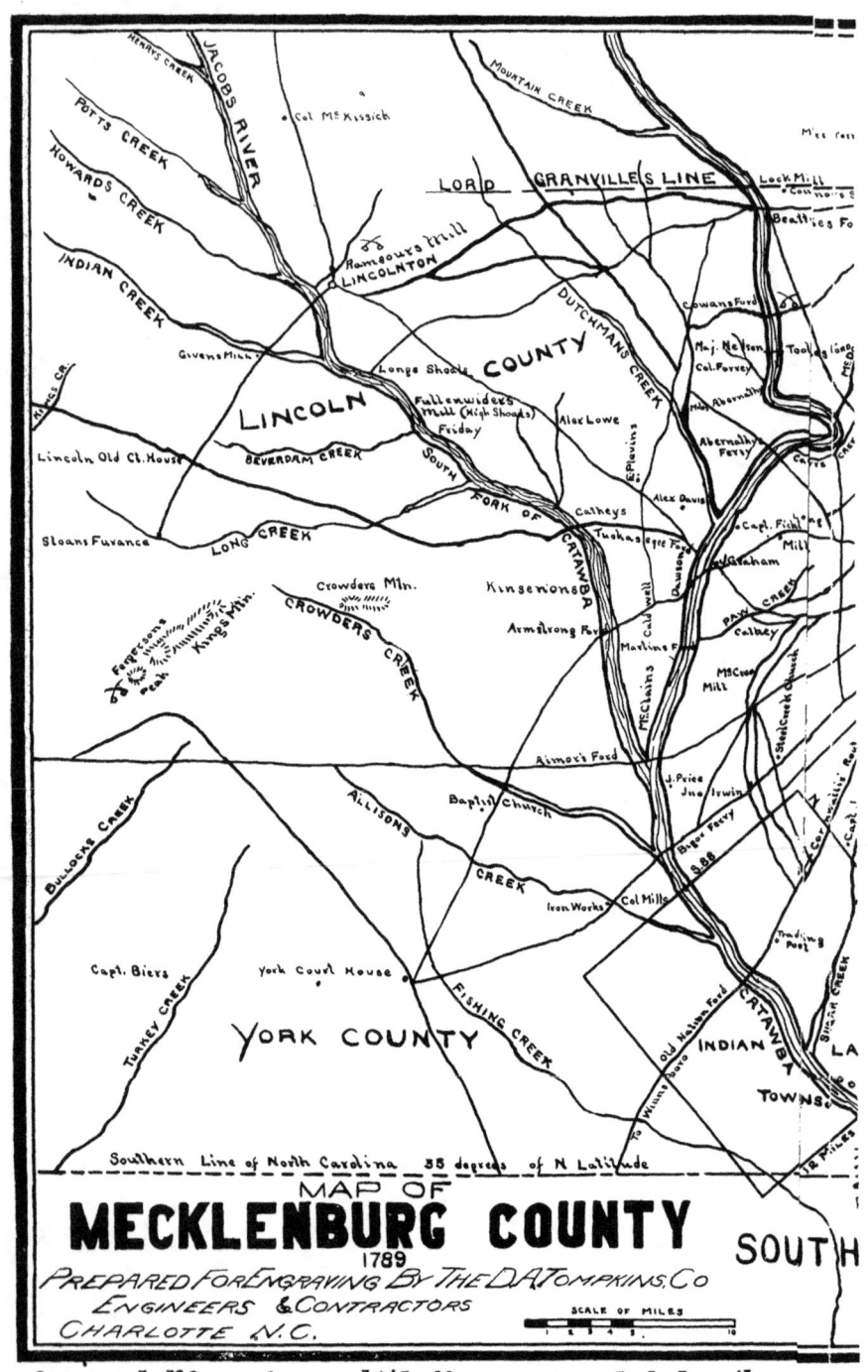

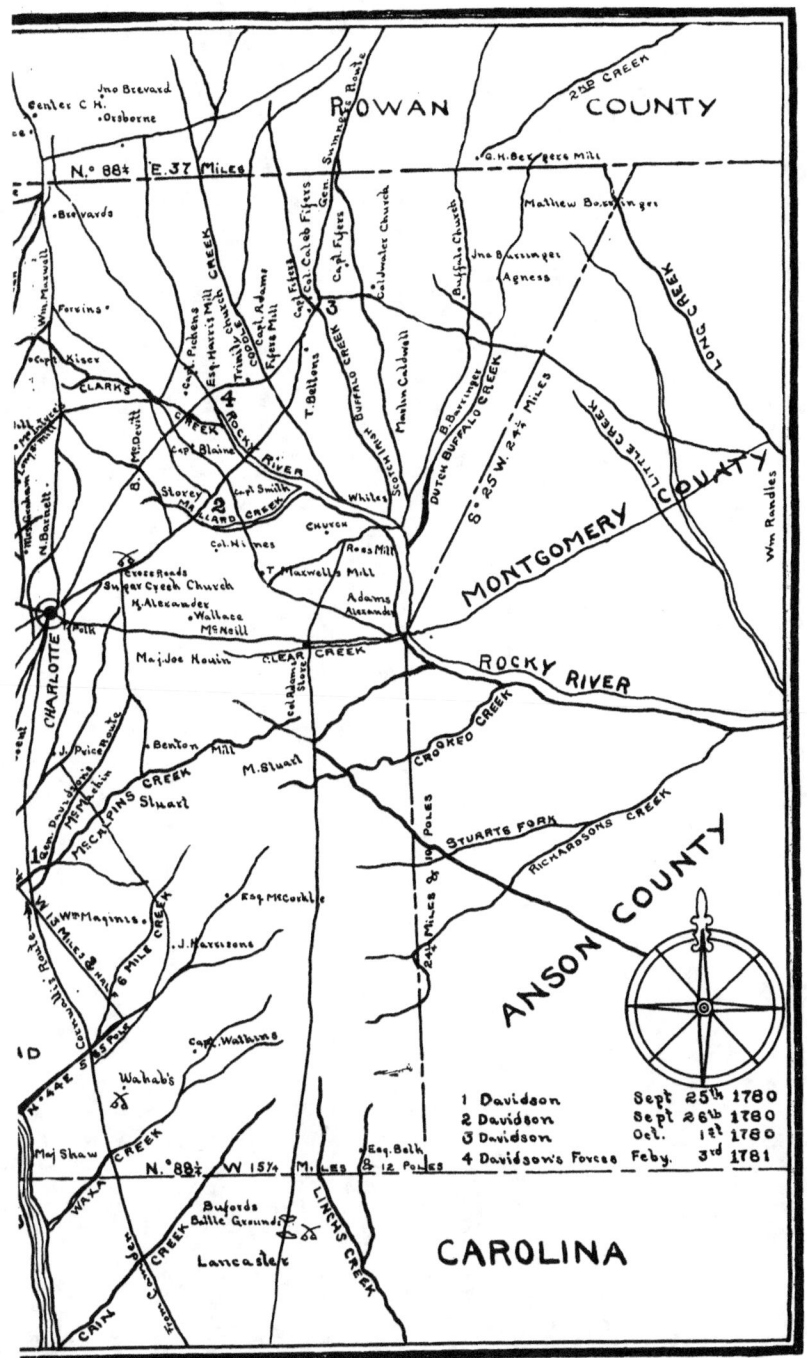

PREFACE

To those who do me the honor of reading the history as prepared, it is necessary that I should say I am indebted in greater or less degree, to Foot's Sketches of North Carolina, Wheeler's History of North Carolina, Martin's History, written between 1791 and 1809, but not published till a later date; also I am indebted to manuscripts of Mrs. H. M. Irvin, deposited in the archives of the Mecklenburg Historical Society; also largely to manuscripts of Lyman Draper, of Wisconsin. Prof. Draper spent much time and took great pains in looking up the early history of Mecklenburg, and left no stone unturned that might throw light on the character of those early patriots, who risked everything to establish independence. This was indeed a bold act, to sever all relations with the mother country, knowing that not to succeed, meant death on the gallows. The Rubicon was crossed, and they could not go back. Patriots of the county held many meetings and debated the question earnestly before the final meeting in Charlotte on the 19th and 20th of May, 1775. All the costs were counted, and each one knew what the consequences would be if they should fail. They were in desperate straits—either to live as slaves and submit to all the indignities of a subjudicated province, or make a declaration of independence, maintain their freedom by force of arms, trusting in the God of right. This last resolve was adopted, success was achieved, and Mecklenburg occupied the foremost place for patriotism in all this mighty continent. Strange that a history of so remarkable a country should have been neglected so long, and only here and there a fugitive piece has been preserved; many things of note were enacted by patriots more than a century ago that are now faded from memory, that should have been preserved by those who lived at that time. It has been characteristic of North Carolinians to *make* history, but not to write it.

In writing the History of Mecklenburg County, I find it very difficult not to trespass on the confines of neighboring counties, and not to follow people who have gone out from our borders. The history of a State, or a county, is almost entirely the history of the people who constitute the inhabitants; all that part of Mecklenburg county, or the greater portion of the county, was settled with the Scotch-Irish, but the part that was given to form Cabarrus, had many of German extraction. This eastern border was trimmed in 1791, and the southeastern section was lopped off to form Cabarrus county, was peopled with the Scotch-Irish, the same people that populated Mecklenburg.

In the years 1830 to 1855, quite a large emigration of our people to all of the Western States was effected, that was to the detriment of our county, but tended to the advancement of all the interests of the States to which they migrated. From the latter period, but a small per cent. moved away—in comparison to the number that moved previously. From the location, being placed in the southern part of the Piedmont section, filled with the best of immigrants from Ireland and Scotland, inheriting a love of freedom that had come to them through a long line of ancestors who had suffered much, for their love of freedom to worship God according to the distates of their consciences, they were exceedingly fortunate in having Mr. Alexander Craighead, providentially sent to instruct them how to resist all kingly oppression, both in ecclesiastical and civil affairs. Notwithstanding he ceased from his labors nine years before the great convention of May 20, 1775, the doctrines he advocated with so much earnestness from the pulpit, and in his pastoral visits, found lodgment in good and honest hearts of all the people who sat at his feet and learned of him. Through the instruction given by this great man, though rejected by Maryland and Pennsylvania, and urged to leave these States, was gladly accepted by the people here, whereby the county of Mecklenburg became the cradle of liberty for the Western world. The seven churches he was instrumental in forming, contributed most of the men who signed the immortal Declaration of Independence.

It is now the part of patriotism for the descendants of those who endorsed the work of that ever memorable 20th of May, as well as the descendants of the committee who signed the famous resolutions then adopted, to hold them up as patriots in deed, who took a decided stand for liberty more than a year before the colonies declared themselves free and independent of Great Britain.

This act is enough for any people to be proud of, and had it occurred in ancient times, the participants would have been knighted, if not deified. And it is with sincere regret that any citizen of Mecklenburg county should deny the truth of so well established a fact, by records of court, the statements of several of the signers themselves, and by men who were not participants but were present; two of whom were Maj. Gen. Joseph Graham and Rev. Dr. Humphrey Hunter, both of whom were present, but not signers, both being under age, but both in the patriot army.

The love of country, which has always been a crowning virtue in the people of Mecklenburg, could be seen in the Revolutionary period, and in the war of 1812-14, when England claimed the "right of search;" in the war with Mexico, and last but by no means least, the war between the States, when our county sent to the front more than 2,700 men. She is always first in a good cause, and last to let go. For the last forty years she has devoted her whole attention to building up her shattered fortunes, and educating her children. For seven years after the close of the war between the States, not a public school was taught in the county; our people needed schools, but we lived for a while under the iron heel of despotism. But, now we hear of education on every side, and civilization is progressing with steam and electricity, so it is hard to keep up with the procession. Our old civilization is fast disappearing, giving way for the new. War is no longer a coveted art in the South, but its opposite is in the lead, and peace will soon have her victories that will far exceed those that formerly belonged to the red flag of war.

The middle of the last century brought in many changes in the workings of our civilization; our people till then nearly all lived on their farms, raised their own supplies, save their sugar, coffee, salt, molasses, etc. All of our ordinary clothing was spun and woven at home. Every community had its own tanyard, and every farmer (of consequence) had their own shoemaker. In fact we were able to live within ourselves. The women knit all our hose; if flannel shirts were needed, they were made of home-made flannel. A great deal of attention was paid to the raising of sheep; fine wool was in demand for making fine flannel, and for making wool hats. Much attention was given to procure the best breed of hogs, cows, horses; even attention was given to the best strain of poultry, chickens, turkeys, geese and ducks. We did not have such a variety to select from, but the poultry and hogs did not have cholera; and I never heard of cows being affected with phthisis, or consumption. The last twenty-five years have added to the ills of humanity, as much as to the sufferings of the domestic animals.

The affection known as "appendicitis," was unknown twenty-five years ago, even in the medical books, but has become quite common not only in Mecklenburg, but throughout the country. This is probably offset by smallpox becoming mild, and is dreaded not so much as measles; hence it is but little talked about, although it has scarcely been absent from Charlotte in the past six months.

It is well for the children to know the history of Mecklenburg, for no other territory of the same size in the United States has such a glorious record to hold before her people. Charlotte was properly named by Lord Cornwallis, "A Veritable Hornets' Nest," and she will ever be jealous of her rights, in whatever way or form she may be attacked. Let her children learn her history, and it will be safe from those who would traduce her fame. There is no safer custodian to preserve her priceless treasure than the descendants of those heroes who won for us the Constitutional Liberty we enjoy to-day.

J. B. A.

Charlotte, N. C., August, 1902.

THE HISTORY OF MECKLENBURG COUNTY.

Early Settlement.

With what complacency we could look back upon the early years of our county, if a memorandum had been kept of the first inhabitants, what they did, how they educated their children, how far apart the neighbors lived, their first temples of worship, how services were conducted, did the aborigines join in the praise to God, the giver of life and every blessing, or did they sullenly look on as if they were infringing upon their inalienable rights, as if they were taking unwarranted liberties that no one had ever dared to do before. The settlement of the State began near the coast and gradually extended west. The eastern section of the State was populated a century before Mecklenburg was named, or steps were taken to lay off meets and bounds to form a county. In that early period there was no occasion for hurry, and everything moved slowly.

But few people moved to this section of the State prior to 1740, that is between the Yadkin and Catawba rivers. The boundary of Mecklenburg was marked off in 1762—that is, the eastern, southern and western borders; the northern or northwestern was not marked off, but was left open to see where it would be settled up, so as to draw the boundary line. In the next twenty years there was a great immigration to this settlement from Maryland and Pennsylvania, and a few from Ireland and Germany. And in 1762 when the boundary lines were run, quite a population occupied the territory that was called Mecklenburg county, and its county seat was called Charlotte in honor of the reigning family.

Not until 1742 did the tide of immigration turn toward this part of North Carolina, and even at this period it was light to what it was twenty years later. In 1750-56, many people of more than ordinary standing, thought to improve their condition in many ways by seeking homes in the Piedmont region that is now traversed by the great Southern Railway, between the Yadkin and Catawba. In this early period, about 1740, a man by the name of Thomas Spratt, said to be the first who ever crossed the Yadkin with wheels, settled near where Pineville is now located; and his daughter, who married William Polk, the first white child born in what was afterwards called Mecklenburg, between the Yadkin and Catawba rivers.

This must have been a lovely picture, when the whole country was covered with tall grass, the wild pea vines and the flora that was indiginous to the soil, disturbed only by the wild Indian and the great herds of buffalo and deer, and such wild animals and fowls as found a congenial home in so temperate a climate. At this period every branch, creek and river was alive with fish; and as they sported in the clear waters in the balmy springtime, they seemed to join in with all nature to invite immigrants into this lovely country.

In 1740, this part of the State was wholly unorganized, with only here and there an immigrant or settler. A school house or a house of worship was then not dreamed of. In 1752, Rev. John Thompson, a preacher of the Presbyterian faith, held service under a wide-spreading oak near the house of Richard Barry, fourteen miles northwest of where Charlotte was ten years later laid off, and established as the county seat of Mecklenburg. This was on the Beattiesford road in the direction of the mountains.

About this time several young men came into this neighborhood and located. The most prominent of whom was Samuel Wilson, from England. He was highly educated, a man of considerable wealth; in fact he belonged to the upper class in England, and was visited by his kinsman, Sir Robert Wilson, of aristocratic lineage; but in those days it took so long to cross the ocean, the visit was never repeated.

Samuel Wilson's first wife was Mary Winslow, a daughter of Moses and Jean Osborne Winslow. His second wife was the widow Howard (we could not find out her maiden name). His third wife was Margaret Jack, a sister of James Jack. His first and third wives were of the best families in America, and I have reason to believe his second —from her posterity—was equal to his first and last. Maj. John Davidson married Violet, a daughter of the first wife. John and Mary Davidson, children of Robert Davidson and Isabella Ramsay Davidson, of Pennsylvania, after their father's death, moved into North Carolina on the Yadkin near where the town of Salisbury now stands. Here the widow Davidson married Mr. Henry Henry, a graduate of Princeton, who was engaged in teaching in that section. Here John and Mary were educated, and John learned the blacksmith trade, and when he reached his majority he and his sister Mary moved from Rowan to Mecklenburg in 1760, just in time to secure an elegant home on the Catawba river, four miles west of where Hopewell church was built two years later. From this alliance of John Davidson and Violet Wilson sprang, a posterity of as good people, and probably as numerous as can be found in the State. They were very intelligent, believers in education, were very industrious and were noted for accumulating property. They exercised quite a beneficent influence in their section of the county, and were friends to internal improvement.

Early Recollections of Charlotte.

My earliest recollections of Charlotte and the inhabitants of the town will scarcely go back to the fortieth mile-post of the Nineteenth century. I was born ten miles north of the town, one mile from where Alexandriana Postoffice was kept for one hundred years. But alas, alas, the time came when the people could no longer spell Alexandriana, and the old revolutionary postoffice had its name changed to Croft. It has but one redeeming trait—it is short and easy to spell, and that is considered of vast importance in this money-loving age. But it is lacking in euphoney, and more than that, the first original name of the postoffice had many interesting reminiscences clustering around its antiquity that were interesting to those who cared to preserve historic facts. But we live in an age that cares for none of these things. It is only here and there that we meet with those who love to look towards the setting sun and gather up his effulgent rays as he goes down and bids good night to the gorgeous day of a well-spent life, where these glories will forever bloom and be appreciated by those spirits who dared to be free. I am aware that many persons have but little respect for what they are pleased to call a rehash of olden times, that are now considered antiquated fables. But in speaking of my earliest recollections of Charlotte and the people who lived in the town, I know you will excuse me if I also bring forward the names of some who lived in the county. In fact, when I first remember the town, it was a small affair, although it had been in existence eighty years. At this time I presume it numbered not more than 1,500 inhabitants, counting slaves and all. For the first fifty years of Charlotte's existence, not a denominational church was established in the town, but all denominations used one church in common.

The Hon. William Davidson gave the lot for a cemetery

and I presume he gave the lot where now stands the First Presbyterian church; at any rate a house for any person to worship, without regard to what denomination should conduct worship. What year this was begun, I cannot say; but it was prior to 1818. The lot and church did not pass into the hands of the Presbyterians until the summer of 1832.

While the congregation enjoyed the stated preaching of Mr. Morrison once in three weeks, an interesting revival occurred among the people in which he was assisted by Messrs. Furman and Barns, of the Baptist Church, and by Rev. Mr. Levenworth. On the fourth Sabbath of August, 1833, thirty-six persons connected themselves with the church, which was at that time organized, and David Parks and Nathan B. Carroll were appointed elders. Rev. Mr. Levenworth was engaged in teaching a female school of a high order. The academy—a large brick structure—occupied the lot now owned by Mr. J. H. Carson. He was employed as stated supply, or pastor of the Presbyterian church. At this time no other denomination had a foothold in the town. About 1840 a Baptist church was built on Fourth street (which in a few years was sold to Alexander Springs and moved to Third street, nearly opposite the new court house), and a new brick church built on the corner of Brevard and Seventh streets. The prominent members when first started were Rev. Joe Pritchard, father of the late Rev. Dr. Pritchard (and I will mention the fact that he was a great believer in Millerism; he afterwards moved west). Rev. Dr. Pritchard, who recently died, served the church very acceptably for several years and was much esteemed by all classes.

Dr. Steven Fox and his family, Dr. Torrence, Wm. Cook, Mr. Boon (who kept a shoe store), Benjamin Smith, and Leonard Smith, with their families, were prominent members of the Baptist church about 1855, and later Rev. ——— Jones organized the Baptist church at this point. During the days of reconstruction, 1865-'71, great uneasiness was felt for fear the negroes should be influenced by the Yankees to appropriate the church and all its property for their use.

That was a time in which *might made right* in ecclesiastical affairs as well as State rule. But they fortunately were induced to build in another quarter of the town. They (the white people) had about seven white heads of families and several hundred negroes—together the whites were in a hopeless minority. However, the denomination has prospered as a Christian people should.

The Methodist church here appears to have started about 1845. Dr. David R. Dunlap, a highly educated gentleman of the old school, had been raised and trained in the Presbyterian Church, married a Miss Jennings, and after her death he was so well pleased with her family, that he married a sister of his first wife, which was against their rules of church government, and consequently he was turned out of the church. He therefore cast about in his mind where he should go; he did not wish to join the Baptists, and he could not ask the Presbyterians for reinstatement, consequently he believed the time had come for the establishment here of the Methodist Church. Dr. Dunlap and Mr. Leadwell were probably the first members, and in a short time more were added to their numbers; and they built a church on the corner of College and Seventh streets, and have continued to flourish as an evangelical church should do, Although they had much to contend with, they have been abundantly blessed.

The Episcopal church commenced laying the foundation for a local habitation three quarters of a century ago. They occasionally had preaching in the common house of worship, which was for all and every one who chose to worship, until 1832; after this they were without a place till a lot and small house on West Trade street was secured about 1845.

The A. R. Presbyterians and Lutherans were last getting a start, but in later years have made a growth that has been by no means disheartening. The Roman Catholic Church, as an organization at least, is second only to the Presbyterians in having an early start. In the latter part of the Eighteenth and first part of the Nineteenth century, no great progress was made in the religious life. On a page close to the beginning of the Twentieth century, I will have more to say with regard to the religion of the town.

PHYSICIANS.

Charlotte has never been afflicted with a dearth of physicians, as far back as we can trace a doctor's practice. In 1815 Dr. McKenzie was the leading physician for a number of years; and from the reputation that he sustained, it is inferred that he was well qualified for the responsible position he occupied. In 1822, Dr. D. T. Caldwell commenced the practice of medicine. He formed a partnership with Dr. McKenzie. One of the partners would go and see the patients on the south of town, and the other would go and see those on the north side. They would see all the patients every other day. This was the era of bleeding. Dr. Caldwell said that if he met a fresh case and failed to bleed from any cause, he felt sure McKenzie would bleed him to-morrow. If any case was doubtful, they would compromise by leeching. Forty years ago it was a common sight to see two or more jars two-thirds full of water with a quantity of leeches floating about ready for use, in the drug store.

Dr. Dunlap came later to Charlotte, and built up a lucrative practice, which he held for many years. He told me he was once sent for to see a man who had been tapped for dropsy, and his doctor got tired going so often to tap him, and had roughened a goose quill by scraping it both ways and then inserted it so the fluid would run out as fast as it would collect. Of course it lighted up an inflammation that soon carried him off.

Dr. Tom Harris came about 1840, or probably earlier. He was a large, fleshy man, immensely popular, did a large practice. He died early, in the midst of his usefulness. He and Drs. D. T. and P. C. Caldwell had formed a partnership that was not only pleasant, but profitable. They had several young men prepare for the medical college, and I never knew one to fail that had this trio for preceptors. Dr. C. J. Fox, Dr. Robert Gibbon, Dr. Macilwaine, were all just budding into practice as the century was half over. Drs. Gibbon and Fox were active members of the profession, and lived long to enjoy the honors of their patrons and reap the benefits of a well-spent life. Dr. Macilwaine did not remain long in Charlotte—went to Florida.

Dr. J. M. Davidson spent a long life here, but only engaged in the practice of medicine more as a past-time than as a life pursuit. Gibbon and Fox were the only ones who pretended to surgery, or were equipped for whatever came along. It was my fortune to be with Dr. Gibbon during the war between the States—in the same brigade with him— and I can say without hesitation, he was the finest operator in surgery that I have ever met with. He was ambidextrous, never thought of turning the patient around, but would simply take the knife in the other hand.

Dr. E. H. Andrews, a dentist, came to Charlotte about 1846, from Virginia—educated in Baltimore. He was a man of pleasant manners, and well qualified for dental work. He kept his home office here, but traveled over several counties. He was quite a mineraligist, had a collection worth several thousand dollars. He was fond of talking mineralogy, and spent much time conversing with his friends. In his time there was not much dental work to do. The civilization of the present era will have much to be thankful for, for the work furnished the dentists of the Twentieth century.

About this time (say in 1845) the business part of town was small indeed. The grocery business was undeveloped, or rather we should say was unthought of. Salt, whiskey, molasses, sugar, and cheese was about all the groceries that were usually kept in an inland town. These were kept in a dry goods house. Nearly everything that a farmer wanted could be found in an ordinary store. Irwin & Elms kept where Woodall & Sheppard now have a drug store; Leroy Springs in the east corner, where R. H. Jordan's drug store is now; H. B. & L. S. Williams, Richard Carson, one door south; Mr. Allison, where Burwell & Dunn now have a drug store; David Parks, where Gray-Reese Drug Co.'s store is now. I think these about all the mercantile houses in the town. At this time probably every store was hung overhead with bales or bunches of yarn for the chain or warp of a web; nearly every farmer's wife had a loom to weave cloth for all on the farm. In the early part of the century nearly ever article of clothing was spun and woven at home; and during the Confederate war our soldiers were largely clothed with the "fruit of looms," made by the good women of the South. The old fashioned loaf sugar wrapped with twine around blue paper, was hung overhead. This sugar was known as loaf sugar, and used on Sunday morning to sweeten "bought" tea, and probably a little of it was used to sweeten morning dram of brandy or rum. Before the middle of the century almost every gentleman kept his decanters filled up and every person (of respectability) was invited to take a social glass. But those days of close friendship by neighborhoods have passed, and the young people know but little of the customs that ceased fifty years ago. Dry goods stores all kept iron—that is bars of iron, slabs of iron for making bull-tongues; large slabs, eight to twelve inches wide by one inch thick, for big, heavy plows, one or two-horse plows. These were for breaking the ground and preparing it for crops. At this time the blacksmith was looked upon as an artist. There was no such thing as a hardware store. The smith had to forge out of the raw material every tool that was used in cultivating the farm; shoes and nails to protect the horse's feet; and every hinge for the doors and window shutters, and every nail to build the house, and to put on the roof with. It was a tedious job to make nails for a large roof and all the fastenings. All large farmers had a screw plate for cutting screws for their plows and wagons. The civilization is very different now from what is was in the early years of the century. Cooking pots and ovens and lids, a big fireplace and sometimes a

Dutch oven, were the only cooking vessels then in use in either town or country. Often the cooking utensils were so scarce that the same skillet would have to do double duty, as heating coffee water, then bake the bread, and last, fry the ham. But the people never thought it a hardship, for they never heard of any other way and were happy to continue in the way their parents trod many years before. It is only the restlessness and dissatisfaction with their condition that make improvements.

As the women of our country constitute the best part of our population, I will mention names and facts of those who exercised an untold influence on the fashions and learning of both town and county, in the first half of the Nineteenth century. There may have been an earlier caterer to ladies' fashions than Mrs. Porter, but if so no record has been preserved. She had her millinery shop on the west side of North Tryon street, near the Hunt building. She had a great many hot house plants in boxes, a lemon, an orange tree—in fact the house was filled with rare plants, besides a feathered songster that appeared to be the pet of the shop. I was 8 or 10 years old, and probably rode behind my aunt for company, hardly for protection, to town to get the latest and prettiest fashions for ladies wear, and probably to have some work done. Ladies in town and country were in the habit of doing their own sewing, except on rare occasions, when they would call on an expert. Weddings were as popular in the first half of the century as in the closing years. It was a rare occurrence to marry in a church, or to go on a bridal trip after marriage. Horseback riding was the only way of traveling sixty years ago, and but few ladies would prefer a trip of this kind to rounds of pleasure, as were frequently given in many houses in a neighborhood, lasting a week.

Female education was not encouraged with much spirit during the first seventy-five years of Charlotte's existence. In this early period, when children of school age were not so plentiful as in later years, they always had mixed schools.

People who were in affluent circumstances, and could afford to give their daughters a higher education than could be obtained in the common schools of the country, had a fine opportunity to patronize the Moravian school in Salem. This institution was much sought after and patronized from the Potomac to the Rio Grand, in the first half of the century. But here for the same reason that male schools did not flourish, we might say that female schools lagged behind. Mrs. S. D. Nye Hutchison, a Northern lady who had earned quite a reputation as a teacher in Raleigh and other places, was induced to teach here, with Miss Sarah Davidson as music teacher. A suitable house was erected on the square now occupied by Mr. J. H. Carson, and the school commenced in 1836. For some three years the school was well attended, and was regarded as very prosperous. After Mrs. Hutchison ceased to teach, Miss Sarah Davidson continued to teach music for many years. In May, 1846, the Rev. Cyrus Johnston was called to the pastorate of the Presbyterian church and also took charge of the female school, with Miss Sarah Davidson. This school was run with more or less regularity till Mr. Johnston was removed by death.

Male schools in the town were not first-class. Occasionally an excellent teacher was employed for a term or two, but not for a permanent school. A teacher by the name of Murphy, in the early forties, gave general satisfaction for a term or two; then a man by the name of Denny for a short time gave general satisfaction, but thinking that a better paying school could be had out in the county, he engaged a school in Steel Creek, but being under the influence of an evil star, he unmercifully whipped a small boy, for which his father fell afoul of him with a wagon whip and lifted him every step for fifty yards, when the father gave out; but our quandam teacher did not stop this side of Guilford.

Also the services of Mr. Alison were secured for a short time, and several others whose names I cannot now recall. To perpetuate the history of a town, county or State, it is necessary that a chair of history, or some fundamental law of the land be enacted to take note of the passing events in each county of the State, so that important steps or epochs be not lost, and the people be posted as to what is good, and warned against what is bad.

Gen. D. H. Hill, Gen. Jas. H. Lane, and Col. C. C. Lee taught a first-class military school here just before the Confederate war, in which not only the teachers, but their pupils took a very active part. Col. Thomas was principal of the military academy after the war, when the reconstruction times were over. Before we have finished this episode, in a more appropriate place, we will recur again to this most remarkable time that has never had its parallel since civilization dawned upon the Anglo-Saxon race.

In the earlier years of the country—say from 1780 to 1840—there was a fine school run at all the seven churches through the county, and consequently when these congregational schools were kept in full blast, but little opportunity was left for a school in the village. From the location of these seven churches it is evident that Mecklenburg was better off in the way of schools than probably any other county in the State.

In this day of the most advanced civilization the world ever saw, if our people would only reflect that their ancestors one hundred years ago eat out of pewter dishes, drank their dittany or sassafras tea out of the plainest delft, used an iron or pewter spoon, the most ordinary knives and two-prong forks made of iron with buck-horn handles. A family was fortunate to have any kind of table cutlery. Most people used their fingers. Up to 1845 steel knives and two prong forks were used by the most fashionable and wealthy people in our midst. All the silverware used prior to 1850 was made at the homes of wealthy people. Silversmiths traveled about and got jobs wherever they could find work, carrying their tools with them. The inhabitants of Charlotte town were like their country cousins, only dependent on them for what they had to buy. But in the olden times every good citizen expected to cultivate a farm, raise his own cows, hogs and chickens. Up to the middle of the last century, Charlotte furnished a very limited market for country produce. Until the advent of the railroad, which first entered the town in 1852, but little was brought here for sale. Ever since then it has grown to be a market for every thing that is raised, for home consumption or shipped to larger markets. During the first half of the Nineteenth Century cooking utensils were as scarce and as difficult to get as convenient tableware. When brass kettles were first used only the wealthy, or those in easy circumstances could afford to use them, but had to be careful not to leave anything acid in them, but were useful in many things around the fireplace where cooking was being done. The Johnnie Cake was extremely fashionable by the well-to-do, but it has almost disappeared as cooking utensils have multiplied. It was made of corn meal, salt, lard, and made up with hot water or milk, and baked on a board set before the fire leaning against a sad iron, rock or brick. As soon as well browned, it was buttered and served hot.

Waffle irons were considered necessary before you could have a well appointed cook-kitchen. People were as expert at preparing an elegant dinner, or setting a beautiful supper table one hundred years ago as now, although they did not have the conveniences that we now think are necessities.

It is important to mention the court house, the place where justice has been meted out between man and man for such a length of time, and punishment for offences against the peace and dignity of the State. The first court house ever built in the county was in the public square where Trade and Tryon streets cross. It was built upon square posts, or columns, some eight or ten feet high, then built up with hewn logs a convenient height. This house was honored with being the birthplace of the first Declaration of Independence that was ever flung to the breeze in the western world. It afterwards witnessed a hard fight and bloodshed between the American and British forces on the 26th of September, 1780. By being built upon posts, any one in passing could have a shelter to protect them from sunshine or rain. This house was built about 1767, and was replaced by a brick one in the year 1810, when it gave way to an up-to-date one on West Trade street, in 1845. Here the courts were held for more than fifty years. This house was used for public meetings of various kinds, such as county political conventions, public speakings, railroad meetings and railroad speeches; in fact for a long time it was as a public hall, and was free to all.

The new court house just finished as the Nineteenth Century was about to close, was built on the ground where formerly stood Queen's Museum, an educational institution that the patriotic people of Mecklenburg tried hard to establish on a firm basis, but England refused to grant a charter. Although it was in charge of graduates of Princeton, Dr. McWhirter and Ephraim Brevard, M. D., and other men of ability, but it had not encouragement from home influence But one young man ever received a diploma from the institution, and in September, 1780, when Lord Cornwallis visited town, Queen's Museum was used as a hospital, and the yard as a burying ground for their soldiers that were killed in battle, and were picked off by the ever vigilant patriots. In digging the foundation for the present court house, several skeletons were exhumed which called to mind the stirring times that occurred one hundred and twenty years ago. Now the grounds are graced by a handsome court house, with all the recent apartments for filing away papers, court records in fireproof vaults, that will probably answer all purposes for another century.

MONUMENT TO SIGNERS.

Immediately in front of this majestic building has been erected a handsome monument commemorating the memory of those immortal signers of the Declaration of Independence of May 20, 1775.

This monument ought to have been erected one hundred years ago, before those old heroes who participated in the great event had all passed away.

In the first fifty years of the Nineteenth Century there was not a man in the county who had the bold effrontery to deny the action of those patriotic men; but now to deny the declaration of May 20, 1775, is fashionable with those who do not want to know the truth.

The old pillory and stocks passed away with State's rights, so with the whipping post. The people who triumphed in the war between the States—who believed that "might made right," and acted accordingly, and so many thousands, or I say truthfully, hundreds of thousands were guilty of stealing, thinking that some day they would be held amenable to the law, they forbade corporal punishment, such as whipping or cutting off the ears, putting them in the stocks lest they should start a race whose backs and ears wore the brand of infamy. The penitentiary has been substituted for all these forms of punishment, and has proved much less effective than the old fashioned way of applying the lash to the bare back, as in ante-bellum times. Since our people have become somewhat Yankeeized, there is considerable opposition to capital punishment or hanging; but the common people are disposed—in flagrant cases—to take the law into their own hands and mete out justice swiftly. We cannot say when the old jail, at the corner of Tryon and Sixth streets, was built, but it served the purpose for many years, with stocks and whipping post in the yard, where every one who wanted could see. The gallows was out in the eastern part of the city, at that time an old field. Up to the war all executions were public, believing the example would have a wholesome effect on the multitude; but it is not a settled question yet how the extreme penalty of the law should be carried out, so as to be a warning to others. The old prison has been converted into two handsome stores on the ground floor, and the second and third stories for a first-class boarding house. All west of this point fifty years ago, except the First Church lot and cemetery, was old field and chinquapin bushes.

May 20, 1775.

Mecklenburg county was populated with a race of people not a whit behind any others on the American continent. They were independent by nature, having no one to lean upon or to appeal to; they were considering well the question if they had not paid taxes long enough to the mother country, and had received but oppression when protection was looked for; they got weary of being taxed and never represented in their Parliament. In 1758, Rev. Alexander Craighead was driven from Maryland for preaching against kingly authority. He supposed that he would find friends in Pennsylvania, but his hopes were soon dispelled, for he was promptly told that such doctrine was disagreeable, and that he must move on. The tendency at that time was to move South, not to get too far away from the coast. Mr. Craighead came down into North Carolina and accepted a call from Rocky River and Sugar Creek churches. This was three years before any church was organized in all this section of country. With the help of Revs. McWhirter, McAden and other missionaries, the noted seven churches were organized in 1762 or thereabouts, at all of which places it is more than probable that Mr. Craighead preached. He was a man of great energy. Wherever he could get a congregation he would preach the Gospel of Jesus Christ, and instruct the people that it was their duty to resist tyranny; that we should resist paying taxes without representation. Here he found willing and eager listeners. In 1762 the county was surveyed and soon a county government was organized. Among the first things done was to lay off military precincts, and enrol all the males from 18 to 45 to bear arms as the militia of the colony. These companies were permitted to elect their own officers, to serve as long as their physical condition permitted.

The best men in the county were elected officers in the

militia. Another committee was appointed called "The Committee of Safety," to look after the safety of the country. When the county was well organized, the great leader, Mr. Craighead, was called home after a life well spent in laying the foundation for American independence, 1766. His body was laid to rest in the first graveyard of Sugar Creek church. Has Mecklenburg ever had his equal to point out the way to independence, to a representative government, one that is the friend of the oppressed and that has grown in one hundred and twenty-five years to be the first power in wealth and influence in the world? Mr. Craighead's influence can only be measured by what followed. He laid the foundation of its future greatness. After his demise, the good men that he had trained in both religion and patriotism, consulted often, in regularly appointed places, what would be best for the country, which was fast ripening into freedom, and soon to take her place in the great family of free and independent States.

Mecklenburg was more fortunate than other counties, in that her citizens had been taught that liberty and independence were necessary to achieve the highest aims in life. The frequent conferences were held by the leaders of public opinion where it was convenient. Three of the noted places where this Committee of Safety were in the habit of meeting was at the residences of Robert Irwin, of Steel Creek; Abram Alexander, of Sugar Creek; and John McKnitt Alexander, of Hopewell. Here at these places was the question of independence discussed, and the people were gotten ready for action. The militia officers were men of rank, elders in the church, were leading men, justices of the peace, ministers of the Gospel, etc.

Everything, both public and private, tended to Independence. In the year 1771, the people of Alamance were so oppressed with high taxes that they rebelled against Governor Tryon. The country was wild with excitement, and the men organized companies to defend themselves against the royal troops from New Bern. In the meantime Mecklenburg was not idle, but sent troops to aid the patriots of Alamance; but the battle was over and the patriots routed before the Mecklenburg contingent arrived. Hence our troops returned, and as evidence that they would bear true allegiance to Great Britain in the future, the governor had them sworn to support the crown. This oath was the source of much trouble to the conscience of many good people, when, a few years later, they were about taking steps to dissolve all ties that bound us to the mother country. They were at last persuaded that when England had ceased to protect them, they were under no obligations to abide by the oath formerly taken; that a contract broken by one side ceases to be binding on the other. This solution gave general satisfaction to every true patriot.

In the summer of 1771, the good people of Lincoln county gave a picnic to the people of that county. The excitement in Mecklenburg arising from swearing her militia to bear true allegiance to the crown, could not be passed over in silence. So, when the day for the picnic came, a large party from Mecklenburg rode over with flags flying, made of white cloth with black letters, so that they could be seen, "Independence." This was received as an insult, whereupon a general fisticuff fight ensued, which shows plainly that Mr. Craighead had not labored among the Dutch of Lincoln county, to show them the truth as it appears from Scripture and common sense.

This was a time that required the services of the best of men to be on the Committee of Public Safety, to be at the head of the militia, and at every position in the county. The county had great reason to be proud of her men, and loves to point back to her noble women who sacrificed every comfort to aid her soldiers in gaining her independence. The Committee of Public Safety notified the commissioned officers when they were expected to meet in Charlotte, to take specific action on the state of the country. Matters seemed to grow more threatening with each year; whatever part of the country was oppressed, was considered a thrust at Mecklenburg, for whatever was hurtful to one part was felt by all. In other words, we felt the necessity of making common cause against a common enemy.

The Committee of Public Safety notified the commissioned officers and as many others as could attend to be in Charlotte on the 19th of May, 1775.

[*Copied From Francois Xavier Martin's History of North Carolina, From the Earliest Period.*]

"Imperfect as the present publication is, it began to engage the attention of the writer as early as the year 1791. At that period the Legislature of North Carolina afforded him some aid in the publication of a collection of the statutes of the Parliament of England then in force and use within the State. In preparing that work, he examined all the statutes from Magna Charta to the Declaration of Independence, and an arrangement of all those which related to America, afforded him a complete view of the colonial system of England. In 1803 he was employed by the same Legislature to publish a revisal of the acts of the General Assembly, passed during the Proprietary, Royal and State Governments, and the local information he acquired in carrying into effect the intentions of those who employed, suggested the idea of collecting materials for a history of the State; and when afterwards he had the honor of representing the town of New Bern in the House of Commons, he was favored with a resolution of the General Assembly, authorizing the Secretary of State to allow him access to the records of his office. In the speeches of the Governors at the opening of the sessions of the Legislature, he found a reference to the principal transactions during the recess, and there were few important events particularly relating to the State, which left no trace on the Journals of the Legislature or the proceedings of the executive. * * * The writer imagined he had collected sufficient materials to justify the hope of producing a history of North Carolina worth the attention of his fellow citizens, and he had arranged all that related to transactions, anterior to the Declaration of Independence, when, 1809, Mr. Madison thought his services were wanted, first in the Mississippi territory and afterwards in that of Orleans; and when the latter territory became a State, the new government thought proper to retain him. He had entertained the hope that the time would arrive when disengaged from public duties, he might resume the work he had commenced in Carolina; but years have rolled away without bringing on this period; and a shock his health lately received during the year of his great climacteric, has warned him that the moment is arrived when his intended work must engage his immediate attention, or be absolutely abandoned. * * *. The determination has been taken to put the work immediately to press in the condition it was when it reached New Orleans. This has prevented any use being made of Williamson's History of North Carolina, a copy of which did not reach the writer's hands till after his arrival in Louisiana. The expectation is cherished that the people of North Carolina will receive, with indulgence, a work ushered to light under circumstances so untoward."

Martin, the historian, further states the conditions which led up to the appointing of delegates to the convention that paved the way to independence. This all occurred prior to 1809, after which date he ceased to write any historical reminiscences of the country, being so engaged for the welfare of the purchase; being a native of France, and otherwise well qualified for the position, he was kept until all difficulties were adjusted and amicably settled. His health gave way, and he was unable to return to historical work, as he desired to do.

In the western part of the province the people were still eager in their resistance. In the months of March and April, 1775, the leading men in the county of Mecklenburg held meetings to ascertain the sense of the people, and to confirm them in their opposition to the claim of the Parliament to impose taxes and regulate the internal policy of the colonies.

At one of those meetings, when it was ascertained that the people were prepared to meet their wishes, it was agreed that Thomas Polk, then colonel commandant of the county, should issue an order directed to each captain of militia, requesting him to call a company meeting to elect two delegates from his company, to meet in general committee at Charlotte, on the 19th of May, giving to the delegates ample power to adopt such measures as to them should seem best calculated to promote the common cause of defending the rights of the colony, and aiding their brethren in Massachusetts. Col. Polk issued the order, and delegates were elected. They met in Charlotte on the day appointed. The forms of their proceedings and the measures to be proposed had been previously agreed upon by the men at whose instance the committee were assembled. The Rev. Hezekiah Jones Balch, Dr. Ephraim Brevard, and William Kennon, an attorney-at-law, addressed the committee, and descanted on the causes which had led to the existing contest with the mother country, and the consequences which were to be apprehended, unless the people should make a firm and energetic resistance to the right which Parliament asserted, of taxing the colonies and regulating their internal policy.

On the day on which the committee met, the first intelligence of the action at Lexington, in Massachusetts, on the 19th of April, was received in Charlotte. This intelligence produced the most decisive effect. A large concourse of people had assembled to witness the proceedings of the committee. The speakers addressed their discourses as well to them as to the committee, and those who were not convinced by their reasoning, were influenced by their feelings, and all cried out, "Let us be independent! Let us declare our independence and defend it with our lives and fortunes!" A committee was appointed to draw up resolutions. This committee was composed of the men who planned the whole proceedings, and who had, already, prepared the resolutions which it was intended should be submitted to the general committee.

Dr. Ephraim Brevard had drawn up the resolutions some time before, and now reported them, with amendments, as follows:

Resolved, That whosoever directly or indirectly abets, or in any way, form or manner, countenances the invasion of our rights as attempted by the Parliament of Great Britain, is an enemy to his country, to America and the rights of man.

Resolved, That we, the citizens of Mecklenburg county, do hereby dissolve the political bonds which have connected us with the mother country; and absolve ourselves from all allegiance to the British crown, abjuring all political connection with a nation that has wantonly trampled on our rights and liberties, and inhumanly shed the innocent blood of Americans at Lexington.

Resolved, That we do declare ourselves a free and independent people; that we are and of right ought to be a sovereign and self-governing people, under the power of God and the general congress; to the maintenance of which independence we solemnly pledge to each other our mutual cooperation, our lives, our fortunes and our most sacred honor.

Resolved, That we do hereby ordain and adopt as rules of conduct, all and each of our former laws, and the crown of Great Britain cannot be considered hereafter as holding any rights, privileges or immunities among us.

Resolved, That all offices, both civil and military, in this county, be entitled to exercise the same powers and authorities as heretofore; that every member of this delegation shall henceforth be a civil officer, and exercise the powers of a Justice of the Peace, issue process, hear and determine controversies according to law, preserve peace, union and harmony in the county, and use every exertion to spread the love of liberty and of country, until a more general and better organized system of government be established.

Resolved, That a copy of these resolutions be transmitted

by express to the President of the Continental Congress, assembled in Philadelphia, to be laid before that body.

These resolutions were unanimously adopted and subscribed by the delegates.

Signers of the Declaration of Independence, 20th of May, 1775:

ABRAHAM ALEXANDER, *Chairman.*
JOHN MCKNITT ALEXANDER, *Secretary.*
EPHRAIM BREVARD, *Secretary.*

REV. HEZEKIAH J. BALCH,	CHARLES ALEXANDER,
JOHN PHIFER,	ZACCHEUS WILSON, JR.,
JAMES HARRIS,	WAIGHTSTILL AVERY,
WILLIAM KENNON,	BENJAMIN PATTON,
JOHN FORD,	MATTHEW MCCLURE,
RICHARD BARRY,	NEILL MORRISON,
HENRY DOWNES,	RORERT IRWIN,
ESRA ALEXANDER,	JOHN FLENNIKEN,
WILLIAM GRAHAM,	DAVID REESE,
JOHN QUEARY,	JOHN DAVIDSON,
HEZEKIAH ALEXANDER,	RICHARD HARRIS, JR.,
ADAM ALEXANDER,	THOMAS POLK.

James Jack, of Charlotte, but afterwards living in Georgia, was engaged to be the bearer of the resolutions to the President of Congress, and directed to deliver copies of them to the delegates in Congress from North Carolina. The President returned a polite answer to the address, which accompanied the resolutions, in which he highly approved of the measures adopted by the delegates of Mecklenburg, but deemed the subject of the resolutions premature to be laid before Congress. Messrs. Caswell, Hooper and Hewes forwarded a joint letter, in which they complimented the people of Mecklenburg for their zeal in the common cause, and recommended to them the strict observance of good order; that the time would soon come when the whole continent would follow their example.

On the day the resolutions were adopted by the delegates in Charlotte, they were read aloud to the people, who had assembled in the town, and proclaimed amidst the shouts and huzzas, expressing the feelings and determination of all present.

When Capt. Jack reached Salisbury on his way to Philadelphia, the general court was sitting, and Mr. Kennon, an attorney-at-law, who had assisted in the proceedings of the delegates at Charlotte, was there in Salisbury. At the request of the judges, Mr. Kennon read the resolutions aloud in open court to a large concourse of people. They were listened to with attention and approved by all present. The delegates at Charlotte being empowered to adopt such measures, as in their opinion would best promote the common cause, established a variety of regulations for managing the concerns of the county. Courts of justice were held under the direction of the delegates. For some months these courts were held in Charlotte, but for the convenience of the people (for at that time Cabarrus formed part of Mecklenburg), two other places were selected and the courts were held at each in rotation. The delegates appointed a committee of their own body who were called a "Committee of Safety," and they were empowered to examine all persons brought before them charged with being inimical to the common cause, and to send the military into the neighboring counties to arrest suspected persons. In the exercise of this power, the committees sent into Lincoln and Rowan counties and had a number of persons arrested and brought before them. Those who manifested penitence for their Toryism, and took an oath to support the cause of liberty and the country, were discharged. Others were sent under guard into South Carolina for safe keeping. The meeting of the delegates at Charlotte and the proceedings which grew out of that meeting produced the zeal and unanimity for which the people of Mecklenburg were distinguished during the whole of the Revolutionary War. They became united as a band of brothers, whose confidence in each other and the cause which they had sworn to support was never shaken in the worst of times.

The history of the convention that convened in Charlotte on the 19th and 20th of May, 1775, is detailed by an educated lawyer—Francois Xavier Martin—a native of France, lived in New Bern, was frequently a member of the North Carolina Legislature, was in close contact with the history of North Carolina from 1791-1809, when he was employed by Mr. Madison, as an attorney, to proceed to New Orleans and the Western purchased territory; that he was well qualified for the work, and also to write history. And we understand that previous to 1819, the Mecklenburg Declaration of Independence had never been called in question in any manner. Some of the signers lived and were able to travel around in the county for nearly fifty years after the great epoch. Maj. John Davidson lived till 1830. Surely the people of Mecklenburg, with all of its boasted intelligence, would have discovered the fraud before forty years had passed over us, or if it was necessary to bolster up the famous son, Mr. Jefferson, of an adjoining State. Another quotation and that will suffice:

The following persons attended the meeting at Hillsboro August 21, 1775, to consider the state of the country: Thomas Polk, John Phifer, Waightstill Avery, Samuel Martin, James Houston, and John McKnitt Alexander.

To the meeting at Halifax, 4th of April, 1776, she sent John Phifer, Robert Irwin, and John McKnitt Alexander. (The county was ever jealous of her rights, in sending her best men as delegates to see that her rights were maintained at all hazards. The following instructions were given to the delegates from the people, being found among the old surviving papers of John McKnitt Alexander. He is the author of them, dated 1st September, 1776.)

Instructions for the delegates of Mecklenburg county:

"1. You are instructed to vote that the late province of North Carolina is and of right ought to be, a free and independent State, invested with all the powers of legislation, capable of making laws to regulate all its internal policy, subject only in its external connections, and foreign commerce, to a negative of a Continental Senate.

"2. You are instructed to vote for the execution of a Civil Government under the authority of the people for the future security of all the rights, privileges and prerogatives of the State, and the private, natural and unalienable rights of the constituting members thereof, either as men or Christians. If this should not be confirmed in Congress or Convention, protest.

"3. You are instructed to vote that an equal representation be established, and that the qualifications required to enable any person or persons to have a voice in legislation, may not be secured too high, but that every freeman who shall be called upon to support government either in person or property, may be admitted thereto. If this should not be confirmed, protest and remonstrate.

"4. You are instructed to vote that legislation be not a divided right, and that no man, or body of men be invested with a negative on the voice of the people duly collected, and that no honors or dignities be conferred, for life, or made hereditary, on any person or persons, either legislative or executive. If this should not be confirmed, protest and remonstrate.

"5. You are instructed to vote that all and every person or persons seized or possessed of any estate, real or personal, agreeable to the last establishment, be confirmed in their seizure and possession, to all intents and purposes in law, who have not forfeited their right to the protection of the State by their criminal practices towards the same. If this should no be confirmed—protest.

"6. You are instructed to vote that deputies to represent this State in a Continental Congress be appointed in and by the supreme legislative body of the State, the form of nomination to be submitted to, if free, and also that all officers the influence of whose is equally to extend to every part of the State, be appointed in the same manner and form—likewise give your consent to the establishing the old political divisions, if it should be voted in convention, or to new ones if similar. On such establishments taking place, you are instructed to vote, in the general, that all officers who are to exercise their authority in any of said districts, be recommended to the trust only by the freemen of said division—to be subject, however, to the general laws and regulations of the State. If this should not be substantially confirmed—protest.

"7. You are instructed to move and insist that the people you immediately represent be acknowledged to be a distinct county of this State as formerly of the late province, with the additional privileges of annually electing in their own officers, both civil and military, together with the election of clerks and sheriffs, by the freemen of the same. The choice to be confirmed by the sovereign authority of the State, and the officers so invested to be under the jurisdiction of the State and liable to its cognizance and inflictions in case of malpractice. If this should not be confirmed, protest and remonstrate.

"8. You are instructed to vote that no Chief Justice, no Secretary of State, no Auditor-General, no Surveyor-General, no practicing lawyer, no clerk of any court of record, no Sheriff, and no person holding a military office in this State, shall be a representative of the people in Congress or Convention. If this should not be confirmed—contend for it.

"9. You are instructed to vote that all claims against the public, except such as accrue upon attendance of Congress or Convention, be first submitted to the inspection of a committee of nine or more men, inhabitants of the county where said claimant is a resident, and without the approbation of said committee, it shall not be accepted by the public, for which purpose you are to move and insist that a law be enacted to empower the freemen of each county to choose a committee of not less than nine men, of whom none are to be military officers. If this should not be confirmed—protest and remonstrate.

"10. You are instructed to refuse to enter into any combination of secrecy as members of Congress or Convention, and also refuse to subscribe any ensnaring jests binding you to an unlimited subjection to the determination of Congress or Convention.

"11. You are instructed to move and insist that the public accounts fairly stated shall be regularly kept in proper books, open to the inspection of all persons whom it may concern. If this should not be confirmed—contend for it.

"12. You are instructed to move and insist that the power of County Courts be much more extensive than under the former Constitution, both with respect to matters of property and breaches of the peace. If not confirmed—contend for it.

"13. You are instructed to assent and consent to the establishment of the Christian religion as contained in the Scriptures of the Old and New Testaments, and more briefly comprised in the thirty-nine articles of the Church of England, excluding the 37th Article, together with all the articles excepted and not to be imposed on dissenters by the act of toleration, and clearly held forth in the Confession of Faith compiled by the assembly of divines at Westminster, to be the religion of the State, to the utter exclusion forever of all and every other (falsely, so-called) religion, whether Pagan or Papal, and that the full, free and peaceable enjoyment thereof be secured to all and every constituent member of the State as their unalienable right as freemen, without the imposition of rites and ceremonies, whether claiming civil or ecclesiastic power for their source, and that a confession and profession of the religion so established shall be necessary in qualifying any person for public trust in the State. If this should not be confirmed—protest and remonstrate.

"14. You are instructed to oppose to the utmost any particular church or set of clergymen being invested with power to decree rites and ceremonies and to decide in controversies of faith to be submitted to under the influence of penal laws; you are also to oppose the establishment of any mode of worship to be supported to the opposition of the rights of conscience, together with the destruction of private property. You are to understand that under modes of worship are comprehended the different forms of swearing by law required. You are moreover to oppose the establishing of an ecclesiastic supremacy in the sovereign authority of the State. You are to oppose the toleration of the popish idolatrous worship. If this should not be confirmed, protest and remonstrate.

"15. You are instructed to move and insist that not less than four-fifths of the body of which you are members shall, in voting, be deemed a majority. If this should not be confirmed, contend for it.

"16. You are instructed to give your voices to and for every motion and bill made or brought into the Congress or Convention, where they appear to be for public utility and in no way repugnant to the above instruction.

"17. Gentlemen, the foregoing instructions you are not only to look on as instructive, but as charges to which you are desired to take special heed as the general rule of your conduct as our representatives, and we expect you will exert yourselves to the utmost of your ability to obtain the purposes given you in charge, and wherein you fail either in obtaining or opposing, you are hereby ordered to enter your protest against the vote of Congress or Convention as is pointed out to you in the above instructions."

Never was there advice more timely given than is recorded in the above seventeen paragraphs, by John McKnitt Alexander, the secretary of the noted and eminently patriotic Convention, that cut loose all the bonds that united us with England, the first convention of the kind ever held in America or the world. The declaration issued by this Convention is the admiration of the present generation, and will be of generations to the end of time—the first Declaration of Independence in America. At a hasty view, this declaration made by a colony on the Western frontier of our American province, may seem rash and unreasonable; but when the race and the creed of the people, and their habits, are taken into consideration, we wonder at their forbearance. This classic declaration expressed a deep settled purpose, which the ravages of the British army, in succeeding years, could not shake. Neither the Congress of the United Provinces, then in session, nor the Congress of the Province of North Carolina, which assembled in August of the same year, were prepared to second the declaration of Mecklenburg, though the latter appointed committees of safety in all the counties, similar to the committee of Mecklenburg. The papers of the Convention were preserved by the secretary, John McKnitt Alexander, till the year 1800, when they were destroyed, with his dwelling, by fire. But the Rev. Mumphrey Hunter and Gen. Graham, who both had heard the Declaration read on the 20th of May, 1775, had obtained copies, which had been preserved, and Mr. Alexander gave one himself to Gen. Davie sometime previous to the fire.

The reason for the obscurity in which the proceedings of the Convention in Charlotte were for a time buried may be found in the facts—first, the county in which they took place was far removed from any large seaport or trading city; was a frontier, rich in soil and productions, and men, but poor in money; with no person that had attracted public notice, like the Lees and Henry, of Virginia, for eloquence; or like Hancock, of Massachusetts, for dignity in a public assembly, or Jefferson, for political acumen; and, second, the National Declaration in 1776, with the war that followed, so completely absorbed the minds of the whole nation that efforts of the few, however patriotic, were cast into the shade. In the joy of National Independence, the particular part any man or body of men may have acted, was overlooked; and in the bright scenes spread out before a young republic, the colonial politics shared the fate of the soldiers and officers that bore the fatigues and endured the miseries of the seven years' war.

Men were too eager to enjoy liberty and push their speculations to become rich, to estimate the worth of those patriots whose history will be better known by next generation, and whose honors will be duly appreciated.

Some publications were made on this subject in the Raleigh *Register* in 1819, and for a time public attention was drawn to the subject in different parts of the country.

About the year 1830,, some publications were made, calling in question the authenticity of the document as being neither a true paper, nor a paper of a true convention. Dr. Joseph McKnitt Alexander, a son of the old secretary, inheriting much of the spirit of his father, felt himself moved to defend the honor of his father and the noble men that were associated in the county of Mecklenburg. Letters were addressed to different individuals who either had taken a part in the spirited transactions of 1775, or had been spectators of those scenes that far outstripped in patriotic daring the State at large, or even the Congress assembled in Philadelphia. The attention of all the survivors of revolutionary times was awakened; their feelings were aroused, and they came on all sides to the rescue of those men who had pledged *"their lives, their fortunes, and their most sacred honor."*

The Rev. Humphrey Hunter, who had preached in Steel Creek many years, within a few miles of Charlotte, and for a number of years in Unity and Goshen, in Lincoln county, sent to the son a copy of the Declaration, together with a history of the Convention, of which he was an eye witness. Gen. Graham, who had grown up near Charlotte, had been high sheriff of the county, and was an actor in the Revolution, and an eye-witness of the Convention, did the same. Captain Jack, who carried the Declaration to Philadelphia, gave his solemn asseveration to the facts as an eye-witness of the Convention, and as its messenger to Congress. John Davidson, a member of the Convention, gave his solemn testimony, writing from memory, and not presenting copy of the doings, but asserting the facts and general principles of the Convention. He also had a son born on the 20th of May 1787—the twelfth anniversary, whom he called "Independent Ben," in honor of the day. The Rev. Dr. Cummins, who had been educated at Queen's Museum, in Charlotte, and was a student at the time of the Convention, affirmed that repeated meetings were held in the hall of Queen's Museum by the leading men in Mecklenburg, discussing the business to be brought before the Convention when assembled. Colonel Polk, of Raleigh, who was a youth at the time, and who repeatedly read over the paper to different circles on that interesting occasion, affirmed and defended the doings of his father, at whose call, by unanimous consent, the delegates assembled. Many less known to the public, sent their recollections of the events of the 19th and 20th of May.

Mrs. Susan Smart, whose maiden name was Barnett, was born between Charlotte and Pineville, afterwards married Smart. When this noted convention met in Charlotte, she being 13 years old, was present with every one else able to get there, and bore witness to the enthusiasm of the crowd in "throwing up of hats," many of them falling on house roofs, where it was difficult to get them down.

The Celebration of the 20th of May, 1775, in the Year 1825, and What Took Place on that Date.

A description of a celebration of the 20th of May as given in the Catawba *Journal,* Charlotte, 1825, which was a weekly paper published under the direction of Lemuel Bingham. The description is as follows:

Charlotte, Tuesday, May 1825.—*Mecklenburg Independence.*

"The celebration which took place in this town on the 20th instant was equal to, if it did not surpass, anything of the kind ever before witnessed here. The day was fine and not uncomfortably warm, and at an early hour a large concourse of people, strangers and citizens, had assembled to honor the day. At 11 o'clock a. m. a procession was formed under the direction of Col. Thomas G. Polk, on the street south of the court house. Capt. Kennedy's company of cavalry and the Fayetteville Artillery, under the command of Capt. Thomas Polk, in front, citizens and strangers next, and lastly, a band of Revolutionary veterans, sixty or seventy in number, wearing badges with the figures '75 stamped on them. The procession then moved to the Presbyterian church, which, though spacious, was crowded to overflowing, and numbers found it impossible to procure seats. The exercises at the church commenced with prayer, replete with genuine piety and ardent patriotism, by the venerable Dr. Humphrey Hunter. This was succeeded by appropriate music from the band, after which the Declaration of Independence by the citizens of Mecklenburg was read by the same reverend gentleman. An oration was then pronounced by Mr. Monson, which rivetted the attention of the audience and caused tears to trickle down the furrowed cheeks of numbers of the war-worn and hoary-headed veterans. The orator did ample justice to his subject. He depicted in animated colors the undaunted patriotism of our forefathers, whom no difficulties could dishearten, no terrors dismay, no privations subdue; who, looking only to the justice of their cause and the wrongs they had received, indignantly renounced their allegiance to a government whose protection was felt only in the injuries which it inflicted, and whose paternal regard was evinced only in systematic attempts to wrest from them all that they held valuable as men who claimed freedom as a birthright and to reduce them to a stage of bondage worse than death. His address to the patriotic band whose venerable forms were before him, and whose snowy locks and bended frames formed such a striking contrast to the picture he had sketched of their youthful strength and vigor, was peculiarly appropriate and pathetic, and excited emotions in every breast which may be easily imagined, but not described. The address, in short, was well conceived and happily executed, and we regret that it will not be in our power to lay it before our readers, as the author has declined the request of the committee to furnish a copy for publication. The exercises at the church were closed with music and discharges of cannon, and the Revolutionary veterans returned in procession, escorted by the military.

"No one present at this celebration could have been entirely unmoved by the recollections and associations connected with it. The occasion was peculiarly calculated to produce an intensity of feeling, and to elicit reflections at once pleasurable and profitable. It was the fiftieth anniversary of an event of which the citizens of Mecklenburg, without the imputation of vanity, might justly be proud; it was a fit occasion of joy and gratitude, rejoicing and praise; but at the same time the reflection could not but arise in many a bosom that but few, very few, of the numbers then assembled to commemorate it, would live to witness its return. Fifty years hence, and of the multitude then present, the greater part will be reposing beneath the clods of the valley; dust will have returned to dust, and the spirit to Him who gave it.

Such a reflection was well calculated to moderate the feelings, to induce a soberness of mirth, and to impart an interest to the scene at once peculiar and impressive. About 4 o'clock p. m., a large number sat down to a dinner prepared by Dr. Henderson, in the beautiful grove on the college green. Gen. George Graham officiated as president, and Mr. Isaac Alexander as vice president. After the cloth was removed, the following toasts were drunk, interspersed with patriotic songs and accompanied with discharges of cannon:

1. "The day we celebrate." On that day the republican banners were unfurled in Charlotte, independence declared by the patriotic citizens of Mecklenburg, absolving themselves from all allegiance to Great Britain. May the noble deed be engraven on the hearts of all present, and the guilded pages of history transmit it to posterity.

2. "The patriots who signed the Mecklenburg Declaration of Independence, the 20th of May, 1775." We honor them for their firmness, love them for their virtues and venerate them for their patriotism.

3. "The memory of those heroes of Lexington, Mass., who first sealed the broken covenant with their blood, and absolved all allegiance with mother Britain."

4. "Our country and our government." The genius of Columbus, the patriotism of Washington, the philosophy of Franklin, the wisdom of Jefferson and compatriots, have erected a fabric that will last till time shall be no more.

5. "The heroes of the Revolution." While we hold in sacred remembrance those that are gathered to their fathers, let us not fail to cherish in our heart's core the scattered remnants that yet survive.

6. "The Presidents of the United States." An able statesman, may the administration prove that the confidence of Congress was not misplaced.

7. "The descendants of the patriotic members of the Mecklenburg delegation who declared independence."

> Let no mean hope your souls enslave,
> Independent, generous, brave,
> Your fathers such examples gave—
> And such revere.

8. "Popular elections." There purity and frequency are the best security for the safety of our republican institutions and the strongest barrier against the encroachments of tyranny.

9. "Internal improvements."

10. "Andrew Jackson." He has filled the measure of his country's story; he is the friend of the people—the people are his friends.

11. "Bolivia and the independent provinces of South America."

12. "Washington and Lafayette."

13. "The Fair Sex." Beauty and booty, the war cry of slavery—protection to beauty, the watchword of freemen.

By Dr. James G. M. Ramsay, of Tennessee: "Gen. Thomas Polk and Dr. Ephraim Brevard."—The first bosoms that ever glowed with the joyous anticipation of American independence.

By Wm. Davidson, Esq: "Henry Clay."—The great orator of the west, an able statesman and independent as a man—shielded by virtuous patriotism, he is impregnable to the shafts of malice.

By Col. T. G. Polk: "The political prospects of Henry Clay."

> Like the dew on the mountain,
> Like the foam on the river,
> Like the bubble on the fountain—
> They are gone and forever.

By the Hon. H. W. Conner: "General William Davidson," who fell at Cowan's Ford, bravely fighting for the rights and liberties of his country.

By J. H. Blake, Esq.: "Henry Clay."—The undaunted champion of universal liberty.

By Capt. Thomas I. Polk: "The next President of the United States."

By L. H. Alexander: "Andrew Jackson and Wm. H. Crawford."

Copied from the same journal of May 24, 1825.

"The fiftieth anniversary of the Mecklenburg Declaration of Independence was celebrated in this place on the 20th instant. Not being able to procure a copy of the toasts in season for this week's paper, and other causes intervening to render a postponement necessary, we shall defer a particular account of the proceedings until our next, barely mentioning at this time that the celebration throughout was worthy the occasion and honorable to the public spirit and patriotism of Mecklenburg. The "toasts" indicate the presence in this semi-centennial celebration of men of both parties, who, however much they differed on other matters, seemed to have met on common ground. Of the participants in these memorial ceremonies a large number appear to have been old soldiers of the Revolution."

At that date, as I ascertain by a paragraph in the *Journal* of May 10, 1825, the only survivor of those who issued the resolutions of May 20th was David Reese, then living in Cabarrus. It is also evident that the 20th of May had been commemorated in a similar manner in previous years.

A Historical Fact Not Generally Known.

The fate of the original Declaration of Independence, enacted in Charlotte on the 20th of May, 1775, to be of any historical importance, is not without its parallel in history, for in an article by W. L. Stone, in the July number of Harper's Magazine (1883) we find the following recited on the subject of signing of the Declaration of Independence of July 4, 1776:

"In thinking of that instrument, one is apt to call up before him an august assemblage gravely seated around a table, with declaration spread out upon it, and each member of the Continental Congress in turn taking a pen and with great dignity affixing to it his name. Nothing, however, can be further from that which actually took place, very few of the delegates, if indeed any, signed the original document on the 4th, and none signed the present one now in Independence Hall, for the very good reason that it was not then in existence.

"On July 19th, Congress voted that the Declaration be engrossed on parchment. Jefferson, however, says that New York signed on July 15th. Consequently, New York must have signed the original Declaration before it had gone into the hands of the engrosser. On what day the work was done by the copyist, is not known. All that is certainly known, is that on August 2nd Congress had the document as engrossed. This is the document in existence now in Independence Hall. It is on parchment or something that the trade calls parchment. On that day (August 2nd) it was signed by all the members present. The original Declaration is lost, or rather was probably purposely destroyed by Congress. All the signatures were made anew. When the business of signing was ended, is not known. One, Matthew Thornton, from New Hampshire, signed it in November, when he became a member for the first time.

And Thomas McKean, from Delaware, as he says himself, did not sign till January, 1777. Indeed, this signing was, in effect, what at the present day would be called a 'test oath." The principles of many of the new delegates coming into Congress from the different States, were not known with certainty—some of them might be Tories in disguise—and thus each one was required, on first entering Congress, to sign the Declaration. In January, 1777, an authenticated copy, with the names of all the signers, was sent to each State for signatures—a fact which may have put a stop to the business of signing. It shows, however, the little importance that was attached to this ceremony, that Robert R. Livingston was one of the committee of five that reported the Declaration, and yet did not sign it, unless his signature is lost with the original document.

"The truth is the Declaration of Independence was considered at that time of much less importance than now, nor did the signers dream of its becoming a shrine almost of worship at the present day. It was like the Scottish Covenants of the previous century, which so strongly tinctured the Mecklenburg Declaration of May 20, 1775."

The Mecklenburg Declaration of Independence is so well authenticated that it takes a man of more than ordinary nerve power to deny, in the presence of the descendants of those great and good men, who sat at the feet of Alexander Craighead and learned of him those Bible and political truths that were established with the freedom and independence of our happy country. Bancroft says: "The first public voice in America for dissolving all connection with Great Britain, came not from the Puritans of New England, the Dutch of New York, nor the planters of Virginia, but from Scotch-Irish Presbyterians."

Rev. Alexander Craighead exercised a most wonderful influence in Mecklenburg county—before the county was laid off—both for Church and State. In 1755 he and his friends came to Rocky River and Sugar Creek, and there he taught the people the great truths of the Gospel and of

Liberty, which are indissolubly connected. Presbyterianism and Republicanism best flouish together. In the decayed monarchies of Europe, the hard and rigorous laws by which the people are held under priestcraft, are inimical to the growth of free governments. Mr. Craighead was the main leader in building the seven first churches in this county. They were all established about 1762, but it is more than probable that they had *stands,* or *groves,* for three or five years earlier. "Over twenty of the members of the Convention of Charlotte, who on May 20, 1775, produced the Mecklenburg Declaration of Independence, were connected with the seven Presbyterian churches of the county, two of which were Rocky River and Sugar Creek. From these two the other five took "life and being." Such were the men who, when informed of the troubles "to the eastward," rallied to the cry: "The cause of Boston is the cause of all."

With Craighead they held that the right of the people were as divine as the rights of kings, for their fathers, and they themselves had often listened in rapt attention to his thrilling eloquence, and felt as if himself were he on whose sole arm hung victory. Although Mr. Craighead died before the convention of May 20, 1775, at Charlotte, yet to the whole American Nation should revere his memory as the fearless champion of those principles of civil and religious freedom, which they now enjoy, and which first found expression from his old comrades in the immortal Declaration, the true date of which, in the language of another, "Has been as clearly established as the given name of any citizen then living in the county."

The Rev. Dr. A. W. Miller in a sermon delivered at Charlotte on May 14, 1876, most truthfully used the following language:

"If to the people of Mecklenburg county Providence assigned the foremost position in the ranks of patriots, a century ago, let them never cease to hallow the memory of that illustrious hero, the Rev. Alexander Craighead, who prepared them for it, at so great toil and pain, and for years and years diligently sowed the seed that produced the glorious harvest. No ordinary work was given him to do, and no ordinary training and discipline fitted him for it.

"Deeply imbibing the spirit of the Scottish Covenant, contending earnestly for the descending obligations of those covenants upon all whose ancestors were parties to the same, and insisting upon making the adoption of the solemn League and Covenant a term of communion for members of the church in the colonial as well as the mother country, testifying continually to the Headship of Christ over the State, and the responsibility of all kings and rulers to Him, a failure of whose allegiance to Him would forfeit the allegiance of the people to them; proclaiming everywhere these good old doctrines, with a fidelity, and a courage, and a zeal, and a constancy, that ought to have secured sympathy and commanded admiration. Instead of this, he experienced the usual fate of those who are in advance of the age. He was opposed, resisted, denounced as an extremist and ultra reformer, calumniated as an agitor, and even censured by the General Synod of the Presbyterian Church. It was not until he came to North Carolina that he found a congenial element which he could mould and train successfully in devotion to principles bearing fruit in splendid achievements, which now, at this anniversary season, in another city, are commanding the homage of the representatives of the world—*so successfully trained*—that Charlotte occupied the front rank more than a year in advance of Philadelphia, the latter on May 20, 1775, counselling submission, the former declaring independence, and so Mecklenburg became the leader of the land."

Among the notable celebrities of Mecklenburg county was Susan Smart—nee Barnett—remarkable for her great age and her accurate and vivid recollections of the events of the Revolution. Her father was John Barnett, who imigrated from Ireland, and who married Ann, the daughter of Thomas Spratt, one of the earliest settlers of this county.

Thomas Spratt was the first who crossed the Yadkin river with a wagon; and the first court ever held in Mecklenburg county was convened at his house. Susan Barnett was born in 1761, and her sister Mary was the first white child born between the two rivers, the Catawba and the Yadkin. She married Capt. Thomas Jack, who has been previously spoken of. Capt. Jack was the bearer of the Mecklenburg Declaration of May 20, 1775, to the Continental Congress at Philadelphia. Mrs. Smart was present at Charlotte on this glorious occasion, and many persons now living have listened with great pleasure to her glowing and graphic accounts of the enthusiasm which pervaded the whole community. It was truly a day of "throwing up of hats,". many of which she stated, fell on the roof of the court house.

Miss Susan Barnett married in 1775, George W. Smart, who died in May, 1809. The house she occupied was built by him. She had always been in the habit of entertaining travelers, as she lived on the public road. William H. Crawford always stopped at her house on his way to and from Washington, and was highly esteemed by her. She used to say, "I have rarely been from home, but I have known well two of our Presidents, Andrew Jackson and James K. Polk. Little Jimmy Polk used to pass along this road often to school, barefooted, with his breeches rolled up to his knees. He was a mighty bashful little fellow." George W. Smart was elected to the Legislature in 1804-'5-'6, served three terms, and had for his colleagues Gen. George Graham and Judge Samuel Lowrie. Mecklenburg had giants in those days.

The War of 1812-1814.

The war between England and the United States was caused by English sailors deserting their vessels and applying for positions in America's merchantmen. The English Government claimed the right to search American ships for their deserters. This was resisted, and war resulted, which lasted till the 8th of January, 1815, when Jackson won his signal victory at New Orleans. This is not the time or place to give history other than what pertains to our county, but will run the risk of adverse criticism.

The six New England States were opposed to this war, and refused to give either men or money to prosecute it; and towards the close they determined that if the government did not stop the war *they would secede*. (If secession was right in 1814, what was wrong with it in 1861?) We wish to perpetuate the memory of those who were patriotic enough to fight for the United States, hence we insert the roster of Mecklenburg's five companies that participated in the war of 1812-1814.

SEVENTH COMPANY.

(*Detached from the First Mecklenburg Regiment.*)

Douglass, Joseph, *Captain;* Kary, Wm. M., *Lieutenant;* Walker, Wm., *Ensign;* Brevard, Hamden, *First Sergeant;* Gibony, David, *Second Sergeant;* Brown, Samuel, *Third Sergeant;* Barrett, Wm. M., *Fourth Sergeant;* Allen, Thomas, *First Corporal;* Solon, John, *Second Corporal;* Pitt, Isaac V., *Third Corporal;* Duckworth, Robert, *Fourth Corporal.*

Private Harrison, Adam,
    Wiley, Hugh,
    Moore, James,
    Caldwell, John,
    Hood, Junius,
    Alexander, David,
    Parker, James,
    Wallace, Matthew,
    McRea, Thomas,
    Phillips, John,
    Farr, Henry,
Todd, Hugh,
Elliott, Hugh,
Jimison, Arthur,
Parish, Nicholas,
Walker, Andrew,
Roden, Upton,
Wilson, David B.,
Love, Joseph,
Cunningham, Jacob I.,
Harris, Hugh,
Alexander, Eli,

MECKLENBURG COUNTY. 53

Johnston, Mitchell,
Lucas, Allen,
Downy, William,
Graham, Samuel,
Bushbey, Will.,
Shepherd, Thomas,
Lane, Andrew M.,
Worsham, Alexander,
Weir, Howard,
Sullivan, William,
Beaty, Isaac,
Bingham, Joseph,
Sharply, William,
Greggs, Hugh,
Erwin, Francis,
Mason Richard,
Elliott, John B.,
Darnell, John L.,
Cameron, William,
Hutchison, Samuel J.,
Clark, Joshua,
Hutchison, James,
McLure, John,
Darnell, John.,
Thompson, Benjamin,
Moore, Alexander,
Smith, Alexander,
Darnell, William,
Darnell, David,
Sloan, Allen,
Fat, John,
Ferret, John,
Henderson, David,
Garreston, Arthur,
Robertson, Will.,
Summimer, James,
Solomon, Drury,
Holmes, Hugh,
McLilie, ———,
Stevenson, Hugh,
Munteeth, William,
Scott, Will,
Alexander, Palan.—76.

EIGHTH COMPANY.

(*Detached from the Second Mecklenburg Regiment.*)

Wood, Robert, *Captain;* Shever, Jacob, *Lieutenant;* Mape, Peter. *Second Lieutenant;* Wilson, John, *Ensign;* Flenigan, William, *First Sergeant;* Hooker, John, *Second Sergeant;* Barns, John, *Third Sergeant;* Watson, James, *Fourth Sergeant;* Hammons, John, *First Corporal;* Dafter, Obed, *Second Corporal;* John, Will, *Third Corporal;* Hart, Charles, *Fourth Corporal;* Stewart, Allen, *Drummer;* Rice, John, *Fifer.*

Private Walker, James,
Brown, John,
Flenigan, Robert,
Sharp, William,
Flenigan, Elias,
Cheek, Randolph,
Flanigan, Samuel E.,
McCallok, Elias,
Stewart, W. Andrew,
Wiley, Samuel,
John, Ash,
Sharp, Cunningham,
Wiatt, John,
Black, John,
Benbow, Paten,
Bryan, Joseph,
Purvis, Antheris.
Clontz, Henry,
Crowell, Charles.
Cuthbertson, John,
Lemmon, Wm. L.,
Flow, John,
Starns, Jacob,
Boid, Robert,
McLoyd, Daniel,
McReley, Roderick,
Stunford, Moses,
Broom, Allen,
Lancey, Charles,
None, John,
Belk, Brelon,
Holden, Samuel,
Prifley, Valentine,
Flenigan. Michael,
Moser, Henry,
Coughran, Eli,
Robertson, James,
Redford, William,
Shanon, Robert,
Barns, William,
Morris, Solomon,
Pirant, William,

Pool, William,
Jesse Yandles,
Rea, Will,
Henley, Thomas,
Ormand, Samuel,
Fobes, John,
Ormand, Adam,
Howard, Lewis,

McCorcle, John,
Levey, Will M.,
Thompson, James,
Long, John,
Miller, Thomas,
Givens, Samuel,
Martin, William.—71.

NINTH COMPANY.

(*Detached from the Second Mecklenburg Regiment.*)

Garretson, John, *Captain;* Wiley, Isaac, *Lieutenant;* Sims, Nathaniel, *Ensign;* Lawyer, Archibald, *First Sergeant;* Dixon, Ire. B., *Second Sergeant;* Smith, William, *Third Sergeant;* Kimmons Joro, *Fourth Sergeant;* Mays, William, *First Corporal;* Holbrooks, John, *Second Corporal;* Kiser, Frederick, *Third Corporal;* Grady, Andrew M.,*Fourth Corporal;* Kenty, George, *Drummer;* Jaccour, John, *Fifer.*

Private Irwin, John,
Harris, Samuel H.,
Ross, James,
Harris, Houston,
Alexander, John,
Harris, Isaac,
Alexander, Laird,
Campbell, Cyrus,
Cochran, Robert M.,
Morrison, John,
Morrison, Robert C.,
McCain, Hugh,
Bost, Daniel,
House, Jacob,
Miller, Henry,
Rinehart, Jacob,
Rowe, Henry,
Bost, Michael,
Light, John,
Carrigan, Robert, Sr.,
Carrigan, Robert, Jr.,
Gayler, Theophilus,
Carrell, John,
Hamilton, Joseph,
Houston, David,
Neels, Andrew,
Neele, James,
Flemming, George,
Icehour, Martin,
Dove, George,
Smith, William,
Linker, George,

Smith, Daniel,
Barnhard, John,
Fink, Son,
Carriher, Andrew,
Fink, Phillip,
Taylous, John S.,
Johnston, John,
Johnston, Rufus,
Black, David H.,
Black, John,
Biggers, Johnston N.,
Newitt, William,
Right, George,
Gilmore, Josiah,
Martin, Edward,
Kelley, William,
Wines, William,
Keelough, Ebenezer,
Hall, James,
Gaugus, Jacob,
Goodnight, John,
Adam, Freeze,
Fereland, John,
Click, John,
Chapie, Jesse,
Sneed, Reuben,
Goodman, John,
McGraw, James,
Walter, Charles,
Shank, Martin,
Luther, Daniel,
Simmon, Jacob.—78.

MECKLENBURG COUNTY. 55

MUSTER ROLL.

Of the Detached Militia, Organized in August, 1814.
Montford Stokes, *Major-General*; Jeremiah Slade and J. A. Pearson, *Brigadier-Generals.*

MECKLENBURG COUNTY TROOPS—FIRST REGIMENT.

Wilson, James, *Captain;* Boyd, Thomas, Esq., *First Lieutenant;* Blacwood, Joseph, *Second Lieutenant;* Price, Isaac, *Third Lieutenant;* Hutchison, Charles, *Ensign.*

Private Carson, William,
Winens, John,
Garner, Bazilla,
McCombs, James,
Barnett, John,
McKelvia, William,
Hawkins, John,
Barnett, Amos,
Alexander, Ezekiel,
Shelvey, William,
Harrison, John C.,
Means, James,
Hope, Thomas,
Caldwell, Robert,
Price, John,
Parkes, John, Sen.,
Johnston, Samuel, Jr.,
Wallis, William, Jr.,
Wallis, Matthew, Jr.,
Parks, Samuel,
Caldwell, Robert, Jr.,
Wynns, Ann,
Sadler, John,
Barnhill, John,
Julin, Jacob,
Henderson, James,
Love, Christopher,
McCracken, Elisha,
Dunn, Robert, Jr.,
Parish, Andrew M.,
Dunn, William,
Lewing, Andrew, Jr.,
Perry, Francis,
Farra, John,
Lewing, John,
Carothers, James,
Dinkins, James,
Bingham, Robert, Jr.,
Johnston, John,
Johnston, William,
Neely, Samuel,
Reed, David,
Whitesides, Joseph,
Miles, Augustus,
West, Matthew,
Connel, Thomas,
Benhill, William,
McKnight, Robert,
Michael, Baker,
Baker, Abel,
McDowell, Hugh,
Kerr, William,
Foard, John,
Baker, Aaron,
Walker, Andrew,
Porter, James,
Beaty, John,
Bigham, Samuel,
Pelt, Simon V.,
Beaty, John,
Jackson, Peavon,
Blackburn, John,
Wilson, John, Jr.,
Brown, John,
Norman, Wm. S.,
Baxter, Daniel,
Wilson, Benjamin,
Elliott, Thomas,
Conner, James,
Davis, Daniel,
Elliott, William,
Hartly, Richard,
Duckworth, George,
Meek, James,
Alexander, James,
Jones, Joel,
Sloan, James,
Morrison, Isaac, Jr.,
Parker, John,
Mentith, James,
Williams, Joseph,
Prim, Andrew,
Osborne, Robert A.,
White, John,
Chanels, Michael,
Steel, John,
McKellerand, Joseph,
Goforth, George,

Alexander, John D.,
Ferrell, Gabriel,
Irwin, Giles,
Ferrell, John,
Wallis, Joseph,
Hunter, Henry, Jr.,
Ferrell, William,
Steel, James,
Gray, Nelson,
Montgomery, Robert,
Peoples, Richard,
Braddy, James A.—105.

MECKLENBURG COUNTY—SECOND REGIMENT.

Moore, David, *Captain;* Wilson, John, *First Lieutenant;* Reed, Solomon, *Second Lieutenant;* Williams, John, *Third Lieutenant;* Alexander, Albertes, *Ensign.*

Private Barfleet, Richard,
McCall, Matthew,
McCall, James,
Thompson, Henry,
Stewart, Alexander,
Cherry, William,
Robertson, James,
Yandles, Samuel,
Harbeson, James,
Shelbey, William,
Freeman, Gideon,
Morrison, John,
Allen, John,
Forsythe, John,
Barnes, James,
Purser, Moses,
Barns, Micajah,
Wilkinson, Osburn,
Allen, Robert,
Vinsent, Groves,
Helmes, William,
Helmes, Charles,
Starns, Frederic,
Starns, Nathaniel,
Shehorn, Morris,
Yerby, William,
Rone, James,
Belk, John,
Rich, Daniel,
Junderbusk, John,
Flowers, Henry,
Yandles, David B.,
Alexander, Salamacnus,
Alexander, Abdon,
Smart, Osburn,
Smart, Elisha,
McCullock, John,
Cook, Robert,
Hanson, Steven,
Craig, Moses,
McCoy, William,
Howard, Robert,
Woodall, William,
Gray, Jacob,
Howie, Aaron,
King, Andrew,
Finsher, Joshua,
Rape, Samuel,
Rener, Samuel,
Hambleton, James,
Vick, Moses,
Phillips, John,
Train, James,
Berns, George,
Fisher, William,
Button, Daniel,
McAlroy, Hugh,
Ivey, Jesse,
Hanley, John,
Spravey, Benjamin,
Reed, Joseph,
Karr, Adam,
Matthews, John,
Parks, George,
Reed, William,
Downs, William,
Taylor, Wilson,
Maglauchlin, Joseph,
Maygeehee, William,
Hargett, Henry,
Hargett, William,
Helmer, Joel,
Crowell, John,
Chainey, Peter,
Harkey, David,
Tuter, George,
Stilwell, Elias,
Morrison, James,
Harkey, John,
Rogers, James,
Harrison, Robert,
Hodge, John,
Lambert, Richard,
Story, David W.,
Tomberlin, Moses,
Reak, Edward,

Morrison, Neel,
Costley, James,
Cochran, Thomas S.,
Houston, Wm., Jr.,
Cochran, Robert,
Wilson, Hugh,
Hood, Reuben,
Dennis, Charles,
Neel, Samuel,
Fuller, John,
Shaw, James,
Webb, Lewis,
Story, James, Sen.—105

The younger class of those who may see proper to peruse this History of Mecklenburg, cannot but see that this glorious county has always done her duty when the honor of the country was assailed, or our liberties were in jeopardy. She promptly sent forward 425 men, and participated in the strife till the war closed at New Orleans, more than two weeks after peace was made. Neither steam nor electricity had then been harnessed for the civilization of this country. We were then but getting started in the race of nations.

The Members of the General Assembly From 1777 to 1902, Inclusive, and Time of Service.

YEARS.	SENATE.	HOUSE.

1777..Jno. McK. Alexander...Martin Phifer, Waightstill Avery.
1778..Robt. Irwin.............Caleb Phifer, David Wilson.
1779..Robt. Irwin.............Caleb Phifer, David Wilson.
1780..Robt. Irwin.............Caleb Phifer, David Wilson.
1781..Robt. Irwin.............Caleb Phifer, David Wilson.
1782..Robt. Irwin.............Caleb Phifer, David Wilson.
1783..Robt. Irwin.............Caleb Phifer, David Wilson.
1784..James Harris ....Caleb Phifer, David Wilson.
1785..James Harris ....Caleb Phifer, George Alexander.
1786..James Mitchell . ...Caleb Phifer, George Alexander.
1787..Robt. Irwin.............William Polk, Caleb Phifer.
1788..Joseph Graham.........Joseph Douglas, Caleb Phifer.
1789..Joseph Graham.........Geo. Alexander, Caleb Phifer.
1790..Joseph Graham.........Robert Irwin, William Polk.
1791..Joseph Graham ....Caleb Phifer, William Polk.
1792..Joseph Graham.........Caleb Phifer, Jas. Harris.
1793..Joseph Graham.........Charles Polk, Geo. Graham.
1794..Joseph Graham.........Charles Polk, Geo. Graham.
1795..Robt. Irwin............ Charles Polk, Geo. Graham.
1796..Geo. Graham ....David McKee, William Morrison.
1797..Robt. Irwin............ James Connor, Nathaniel Alexander.
1798..Robt. Irwin.............James Connor, Hugh Parker.
1799..Robt. Irwin.............James Connor, Sherrod Gray.
1800..Robt. Irwin........... .Charles Polk, Hugh Parker.
1801..Nathaniel Alexander ...Charles Polk, Alexander Morrison.
1802..Nathaniel Alexander ...Thos. Henderson, Alexander Morrison.
1803..Geo. Graham ....Thos. Henderson, Alexander Morrson.
1804..Geo. Graham ....Samuel Lowrie, Thomas Henderson.
1805..Geo. Graham ....Samuel Lowrie, Geo. W. Smart.
1806..Geo. Graham ....Samuel Lowrie, Thomas Henderson.
1807..Geo. Graham .... John Harris, Thomas Henderson.
1808..Geo. Graham ....John Harris, Geo. W. Smart.
1809..Geo. Graham ....Thomas Henderson, Hutchins G. Burton.

MECKLENBURG COUNTY.   59

YEARS.	SENATE.	HOUSE.
1810	Geo. Graham	Thomas Henderson, Hutchins G. Burton.
1811	Geo. Graham	Jonathan Harris, Henry Massey.
1812	Geo. Graham	Jonathan Harris, Henry Massey.
1813	William Davidson	Cunningham Harris, Jonathan Harris.
1814	Jonathan Harris	William Beattie, Geo. Hampton.
1815	William Davidson	John Ray, Abdon Alexander.
1816	William Davidson	Joab Alexander, John Wilson.
1817	William Davidson	John Rhea, Jno. Wilson.
1818	William L. Davidson	John Rhea, Jno. Wilson.
1819	Michael McLeary	John Rhea, Miles J. Robinson.
1820	Michael McLeary	John Rhea, Miles J. Robinson.
1821	Michael McLeary	John Rhea, Samuel McCombs.
1822	Michael McLeary	John Rhea, Matthew Baine.
1823	Michael McLeary	Thomas G. Polk, Matthew Baine.
1824	Michael McLeary	Thomas G. Polk, Matthew Baine.
1825	William Davidson	Thomas G. Polk, Matthew Baine.
1826	Michael McLeary	Wm. J. Alexander, Matthew Baine.
1827	William Davidson	Wm. J. Alexander, Joseph Blackwood.
1828	William Davidson	Wm. J. Alexander, Joseph Blackwood.
1829	William Davidson	Wm. J. Alexander, Evan Alexander.
1830	Joseph Blackwood	Wm. J. Alexander, Evan Alexander.
1831	Henry Massey	James Dougherty, Jno. Harte.
1832	Henry Massey	James Dougherty, Jno. Harte.
1833	Washington Morrison	Wm. J. Alexander, Andrew Grier.
1834	Wm. H. McLeary	Wm. J. Alexander, J. M. Hutchison.
1835	Stephen Fox	J. A. Dunn, J. M. Hutchison.
1836	Stephen Fox	J. A. Dunn, J. M. Hutchison, G. W. Caldwell.
1838	Stephen Fox	G. W. Caldwell, Jas. T. J. Orr, Caleb Erwin.
1840	J. T. R. Orr	G. W. Caldwell, Jno. Walker, Benj. Morrow.
1842	Jno. Walker	Jno. Kirk, Jas. W. Ross, Caleb Erwin.
1844	Jno. Walker	Robt. Lemmons, J. A. Dunn, Jno. Kirk.
1846	Jno. Walker	Jno. W. Potts, Jno. N. Davis, Robt. Lemmons.
1848	Jno. Walker	J. K. Harrison, J. M. Davis, J. J. Williams.

HISTORY OF

YEARS.	SENATE.	HOUSE.
1850	Green W. Caldwell	Jno. K. Harrison, J. J. Williams, E. Constantine Davidson.
1852	Green W. Caldwell	W. Black, J. A. Dunn, J. Ingram.
1854	Jno. Walker	W. R. Myers, W. Black.
1856	W. R. Myers	W. Matthews, W. F. Davidson.
1858	Wm. F. Davidson	H. M. Pritchard, W. Wallace.
1860	Jno. Walker	S. W. Davis, J. M. Potts.
1862	Jno. A. Young	J. L. Brown, E. C. Grier.
1864	W. M. Grier	J. L. Brown, E. C. Grier.
1866	J. H. Wilson	R. D. Whitley, J. M. Hutchison.
1868	Jas. W. Osborne	R. D. Whitley, W. M. Grier.
1870	H. C. Jones	R. P. Waring, J. W. Reid.
1872	R. P. Waring	Jno. E. Brown, S. W. Reid.
1873	R. P. Waring	Jno. E. Brown, S. W. Reid.
1874	R. P. Waring	Jno. E. Brown, S. W. Reid.
1875	R. P. Waring	J. L. Jetton, J. Sol. Reid.
1877	T. J. Moore	Randolph A. Shotwell, W. E. Ardrey.
1879	S. B. Alexander	W. E. Ardrey, J. L. Brown.
1881	A. Burwell	A. G. Neal, E. H. Walker.
1883	S. B. Alexander	J. S. Myers, T. T. Sandifer, W. H. Bailey.
1885	S. B. Alexander	W. E. Ardrey, H. D. Stowe, R. P. Warring.
1887	S. B. Alexander	J. T. Kell, J. W. Moore, E. K. P. Osborne.
1889	J. Sol Reid	N. Gibbon, J. Watt Hood, Jas. C. Long.
1891	W. E. Ardrey	R. A. Grier, J. Watt Hood, W. D. Mayes.
1893	F. B. McDowell	Jno. R. Erwin, Hugh W. Harris, J. L. Jetton.
1895	W. C. Dowd	J. T. Kell, J. D. McCall, Jno. G. Alexander.
1897	J. B. Alexander	M. B. Williamson, W. S. Clanton, W. P. Craven.
1899	F. I. Osborne	Heriot Clarkson, R. M. Ransom, J. E. Henderson.
1901	S. B. Alexander	C. H. Duls, W. E. Ardrey, F. M. Shannonhouse.

The County Officers and the Time They Served.

SHERIFFS OF MECKLENBURG COUNTY.

Thomas Harris was the first sheriff of Mecklenburg. How long he served cannot be positively stated, as the books were not kept accurately for a number of years.

The following list is probably the best that can be given:

Thomas Harris was appointed sheriff "in good old colony times, when we lived under the king," just at what date we cannot say, but he performed the duties of the office before 1774, and for some time afterwards.

James White, Esq., was elected sheriff in July, 1779, by the County Court, which was composed of twelve magistrates. They required a bond of $2,000, to be given once a year.

The following is a list of those who constituted the court: Abraham Alexander, Hezekiah Alexander, David Reese, John McKnitt Alexander, Edward Giles, Robert Irwin, John Ford, Adam Alexander, Robert Harris, Robert Harris, Jr. These were present at the court, and they elected the sheriff; in fact, they took the oversight of the entire county. There was ten or twelve men in the county who appear to have taken control over the courts and administer justice as they deemed right and proper. They were certainly wise men, and did that which was for the best interests of all the people. John McKnitt Alexander, Thomas Harris and David Wilson were appointed by the court to dispose of the confiscated estates in Mecklenburg county— the estates of Tories. Money was depreciated to a great extent. The county Court allowed the assessor $30 per day in 1779. In 1780 and 1781, $100 per day. It was worth about $1.00 to $100.

Thomas Polk was elected sheriff in 1781, and resigned in 1782.

Major-General Joseph Graham became sheriff of Mecklenburg county some time after the Revolutionary war was over, and it is not known how long he served, but it is more than probable that he served only four or five years, for he was State Senator from this county in 1788-'1794, seven years. (In the year 1814 he received the strong solicitations of the Governor of North Carolina to command a body of men, with the rank of General, to aid Gen. Jackson in quelling an outbreak of the Indians, which he did at the battle of the Horse Shoe.) He moved over into Lincoln county, where he engaged in the iron business.

Sheriff Wilson probably succeeded him for quite a number of years, and gave satisfaction to the people of the county.

Col. John Sloan came next into office, with like results; that is, satisfaction to the tax payers.

Joseph McCaughneyhey ruled as sheriff, with old "Uncle Billy Todd" as deputy, for a number of years. We can be more particular in recent dates.

Thomas N. Alexander, from 1838 to 1854.

E. C. Grier, from 1854 to 1860.

W. W. Grier, from 1860 to 1862.

R. M. White, from 1862 to 1872.

M. E. Alexander, from 1872 to 1884.

L. A. Potts, from 1884 to 1885 (died).

W. F. Griffith, from 1885 to 1886.

T. S. Cooper, from 1886 to 1888.

Z. T. Smith, from 1888 to 1898.

N. W. Wallis, 1898.

The people of Mecklenburg county have reason to be proud of their chief executive officers for more than one hundred years. Every one has gone out of office doubly as strong as he entered on his duties.

COUNTY TREASURERS.

Prior to the year 1868, the duties of taking care of and disbursing the money of the county devolved upon the sheriff, or some one appointed by the old County Court, which never ceased until the rights of the county, with those of the State, were denied the people, when the government was torn up by the roots in 1865, then everything was changed.

Then they elected their first county treasurer, and it would be only justice to say the county never did herself more honor than when S. E. Belk was put in charge of the finances of the county.

The first treasurer was a soldier in the war with Mexico in 1846 and 1847. He came out of the war with a clean record and stood well with the people. In 1861 he volunteered in the Confederate army, was elected Captain of a company from Mecklenburg county and assigned to the Fifty-third Regiment, North Carolina Troops, where he acquitted himself most gallantly. Towards the close of the war Capt. Belk had the misfortune to lose an arm at the shoulder, from which wound he suffered a great deal, and at times would become irritable, for which he would apologize most humbly.

Capt. S. E. Belk, from 1868 to 1884.
J. H. McClintock, from 1884 to 1894.
E. H. Walker, from 1894. He is still in office.

J. H. McClintock served for ten years and, like his predecessor, fought in the Confederate army till he lost an arm in the service of his country. He went to school, graduated at Davidson, then taught school, and served his country in whatever way the county desired his services.

REGISTER OF DEEDS.

The office of Register of Deeds was probably the first office ever established in Mecklenburg county. We see it stated in the court house records that Robert Harris was appointed in 1763, in the year when Mecklenburg county was legally set apart from Anson. The county was recognized, the meets and bounds declared by the surveyor in 1762, but not confirmed by the authority of the colony of North Carolina until 1763, when the machinery of the county was put in motion. Hence we find that—

Robert Harris was appointed in 1763; served till 1792.
John McKnitt Alexander, from 1792 to 1808.
Wm. B. Alexander, from 1808 to 1836.
The next four years were filled by the sheriff.
F. M. Ross, elected, 1840 to 1870.
Wm. Maxwell, from 1870 to 1884.
J. W. Cobb, from 1884 to 1898.
A. M. McDonald, from 1898; continues in office.

The seven men who have held the office of Register of Deeds for one hundred and forty-five years show plainly that patriots indeed had the oversight of all that pertained to the welfare of the county. The men who have exercised the functions of office for the last fifty years, were equal in point of integrity to any men in any period of the county's history. Mecklenburg is exceedingly fortunate in always being able to furnish men capable to fill any position with honor to themselves and credit to their county. May she ever be so fortunate.

CLERKS OF THE COUNTY COURTS.

The system of keeping the records of court previous to 1836, makes it very difficult to know for a certainty who was clerk of court at a given time; hence the clerks of the County Court will be given only from 1836:

Mr. Brawley Oates served from 1836 to 1842.
Charles T. Alexander from 1842 to 1845.
Brawley Oates, from 1845 to 1854.
W. K. Reid, from 1854 to 1862.
Wm. Maxwell, from 1862 to 1868.

MECKLENBURG COUNTY.

After this date the old county Court, known as the Peoples' Court, was done away with by the order of Gen. Canby, the Yankee general who happened to be in command at the time, although his headquarters were in Charleston, S. C. All the duties of this court were merged into the Superior Court. Soon the docket was so large we had an Inferior Court established to try the smaller cases. Then afterwards the Criminal Court was inaugurated. Now we have these two courts in the county.

SUPERIOR COURT CLERKS.

Jennings B. Kerr served from 1842 to 1865.
Mortimer D. Johnston, from 1865 to 1866.
E. A. Osborne, from 1866 to 1875.
John R. Erwin, from 1875 to 1886.
J. M. Morrow, from 1886 to 1899.
J. A. Russel, from 1899; still in office.

The county is to be congratulated on her long line of good men for clerks. In all the multiplicity of clerks and other county officials since the county was first formed, we have had none but the best of men. Every officer has rendered a satisfactory account of his stewardship.

Rev. Alexander Craighead.

Mr. Craighead came to America in a time that was auspicious for the work that the march of events was marking out for him to engage in. From the most reliable authority we are led to date Mr. Craighead's admission into the ministry in 1736. He was born in Ireland, and possessed in a large degree the characteristics that are peculiar to the Irish people. Being an exceedingly zealous man, of an ardent temperament, devoted to the work of the ministry, he was noted for preaching sermons peculiarly calculated to awaken careless sinners. He was accused of irregularities before his Presbytery in 1740. No immoralities were alleged against him, or false doctrines charged on him; the complaint was against various proceedings thought to be irregular. The Presbytery was unable to make any conclusion of the matter, for while the majority were against him, his vehement appeals to the public turned the sympathy of the community in his favor. The charge of irregularity he rebutted by the recriminating charge of Pharisaism, coldness and formality, and in the ardor of his defence he was not very measured in his epithets and comparisons. Probably the principal cause of the disagreement was Mr. Craighead was opposed to British rule, opposed to one church having advantages over another. He believed in a separation of Church and State. About this time he was directed by the Presbytery in Cumberland, January, 1758, to preach at Rocky River, on the second Sabbath of February, and at other vacant churches till Spring.

At the meeting of the Presbytery in April, a call from Rocky River was presented for the services of Mr. Craighead. He accepted the call and requested installation, which was attended to soon afterwards. It appears that this was the first church established in the upper country.

"In this beautiful, fertile and peaceful country, Mr. Craighead passed the remainder of his days in the active duties of a frontier minister of the Gospel, and ended his successful labors in his Master's vineyard in the month of March, 1766, the solitary minister between the Yadkin and Catawba. In this retired country, too, he found full and undisturbed exercise for that ardent love of personal liberty and freedom of opinion which had rendered him obnoxious in Pennsylvania, and was in some measure restrained in Virginia. He was ahead of his ministerial brethren in Pennsylvania in his views of civil government and religious liberty, and became particularly offensive to the governor for a pamphlet of a political nature, the authorship of which was attributed to him. The Synod disavowed both the pamphlet and Mr. Craighead, and agreed with the justice that it was calculated to forment disloyal and rebellious practices, and disseminate principles of disaffection.

In Carolina he found a people remote from the seat of authority, among them the intolerant laws were a dead letter, so far divided from other congregations, even of his own faith, that there could be no collision with him on account of faith or practice; so united in their general principles of religion and church government that he was the teacher of the whole population, and here his spirit rested. Here he passed his days; here he poured forth his principles of religious and civil government, undisturbed by the jealousy of the government, too distant to be aware of his doings, or too careless to be interested in the poor and distant emigrants on the Catawba. Mr. Craighead had the privilege of forming the principles, both civil and religious, in no measured degree, of a race of men that feared God, and feared not labor and hardship, or the face of man; a race that sought for freedom and property in the wilderness, and having found them, rejoiced—a race capable of great excellence, mental and physical, whose minds could conceive the glorious idea of Independence and whose convention announced it to the world in May, 1775, and whose hands sustained it in the trying scenes of the Revolution."

Previous to the year 1750, the immigration to this beautiful, but distant frontier, was slow and the solitary cabins were found upon the borders of prairies and in the vicinity of canebreaks, the immense ranges abounding with wild game, and affording sustenance the whole year, for herds of tame cattle. Extensive tracts of country between the Yadkin and the Catawba, now waving with thrifty forests, then were covered with tall grass, with scarcely a bush or shrub, looking at first view as if immense grazing farms had been at once abandoned, the houses disappearing, and the abundant grass luxuriating in its native wildness and beauty, the will herds wandering at pleasure, and nature rejoicing in undisturbed quietness. At the time of the settlement of Mr. Craighead, the county of Anson extended indefinitely west, having been set off in 1749 as a separate county. In the year 1762, the county of Mecklenburg was set off from Anson, and took its name in honor of the reigning house of Hanover; and the county seat, in the bounds of Sugar Creek congregation, and about three miles from the church, was called Charlotte, in honor of the Princess Charlotte of Mecklenburg. There were seven congregations in a short time, in Mecklenburg, except a part of Centre, which lay in Rowan—now Iredell—and in their extensive bounds comprehended almost the entire county, viz.: Steel Creek, Providence, Hopewell, Centre, Rocky River, Poplar Tent and Sugar Creek. From these came the delegates that formed the celebrated convention that met in Charlotte on the 20th of May, 1775. In this old graveyard of Sugar Creek church, where Mr. Craighead preached the most of his time, is certainly a spot of remarkable interest. It was here in 1766 that this wonderful man was given sepulcher. Borne to his grave on two sassafras hand-spikes, and one placed at the head and one at the foot of the grave, both grew into large trees; but in the course of time they have fallen; they have been sawed up into lumber and church furniture made of them. The grave is now marked by a neat slab of marble, with an iron fence around the grave. A cenotaph has been erected in the cemetery in Charlotte to his memory, but not one person in a thousand of those who visit the city are ever told that such a man ever lived, or see the monument to inquire "What does this mean, or what good did he effect?" We hold that much of the spirit of Independence that was exhibited in Charlotte in May, 1775, was the result of his teaching.

Although he died nine years before this convention met, yet his doctrine was gladly received, and bore fruit to the good of this people. His grand-son, Rev. S. C. Caldwell, preached in Sugar Creek from 1792 to 1826, and did much work in building up Hopewell and Mallard Creek, organized and built up Paw Creek, and devoted considerable toward building the church in Charlotte, although the church in Charlotte was not organized till 1832. Rev. Dr. Hall Morrison preached at Sugar Creek for several years after Mr. Caldwell died in 1826, and then in 1837 was elected President of Davidson College. The next minister at Sugar Creek was Rev. J. M. M. Caldwell, a great-grand-son of the first minister, Mr. Alexander Craighead. Who shall say that the covenant of God is not visited from the fathers to the children, in the infinite mercy of God? Another name, which will never be forgotten in Mecklenburg, although on a very humble stone in "this city of the dead," is Abraham Alexander, the chairman of the convention of the 20th of May, 1775. Not only was he an active patriot, but an active member of Sugar Creek church.

A large number of the descendants of Hezekiah Alexander—a brother of John McKnitt Alexander—still live in the county, but are not sure whether their ancestor was buried in Sugar Creek or Hopewell. Strange that such carelessness should have been permitted, but such is the fact in every church yard in the county. The posterity of these early patriots have ever been our best class of citizens, as pertaining to both Church and State. And it is a noted fact that no descendant of a Revolutionary hero bore arms against his home, or took sides with the Federals to destroy the civilization of the South. The blood of 1775 continued to tell from 1861-'65. People who were Tories in the first revolution had descendants who were Tories in our last. In the early part of the Nineteenth century, Archibald Frew built probably the finest house in the county. Mr. Frew was visited by misfortune, and the residence passed into other hands. Dr. D. T. Caldwell became owner of the place, and his son, R. B. Caldwell, and his sister, Miss Alice, live there. The place now appears to be of the fashion that was in vogue three quarters of a century ago. Descendants of some of the old settlers are still in the neighborhood, viz.: Robinsons, Barnetts, Alexanders, Hendersons, etc. It was here, on the highway that Col. Locke was killed September 26, 1780, after the fight in Charlotte; also where Gen. Graham was severely wounded, and was taken care of by "Aunt Susey," when quite a young girl..

DR. D. T. CALDWELL.

Dr. D. T. Caldwell.

Dr. D. T. Caldwell was the son of that eminent divine, Rev. S. C. Caldwell, and Abagail Bain, daughter of John McKnitt Alexander. Dr. Caldwell was born about 1796. He was educated by his father at Sugar Creek church. From there he went to the University. He was in college with President Polk and other men who occupied high positions in both church and State; he graduated about 1820. He studied medicine under Dr. McKenzie, and after attending lectures in Philadelphia, he practiced with him. He often said one of them would go on the north side of town one day, and on the south next day. By this arrangement each one would see all the cases every other day. Bleeding was the order of the day, and if Dr. Caldwell failed to bleed a fresh case, he felt sure Dr. McKenzie would not pass him by. Doctors were not plentiful in those early days, and a man who was qualified for the profession had no idle time. Dr. Caldwell would frequently ride out to his father's to get a night's sleep. In 1826 he married Harriet, a daughter of Hon. William Davidson, who filled many offices of public trust. Dr. Caldwell continued to do a large practice for many years, was very popular and much respected. Has now but three of his children living. His son, Dr. William D., died many years ago. He was a soldier in the Trans-Mississippi army. Baxter was in the army of Northern Virginia. He lives on the old homestead, never married; is an excellent farmer. His sister, Miss Alice, keeps house for him. Mrs. S. J. Donald, nee Miss Sarah Jane Caldwell, lives in Greensboro, happily situated. Dr. D. T. Caldwell lost his wife in the terrible epidemic of erysipelas in 1845 that proved a scourge to the people of the northern part of the county, that will be talked of till all the witnesses are removed by death. He was an elder in Sugar Creek church from an early period, and was a most exemplary man in all the walks of life. His second wife was a Miss Hutchison, of Rock Hill, S. C., a most excellent woman. She had but one daughter, who married Mr. Walter Rawlinson. She left three children and died young. Dr. Caldwell died December 25, 1861. A good citizen.

The Lives and Peculiarities of Some of the Signers of the Declaration of Independence of May 20, 1775.

As Col. Tom Polk lived ten years after the independence of the United States was established, he entertained Gen. Washington in 1791, in Charlotte, when on his southern tour; was one of the most prominent and popular citizens of our county, his reputation was cleared of every stain, and no one dared to calumniate his revolutionary record. He died in 1793, and his wife Susannah, who preceded him many years, was buried in the old cemetery of Charlotte back of the old church. He had much to do with those early patriots in securing independence for the people of Mecklenburg, and through them for the people of the Western world. Sufficient credit cannot be given the plain people for the noble stand they maintained in those years of trial.

MAJ. JOHN DAVIDSON.

As for Maj. John Davidson, a signer of the Declaration of Independence of Mecklenburg, every one who knew him could attest that he was not only the truest of patriots, but one of the most devoted of Christians. He lived to extreme old age, far into the Nineteenth century, lacking but three years of attaining his one hundredth birthday. He was born in Cecil, Md. While but a small boy he lost his father, and his mother, whose maiden name was Isabella Ramsay—with her two children, John and Mary, moved to Rowan county and purchased a farm. Here she found a fine school to educate her children, and for the teacher there was a mutual attraction, which resulted in a marriage between Mrs. Davidson and Mr. Henry. When John became of age he moved to Mecklenburg with his sister Mary, to keep house for him. He was a skillful blacksmith, and for many, many years followed the trade. Blacksmithing at that period was a lucrative business, and competition was not close as it got to be in after years. He married an English lady—Violet, a daughter of Samuel Wilson—who was a near kinsman of Gen. Wilson, in whose veins flowed the blood of royalty. Their royal kinsman, Sir Robert Wilson, made them a visit once before the Revolutionary war, but never repeated it. He prospered far beyond his compeers, and took a great interest in developing the iron industry of the country after the war. He appears to have lived an exemplary Christian. Some incidents are related illustrative of his character. His oldest grand-daughter (a noted beauty) married a distinguished and wealthy South Carolinian, William Edward Hayne. This led to more gay company in the old homestead than usual; and sometimes the guests differed widely from their host in manners and opinions. On one occasion a party of gentlemen who had adopted the principles of French philosophy then so prevalent, were visiting at his house. Knowing that they were avowed atheists, and believing that his father's evening devotions would only subject him to ridicule, one of the younger Davidsons suggested that, for once, they be omitted. But such was not in keeping with the independent and conscientious character of Maj. Davidson. When the hour for retiring came, he said quietly, "Gentlemen, it is always my custom to close the day with Scripture reading and prayer in my family. If you choose to be present, you are most welcome to do so. If not, you can retire to your own rooms." They decided to remain, and for once in their lives listened respectfully on bended knees to an earnest prayer from the lips of a very earnest worshipper.

Another grand-daughter, a gay young girl who was motherless and consequently much at his house, had the usual dislike of young ladies for early rising, and consequently she was sometimes late at morning prayers. The grandfather was usually very patient, but at last administered a mild rebuke. He said: "Mary, I hope you will marry some one who will *make* you come to prayers." The hope seemed to be prophecy, for she married the Rev. Dr. R. H. Morrison, who during his long life, was especially strict in requiring every member of his family to be present, at both morning and evening prayers. Notwithstanding this (or let us say, in consequence of it) he was the most tender and devoted of husbands and fathers. Maj. Davidson's last years were spent at the home, and in the devoted care of his youngest daughter, Elizabeth. She married William Lee Davidson, the youngest son and namesake of her father's old friend, the officer who fell at his post of duty at Cowan's Ford, and whose death at the hands of a Tory, ought to protect him from all subsequent misrepresentations.

Maj. Davidson was a man of wealth, attended strictly to his own business, and was very industrious and spent no money foolishly. His slaves were native Africans, bought from the New England slave ship which landed their pitiful cargoes on the wharfs of Charleston, S. C. That was the Pandora's box from which issued untold evils to our people one hundred years later. Although it was a master stroke to civilization and Christianized the cannibal tribes of Africa.

During the time of African slavery in the United States, there was 700,000 converted to Christianity from "hoodooing" cannibals. Greater progress was made here with the slaves than was effected by the missionaries of all other Christian nations in their home country. But their freedom was a great blessing to the white people of the South. How gentle and faithful and affectionate they became to their Christian masters and mistresses. And it seemed natural for them to hate "poore white trash." In fact the negroes of the rich had but little time for the negroes of those who owned but two or three.

Maj. Davidson's title was first conferred upon him by Gov. Tryon, and afterwards re-conferred upon him by the Provincial Congress. His home was about fifteen miles northwest of Charlotte, near the Catawba river; and his sons located themselves on adjoining plantations. The oldest son, Robert (called Robin), married Margaret Osborne (known far and near as "Aunt Peggy"). She was the granddaughter of Alexander Osborne and Agnes McWhirter. The second son, John, (commonly called Jacky), married Sarah Brevard, grand-daughter of John Brevard and Jane McWhirter. "Jackey" had the most stentorian voice in the State. He could deliver a message two miles by calling out. The third son, Benjamin Wilson (named in honor of his grand uncle, Benjamin Wilson, of England, who was the father of Gen. Sir Robert Wilson), married Elizabeth Latta, and lived about seven miles east of his father. Benjamin was called "Independence Ben" because he was born on May 20, 1787. The three elder daughters of Maj. Davidson married distinguished rebel officers, Captain Alexander Brevard, Gen. Joseph Graham, and Dr. William McLean, who was an army surgeon. Another daughter, Sarah, married Rev. Alexander Caldwell, son of Rev. David Caldwell, D. D., of Guilford, who suffered almost martyrdom for the sake of independence.

They had two sons and one daughter—probably the most remarkable family, not only in Mecklenburg county, but in North Carolina. They were noted for their mental calibre, their mind appeared to grasp whatever subject or problem came within their reach, and when once fixed in their mind, was there never to be forgotten. Their energy and industry was unsurpassed, and their influence was felt for miles around them. Mr. D. A. Caldwell, one of the brothers, was a man of great determination, always ready to contend for what he considered was right; he was anything else than a policy man. He possessed that mould of features that was peculiar to men of a former day, that denoted friendship, decision of character, and did not know what fear was; and was the very soul of honor.

When the Confederate soldiers were wending their way home, the war being over, a captain and twelve men—cavalry—rode up and said they would stay all night with him; in the meantime one of their horses became so badly foundered that it was impossible for it to travel, so the captain looked around at Mr. Caldwell's stable and selected his family carriage horse, and said he would be obliged to take it. Mr. Caldwell told him he could not spare that horse, but was willing to let them have another horse that was not so valuable. The captain said no, "I must have the bey horse." I was immediately sent for, and hastened to his aid. He met me at the back door and told me he wanted me to witness what was about to transpire. We walked to the front door where the captain and his men were saddling their horses. The captain spoke kindly, or rather I should say, politely, "Mr. Caldwell, you have entertained us kindly, fed our horses, showed us all the courtesies we could expect, but necessity knows no law; I will certainly take the bey horse." Mr. Caldwell replied, "I will kill whoever puts his hand on my horse." The captain said, "There is thirteen of us and but one of you. Would you sacrifice your life for a horse?" "Not for a horse, but for the principle of the thing, I will do it quick." The captain told his troopers to let the horse alone. These three—the Caldwell branch—lived to an average age of 90 years, and their offspring still inherits all the fine qualities of their ancestors.

The youngest daughter, as before stated, married William Lee Davidson. So that no family in the county was more thoroughly identified with the achievement of national independence. Maj. Davidson shared the labors of his newly purchased slaves, and instructed them personally in every branch of plantation work. And he did everything so well with his own hands that his grand-sons would laugh and say: "Grand-father can do everything in the world, except shear a sheep." He had tried to assist in the sheep-shearing, and failed so signally that it was a standing joke in the family ever afterwards. His handsome old brick mansion, built after the close of the war, was unfortunately destroyed by fire a few years ago, but his plantation is still in the hands of his descendants. His grave and that of his wife may still be seen near his homestead.

HEZEKIAH ALEXANDER.

Four of the six Alexanders who signed the Mecklenburg Declaration were so well known in the county that they are still spoken of with reverence and affection. We know just where their homes were, and their graves are with us to this day. The principal transactions of their lives are recorded in history. But of the other two, Ezra and Charles, diligent enquiry has revealed nothing that is satisfactory from the oldest citizens. One informant was under the impression that they lived within the bounds of Providence, and were neighbors of Ezekiel Polk, and like him, were atheists. If this is true, they probably emigrated with him to Tennessee, carrying with them their circulating library or infidel literature, and so both they and their books disappeared and were a good riddance to their fellow citizens. Hezekiah and John McKnitt Alexander were brothers, and were near kinsman of the Brevard family. Hezekiah Alexander was born in Pennsylvania the 13th of January, 1722. By the Provincial Congress at Hillsboro (21st August, 1775) he was appointed with Griffin Rutherford, John Brevard and Benjamin Patton and others a Committee of Safety for the Salisbury District, which included Mecklenburg within its bounds. In April, 1776, he was appointed with William Sharp, again on a Council of Safety—an evidence of the great respect inspired by his intellect and integrity. He afterwards held the position of paymaster to the Fourth Regiment of North Carolina Continentals, of which Thomas Polk was colonel, James Thackston lieutenant-colonel, and William Lee Davidson major. In November, 1776, he was elected a member of the Provincial Congress from Mecklenburg with Waightstill Avery, Robert Irwin, John Phifer, Zaccheus Wilson as colleagues, which assembly formed the Constitution of North Carolina. He died in

1801, and is buried in Sugar Creek church graveyard. His house, a stone building of good proportions, is still standing, about four miles from Charlotte, near the old Potter road, a highway that was in use before our town was laid off or located. The old house has a great cavern of a cellar where tradition says Mrs. Hezekiah Alexander used to store the rich products of the farm, many jars of honey being part of their contents. Just in front of the cellar door is, or used to be, a large flat stone; and upon this stone the British soldiers broke all the jars of honey which they could not carry away with them. They would not leave anything for the old rebel and his family. There is a beautiful spring near the house with a stone arch built over it, a stone spring house for dairy purposes, whose size indicates that milk, butter and cheese must have been so abundant as to require considerable room.

Like all the colonial homes, a meadow was near by—probably once smooth and green and a thing of rare beauty; but now defaced with corn furrows and rough stalks of stubble left by the last crop. Tradition states that the two daughters of Hezekiah Alexander were very beautiful women. Mrs. Captain Cook, who was deputed by the town to entertain Gen. Washington when he was the town's guest in 1791, was considered a good judge of female beauty, having seen much of the world, and she said she had never seen any beauties who equaled these two Misses Alexander. One of them married Charley Polk and met a very tragic fate. Her husband was cleaning his gun in her room (where she was sitting with her child in her arms), when it went off and killed her. He subsequently announced his intention of marrying his beautiful sister-in-law, but her brothers objected very decidedly, and his own brothers also interfered to prevent the marriage, and he had to give it up. Daredevil as he was, he could not dare everything. The lady died unmarried. Waightstill Avery, the friend of Hezekiah Alexander, made his home at his house during his residence in Mecklenburg, and rode into town every day to his law office. The sons of the family did not think it safe to remain at home during the occupation of Charlotte by the British, as foraging parties might be expected at any time, but of course had to return occasionally for their supplies; and their mother used to hang a signal from one of the upper windows when she thought it safe for them to come home. On the walls of the house may be seen the date of its erection, 1774.

JOHN M'KNITT ALEXANDER.

No man in Mecklenburg county in Colonial times seems to have had more of the confidence and love of his fellow-citizens (or rather fellow sufferers) than John McKnitt Alexander. His devoted piety, his open-handed and never-ceasing hospitality, and excellent good sense made him a leader among the best class of the community. His grandson, Dr. J. G. M. Ramsay, the well-known historian of Tennessee, tells that when Ochiltree, the traitor, found that Cornwallis was preparing to leave Charlotte, he knew that the citizens would punish him as he deserved, for accepting from the enemies of his country the office of Quartermaster after having signed the Mecklenburg Declaration of Independence. He had grown rich in his mercantile dealing with the Mecklenburg people and was loath to leave the property he had accumulated here. He determined to appeal to John McKnitt Alexander for protection, as being the kindest-hearted and most influential man in the county. So, on the night previous to the evacuation he mounted his horse and rode nine miles up what is called the Statesville road to the house of Alexander, but found no one at home except Mrs. Alexander and her children and servants. She knew him well, having bought goods from him for years as a merchant, and refused to admit him and refused to tell him where her husband was. He pledged the honor of a British officer that his intentions were good, and reached his sword to her through the window as a guarantee of his truth. Mrs. Alexander's pity was aroused and she agreed to send for her husband, who was at one of the many military camps then dotting the country. This one was Maj. Sharp's, the one nearest his own house. Her little daughter Peggy, a girl of thirteen, attended by a faithful slave, Venus, was sent to bring her father. On returning home with the child, Ochiltree threw himself upon his protection, asking security for person and property, after the British army had left. But all the milk of human kindness had been turned to gall in the patriot's heart. The former friend and colleague had sinned too deeply to be forgiven. He said: "Ochiltree, if I had met you anywhere else, I would have killed you; in my own house your life is safe. But I advise you to cross the Yadkin before daylight, otherwise you will never witness another daylight. Your life is forfeited." The panic-stricken traitor knew that if John McKnitt Alexander had no pity on him, nobody else would, and he took his advice and fled. That was the last seen of Ochiltree. It was reported that he reached Wilmington safely and afterwards escaped to the coast of Florida. Previous to this time, Ochiltree had been sending out foraging parties to every plantation which he knew so well, to obtain supplies for the British troops. No man was base enough to sell to him, and many poor soldiers paid their lives for being his messengers. McKnitt Alexander was wealthy, and the produce of his plantation was very great. He said to his foreman, "Cato, the moment you see the red-coats enter our lane, run quick and set fire to the stock yard and barn. Duncan Ochiltree shall not have one bundle of my fodder." And in loyalty to his master, Cato and Ruth did actually burn to ashes the whole result of a year's labor.

The delegates from Mecklenburg who were elected to the Provincial Congress which met at Halifax 1776, were John Phifer, Robert Irwin, and John McKnitt Alexander. He was secretary to the convention in Charlotte which declared independence. He was treasurer for the two Synods (then united in one) of North and South Carolina. His house was headquarters for the clergymen of his church, and hence his daughters naturally married the pastors of the surrounding congregations, Rev. James Wallis, of Providence, and Rev. Samuel Craighead Caldwell, of Sugar Creek.

Like the other colonists of means, he educated his oldest son Joseph McKnitt Alexander, at Princeton. A list of the Princeton graduates of Mecklenburg would be quite a long one. The Alexander plantation when Cato and Ruth burned the stock yard and barn, was said to be the largest in the county; and in those days large estates in land was the rule rather than the exception. Wheeler calls Thomas Polk's estate "princely." But the McKnitt Alexander place was said to be ten miles square. John McKnitt Alexander was a member of the convention which formed the State Constitution; and in 1777 we find him in the State Senate, while Waightstill Avery and Martin Phifer were members, the same date, of the House of Commons. This was his last appearance in public life. He was buried at Hopewell church, one of the seven noted churches of Colonial times. His sister, Mrs. Jamima Sharp, is buried at Sugar Creek. She used to say her nearest neighbor on the north was eight miles distant, and southward and eastward, fifteen miles. Just think of the loneliness and desolation of that Indian-haunted region and what these people were willing to endure for conscience sake.

John McKnitt Alexander's eldest son Joseph, a graduate of Princeton, married Dovey, the daughter of Moses Winslow, and the grand-daughter of Alexander Osborne and his wife Agnes McWhirter. The second son, William Bane, married Violet, a daughter of Maj. John Davidson. Both are said to have been very beautiful women. In Colonial days, Mecklenburg was renowned for beautiful women.

"SACRED TO THE MEMORY OF JOHN M'KNITT ALEXANDER, WHO DEPARTED THIS LIFE JULY 10, 1817, AGED 84."

By his side is buried his wife, Jane Bain, who died March 16, 1798, aged 30 years. Two sons, Joseph McKnitt, M. D., and William Bain Alexander. The first married Dovey Winslow, who died September 6, 1801, aged 25, leaving one son, Moses Winslow Alexander, M. D.

Dr. Joseph McKnitt Alexander was born in 1774 and died October 18, 1841. His son, Moses Winslow Alexander, was born May 3, 1798, and died February 27, 1845. The children of William Bain Alexander, who married Violet Davidson, a daughter of Maj. John Davidson, were fourteen in number, seven sons and seven daughters:

1. Joseph, married Nancy Cathy; moved to Alabama in 1835.
2. William B., married Clarissa Alexander.
3. Robert D., married Abigail Bain Caldwell.
4. Benjamin Wilson, married Elvira McCoy.
5. James McKnitt, married Mary Wilson.
6. George Washington, married first Sarah Harris; second, Gillespie; third, Jetton.
7. John Ramsay, married Harriet Henderson.
8. Jane Bain, married Capt. John Sharp.
9. Margaret Davidson, married David R. Henderson.
10. Rebecca, married Marshall McCoy.
11. Sally Davidson, never married.
12. Abigail, married Henderson Robertson.
13. Betsy, married Dr. Isaac Wilson.
14. Isabella, married Dr. Calvin Wier.

This is copied from Wheeler's Reminiscences, published in 1884. Persons desiring it carried out still further, have plenty of data to draw from.

ABRAHAM ALEXANDER.

The home of Abraham Alexander was about three miles northeast of Charlotte, and was known in the neighborhood as Alexander's Mill. It is now very difficult to locate the exact spot; it is only by referring to old papers and land deeds that the old place can be recognized. An old excavation almost filled with the washings of the surrounding soil, is the only vestige of the Colonial home. It is now a very desolate looking spot; but when forest trees crowned the hills around the little valley, once smooth and green, and the now vanished spring bubbled at the foot of a gentle slope upon which the dwelling stood, and sent forth its sparkling brook to meet the larger stream which turned the mill wheel it may have been a very charming place. The grand-son, Elias Alexander, built a handsome brick house on another portion of the estate which is still standing. From all we can learn of Abraham Alexander, he was a quiet, God-fearing man, and much beloved and respected by his neighbors. When he rode through the forest on that balmy May morning to take his seat as chairman of the Mecklenburg Convention, he probably had not the faintest idea that he was making a name in history for himself and his family. He no doubt thought he was doing his simple duty as an humble Christian citizen. Verging upon three score years of age, he had no youthful enthusiasm for new ways. But he had sat reverently under Craighead's ministry, and probably imbibed every one of his political opinions. We can imagine his soliloquy as he jogs along to the stormy meeting before him. He may be saying to himself: "The Bible certainly commands us to submit ourselves to 'the powers that be;' yes, yes, to 'the powers that be.' But the question is, what and who are the powers that be! If we are stronger than our oppressors, are not we ourselves the powers that be? And is it not sinful supineness to neglect to exercise the powers that God gives us? We can try it any how, and the effort to free ourselves will be an appeal to God, and He himself shall decide the question." And here we will imagine that he meets his neighbors Hezekiah Alexander from the neighboring farm, bound like himself, to the meeting in Charlotte and they begin to discuss the question, "I wish our old pastor Craighead was alive now to advise us what to do." "I know very well what he would advise us to do," answered Hezekiah. "He would preach us a sermon on the duty of putting down bad rulers and substituting good ones. We are commanded to put men into power who hate covetousness. Now you know very well, neighbor, that sole object of the many deputies who rule us in the King's name, is to enrich themselves as fast as possible at the expense of the public. We are commanded to have men of truth as rulers—our royal governors are liars, promising redress and never keeping their word. We are commanded to have able men to rule us. And according to all accounts, our King George is anything but an able man. At least he is not able enough to save us from oppression by his deputies." And so these Bible taught men come prepared to do their duty—humbly, reverently, we hope prayerfully. They ride together into Tryon street and dismount at the gates of Queen's College. (The people never took kindly to the new name of Liberty Hall, and through all subsequent changes called their institution Queen's College.) Had the men who met them that day been endowed with the gift of second sight, they would have looked forward to the death of State's Rights upon the very spot where Independence was born; for here in Tryon street, Charlotte, Jefferson Davis made his last public address as President of the Confederate States. State's Rights lived less than one hundred years, and died an awful death, including various battles at the North, but their full strength was only shown when their own colony was invaded. Abraham Alexander was too old for military service, but he was none the less a hero and true patriot. He lived long enough to see his hopes realized in the establishment of American Independence. His tombstone may be seen in the cemetery of Sugar Creek church, overshadowed by a splendid oak, and bearing the inscription, "Let me die, the death of the righteous and let my last end be like his."

DR. EPHRAIM BREVARD.

The Brevards were a Rowan family, and the only member that we can claim is Dr. Ephraim, who married in Mecklenburg and became a citizen of this county. The Osbornes were also Rowan people, and the Lockes and Brandons and Sharps and Winslows. George Locke, however, we may partly claim, as he died upon our soil and in defence of our county. The saddest history in our revolutionary annals is that of Dr. Brevard, our martyr. Locke died a fearful death, cut to pieces by the sabres of Tarleton's dread and merciless drgoons, while vainly trying to shield himself by holding up his rifle. His death agony, however, was short, while Brevard died by inches in all the long anguish of a barbarous imprisonment. The horrible prison ships of Charleston were meant to be death-traps. Bad food, worse water, and still worse air, were the fiendish agencies used to kill hundreds of men and unnumbered broken hearts of widowed women and orphaned children. So strange and terrible are the vicissitudes of nations.

So many truthful and able pens have told the history of the convention, that it need not be repeated here, as it has a place set apart for it, separate and distinct, as this chapter tells more of those who participated in this wonderful convention. After it the people felt themselves free of all royal authority; and they arrested and punished all who maintained that the British government was still in force.

The Queen's College students were full of republican ardor, and formed themselves into a military company in the following year, February, 1776, to assist in defending our maritime frontier. The victory at Moor's Creek, intelligence of which met them at Campbleton, rendered their campaign and their vacation a short one. But each one of these students did good service in other fields subsequently. Wm. Richardson Davie, John George and Joseph Graham, Francis Locke, Paul Phifer, Wm. McLean were only a few of the youths who were educated in Charlotte, although some of them afterwards supplemented their education at Princeton and Philadelphia. The snow campaign under Gen. Rutherford kept our county busily excited for some portion of the same year. Rutherford was a Rowan citizen, and therefore we make no claim to one leaf of his brilliant laurels, but many Mecklenburg men fought under him (our county and Rowan forming one military district) and helped in putting down the Scovillite Tories and the Cherokee Indians. The campaign was sharp and bloody, but completely successful.

In the three or four following years Mecklenburg men fought the Tories wherever found. The longing for home killed some, for people in those days loved home with a tenderly passionate affection, which we migratory, travel-loving people can scarcely understand. How often I have heard of old people longing to behold the old spring which ran near the father's door; and shedding tears of joy at again listening to the old familiar hymns sung in the country churches when they were children. They were like the old Scotch woman, dying in the slums of London and asking her pastor with her failing breath if he thought the dear Lord would allow her to go by her old highland home on her way to heaven. An old woman in Mecklenburg county, who was married while young and moved West, spent her life in the far West, returned in her old age and was so rejoiced to get *home* that she said now she was ready to die. The wish was granted, and she was buried with her kindred and friends in the old cemetery in Charlotte. Dr. Brevard was one of these tender, loving natives. In his childhood his love for his little sister led him to perform an act of heroism which cost him the loss of one of his eyes. Returning from school one evening, he heard his sister scream; her clothing had caught fire from one of the numerous brush-heaps which always made the pioneer's newly cleared ground so picturesque a scene. Rushing to her assistance, and entirely forgetful of his own safety, he struck his eye against a bough and received so severe an injury that the sight was destroyed, and he went through life with only one eye. Of course, a man of such loving and self-sacrificing disposition would naturally have devoted friends; yes, friends who were ready to die for him. One of his patients —an old woman—hearing of his sufferings in prison, determined to go to Charleston and do what she could for him. Other women in Mecklenburg had sons and brothers in the dreadful prison ships, and they formed a party to go down and offer themselves as nurses. They set out on foot, traveling through a thinly settled country which afforded little or no accommodations to wayfarers; but they struggled bravely on, laden with medicines and hospital stores, and at length reached their destination. Oh, the brave, tender, noble women of revolutionary days; working women, homespun-clad, but rich with all the sweet attributes of sanctified womanhood. Bible-loving, church-going women, who were willing to endure all things in the path of duty. Mrs. Jackson, the mother of a subsequent President, was one of these Charleston nurses, and was so broken down by her efforts that she died on the way home. Died in a tent which had probably been furnished them by some of our own soldiers, to shelter them from the weather. She was buried by the roadside, and the spot is now forgotten. The British evacuated Charleston in May, 1782, but our local historians say that Dr. Brevard was released in 1781, and if that is true, he was probably exchanged for some noted prisoner in the hands of the Americans. Once free, his great desire was to reach his loved home, his reverend old mother and his motherless child. In those days there were no conveniences for travel. Our hardy ancestors made long journeys on foot—at best they traveled on horseback, or wagons without springs. So our dying hero set out from Charleston to reach home. The long, wearisome journey, with failing strength and failing nerves and no hope of rest until he reached home. What a tedious, suffering struggle it was. But love conquers all obstacles. He must get home—must see his mother and his child, and the beloved scenes of his childhood. He reaches Charlotte at length, where his happy young married days had been spent, and where his wife, Mary Polk, was buried; but his mother's house was still twenty-five miles further on—the original home had been burned by the British soldiers, but another stood upon the loved spot.

Thank God the vandal avengers could not destroy the landscape of wood and meadow and of firm, white sand where his mother, in the absence of primary books, had taught her children to read by drawing the letters and words with a pointed stick. The mother, Jane McWhirter, came of a noble family whose blood had flowed in martyrdom before they crossed the Atlantic. She and her sister Agnes (Mrs. Alexander Osborne) lived on neighboring plantations in Rowan—now Iredell county. Their old mother lived with them, and their brother, Rev. Dr. McWhirter, an intimate friend of Gen. Washington, was sent south by Congress to animate the Southern colonies in defence of their homes and their religion. And here we would say that to be consistent, Christian ministers must always preach against war, except in extreme cases. Undoubtedly our Lord commands us to resist not evil, but in defence of home and women and children and Bible truth, we may resort to arms. The Scotch, the Scotch-Irish and the English Puritans held the same views on these subjects.

To talk to them of the "pomp and circumstance of war" was useless labor—mere clap-trap. Glory won by conquest was equally opposed to these principles. Brute courage was essentially unmanly. But to die in defence of God's Bible truth, that was another thing. They could not obey God unless they had political and religious liberty. Dr. Brevard and his fellow prisoners had the comforts of believing that their martyrdom, cruel as it was, was securing for their fellow countrymen the great boon of a righteous government and an unfettered church.

Dr. Brevard was one of the leading spirits of the Mecklenburg Convention that set in motion the liberty we achieved in the eighteenth century. He thought much and clearly upon the subject, and Foote gives a long paper of instructions to our legislative delegates, written by him. Worn out by disease and fatigue, he reached the house of his friend and kinsman, McKnitt Alexander, and could go no further. We hope his mother and daughter reached his bedside before his death, but history gives us no particulars. His long sufferings ended there, and Foote says he was buried at Hopewell church. Others say his body was brought to Charlotte and buried beside his wife in the grounds of Queen's College. As these grounds were used for a burying place for the Cornwallis soldiers, it seems scarcely probable that our noblest hero should be laid beside them. Especially as the town had a cemetery of its own in which his wife's mother was buried, and two years later her father, Gen. Tom. Polk. So we are compelled to think there is some mistake about it, and that both he and wife are buried in our old church cemetery in Charlotte.

Some of the Bar One Hundred Years Ago.

HON. SAMUEL LOWRIE.

He was a native of New Castle county, State of Delaware, born May 12, 1756; son of Robert and Elizabeth Lowrie. When a child his parents moved to Rowan county and he was educated at Clio Academy, Iredell county, by Rev. James Hall. He studied law in Camden, S. C., and was elected to the House of Commons from this county in 1804, 1805 and 1806, when he was elected a judge of the Superior Court, which he held until his death, on the 22nd of December, 1818. He married in 1788 Margaret, daughter of Robert Alexander, who left him with several children; and second time, 1811, he married Mary, daughter of Marmaduke Norfleet, of Bertie county. He was a man of most engaging manners, a fine conversationalist, very learned in the law. His judicial district covered a great deal of territory, extended down into the eastern counties. Some of his descendants still live in Mecklenburg. The family were noted for intellect, both men and women, and were looked up to as leaders of thought, and were critics of more than ordinary ability, especially the female members of the family.

JOSEPH WILSON, ESQ.

A most distinguished lawyer and statesman, resided and died in Charlotte, which for many years was the scene of his services and honors. Joseph Wilson's early education was as good as the country afforded. He was under the care of Rev. David Caldwell, and by the advice of Reuben Wood, he studied law. He was licensed in 1804, and came to the bar at the same time with Israel Pickens, of Burke county, afterwards Governor of Alabama. By the perseverance of his character, the force of his intellect and steady application he arose to eminence in his profession. He settled for a while in Stokes county; he represented that county in the State Legislature in 1810-'11-'12. He distinguished himself by his warm advocacy of the war with England. About this time he made his home in Charlotte; was elected Solicitor of the Mountain Circuit, then embracing nearly all the western part of the State. His unsurpassed zeal and indomitable energy with which he discharged his duties of this responsible position, when the country was swarming with law-breakers, in bringing them to punishment, was indeed a hazardous undertaking. More than once was his life threatened for upholding the majesty of the law. He continued in this office until his death, which occurred in August, 1829. He left quite a large family, who inherited largely their father's talents. His daughter, Catharine, married William J. Alexander, Esq., who was as profound a lawyer as his accomplished father-in-law. Another of his daughters, Miss Roxana, married Dr. P. C. Caldwell, the most distinguished physician in the county. Miss Cousa Wilson, another daughter, who was never married, but partook largely of the intellectual qualities of her father. Of Mr. Wm. J. Alexander's family much could be said of the mental attainments, and of the brilliancy and beauty of the women. Miss Mary Wood Alexander was admired by the most talented young men of the town, but she thought best to remain heart-whole and fancy free, and applied herself to the education of young girls, fitting them to fill useful stations in life. Miss Laura also remained single, and applied her talents on the stage, where she shone brilliantly for a while, but her sun went down when her friends thought she had scarcely reached half way to her meridian. Both sons, William and Joseph, attained honorable positions in the Confederate army, and proved themselves worthy of their parentage. Their father, W. J. Alexander, attained a reputation as a lawyer, but few men ever reach. Early in the latter half of the last century he and his family moved to Lincoln county, where he remained until he died. His brother, Washington Alexander, also a lawyer, lived here, was well known as an advocate, did much practice in the forties, but did not have the great reputation of his brother Julius.

In 1846, at a gala day in Charlotte, when the town was crowded with negroes, one man was overheard to say: "I believe there are negroes enough here to pay all of Julius Alexander's debts," and some one replied, "I think it doubtful."

JAMES W. OSBORNE.

James W. Osborne began the practice of law about 1830. He was much sought after to take capital cases. It was conceded that if Mr. Osborne could not clear a case of murder, or any other capital case, he must be guilty. Besides his logical powers of reasoning, he was the most eloquent lawyer that ever appeared at the bar in the western part of North Carolina. He was an elder in the Presbyterian Church and often attended church courts, and was by no means a silent member, but took an active part in whatever pertained to the spiritual welfare of the church. He left a record as a jurist that any man might well be proud of. His memory should be cherished by the people of the town and county, and his character emulated by the youth of the State. His widow still lives in the city at a good age, surrounded by her son's family and hosts of friends to cheer her in her declining years.

J. HARVEY WILSON.

Mr. J. Harvey Wilson, another lawyer of eminence, came to the bar about the same time and took a high stand with his brethren, and also with the people.

He came of a lineage that would have pushed to the front

a man of less natural ability. He was a son of the Rev. John McCamie Wilson, D. D., who was regarded as a preacher of wonderful power, and had much to do in forming the sturdy character of the people of this section. Blood will tell by cropping out in after generations; so we are always glad to know that our ancestors were of good blood.

At this time we will only speak of those who held prominent positions before the century was half over.

President James Knox Polk.

When 11 years old his father, Samuel Polk, moved to Tennessee, and sent his son James K. Polk, at a proper age, back to North Carolina to the University at Chapel Hill, where he graduated with the highest honors of the University. It is said that he never missed a college duty in four years. In those *honest* days no wonder he became President of the United States. There is no other man, for whom is claimed three distinct places of birth, in Mecklenburg county. Each one appears to be well authenticated. On the south side of Big Sugar Creek, near the present town of Pineville, was where Samuel Polk lived; that was the place he took his wife when married; hence the neighbors say here was the birthplace of President Polk. Again, Mrs. Susan Smart, the same girl who was present on the 20th of May, 1775, then known as Susan Barnet, in 1848, told Harvey Wilson, Esq., an eminent lawyer, that President Polk was born in the house occupied by Richard Carson, now owned by L. W. Saunders. The child had an enormously large head when born—so much so that all the old women and the doctors thought that he would be an idiot, or had dropsy of the brain. When old Mrs. Smart heard the report of the child being an idiot, she at once ordered her carriage and drove up to Charlotte to see the baby for herself. When she went into the house she saw no signs of a baby, and she asked the young mother where the baby was. She told her it was in bed. "Well, I want to see it." Mrs. Polk went to the bed and brought the child out for Mrs. Smart's inspection. After a thorough inspection, Mrs. Smart said: "Your child is all right, and will some day be President of the United States." Mrs. Polk was delighted at the prophecy, and fifty years later Mrs. Smart was equally elated at the young man's success.

Mr. James P. Wilson has just given me this version,

and was 16 years old when he heard Mrs. Smart relate the story to his father.

An Irish family by the name of Alcorn, living fifteen miles northwest of Charlotte, who came to this country about a century ago, with three children; when the oldest girl was about 13 years old, she was hired to nurse the baby, and wait on Mrs. Polk when not busy with the child. Many years afterwards, when the girl had become an old woman, she said it was a common thing for a young woman to go back to her *mother* to be confined with her first child. Mrs. Polk came back to be with her parents, Mr. and Mrs. James Knox, between Hopewell and Huntersville. This is where they lived and died. A tombstone in Hopewell graveyard marks the place where they were buried.

This very plausible version of his birthplace was given by my venerable friend, E. A. McCaulay, Esq., who married a daughter of the nurse of the President. The child and nurse are now both in the spirit land, where no anxiety about the place of either birth or death will cause a trouble to disquiet their never ending repose.

William Davidson.

William Davidson lived and was a very active man in the first half of the Nineteenth century. He was a man of much wealth, owned many negroes, was public spirited, and did much for the county. Mr. Davidson represented Mecklenburg in the State Senate for several years; first in 1813, then in 1815-'16-'17-'18, again in 1825, and then in 1827-'28-'29. He also served several sessions in Congress. His family moved in the best circles. His daughter, Harriet, married Dr. D. T. Caldwell, who practiced medicine in Charlotte for many years, and raised a worthy family. Another married a Mr. Blake. They had one son and two daughters. They were a handsome trio. The son was educated at Annapolis and served in the United States navy in the war with Mexico, and afterwards till 1861, when he joined the Confederate States navy, and soon died with hemorrhage of the lungs. The young ladies passed away early in life. Miss Sarah Davidson, another daughter, was gifted with more than ordinary talents; she was well educated and admired for her mental attainments, especially in music. She taught music for a number of years, and gave such satisfaction that she held a high place as a teacher of music in the opinions of eminent people. He left one son, William, who was not equal to his father, either mentally or physically, yet he was in the Legislature, a lawyer, and later in life a Justice of the Peace, who did a great deal of business. All the older members of the family have passed away, and but few people now living in the county have any knowledge of the Davidson family. Something more than half a century ago the Davidson family lived in a large frame building on the southwest corner of Trade and Tryon streets, now occupied by Burwell & Dunn's drug store. All that property—the entire front on Trade street down to Church street, has long ago changed owners, and is now busy with a rushing trade.

Governor Nathaniel Alexander.

Of all the eminent men raised or lived in Mecklenburg county, but two were ever elevated to the executive chair. Z. B. Vance, the pet of the State, when the man with the Iron heel had the State by the throat in 1876, was elected Governor. At this juncture the State was drawn from the clutches of those who were thriving upon her downfall and humiliation.

Gov. Nathaniel Alexander was a native of Mecklenburg. He was a physician by profession, but there is no evidence that he ever practiced. He appears to have been politically inclined, for he was elected a member of the House of Commons in 1797; a member of the Senate in 1801, and re-elected in 1802. In 1803 to 1805 he was a member of Congress, and he was in 1805 elected Governor of the State. He served but one term, and there is no evidence that he ever courted popular favor after this. He married a daughter of Col. Thomas Polk, of more than ordinary fame in Mecklenburg county. He left no children—neither son or daughter—to inherit his name, or to keep his fame fresh as it passes down the stream of time. He was a man of much personal worth and respectable talents. He died and was buried in the old cemetery in Charlotte.

Gov. Nathaniel Alexander was one of five sons of the famous Moses Alexander. Gov. Alexander had a brother, William Alexander, who married Elizabeth Henderson.

From such a parentage, we are not surprised that Gov. Alexander should have been the peoples' choice for Chief Magistrate, as Gov. Vance was in 1876, when the people did not know which way to turn to preserve our liberty, or escape a doom that was worse than Poland at its last overthrow in 1790. "Man's inhumanity to man has caused countless thousands to mourn."

Maj. Green W. Caldwell.

Maj. Green W. Caldwell, long a resident of Charlotte, but not a native, was born in Gaston, or rather Lincoln county, near Tuckasege Ford, on the Catawba river, the 13th of April, 1811. We have no knowledge of his early education, but he studied medicine with Dr. Doherty near Beattie's Ford, and practiced with success. But, becoming dissatisfied with the early choice of professions, he abandoned it for that of the law. At about this time he moved to Charlotte. In 1836 he was elected a member of the House of Commons, and was re-elected in 1838-'39 and 1840, and in 1841 he was elected to Congress, where he served but one term. His practice of law was eminently satisfactory. In 1844 he was appointed superintendent of the mint in Charlotte. In 1846 he was the unanimous choice of his party (Democratic) for Governor, but this he declined. When the war with Mexico was declared, he at once resigned his appointment of superintendent of the mint, and volunteered for the war. He secured the appointment of captain of a company of dragoons, with E. C. Davidson, J. K. Harrison and Alfred A. Norman as lieutenants. This was a new experience for the men; but Southern patriotism is the ruling passion with our young men. A company of young men was soon formed, and they were soon off "for the wars again," with high hopes and bright anticipations.

The company did not see much fighting, and when the war was over, the most of them returned, and when the South had to defend what their fathers won in the revolution more than seventy-five years before, they entered the Confederate army, where they found real war. To-day there are exceeding few to tell the tales they heard in the capital of the Montezumas. Sergt. D. C. Robinson is the only one of the old guard now living in Charlotte who followed Maj. Caldwell to Mexico. In 1849 he was elected to the Senate, with two of his officers in the lower house, viz., Davidson and Harrison. In a progressive country like ours, how soon are the acts of the foremost citizens forgotten.

THE OPINION OF THE LADIES.

The following paragraph was found in the *South Carolina and American Gazette,* from the 2nd to the 9th of February, 1776:

"The young ladies of the best families of Mecklenburg county, North Carolina, have entered into a voluntary association that they will not receive the address of any young gentleman of that place except the brave volunteers who served in the expedition to South Carolina and assisted in subduing the Scovalite insurgents. The ladies being of the opinion that such persons as stay loitering at home when the important calls of the country demand their military services abroad, must certainly be destitute of that nobleness of sentiment, that brave, manly spirit which would qualify them to be defenders and guardians of the fair sex. The ladies of the adjoining county of Rowan have desired the plan of a similar association to be drawn up and prepared for signature."

Matthew Wallace and George Wallace.

George Wallace, his mother and two maiden aunts, and three orphan children, (their father, John, having died in Ireland, their mother had been raised up in the Roman Catholic faith, remained in Ireland), came over to America and landed in Philadelphia in 1784. The widow appears to have been willing for her children to cross the ocean in pursuit of a better country, and she married a second time in the old country. Matthew Wallace, who was a brother of George, came across the ocean with his wife and six children, and landed in Charleston, S. C., in 1789. They had one child born after they came to this country. We are not informed how the two families came to meet in Mecklenburg, when George came by the way of Charleston in 1784, and Matthew by the way of Philadelphia in 1789. But whether by chance or by appointment, they agreed to settle in the fertile region that is watered by the streams that help make McCoffin's Creek. They came over to this country immediately after the Revolutionary war, when the country was wild, the untamed savage still roamed in the great forests and over the prairies, where the buffalo was still seen, and the deer was a frequent visitor in sight of the emigrant's cabin.

One of the noted men of the times was Matthew— "Shacklen" was his nick-name. He was a son of Alexander, a brother of old Matthew ("Wheelright Jimmy") Wallace, who was known far and near by his occupation, who was a son of George Wallace. Boston Wallace, who died in 1897, was a man of fine sense, had no hesitation in expressing his opinion on any subject with which he was acquainted without regard to whom it affected. He was a bold, blunt man; was a prohibitionist from principle, and could not tolerate a man who would run "fast and loose," or who could court favor by sacrificing principle. He was a son of Alexander

Wallace. The Wallace family were fond of perpetuating the names of their ancestors. Mr. "Bob" Wallace, of Eastfield, is a son of Matthew Wallace, who was a son of John, who came across the ocean in childhood.

EXTRACT FROM THE WRITINGS OF ALEXANDER WALLACE.

"The old set of Wallaces first emigrated from Scotland to Ireland, and from Ireland to America just at the winding up of the Revolutionary war. The first set came in 1784, and the next set in 1789. It was said by the old set that they left none of their relations of the name of Wallace in Ireland.

"Jane Alexander was the name of my great-grandmother, which was the great-grandmother of my little boy, William Alexander Wallace; and she was buried at Sugar Creek church, with all her children, except my grandfather, Matthew, and he is lying at Sardis church. Matthew was the name of my great-grandfather. He was buried in Ireland. The tall, the wise, the reverend head, must lie as low as ours." ALEX WALLACE.

"Jane Alexander was the maiden name of my great-grandmother, who married Matthew Wallace, who was the father of the first named Matthew Wallace. Catherine Sullevan was the maiden name of my great-grandmother, who married Alexander, or John Wallace—not certain which name. She was the mother of Margaret, Robert and Alexander. She was left in Ireland; her husband lived there. This was after the Wallaces brought her children to America. The old 'set' brought their certificate of church membership with them. They were Psalm singing Presbyterians, and their descendants to the present day still hold to only the singing of Psalms."

The Wallaces are amongst our best people, but the men were not noted for their piety, but were noted for energy and thrift. All were in easy circumstances, and were noted for their liberality, for being first-class farmers, and several of them became very wealthy. During the war between the States, they acted the part of patriots. Mr. William Wallace, a grand-son of Matthew Wallace, was amongst the finest looking men in Lee's army, and he made a splendid reputation as a cavalry fighter; and, like many of our best men, his body was left on the field. They were a family of large people, many of them were very fleshy—not unusual to weigh 250 pounds.

It was common to distinguish the different members of the Wallace family who were called Matthew by giving them a nick-name, "Shacklen" Matthew, "Bachelor" Matthew, "Devil" Matthew, etc. "Devil" Matthew was a very powerful man, and was selected in 1845 to guard the mint. At that time there were but three mints in the United States, and consequently the mint was looked upon as a place of much more importance then as money was coined here, than it is now, as only an assay office. Fortunately nothing occurred while guarding the mint to test his metal, or we might have quite a racy story to write.

Adam Alexander.

Adam Alexander, one of the signers of the Mecklenburg Declaration of Independence and still further known to history for his military services, was born in Pennsylvania September 28, 1728, of Scotch-Irish parents.

He married Mary Shelby, of Holston county, Maryland, of a family which gave to the cause of independence in the war of the Revolution the names of Gen. Evan Shelby and of Col. Isaac Shelby, one of the heroes of the battle of King's Mountain, and afterwards the first governor of Kentucky.

About 1750, when many settlements of Scotch-Irish Presbyterians were being made in North and South Carolina, the Alexanders came to Mecklenburg county. There were several branches of the family. Adam Alexander settled in that section of the county now known as Clear Creek. He and his family were members of the old Rock Spring Presbyterian church, where before the Revolution a pious congregation worshipped, mingled with their devotions prayerful appeals for the final deliverance of their country from the approaching conflict of arms in a righteous cause.

On December 18, 1775, Adam Alexander was, by the Provincial Congress, held at Johnston Court House, appointed Lieutenant-Colonel of a battalion of minute men, with Thomas Polk as Colonel and Charles McLean as Major. In the latter part of May of the same year, and at the suggestion of Colonel Polk, two delegates from each of the companies of the county militia met at Charlotte with power to take such action as might seem advantageous to the colonies. The name of the subject of this sketch appears in the list of those patriots who drew up and signed the resolutions which constitute the famous Mecklenburg Declaration of Independence.

During the rebellion of the regulators, he, with other

officers, were ordered to bring their troops to join Gov. Tryon in Orange, now Guilford county; but finding their men so averse to fighting against their brother colonists, they sent the following letter to the Governor:

GEN WADDELL'S CAMP,
POTT'S CREEK, 10th May, 1771.

By a council of officers of the Western Detachment: Considering the great superiority of the insurgents in numbers and the resolution of great part of their own men not to fight, it was resolved that they retreat across the Yadkin.

WM. LINDSAY,	ROBERT SHAW,
ADAM ALEXANDER,	GRIFFITH RUTHERFORD,
THOMAS NEEL,	SAMUEL SPENCER,
FR. ROSS,	ROBERT HARRIS,

SAMUEL SNEAD.

On the 4th of April, 1776, he was appointed Colonel of Mecklenburg county by the Provincial Congress held at Halifax. He was a brave and energetic officer and his name is found in nearly every expedition which marched from Mecklenburg county to oppose the enemies of his country.

He was for many years before and after the war an acting Justice of the Peace. His name is frequently seen in records of church as well as of State, and tradition speaks of him as bearing an excellent character.

A stone marking his grave beside that of his wife in the old Rock Spring graveyard bears this inscription, appropriate to his life and character as a patriot and soldier: "Colonel Adam Alexander, who departed this life November 13, 1798, aged 70 years 7 months. The last enemy that shall be destroyed is death."

Adam Alexander had six children, three sons and three daughters—Evan Shelby, Isaac, Charles Taylor, Sarah and Mary.

His eldest son, Evan Shelby, was a graduate of Princeton in 1787, a lawyer and a member of the Ninth Congress from

Salisbury District (1805-'09), vice Nathaniel Alexander elected governor. He died in 1809, comparatively young and unmarried. The other sons, Isaac and Charles Taylor, have descendants now living in this county, some of whom bear the name of Erwin.

Of the daughters, the eldest, Sarah, married Captain John Springs and has many descendants, chiefly through her daughter, Mary A., who married her cousin, John Springs, a son of Captain Richard Springs, of York county, South Carolina. She has descendants also through her son, William Polk Springs, who married another cousin, Margaret Springs.

Some of the descendants of Adam Alexander now living in this section, besides those bearing the names of Alexander, Springs and Erwin, are of the families of Colonel William R. Myers, Colonel A. B. Davidson, Rev. Dr. Samuel Pharr and Dr. Charles Harris.

References: Wheeler's History of North Carolina, Hunter's Sketches of Western North Carolina, Family Record.

—*Contributed by Miss Sophy Myers.*

Humphrey Hunter.

But few persons in North Carolina have deserved more of their country than Humphrey Hunter, in his youth or his young manhood, or in his maturer years. No one is more deserving of a page in history, as one who contended for the freedom of his country, or as a preacher of righteousness. He was born on the 14th of May, 1755, in the vicinity of Londonderry, in the North of Ireland, the native place of his father. His paternal grandmother was from Glasgow, Scotland, and his maternal grand-father from Brest, in France. The blood of the Scotch and the Huguenot was blended in Ireland, and the descendant emigrated to America and flourished in the soil of Carolina.

Deprived by death of his father in his fourth year, young Hunter embarked at Londonderry with his widowed mother for Charleston, S. C., on the 3rd of May, 1759, on board the ship Helena. Arriving on the 27th of August, the family in a few days proceeded to Mecklenburg county, North Carolina, where the mother purchased land in the Poplar Tent congregation, and remained for life. As the enjoyment of civil and religious liberty was one of the principal causes of his mothers emigration, it is not wonderful that young Hunter grew up with a spirit jealous of encroachment from the English crown.

From the time of his reaching Mecklenburg till his twentieth year, little is known of him. We are left to the conjecture that he grew up familiar with all the labors and privations of a frontier life, by which he became fitted to endure the fatigues and sufferings of a military expedition. He attended the convention in Charlotte May 20, 1775, as one of the numerous crowd of spectators assembled on that exciting occasion. In his account of the meeting prefixed to his copy of the Declaration of Independence, he thus writes concerning the battle of Lexington, which took place on the 19th of April:

"That was a wound of a deepening, gangrenous nature,

not to be healed without amputation. Intelligence of the affair speedily spread abroad, yea flew, as if on the wings of the wind collecting a storm. No sooner had it reached Mecklenburg than an ardent, patriotic fire glowed almost in every breast; it was not to be confined; it burst into a flame; it blazed through every corner of the county. Communications from one to another were made with great facility. Committees were held in various neighborhoods; every man was a politician. Death rather than slavery, was the voice comparatively of all."

Soon after the Declaration of Independence, a regiment was raised in Mecklenburg, under Col. Thomas Polk, and Col. Adam Alexander, to march against some Tories who were embodied in the lower part of the State. Mr. Hunter went as a private in the company of Capt. Charles Polk, nephew of Col. Thomas Polk. The Tories dispersed at the approach of this force, and the regiment speedily returned without bloodshed or violence.

Mr. Hunter then commenced his classical education at Clio Nursery (now Iredell), under the instruction of Rev. James Hall. The following certificates, preserved by Mr. Hunter, show the order of the congregation, and the care with which the morals of the youth were watched over by church officers and instructors in schools. The first appears to have been required for his honorable standing at Clio's Nursery:

"This is to certify that the bearer, Humphrey Hunter, has lived in the bounds of this congregation upwards of four years, and has behaved himself inoffensively, not being guilty of any immoral conduct known to us, exposing him to church censure, and is free from public scandal.

"Given under our hands at Poplar Tent this 18th day of October, 1778.

"JAMES ALEXANDER,
"J. ROSS,
"ROBERT HARRIS,
"Ruling Elders."

When General Rutherford collected a brigade from Mecklenburg, Rowan, and Guilford counties to repel the aggressions of the Cherokee Indians, Mr. Hunter received a commission of lieutenant under Capt. Robt. Mayben, in one of the three companies of cavalry that formed part of the corps. The campaign was successful, the Indian forces were scattered, and their chiefs taken. After this campaign, Mr. Hunter resumed his classical studies at Queen's Museum in Charlotte, under the care of Dr. McWhirter, who had removed from New Jersey to take charge of that institution, with flattering prospects. Of the moral and religious character of the young man, the following certificate in the handwriting of his instructor is testimony, viz.: That the bearer, Humphrey Hunter, has continued a student in Clio's Nursery from August, 1778, till last October; that he applied to his studies with diligence; was admitted to the sacrament of the Lord's Supper in Bethany congregation; has during the aforesaid time conducted himself as a good member both of religious and civil society, and is hereby well recommended to the regard of any Christian community where Divine Providence may order his lot—is certified by James Hall, V. D. M., Bethany, January 12, 1780.

In the summer of 1780, Liberty Hall Academy, or Queen's Museum, as it was originally named, was broken up by the approach of the British army under Lord Cornwallis, after the surrender of Charleston, and the massacre of Buford's regiment on the Waxhaw, and the course of study was never resumed under the direction of Dr. McWhirter, who returned to New Jersey. Upon the breaking up of the college, the young students were commended to their parents and guardians, and the older were urged to take the field in the cause of their country. It is not to be supposed that young Hunter required much urging to take up arms with his fellow citizens of Mecklenburg, who five years before had pledged "their lives and their honor." Upon the orders of Gen. Rutherford to the battalions of the western counties of the State, a brigade assembled at Salisbury. For the first three weeks Mr. Hunter acted as commissary, and afterwards as lieutenant in the company of Capt. Thomas Givens. Having scoured the Tory settlement on the northeast side of the Yadkin, the forces under Gen. Rutherford joined the army of Gen. Gates at Cheraw. On the morning of the 16th of August, the unfortunate battle of Camden took place by the mutual surprise of the marching armies; and the forces under Gates were completely routed. Gen. Rutherford was wounded and taken prisoner with many of his men. Mr. Hunter, soon after his surrender as prisoner of war, witnessed the death of the Baron de Kalb. He tells us he saw the baron, with suite or aide, and apparently separated from his command, ride facing the enemy. The British soldiers clapping their hands on their shoulders, in reference to his epaulettes, shouted, "A general, a rebel general." Immediately a man on horseback (not Tarleton) met him and demanded his sword. The baron, with apparent reluctance, presented the hilt, but drawing back, said in French, "Are you an officer, sir?" His antagonist, perhaps not understanding his question, with an oath, more sternly demanded his sword. The baron dashed from him, disdaining, as is supposed, to surrender to any but an officer, and rode in front of the British line, with his hand extended. The cry along the line of "A rebel general," was speedily followed by a volley, and after riding some twenty or thirty yards, the baron fell. He was immediately raised to his feet, stripped of his hat, coat, and neck-cloth, and placed with his hands resting on the end of a wagon. His body had been pierced with seven balls. While standing in this situation, the blood streaming through his shirt, Cornwallis, with his suit, rode up, and being told that the wounded man was DeKalb, he addressed him: "I am sorry, sir, to see you; not sorry that you are vanquished, but that you are so severely wounded." Having given orders to an officer to administer to the necessities of the wounded man as far as possible, the British general rode on to secure the victory, and in a little time the brave and generous DeKalb, who had seen service in the armies of France, and had embarked in the cause of the American States, breathed his last.

After seven days confinement in a prison yard in Camden, Mr. Hunter was taken, with about fifty officers, to Orangeburg, S. C., where he remained without hat or coat, until Friday, the 13th of November, about three months from the time of his captivity. On that day he went to visit a friendly lady who had promised him a homespun coat. On his way he was met by a horseman of Col. Fisher's command, who accused him of being beyond the lines, and sternly ordered him back to the station, threatening him with confinement and trial for breach of his parole. Hunter explained and apologized, and promised, but all to no purpose. "To the station," "Take the road." Up the road went the rebel Whig, sour and reluctant, and made indignant by the frequent goading with the point of the Tory royalist's sword. Passing a large fallen pine, from which the limbs had been burned, he suddenly leaped the trunk. The horseman fired one of his pistols, missing his aim, and leaped his horse after him. Hunter adroitly leaped the other side the trunk, and began throwing at the horseman the pine knots that lay thick around. The second pistol was discharged, but without effect. By a blow of a well directed pine knot, the horseman was brought to the ground, and disarmed by his prisoner. Hunter returned the Tory his sword on condition that he should never, on any condition, make known that any of the prisoners had crossed the forbidden line, or any way transgressed, promising himself to keep the whole matter of the late encounter an inviolable secret.

On the following Sabbath a citation was issued by Col. Fisher, directing all militia prisoners to appear at the court house by 12 o'clock on Monday. The affair had been discovered. During the contest the horse galloped off to the station with the saddle and holsters empty, and when the dismounted rider appeared a little time afterward with the bruises of the pine knots too visible to be denied, the curious inquiries that followed baffled all his efforts to concealment. It was soon noised abroad that one or more of the prisoners had broken parole and attacked an officer. The report reaching the colonel's ears, the order was issued for their appearance at the court house. On Sabbath night Hunter and a few others, expecting close confinement would follow their assembling on Monday noon, seized and disarmed the guard and escaped. He was nine nights in making his way back to Mecklenburg, lying by during the day to avoid the patrols of the British, and sustaining himself upon the greenest of the ears of corn he could gather from the unharvested fields.

In a few days after his return home, he again joined the army, and became a Lieutenant of cavalry under Col. Henry Hampton, and attached to the regiment under Col. Henry Lee, received a wound in the battle at Eutaw Springs, where so much personal bravery was displayed. His military services closed with that campaign, and he returned home with a good name, his bravery unquestioned and his integrity unsullied.

He resumed his classical studies at the school taught by Rev. Robert Archibald, near Poplar Tent, as appears by the following certificate in the irregular hand and crooked lines of his preceptor, which is the only evidence at hand of the classical school in that congregation immediately after the war:

"MECKLENBURG, N. C., ―――――.

"This is to certify that the bearer, Humphrey Hunter, has been some years at this school in the capacity of a student, and during the term has conducted himself in a sober, genteel and Christian manner; and we recommend him as a youth of good character, to any public seminary where Divine Providence may cast his lot. Certified and signed by order of the trustees, this 3d day of November, 1785.

"ROBERT ARCHIBALD, V. B. M."

A college diploma from Mount Zion College, at Winnesboro, S. C., 1785, accredits him with a good preparation to enter upon the study of the ministry, which he had in view for several years, but was more or less interrupted by the war. Having pursued the study of theology about two years under the Presbytery of South Carolina, he received license to preach the Gospel in the following words, viz.:

"The Presbytery having examined Mr. Humphrey Hunter on the Latin and Greek languages, the sciences and divinity, and being well satisfied with his moral and religious character, and his knowledge of the languages, sciences, and divinity, do license him to preach the everlasting Gospel of Jesus Christ; and affectionately recommend him to our vacancies.
"JAMES EDMUNDS, *Moderator.*
"ROBERT HALL, *Presbt. Clerk.*
"Bullock's Creek, Oct. 15, 1789."

For the first fifteen years of his ministry he preached in a number of places in York District, S. C., also in Lincoln county. In 1805 he settled in Steele Creek, and there he remained till the year of his death, 1827. Here he was buried with the people, among whom he had labored for more than twenty years. His tombstone bears the following inscription:

"Sacred to the memory of Rev. Humphrey Hunter, who departed this life August 27, 1827, in the 73d year of his age. He was a native of Ireland, and emigrated to America at an early period of his life. He was one of those who early promoted the cause of freedom in Mecklenburg county May 20, 1775, and subsequently bore an active part in securing the independence of his country.

"For nearly thirty-eight years he labored as a faithful and assiduous ambassador of Christ, strenuously enforcing the necessity of repentance, and pointing out the terms of salvation. As a parent he was kind and affectionate; as a friend, warm and sincere, and as a minister, persuasive and convincing. Reared by the people of Steele Creek Church."

He had certainly deserved well of his country, and it not only was proper, but highly creditable to the citizens of Mecklenburg to keep his memory always green for what he did for his country one hundred years ago.

In his preaching he was earnest, unassuming, and often eloquent. Possessing a strong mind with powers of originality, and trained by the discipline of a classical education under men capable of producing scholars, he consecrated all his talents and acquirements to preach the everlasting Gospel, counting all things but loss for the excellency of the knowledge of Christ Jesus. He possessed in a high degree a talent for refined sarcasm; and his answer to trifles with his office or the great truths of religion, and sticklers for unimportant things was a shaft from this quiver that pierced to the marrow. His benevolence as a minister, and his tenderness as a neighbor forbade its use in his social intercourse. Honest objections and difficulties arising from want of knowledge or proper reflection, he would meet kindly with truth and argument; sophistry and cavils he considered as deserving nothing but the lash which he knew how to apply till it stung like a scorpion. He was a just man. The mould in which he was cast, that peculiarly belonged to men of that period, is now obsolete, and we rarely see one who approaches it.

Hopewell Church and Graveyard.

Among the earliest settlements in the western part of North Carolina, is Hopewell Church. For many months before a building was erected for a place of worship, the people would assemble at or near this place to discuss matters pertaining to the welfare of the country, as well as to hold religious services, as they could get a supply from some passing missionary. The first church was built in the year 1765, ten miles northwest of Charlotte, and two miles east of the Catawba river. The first house was built of logs, and shaded on all sides, so as to be comfortable for women who had young children to look after without disturbing the congregation; also to entertain large crowds who at that time thought it no hardship to ride horseback ten to fifteen miles to church.

In 1830, or thereabout, a very handsome brick house took the place of the first, and about 1860 it was enlarged and capacious galleries were added. The old graveyard is full of historic interest.

Rev. John Williamson was pastor of Hopewell from 1818 to 1842. His wife sleeps beside him. They were worthy people. As far as it is known, he was the only minister who has ever been buried here. Hopewell has always been blessed with preachers well equipped for their work, and gave general satisfaction.

The Hopewell section was thinly populated in 1750, by people moving from Pennsylvania and Maryland hunting a congenial climate to build their home. Richard Barry is said to have moved here many years preceding the Revolutionary war; but we are told that he was 55 years old when he participated in the battle of Cowan's Ford; that he and his friend, David Wilson, carried the body of Gen. W. L. Davidson, who was killed February 1, 1781, and prepared it for burial in Hopewell graveyard. In this spot it has ever rested, without a marble shaft or even an humble stone, to mark the spot where one of the noted patriots of Mecklenburg is buried, who gave his life for the freedom of America. It is a shame that the United States, the richest and most powerful nation on the face of the earth, who pays its most ordinary officers from one thousand to fifty thousand dollars a year, and not contribute one dollar to mark the graves of Gen. Davidson and Gen. Nash. A bill was recently introduced in Congress to erect a monument over each of their graves to cost $5,000 a piece, which was defeated. If they had been from the New England States, government appropriations would have been made, that every school boy or girl would have been familiar with their military powers.

A noted character of the Revolutionary days was Capt. Francis Bradly, a true patriot, who took an active part in the skirmish of McIntyre's Branch and was murdered November 14, 1780, by a small band of Tories. Physically he was said to be the strongest man in the county.

Here also is the grave of John McKnitt Alexander, the secretary of the noted convention that met on the 20th of May, 1775, and made the first and the most defiant Declaration of Independence that ever was thrown to the breeze in America, or in the world. Around his grave are a host of his posterity. His two sons, Dr. Joseph McKnitt, and William Bane Alexander, and one sister, Rev. Mrs. S. C. Caldwell, and a great congregation of their descendants. In the fourth generation from the old secretary, we see the name of Capt. Francis Ramsay Alexander, a great-grandson of John McKnitt Alexander—killed in front of Petersburg, Va., in one of the terrific battles in June, 1864. We see here another evidence that the patriots of 1775 would leave indelible impress of patriotism through many generations. Blood will tell. The most numerous persons are of the name of Alexander in this city of the dead. Now but comparatively few of the old family of Alexanders are in the settlement. They have moved to other sections, and strangers have moved in. The Barrys have all gone; the Davidsons and Torrances, and Sam Wilson's posterity are fast disappearing; and their lands have passed into hands of strangers. All the great forests have been cleared up, "the cattle upon a thousand hills" have disappeared; the fish that stocked every creek and branch in great abundance, are no longer to be seen; and the deer and wild turkey that were in former years so plentiful, now only exist in stories of a past age. The whole face of the country has been changed within the memory of an average life time. Here lived Maj. John Davidson, a signer of the immortal document, the Declaration of Independence. He was in a number of engagements with the British and Tories. In after life he went into the iron business with his son-in-law, Capt. Brevard. From this neighborhood came Gen. Joseph Graham, who was present in Charlotte on the 20th of May, 1775, and testified as to the truth of the Declaration of Independence. After he gallantly served in the war of Independence, he became the sheriff of Mecklenburg county. His brother, Gen. George Graham, was a true patriot. He came from Pennsylvania in 1764. He was educated in Charlotte at Queen's College, and in 1775 he and a few others rode all night to Salisbury, seized the Tory lawyers, Dunn and Booth, brought them to Mecklenburg, thence they were carried to Camden and imprisoned.

When Lord Cornwallis lay in Charlotte (1780), Gen. George Graham was very active in attacking his foraging parties. He was one of the band of twelve who forced the British, who had four hundred in their foraging party, to flee in such haste that they reported to their commander "there was a rebel behind every bush." He was a Major-General of militia of North Carolina. For many years he was clerk of the court of the county, and was frequently a member of the Legislature. He died in 1826, and was buried in the old grave yard in Charlotte.

The Part Mecklenburg Took in the War With Mexico.

North Carolina furnished one regiment of infantry only, to prosecute the war with Mexico, but Mecklenburg took no part in the formation of the regiment. The county raised a company of Light Horse, Capt. A. J. Harrison and Lieut. E. C. Davidson being commissioned to organize a company of Dragoons. When the company was full, they went to Charleston, S. C., and were conveyed by transports to Vera Cruz. They were in no such battles as we had in Virginia in 1861-'65, but did much service in guarding wagon trains and skirmishing with the enemy. The company returned home, having performed their duty, and were honored by the people at home and the officers honored with seats in the State Legislature.

Banks and Banking.

Independence was declared for fifty years before a bank was ever opened in Charlotte to transact business; probably it was not needed at an earlier period. In the earlier years of the century, except in seaport towns, there was comparatively but little money in circulation, and but little trade was effected. The first in Charlotte was a branch of the State Bank in 1834. It did some business, in a general way, but issued no bills less than $3.00. Each State issued bills for its own use, but nearly all were discounted more or less. South Carolina money commanded a higher premium than most any other State.

In 1853, the Bank of Charlotte started to do business, and had a fine beginning. Henry B. Williams was president, with Wm. Lucas cashier. Some changes were made afterwards and all monied institutions went up when the Confederacy fell. We were then poor indeed; no banks, or money deposited of any kind. Those who had been our richest men and were able to help those who were not so fortunate, were now on a par with our poorest.

In the course of a few years our people seemed to take on new life; farm produce commanded good prices, and if the Yankees had not molested our people, we would have seen better times.

Tate & Dewey's Bank started to do a considerable business, put out bills with a free hand, and the people encouraged the bank by depositing there all their surplus. Its career was short. Mr. Dewey died and the bank collapsed; no assets of any consequence were left; many people lost heavily; the bubble burst and a nine-days' wonder was all that was left.

Some of the Prominent Citizens in the First Half of the Nineteenth Century.

About the year 1830, Chevalier de Riva Finola, an Italian nobleman, was sent here as the president of a mining company. He was an expert as a mining engineer, but we are at a loss to know how long his stay was protracted, or what success he had. Probably not a dozen men in the county have ever heard his name. While here he lived in the house that was afterwards occupied by Joseph Wilson, the great lawyer and solicitor, and for many years by W. J. Yates, the well-known editor of The Charlotte *Democrat*. Recently the house has been moved back on West Morehead street. Seventy years ago an Italian of royal blood lived in Charlotte, and employed a mulatto barber by the name of Paulidon Brickett, to shave and dress his hair every morning. So the plain people of Mecklenburg had a live prince among them, who moved about in European fashion.

Humphrey, Titus and Edward Bizzell moved to this county probably somewhat later; but Edward Bizzell was mayor of the town for a short time just after the war. They were natives of New York. They came as mining experts, and were very liberal in spending money for the company. They got possession of several large tracts of land, but did not have good titles. What is known as Bizzell's Mill, was one of their places. This mill was in operation before the Revolutionary war, and is where Lord Cornwallis got his grinding done during his short stay in Charlotte. They have gone the way of the world without leaving any posterity to perpetuate the name. In company with them came a man named Penman. He was a native born Englishman, stood well with the nobility, and was sent over here to take charge of some gold mines that were supposed to be very rich, and some of them sustained the character for half a century that was given them; but probably more money was spent in developing them than they ever yielded their owners.

Penman was a large, red-faced, typical Englishman, and was used to being waited upon. He brought his body servant with him, a man by the name of Goodluck. Every morning the servant would groom his master with as much care as our former slaves would our race horses; then saddle his master's horse and mount his own, riding a respectful distance behind, but near enough to take his master's horse the moment he would light. This was the usual programme. At any rate, this kind of service was kept up for several months. Wherever Penman would turn, Goodluck would have to be on hand to obey every behest.

Mr. David Henderson, a near neighbor, suggested to Goodluck that he was as free as Penman, and he was not obliged to wait on him; in fact, he advised him not to make himself a "nigger" for any man. Goodluck at once quit his employer. James P. Henderson—a distant relative of David Henderson—thought he knew a good thing when he saw it, immediately applied for the vacant place and was accepted, and was duly inducted into the office of 'Squire for the Knight of the Golden Dream around Charlotte. This was an era of gold hunting that has only been rivaled once in fifty years. James P. Henderson was not ashamed to work for money in a legitimate way. This service lasted but a short time. He married a woman of brilliant mental attainments—a daughter of Dr. Matthew Wallace—raised four children far above the average in mental acumen.

Capt. Penman had an associate or fellow helper, by the name of Penworthy, in his mining operations. They were a lively pair, and spent their money most lavishly, not to see how much good they could do, but to see how good a time they could have. It has always been the same old story, that every dollar made by mining, it cost ten dollars to get it.

About 1845, Capt. Penman abandoned mining and set his face towards the ministry, after being converted to the

Methodist faith. He then became a preacher—a winner of souls for the Kingdom of Christ. In the latter part of his life he behaved very civilly and did not need so much waiting on. The two women who lived with him, and whom he passed off as his sisters, are now forgotten, "having neither name nor place" to let those who come after know that they ever occupied a place in the county. Mining for gold was carried on very extensively in the first twenty-five years of the century, but their methods were very crude, and unsatisfactory. Costly machinery was not put in the shafts, as the time for heavy expense had not arrived, for when a profit was not yielded directly, it was considered that much was lost.

The Champions of the Northern and Southern Parts of the County.

In the first part of the century it was the custom of the times for each section of the county to have one man who was noted as the champion, or "bully," of his precinct. At a general muster of the county, in which both the infantry and cavalry participated, in the presence of an immense crowd, in the year 1835, just east of the present site of the Episcopal Orphanage, met the two "best men," or champions of the county. The sporting characters were not long in spotting their game. Arrangements were soon made for "Devil" Matthew Wallace and Frank Nealy to fight till one or the other hollered out "enough." A ring was quickly made, the combatants stripped to the waist, judges were appointed to see that no foul play was taken by either side. It was then announced that the fight would begin at the signal. In a twinkling, the time-honored general muster came to a close, every man seemed to break ranks on his own authority and a grand rush was made for the arena of the athletes, where two modern Hercules were striving for the mastery. Boys and young men climbed trees that grew near the spot that they might witness the terrific combat. Almost at the beginning of the contest Nealy threw (or knocked) Wallace down, and rained terriffic blows in Wallace's face, while Wallace let his blows into Nealy's sides and chest. Nealy was considerably taller than his antagonist, but Wallace was the heaviest, and said to be double-jointed. He had double breasts, well developed. When thoroughly exhausted, Wallace hollered "enough." They were separated, laid in the shade and sponged with cold water. They were both covered with blood. In one hour Wallace proposed to fight it over, but Nealy was too exhausted, and declined.

Blind Dick.

However humble an individual may be, we must not forget that he is a part of the whole, and may be known to all the citizens of a small town, especially if respectful and makes himself useful. Long before the middle of the last century, in the heyday of American civilization, the man blind Dick was probably the most noted negro in the county. He was a slave, the property of Lawyer James Hutchison. He was a noted landmark in the town for more than twenty years before the great civil war, and lived for several years afterwards. His master gave him his time and protected him from evil-disposed persons. He contracted with several persons to feed and water and curry horses, carry fresh water to a number of rooms or offices, black boots, make fires and do sundry turns. He went about everywhere by himself, feeling his way with his stick. Almost every person in the county knew Blind Dick. He was very polite and respectful to every one, and every one wished to help him along, so he was well cared for. Once while carrying a bushel basket of fine apples on his head along the street, a gentleman standing in his door reached up and picked an apple off the basket, which Dick at once perceived, and struck with great force where he supposed the offender was who had taken the fruit that had been entrusted to his care. Dick was regarded as honest, and always bore a good name from white people.

If the great events that occurred in the county should be preserved with fidelity, why should those of lesser grade be passed over in silence. It is our desire to treat all subjects fairly; even slavery that we not only tolerated, but defended for one hundred and fifty years.

Negroes Before the War Between the States.

From the time Mecklenburg county was the home of the Caucasian race—long before the meets and bounds of the county were designated or cut off from Anson, the negro was employed as the slave of white men. At that early day they were not numerous according to population, but as the population increased they became more numerous. The price in the early times for a grown negro, either man or woman, did not exceed three hundred dollars; but before the Nineteenth century was half over, the price of a good looking man or woman would range from $1,000 to $1,800. The market price varied according to the price of sugar, rice, tobacco and cotton. In this county it was no uncommon thing to find the finest blacksmiths, carpenters, tanners, shoemakers, and in fact all kinds of mechanics among the slaves. In the rice plantations of South Carolina, the great cotton fields of the more tropical States of the South, and wherever the negroes were worked under the overseers of the Southern States, they did not have the advantages that were to be had in Mecklenburg, where none of the great crops were raised to the exclusion of the cereals. But few large slave holders—compared to those who owned but a few, or none at all—lived in the county. In the first sixty years of the century, scarcely a half dozen people in the county were fed in the Poor House. Now in the beginning of the Twentieth century about sixty—on an average—find quarters there, of both white and black. The population of both races have increased rapidly in the last forty years. The negroes have increased in an accelerated ratio in the last twenty years, owing to the rapid increase of population of Charlotte as a commercial and manufacturing centre.

The negroes are abundantly provided with church and school facilities, although they were denied the privilege of going to school or acquiring an education when in a state of slavery. Now they are on an equal footing with white children, in educational advantages, as the State provides public schools.

But to speak of the negro in slavery in the county, was the object in view, that the young people might understand they had more real enjoyment prior to 1865 than they have ever had since.

The affection that existed between master and slave was wonderful indeed. It was common when the white children should be sick, for the negroes to show a great deal of solicitude for the little one's welfare. When B. A. Johnston volunteered in the Confederate army, Company C, Thirty-seventh Regiment, Mrs. Johnston sent the family servant, Lige, to wait on and to nurse him in case of sickness. In May, 1864, Lieut. Johnston was killed and the enemy held the part of the field where he fell. When the news was carried to the rear and Lige was told of his master's death, and his body was in the Yankee lines, he cried like a child and said: "How can I go home to mistress and master, and leave Mars Alic's body in the hands of the enemy. I'd rather die than tell them."

They were true to their master's interests during the war. During all these four years of war, when only the old men and women were left at home, not a woman was insulted, or a house was burned by negroes; but things were as quiet and orderly as if the men were at home and no war in the country. Their behavior was unparalleled in the annals of our country for more than one hundred years.

Strange that they should aid in perpetuating their bondage by their good behavior and raising good crops to feed the Southern army.

It is characteristic of the negro to be happy when well fed, well clothed and not oppressed with over work. The fiddle and the banjo were their instruments of music, and when not forbidden, one-half of the night was consumed in social enjoyment. In ante bellum times the principal ration issued the slaves was corn bread, fried bacon and buttermilk for breakfast; boiled bacon, cow peas, corn bread and vegetables for dinner; and for supper, bread and milk. On this diet they were able to do heavy work, viz., cut (with a scythe and cradle) one hundred dozen of wheat, or make two hundred rails in a day, which was an ordinary task. They increased rapidly and their children seldom ever died. Their mistress took the oversight of the babies, while their mothers would be in the field. The negroes were peculiarly subject to typhoid fever epidemics, and proved fatal in many cases. Since their freedom they do not have it. In slavery they were almost free from consumption; now a large part of them die with it. Their diet has a great deal to do with it.

The negroes in the time of slavery were emphatically religious people. Often carried away by their emotions, they were easily thrown into a state of enthusiasm or excitement that rendered them oblivious to all else for the time. Some times they would simulate a condition of trance, and remain in a semi-conscious state for hours. This state of mind would last but a few days, when they would regain their usual happy condition. They attended the churches of the white people. There was no such thing in slavery times as negro churches. It was usual to build a gallery in every church for the accommodation of the negroes. On communion Sabbaths, or other days when camp-meetings were held, very large crowds of them would be present, and dressed in their best clothes, could excel the whites in gallantry and general attention to the women. This was their happiest time. There was not a half dozen cruel masters in all of Mecklenburg county. A man that was cruel to his negroes was tabooed by the white people in general, and would not be received into polite society. In the fall of the year, when their crops would be gathered, long piles of corn drawn into the barn yard and prepared to be shucked by all the hands in the neighborhood—the expectation of the rich supper that awaited them, premised by a treat of the best whiskey or brandy (that could be bought for 35 cents a gallon) that produced lively anticipations. The heap was soon divided, the two captains chose their men, a lively corn song was raised, and with great animation the long pile of corn was quickly shucked, with loud huzzars and great rejoicing of the victors. After their vociferous rejoicings had subsided, they would wend their way to the supper table where a bountiful repast awaited their arrival. When all had partaken of the bounty, they were assigned to a room where the furniture had been removed, when the fiddle and the banjo played "Old Jimmie Suddentie," and other pieces suited for the "light fantastic toe." This was kept up till midnight, when they would all disperse and go to their homes. These were the happiest days of the race; and it is a great consolation to the people of the South that the present deplorable condition of the negro cannot be laid at our doors. "Shake not thy gory locks at me; thou canst not say I did it."

The State Laws in the First Half of the Nineteenth Century.

In the first half of the 19th century the State laws were much more strict and rigid than they were at its close. Many offenses were then not noticed. A thief was more apt to get the penalty of the law than a homicide or even a murderer. As civilization grew older, the branding iron was frequently called in to mark the man guilty of manslaughter. It was also called into requisition for perjury, but more frequently the punishment for false swearing was to nail the lobe of the ear to a whipping post and cut the ear from the head. For manslaughter, the side of the face, or the palm of the hand was strongly bound to the railing by leather straps, when the branding iron, with the letters "M. S." heated red hot, was held on the cheek or in the palm of the hand, till the criminal or his attorney would say three times, "God save the State." But however glib with the tongue the attorney might be, the smoke arising from the quivering flesh would reach the top of the court room, or "The Temple of Justice."

The lash was the only remedy for stealing, and was often made use of for minor offenses. Thirty-nine was the limit, but in bad cases the whipping could be repeated in ten days. Imprisonment for debt was very common, keeping the debtor in prison for thirty days; then if he could swear he was not worth 40 shillings, he was released, and no further prosecution could be had against him, but was free.

The whipping post, the stocks and pillory, branding irons, were institutions that proved a holy terror to law-breakers in general, and were kept on the statute books for the benefit of the unruly until 1867. While we were under military despotism during reconstruction days, our people were forbidden the use of corporeal punishment.

As a substitute, though a poor one, we made use of the

chain gang, and as soon as possible the penitentiary was gotten under way. Then was inaugurated a "School for Scoundrels."

Mecklenburg has reaped her full share of the evils of such an institution. The penitentiary costs very heavy, and is a foot ball to be kicked about by whichever party has the power of filling the offices. But for the last twenty years since the county has engaged in building and constructing Macadamized county roads, wherever the nature of the crime will admit of it, the criminal is made to work for the county. Where the crimes have been very heinous, they are sent to the State prison. But no punishment is so cheap or so effective as the stocks and whipping post. But we have to keep up with the procession. At this stage of civilization it was customary to adopt the easiest and quickest way to take game without regard to damages that may be sustained by other people. In the early part of the century it was very common for people to go deer stalking; that is, to hunt deer with a pan of fire fastened with a strap on the back between the shoulders, with rich pine laid across the pan to make a brilliant light, so that the eye was blinded by the dazzling torch so that the hunter could come up close and "shine their eyes;" could take good aim, and have no difficulty in taking their game. But this plan had its drawbacks as it is impossible to tell by the "shining eyes" whether it was a calf, sheep, colt or deer. Consequently a special law was passed against fire hunting, making it a misdemeanor, punishable with thirty-nine lashes on the bare back. It soon broke up this style of hunting. Many of the little misdemeanors, more annoyances than loss of property, were subject to whipping at the discretion of the magistrate's court. But in many cases the thief was permitted to run away, commonly called "taking leg bail." But old things have passed away and all things have become new.

Biographical Sketches.

GEN. GEORGE GRAHAM.

He was a resident of Mecklenburg, and a brother of Gen. Joseph Graham. He was born in Pennsylvania in 1758, and came with his mother and family to North Carolina when about six years old. He was educated in Charlotte, and at an early age espoused the cause of his country. In 1775, he, with a few others, rode all night to Salisbury, seized the Tory lawyers, Dunn and Booth, brought them to Mecklenburg, and from thence they were carried to Camden and imprisoned. When Cornwallis lay at Charlotte, he was very active in attacking his foraging parties. He was the leader of the attack at McIntyre's, six or seven miles from Charlotte, on the Beattie's Ford Road, and actually, with twelve men, compelled the foraging party of four hundred English, to fall back in utter confusion. He was Major-General of militia of North Carolina. For a long time clerk of the court, and often a member of the Legislature. He died the 29th of March, 1826. He was buried in the old, or first cemetery in Charlotte. The following inscription is upon his tombstone:

"Sacred to the memory of Major-General George Graham, who died on the 29th of March, 1826, in the 68th year of his age."

He lived more than half a century in the vicinity of this place, and was a zealous and active defender of his country's rights in the Revolutionary war, and one of the gallant twelve who dared to attack, and actually drove four hundred British troops at McIntyre's, seven miles north of Charlotte, on the 3d of October, 1780. George Graham filled many high and responsible public trusts, the duties of which he discharged with fidelity. He was the peoples' friend, not their flatterer, and uniformly enjoyed the unlimited confidence and respect of his fellow citizens.

WM. LEE DAVIDSON.

Wm. Lee Davidson, Esq., was a son of Gen. Davidson, who was killed in the battle of Cowan's Ford, and lived near Davidson College; in fact, the college was called for his father, and he did much to help get it in working order. He was a man of fine intellect, and did much for the county, but being a Whig in politics, was in a hopeless minority. In 1850 he moved to Alabama, and engaged in planting cotton. He was a large and successful farmer. He was married twice, but raised no children. He died about the close of the war, in 1865. He was an enthusiast in silk culture in 1845. He planted an orchard of (multicaulis) mulberry trees to feed the silk worms. He was very successful in raising the worms and also in having the cocoons spun, but could not find a market for the product, and of course, the industry was abandoned. This was a great "fad" over the country that yielded but little fruit, but left an experience that has served to warn against indulging in an industry that failed to "pay."

PATRICK JOHNSTON.

Patrick Johnston, a native of Ireland, came to this country in 1787; was an expert weaver by trade. He married Miss Annie Wall. They worked hard and were saving, and soon accumulated a handsome estate. He had three sons and two daughters. James Johnston and Houston Johnston lived near the home place, between Beattie's Ford and Davidson College. They were good citizens, accumulated property, were large tax-payers, but were a short-lived family.

Mary married Samuel Lowrie, a son of Judge Samuel Lowrie, and lived on the Beattie's Ford road, seventeen miles northwest of Charlotte. Mr. Lowrie died in Missouri in 1846, of yellow fever, and Mrs. Mary Lowrie died in 1849, leaving four sons and one daughter. The sons all volunteered in the army. Houston, a captain in the Sixth Regiment, N. C. T., was killed at Sharpsburg, Md., September 17, 1862. Lieut. Jas. B. Lowrie was killed at Gettysburg July 3, 1863. Capt. Patrick J. Lowrie died at Wilmington, N. C., 1862, of yellow fever. Samuel Lowrie, the only one of the four who lived through the war, resided in Florida and died in 1892. Miss Annie Wall Lowrie married Dr. J. B. Alexander and lived near the old homestead for more than thirty years. She was very popular with her neighbors, and was much missed by her friends when she and her husband moved to Charlotte in 1890, to be with their daughter, Annie L. Alexander, who was a graduate in medicine, and located here to practice her profession. And I would mention the fact that she was the first Southern woman to take a degree, or practice medicine in the Southern States. She graduated at the Woman's Medical College of Pennsylvania, in Philadelphia, in 1884. Since the ice has been broken, and women have been admitted to practice medicine on an equality with men, they have now first-class colleges in a great many Northern cities and admit them to all medical colleges in the South on an equality with men.

His two daughters—Rachel married Sidney Houston, who lived in Iredell county, and had two sons, James and George Houston, who were first-class men, and raised families who were useful citizens. Mr. James Houston married a daughter of Wm. Patterson, a prominent citizen, south of Beattie's Ford. Mr. Patterson was an active Justice of the Peace, a man of influence, and was held in repute in this end of the county. His daughter Margaret was well known and appreciated by a large circle of friends. She has spent a long life in doing good to others.

One daughter of Mr. Patterson, Lenora, married Joseph M. Wilson, Esq., who is also a prominent Justice of the Peace and farmer, and has taken an active part in schools and church; and has raised a worthy family of children. His wife is still living, in feeble health, but can look back on a well-spent life.

LOUIS JETTON.

Mr. Louis Jetton, a descendant of the French Huguenots, came into this county in the latter part of the Eighteenth century. His son, Alexander Brevard Jetton, lived to be an old man, who exemplified in his life the religion he professed, was held in much esteem by all who knew him. His name is transmitted by one son, J. L. Jetton, an educated gentleman, and has educated his six children that they may prove to be worthy of such ancestors. Mr. Jetton and his wife are still living, and enjoy the fruits of a well-spent life. He was twice a member of the Legislature, when the honor was forced upon him. He now resides near Davidson.

HUGH TORRANCE.

Hugh Torrance came to Mecklenburg in the latter part of the Eighteenth century, and settled in the Hopewell neighborhood. He was an extensive farmer, and married the widow of Col. Falls, who was killed in the battle of Ramseur's Mill, in Lincoln county, in 1781. He built a very elegant brick mansion that will compare favorably with the most aristocratic residences in the city or county. Mr. Torrance was a native of Ireland, and had the "push" that was characteristic of the early emigrants of the Scotch-Irish people. They were a money-making and church-loving people; consequently they were not willing to stop short of independence, and Mecklenburg will ever be proud of the fact that her early settlers were of the stamp that loved liberty and freedom. One son, James Torrance, was the only fruit of this marriage. Both Mr. and Mrs. Torrance died in February, 1816. Their elegant home was left to Mr.

MISS MARGARET A. LOWRIE.

James Torrance, who added largely to his estate—both in land and negroes. He was married three times, had a large family who have scattered off, till now but two, the youngest sons, live in the county. The old county seats that have been in the family from the time the lands were first entered, are now fast passing into the hands of strangers, and will soon be unknown to the children of the original owners. Richard and John, two of the youngest of the third generation, are now among the oldest men of the county, and will soon have passed from the land holders of the county. As there is now a craze for all the educated classes, and the property holders to move to towns, where they can have the advantages of schools and society. Mr. Richard Torrance and family now live in Charlotte, but cultivates his farm with tenant labor. For more than one hundred years our lands have been cultivated by slave labor, but for nearly forty years freed labor, or free labor, has been depended on, which has been so unreliable that the best element on the farms, with the employers, have moved to the towns.

MARGARET ALEXANDER LOWRIE.

Without an effort on her part there were but few women in the county who exercised a more healthy or helpful influence. When a young lady, rich and beautiful, came of a family of great culture and influence, she was looked up to and courted by the many for her smiles of approbation. Her company was always sought for. She never considered any one an inferior who supported a good name and was careful to preserve it. She was a daughter of Judge Samuel Lowrie, who was a native of Delaware, and was a son of Robert and Elizabeth Lowrie. When a child his parents moved to Rowan county, and he was educated by Rev. James Hall in Iredell county.

In 1804, 1805 and 1816, he was elected a representative in the Legislature of North Carolina. In 1806 he was elected judge of the Superior Court, which position he held until he died, which was in 1818.

He married Margaret, daughter of Robert Alexander. The fruit of this marriage was Robert, Samuel, Polly (married Dr. Dunlap), Lilly (married Brawley Oates), Eliza and Margaret. In 1811 he married Mary, daughter of Marmaduke Norfleet, of Bertie county, N. C. From this marriage there was but one daughter, Rebecca, who married Rev. John Robinson, an Episcopal minister, who located in Huntsville, Ala. But few of the family are now left to speak of their history. Miss Margaret Lowrie was a great favorite with young people, and always had a crowd to visit her. Her sister Eliza, who was never strong, lived with her. She was a great reader just for her own pleasure, and let Miss Margaret do the housekeeping and the entertaining of visitors. In her old age she never forgot that she was once young, and had much charity for the young, and sometimes in a sly way would tell how the boys would come "a-courting." It always appeared to furnish her pleasure to tell about Speight McLean and Joe Alexander coming on Cupid's errand. She received offers of marriage when she was quite old, but she would laugh and say: "It is time now to turn these little episodes over to our juniors." In these prosaic times it would be well to have some of the "old issue" to come along again.

SAMUEL J. LOWRIE, ESQ.

He was one of the most brilliant lawyers that Mecklenburg county ever produced. He was the son of Dr. Robert Lowrie, and he a son of Judge Samuel Lowrie, of Mecklenburg county. He was born to an inheritance of legal talent. The women possessed literary talent of a high order, connected with grace and beauty of person. Mr. S. J. Lowrie's father died quite young, had but two children, Samuel and Robert. Their mother married a second time, and Samuel J. Lowrie came to Charlotte to live with his aunts, maiden

SAMUEL J. LOWRIE, ESQ.

CAPT. JOHN WALKER.

ladies, who lived with their brother-in-law, Dr. David R. Dunlap, and frequently with Brawley Oates, another brother-in-law, who lived in a large lot on the eastern corner of Seventh and Brevard streets. And, by the way, it is said Miss Lilly Lowrie, afterwards Mrs. Oates, was the prettiest woman in Mecklenburg. Mr. Oates was engaged in the office of the County Court Clerk, and took his nephew as a substitute in the office with him, and for several years he worked there and read law. He was not only thoroughly drilled in the science of the law, but was well acquainted with the practical workings of the law. After obtaining his license to practice law, he was taken in partnership by Hon. J. W. Osborne, who was a prince among lawyers. After a few years he took an office by himself, and did not devote himself as assiduously to his practice as his friends desired. He was the peoples' favorite, and his services always in demand. The war came on and he plead his avoirdupois was against his marching. He was too heavy for cavalry service, hence he chose the navy. He was stationed in Charleston harbor, where the duties were light and no marching to do. His legal talents accompanied him to the navy; here he was employed to defend a poor seaman who had stricken an officer. The penalty was death, but he gained an acquittal for his client. Once he wanted a furlough, and he wrote the clerk to know how many cases he was to appear for in the Superior Court. The clerk replied 150 cases; either for or against most every case on the docket. He got his furlough. His opportunities were very great. He outlived his aunts and all of his near kin, yet he was scarce forty when death claimed a most brilliant lawyer, in 1870.

CAPT. JOHN WALKER.

In any State of the Union, Capt. Walker would have taken a prominent position. Nature had chosen him for a leader of men. He was not a polished man, with a surface education, but he had a strong mind, well balanced, fearless in contending for what he believed was right. He was one of the most influential citizens of Mecklenburg county. He entered public life in 1840, as a member of the General Assembly of North Carolina. He there drew the attention of the county, by his close attention to business, particularly to the welfare of Mecklenburg. He was sent to the Senate in 1842-'44-'46-'48. Again Senator in 1854, and the last time in 1860. Six times a Senator from this county betokens great popularity. He was given the pet name of "The Great Wheel Horse of Democracy." He was an active Justice of the Peace; was for a long time chairman of the County Court, and was able to dispense justice without so much red tape. He was a good man to have in a neighborhood. He appealed to reason, and prevented many a trivial law suit by a timely word of advice, that otherwise would have engendered a bitterness that would have lasted more than a generation. He understood the common law, and had no hesitation to enforce it, and believed that all—both rich and poor—should be treated alike. He believed in being fair in debate, and he would force his opponent to be fair, or else he would drive him to the wall. He was strictly in his element when he had a "foeman worthy of his steel."

After the war, in the days of reconstruction, he was shorn of his strength. Much of his property was gone; he was placed under the ban; he was not allowed to vote; if he was worth $20,000, unless he could get a pardon (?) his property would be confiscated. His proud spirit could not brook such treatment. He lived but a short time. Reconstruction laws bore heavily upon him.

It took a man of iron nerves to undergo the so-called reconstruction days. He was elected an elder in Sardis church when but 20 years old. But for the sake of peace and harmony, he, with his son, Rev. James Walker, and several other prominent members, removed their membership to Sharon, where he continued to exercise the office of ruling elder until his death.

Capt. Walker was married three times. First he married

JAS. H. DAVIS.

Miss Susan McCullough. She bore him two children, Rev. James Walker, and one other son who died in childhood. His second wife was a widow—Jane Harris—who bore him no children, although she had two by a former husband. His third wife was Miss Sophonia White. She did not bear any children.

Capt. Walker was a representative man of the old school, when the peoples' verdict was the law of the land, from which no one deemed it a hardship or ever thought of an appeal. He lived in a time when a case of extreme poverty was unknown in the county, unless it was from sickness or self-imposed. During his day the production of cotton was comparatively, in its infancy; raising negroes, hogs, cattle and horses and mules; they did not care so much for money, as to have that which could be turned into money. Our whole system of farming and civilization was changed by the reconstruction. Capt. John Walker was born February 22, 1801, east of Charlotte, about eight miles. Here he kept his home all his life when not engaged in the business of the State. He died September 8, 1876. His life was a useful one. When not engaged for the State, he was looking after the interests of his family, the church, and the county. The county could well say he was jealous of the best interests of Mecklenburg, and of the church.

JAMES DAVIS.

Mr. James Davis was the son of Watson Davis, of Providence congregation, where he lived and died early in the Nineteenth century. James, the subject of this sketch, had one brother who also lived in Providence, named Samuel Davis. He had a daughter who married her cousin, Marcellus Davis, who lives in the town of Charlotte.

Mr. James Davis lived some six miles southwest of Providence church. He married a Miss Lee, an aunt of D. P. Lee, amongst the best people in the county. Mr. Davis was a farmer of splendid attainments. He studied the needs of his soil and put in practice his conclusions. Persons who knew him well, said he was a bold buyer, or seller, as the case might be. He would buy a plantation ready stocked with horses, mules, cattle, sheep and hogs, and farming tools, and negroes enough to cultivate it. A big trade of this kind would not cause him to lose an hour's sleep. He was always cool, and if he could see a fair promise to realize a handsome profit, he was quick to strike a trade. He always rode a magnificent horse, and was a fine rider. He owned several large plantations, and they were well stocked with the best the country afforded. Of course we are speaking of things as they appeared then. The civilization of ante-bellum days was very different from what it was at a later day. In the former period a man of means had no hesitation about making debts; for the number of slaves he had were regarded the best of collaterals, and he could always get as much time as he wanted. He had all his stock, of every kind, well protected against the cold of winter; abundantly fed, so that they were always ready for service. His negroes were well cared for, in sickness and health. It was his opinion that all stock was profitable in proportion to the care that was bestowed upon it. This was before cotton became king of products and king of commerce. In 1852 a wealthy man in south Iredell county said the most profitable stock to raise in this country was "negroes and hogs."

Mr. Davis was a staunch supporter of the war. He believed in raising all the supplies the army should need, both what was necessary to feed the soldiers in the field, and supply their families at home. He first gave his son, a boy of seventeen, to the Confederacy, all the horses and mules he could spare from his farm, paid more than the tenth of all his meat and bread and feed for horses. During the last two years of the war his granaries were so much frequented by the soldiers' wives, especially from Union county, that they called it "going down to Egypt." They would frequently come in large companies, a soldier's wife or daughter driving a one-horse wagon, sometimes an ox, or a mule; and none turned away without a load. Whatever would satisfy hunger and render the people comfortable, was poured out without stint. If the wealthy people of our Southland had been as patriotic as Mr. Davis, there would have been fewer desertions from the Confederate army.

Mr. Davis owned about three hundred negroes, and of course had no hesitation about contracting a debt with all these collaterals behind him; but when the war ended disastrously to the South, and swept away the very foundations on which the finances of the State, or the Confederacy was built, it cast a gloom over the people that they could not shake off at pleasure. The younger people could start in anew, but those who were in the evening of life were not able to stem the adverse current as it rushed madly on to overthrow all of our civilization.

It was morally impossible for a man, a large planter, owning a vast number of slaves, to regain his hold on the financial touchstone, when all had been swept away, an army of adventurers were hanging on his every turn, hoping to pick his financial carcass, as he recuperated his shattered fortune.

Young men endowed with a superabundance of energy can sometimes rebuild a lost fortune under adverse circumstances; but when the evening shadows grow long, and hope is crushed, and only defeat stares him in the face; all incentive to action has subsided, energy is gone, and he gradually sinks into a premature grave. In this way have many entered the future state who otherwise might have reached a green old age. Old age that comes with stealthy steps, hardly pausing as each year goes round, comes naturally, has many sweets to make bright and gladsome the countenances when all goes well; but we can only see poverty and wretchedness, when the bitter cup is pressed to our lips, and we are made to drink to its dregs, and there is nothing left us but the quietude of the grave.

Many cases of this kind will have to be answered for at

the shrine of truth and justice. Our Southern people faced the defeat with wonderful courage. Many of our old men were so paralyzed, not by defeat so much, as by the petty tyrants who thought to lord it over their superiors in virtue and all that constitutes true manhood.

Mr. James Davis was surrounded by the best people in the State—Mr. W. M. Matthews, Wm. McKee, Wm. Ardrey, M. D., Capt. W. E. Ardrey, John Rhea, Robert Grier, Elam Sample, Neil Morrison. The names of such men to constitute the neighbors of James Davis, is *prima facie* evidence that he was more than an ordinary man; and his deeds of charity in cases deserving it, will live long after his face is forgotten.

W. J. YATES—EDITOR AND PRINTER.

Mr. Yates was born in Fayetteville, N. C., in 1827. Work was as natural for him as laziness is for some people. He loved to work to accomplish certain aims. He most cordially despised idlers, and laid to the charge of idleness poverty and all its train of evils. He entered the printing office of the *North Carolinian* at an early age, and by industry and frugality, was enabled to buy the paper, which he again sold and in 1856 moved to Charlotte and bought the Charlotte *Democrat*. This was his idol—the apple of his eye. He could suffer the loss of anything else rather than have his paper evil spoken of. In 1881, October 1st, the *Southern Home* was consolidated with the *Democrat* and published as the *Home-Democrat,* Mr. Yates retiring from active management of the same. In the interval he was restive and his oft repeated assertion, "I cannot stay out of this office," led him in February, 1884, to again assume his wonted possession—a good editor, he loved his profession. He made a financial success of his paper and by economy and judicious business management, accumulated a handsome competency. He earned his money in Charlotte, and invested it here, having no use for any enterprise outside of the State. A loyal North Carolinian, familiar with her history and conversant with the record of her people.

He was president of the Board of Directors of the Insane Asylum at Morganton, and a Trustee of the University at Chapel Hill. Pronounced in his opinion, he held his convictions with a strong and unyielding grasp, his superior judgment wielded an influence in the councils of which he was a member. His individual characteristics were manifest through the columns of his paper. Liberal, he gave unostentatiously; his private charities amounted to a large sum; the veriest tramp never appealed in vain, the gift often accompanied with expressions of his contempt for idleness. The poor will miss his generous hand. Simple in taste, plain in habits, he was intolerant of display and pretence; a good citizen, one whom the community will miss. The press of North Carolina has lost its oldest and most valued editor. Peace to his ashes. He was well suited for the times in which he lived. He died October 28, 1888.

SHERIFF MARSHALL ALEXANDER.

He was one of the most popular men of Mecklenburg county. He was a gentleman of the old school—never forgot the training he received in ante-bellum days; always cheerful, and ever ready to help an old Confederate.

In speaking of Mr. Alexander, we must say that there were in his life and career far more noble qualities than one would suppose who was not intimately acquainted with him. He was a man of fine intelligence, possessing a warm heart. At times he appeared rough and harsh, but it was because you did not know him. There was a vein of quaint humor running through his character that made him friends wherever he moved. He was a gallant soldier in the late war, and occupied the position of Lieutenant in Company B, Fifty-third Regiment, North Carolina Troops, Gen. Daniel's Brigade, Rode's Division. He was captured at Gettysburg and sent to Johnston's Island, and not exchanged, but remained there till the war was over.

In 1872 he was elected sheriff of Mecklenburg county, which office he filled with entire satisfaction for 12 years. He made a faithful officer, always among the first to settle with the State; yet he was indulgent and the tax payers of this county speak of his administration of the office in the highest terms. It was a common saying on the streets that he was "the best sheriff the county ever had." (But the county has never had an inferior officer of any kind since the days of reconstruction.) He was cut down in the prime of life, when his usefulness was at full tide, his wife having preceded him some time. He was about 50 years old. Every one said "Marshall Alexander was an honest man." He was just and straightforward in all his dealings; he was always ready "to render unto Cæsar the things that belonged to Cæsar." He was a conscientious man and was as true to his convictions as the needle is to the pole. He was open and candid. Had no petty spites or harbored a mean revenge. He died peacefully and calmly. His life ebbed out like the fading light of day. The whole county feels the loss of a friend. But everything terrestrial must fade and disappear. He died in 1886.

DR. J. M. STRONG.

John Mason Strong was born in Newberry county, S. C., September 1, 1818. He was the only son of Rev. Charles Strong, of the Associate Reformed Presbyterian Church, and Nancy Harris Strong.

Charles Strong died July 20, 1824. His wife survived him until November 8, 1842. They had five children—but one son—the subject of this sketch. John Mason entered Jefferson College, Cannonsburg, Pa., in 1839; graduated in 1841 under the presidency of Dr. Matthew Brown. He read medicine under Dr. John Harris, of Steele Creek, and attended a course of lectures at Charleston, S. C., but graduated from Jefferson Medical College, Philadelphia, Pa., in 1847. His first and only home was in Steele Creek, where he was reared and where he practiced medicine for over fifty years. He was a ruling elder in Steele Creek A. R. P. Church and throughout his long and singularly useful life was one of the staunchest of churchmen. He was a "pillar of the church," being prominent always in its councils and affairs. He served as a surgeon in the late war, and was considered one of the ablest men, professionally, in the service. He was called in as an expert to settle the difference among the local doctors in the smallpox epidemic of 1850 in Charlotte.

Dr. Strong was twice married. His first wife was Rachel Elenor Harris, daughter of Dr. John Moore Harris. They were married April 7, 1851. She died May 27, 1880, leaving five children. In September, 1883, Dr. Strong married Miss Nancy Grier, of Steele Creek, who survives him. He was one of the most prominent men in the county. His integrity was above question, his piety an example to all, and his ability of the class that made him easily one of the best physicians of the county. He kept up with the progress of the science, held to that which would counteract disease and benefit his patient. He was an all-round man, and was prepared for any emergency. He reached a ripe age, and was an honor to his profession and to the county of his adoption. He died March 22, 1897.

JUDGE SHIPP—BORN NOVEMBER 19, 1819, DIED 1890.

"Judge Shipp was a man of wonderful popularity, both as a judge and as a citizen. In the former capacity he was conceded to be one of the finest judges of law known to the State. He was, on all occasions, a modest man. Oftentimes subject to unjust criticism, he always presented the even tenor of his way and in the end he was always vindicated. It was seldom indeed that one of his decisions was reversed. As a judge he ranked amongst the foremost of the State.

As a citizen, Charlotte was proud of him. A genial man, upright in all the walks of his life, both private and public, his death is a loss to the State and will be mourned not only by Charlotte, but by every town and hamlet in the State. He was graduated at the University in 1840, delivering the salutatory address; was admitted to the bar in 1842; practiced in Lincoln and the mountain district. At the beginning of the Civil War he was elected captain of a volunteer company in Hendersonville, and served in that capacity in Virginia until he was elected Judge. In 1870 he was nominated by the Democratic party for Attorney-General on the ticket with Hon. A. S. Merrimon, candidate for Governor, etc., and was the only Democrat elected. He practiced law in Charlotte from 1872 to 1881, when he was appointed by Governor Jarvis judge of the Superior Court to succeed Hon. David Schenck. He was re-elected for eight years in 1882. He was a member of the Legislature before the war.

He was twice married, first to Catherine Cameron; second, to Margaret Iredell, daughter of James Iredell, at one time Governor of North Carolina and United States Senator.

"Judge Shipp was one of the best informed lawyers in the State. He had a marked legal mind, he reasoned closely, and as a jurist was eminent. He had no superior on the bench. He was fond of history and literature of our language, especially the standard works. He was interesting and alive in conversation, and had much wit and humor."

The Charlotte bar met and attended his funeral in a body, and passed appropriate resolutions on the great loss they had sustained in the death of Judge Shipp. But his usefulness was not confined to Mecklenburg county, but extended to all parts of the State. He died in 1890.

COL. WILLIAM JOHNSTON.

One of the foremost citizens of Mecklenburg county, who was born in Lincoln county March 5, 1817, and belonged to one of the best families in that county. He was educated at the University of the State. He studied law under Judge R. M. Pearson, was licensed in 1842, and located in Charlotte, where he continued to reside to the end of his life. His residence was somewhat of the olden style, very large and roomy and elegant.

He was an ardent Whig during the decade preceding the war between the States, and with great ardor espoused the cause of the South. In 1856 he assumed the presidency of the Charlotte & South Carolina Railroad Co., and by his ability as a financier and manager, put the road in a prosperous condition. This road proved of great benefit to the Confederate government during the war until destroyed by Sherman in 1865.

In 1859 Col. Johnston inaugurated the Atlantic, Tennessee & Ohio Railroad, and completed forty-six miles of construction, when the war came on and put a stop to the work. Col. Johnston was an ardent supporter of the Southern Cause. He was twice sent as a delegate to the conventions called for the purpose of considering Federal relations, and at both he strongly advocated North Carolina withdrawing from the Union.

In March, 1862, he was a candidate for Governor, but he had as an opponent Zebulon B. Vance, then a colonel in the Confederate army, by whom he was defeated. He, however, rendered the Confederacy throughout the war great service in the transportation of men, ammunition and supplies. At the close of the war he succeeded in getting the Charlotte, Columbia & Augusta road completed from Columbia to Augusta, and to-day it stands as a monument to his sagacity and business ability. The story of President Davis' arrival in Charlotte, and the startling news it was destined he should hear in this city, is known by the older citizens; but as a matter of history for the younger generation, as well as being one of the most interesting events in Col. Johnston's life, is told here. Just after peace had been declared, President Davis arrived in Charlotte April 18, 1865, and was met by Col. Johnston. He was taken to the home of a man by the name of Bates, whose guest he was, and who lived on the corner where the express office now stands. A crowd had gathered on the corner to greet Mr. Davis, who stood on the steps of the house making an address. A telegram was passed to him. He read it, and his face assumed a serious expression, and passing the telegram to Col. Johnston, who stood by him, he retired into the house. In the crowd was Bates. He reported to the United States Government that President Davis had spoken exultingly when he read the telegram which announced Lincoln's assassination. Subsequently, Col. Johnston volunteered, when President Davis was under arraignment by the government, to go to New York and furnish the facts to Davis' counsel.

Col. Johnston was married in 1846 to Miss Anna Eliza Graham, daughter of Dr. George F. Graham, brother of Wm. A. Graham, and to them were born Julia M., wife of Col. A. B. Andrews, of Raleigh; Frank G., Cora J., wife of Capt. T. R. Robinson; W. R. Johnston. Mrs. Johnston died in 1881. The children all survive except Mrs. Robinson.

Col. Johnston was one of Charlotte's wealthiest citizens. He owned valuable property here and in Memphis.

Col. Johnston was elected Mayor of Charlotte and served as follows: from May, 1875, to May, 1887—missing two years. He served four terms, giving great satisfaction. The town prospered under his administration very greatly. He was a wise financier, and used the peoples' money most judiciously, solely for the benefit of the town. He died in 1896.

DR. ISAAC WILSON.

DR. ISAAC WILSON.

(A practitioner of Medicine from 1825 to 1875.)

The subject of this chapter was a son of Sheriff Wilson, and a nephew of that eminent minister, Rev. John McKamie Wilson, D. D., who was regarded as one of the greatest preachers of his day. Rocky River was his church and home for a number of years. He was so intimately connected with the people of Mecklenburg that no apology is needed for mentioning his name or his greatness. Dr. Isaac Wilson studied medicine under Dr. D. T. Caldwell. He did not have the advantages of attending a medical college, or one of the recent kinds of hospitals, but he gained his knowledge from medical works and bedside experience. His practice covered a large expanse of territory. One day he would start out on the west side, on the next he would go on the east side—so that he was able to see all of his patients once in two days. He carried a very capacious pair of saddlebags, which were replenished every morning with such things as were expected to be needed. One thing in particular was never left out, viz.: his cupping *horn*. Seventy-five years ago it was very fashionable to bleed in all diseases. Dr. Wilson was not noted for bleeding, but if he did not bleed, he always cupped, hence his horn was never forgotten. It was taken from the head of a two-year-old heifer, scraped so thin you could easily see how much blood was drawn. A nice piece of ivory or horn closed the large end, with a few tacks or wire, and the small end with beeswax, punctured with a pin—through this hole the air is sucked out, and with the teeth the wax is made to fill the hole, and the blood is now poured out in sufficient quantity to relieve the patient.

Dr. Wilson was well known in the northwestern half of the county. In those days when physicians were few and far between, their practice was necessarily extensive; and it was common for a doctor not to see his patients oftener than once in two or three days. In 1830, before quinine was discovered, or had been put on the market, barks (Peruvian) was the great remedy to stop chills with. In virulent cases a "bark jacket" was worn. In many cases grow round (*eupertorium perfolliatum*) a plant growing in marshy places, was extensively used; but we must not suppose the doctor carried all these plants with him, but they could be obtained at almost every house. He was immensely popular, was invited to all the parties, dinings, weddings and entertainments. One hundred years ago a doctor was about on a par with the preacher. Dr. Wilson was a Justice of the Peace, and was often called on to officiate in marriages when the preacher was absent.

Dr. Wilson was married three times. His first wife was a daughter of Wm. B. Alexander—Elizabeth. They had six children. The two youngest—Gilbreth and Thomas—died in the hospital in Richmond, Va., time of the war, 1862. Joseph Mc. and J. A. Wilson have families, and are farming. Their sister, Isabella, of more than ordinary talents, married Mr. Andrew Parks—died a few years ago in Statesville, leaving but three children. Dr. J. M. Wilson, another brother, a polished gentleman, who was well educated, graduated from Davidson in 1853, took a fine stand in class; taught school a short time, studied medicine and graduated in Charleston, S. C., in 1857; did a large and successful practice; was not strong physically, and in 1898 wound up his course, a successful life.

Dr. Isaac Wilson's second wife was Miss Rebecca McLean, a daughter of the revolutionary surgeon, Dr. McLean, who married a daughter of Maj. John Davidson—Mary (or Polly). She had no children. She was a most estimable woman, not of a robust constitution, and lived but a short time. His third wife was a widow by the name of McIntosh, from Alexander county. She was also a lovely woman and adorned the society with which she mingled. The evening of their lives was spent happily together. Having served his generation well, having waited upon the people for half a century, having to call him blessed, at peace with all men, he laid down the burden of life with a bright hope of happiness in that world beyond the grave. He received a very productive farm from his first wife's father, twelve miles northwest of Charlotte, west of the Atlantic, Tennessee & Ohio Railroad. Here he built and improved the place, and had a most desirable residence. Dr. Wilson lived in the best part of the Nineteenth century. The great wilderness which existed at the beginning of the century, gradually began to give way, houses sprang up, fields were cleared, churches and school houses dotted the face of the county, industry accomplished wonders in the lifetime of one man. Dr. Wilson's life of seventy-five years saw wonderful changes in this county, all tending for the good of the county; best of all the changes, was putting up the stock in pastures, and turning out the fields. Timber was getting scarce as he neared the end of life, and it was meet that we should cut off the expense.

The expense of keeping up miles of fencing and annual repairs, amounted to vast sums of money; and our labor being freed, there was no other way left for the people to do but to keep better stock and less in numbers, and throw our cultivated lands outside. After a few years it gave perfect satisfaction. This grand movement in the march of civilization took place about the time the old doctor finished his course. From 1840 to 1850, the shooting match was common for beef or turkey. In this sport Dr. Wilson often indulged. He was not only an expert with the rifle, but was particularly fond of the sport. At this time the people had not learned how to preserve ice, consequently but a small piece of beef could be taken care of by one family; hence the necessity of having a large number to participate in the match.

Fox hunting was another grand amusement that Dr. Wilson often joined in with great pleasure. He kept a good pack of hounds, and any time in the fall or winter months, when not engaged professionally, he would indulge in the chase. Often he has been seen to lead in the chase, with half a dozen sportsmen and twenty dogs. When a red fox was raised, the chase was kept up for several hours, as that species are much longer-winded than the grey. With the passing away of Dr. Isaac Wilson, so also the sports he loved so well have been forgotten, remembered only by the older people. The shooting match is now obsolete, and the fox hunting with the winding horn and pack of dogs is an exercise of the past.

WILLIAM MAXWELL, ESQ.

As a general rule, we do not see or appreciate the true worth of our public functionaries until they are removed from the sphere of their usefulness. While the memory of Esquire Maxwell is still fresh in the minds of the people, it is well to rehearse what endeared him to the people of Mecklenburg.

He passed away on the 26th of October, 1890, after having spent a useful life for his family, for the county, and for the church. His was a well rounded life, devoted both to church and State.

Esquire Maxwell was in his 82nd year. He was born at what is known as the old Maxwell place, seven miles east of Charlotte, on September 9, 1809. He was the third son of Guy Maxwell, who emigrated to this country from County Tyron, Ireland, in 1795. Esquire Maxwell was twice married. His first wife was Mary E. Johnston, a sister of Nathaniel Johnston. She died a year after her marriage. His second wife was Nancy A. Morris, daughter of Col. Zebulon Morris, who with three children—Col. D. G. Maxwell, W. C. Maxwell, Esq., and Miss Carrie Maxwell, survive him. Esquire Maxwell was long in public life in this county, and his official career was untarnished. He was for a long time a member of the old County Court, and was also its chairman. In 1862, Mr. William K. Reed resigned as clerk of the court and Esquire Maxwell was appointed to fill out his unexpired term. That began Esquire

WILLIAM MAXWELL, ESQ.

Maxwell's reign as a court house official. He continued as clerk of this court until it was abolished in 1868. Then he was appointed Register of Deeds to fill the unexpired term of F. M. Ross. He was subsequently repeatedly elected to that office until December, 1884, when, feeling the cares of old age pressing upon him, declined to again become a candidate, and retired to private life. Esquire Maxwell was prominent as a church man. For thirty years he was an elder in Philadelphia Presbyterian church, and was for twenty-five years an elder in the First Presbyterian church of Charlotte.

FUNERAL OF MR. MAXWELL.

"The funeral services over the remains of the late William Maxwell were conducted from the First Presbyterian church. A very large concourse of people turned out to pay the last tribute of respect to the memory of the lamented dead, the main body of the church being crowded. The body was inclosed in a very handsome casket covered in black broadcloth, and the top was hidden under a mass of white flowers. Rev. Dr. Miller, the pastor of the church, preached an impressive sermon, and at its conclusion the body was escorted to Elmwood, where it was interred. The large crowd present eloquently attested the esteem in which the deceased was held by the community."

THE FIFTH REGISTER OF DEEDS.

Mr. Maxwell was the fifth Register of Deeds of Mecklenburg county, which position he held from 1870 to 1884. His immediate predecessor was F. M. Ross, who held the office from 1840 to 1870.

The first register was Robert Harris, who was in office from 1763 to 1782. John McKnitt Alexander succeeded Mr. Harris, and was register ten years. In 1792 Wm. Bain Alexander succeeded his father, John McKnitt Alexander, and how long he had the position there are no records to tell; but between Wm. Bain Alexander's incumbency and that of Mr. Ross, who came into office in 1840, there was a time the duties of Register of Deeds was performed by the county clerk, or the clerk of the Superior Court. It is evident, however, from the great amount of registering done by Wm. Bain Alexander, that he held the office many years.

The registering work done by Mr. Maxwell is in a neat, strong, clear hand, and denotes method and accuracy. The present register, Mr. Cobb, who succeeded Mr. Maxwell, says that the latter was one of the best registers any county ever had. He never left anything undone from one day to another. He was popular with all classes.

SUGAR DULIN.

This account of Sugar Dulin was found among the papers of the late Wm. Maxwell, he having been administrator of Sugar Dulin. It was written upon foolscap paper and doubtless with a quill pen, as that was the only kind then in use. Notwithstanding the bad spelling and the extravagant use of capital letters, the handwriting is plain and of systematical form, and in fact will compare favorably with the handwriting of the majority of the business men of to-day. He was of great individuality. Many of his quaint sayings are to this day quoted by the old people in the neighborhood in which he lived. He often remarked that he had more sense than King Solomon, for Solomon did not know for whom he was laying up riches, but that "he knew that he was laying them up for a set of d—d fools." It is said that Sugar Dulin's father, Thomas Dulin, was so fond of sugar and rice that he gave the name of Sugar to one son and rice to the other. Rice Dulin moved in early life to Charleston, S. C., where he accumulated a considerable amount of property. Sugar Dulin came to Mecklenburg county and bought a large body of land ten miles east of Charlotte, where he lived and died about 1845. He was a member of Philadelphia Presbyterian church, and is buried in the old cemetery at that church, twelve miles east of Charlotte. As the autobiography states, Sugar Dulin had a great many descendants, and in fact, they were so thickly settled near Philadelphia church that the section was called Dulintown. The Dulins were all noted for their physical courage, and while they did not have the reputation of being "bullies," yet if any man was looking for a fight, he could always be accommodated by a Dulin; and in antebellum days at almost every session of our old county courts, some of the Dulins were charged with assault and battery, but one of the name has never been known to have been indicted for a felony.

In the war between the States there were seven Dulins in Capt. D. G. Maxwell's company (H, Thirty-fifth North Carolina Regiment), and but two of them came home after the surrender, and they both were wounded.

The life movements of Sugar Dulin from birth to extreme old age:

He lived in Mecklenburg from 1791 till his death, which was almost a half century. He was a law-abiding man and a good citizen. This brief account is given in his own spelling, and distribution of capitals:

N. B.—I was Born in onslow County, No. Carolina, the 23rd Day of April, 1763 as my parents sd any How Before I mind & they Settled within Two miles of where Trentown in Jones County stands, & they sd Before I mind they moved Ten miles Higher up within one mile of old Daniel Shines & there I was Raised & lived until I went to the army & never father from Home than to Nubern until I went to the army & then I made it my Home until I was married, and then I lived in sd County until 1791. I Removed to Mecklenburg County on the place I now live on. Now this the 1st Day of April, 1835 against the 21st of this Instant I have lived in Mclinburg County, No. Carolina, Forty Two years, &c.

Done with my own Hand & the leading men of this County may Due the Ballance as to my Carretter &c.

SUGAR DULIN.

I Have lived with one wife going on 51 years & we Have Raised Five Sons & five Daughters & we this Day counted our Grand Children & we make them 94 that our Sons & Daughters has had & we Counted 13 great grand Children. This the 20th of March, 1837, SUGAR DULIN.

These people lived in Philadelphia congregation, owned a large tract of land, raised fine crops of grain, hogs, cattle, horses and sheep, were all round good citizens, and raised a numerous posterity; were ever ready to contend for the right. Not one of the name was ever indicted for a disreputable transaction; never gave an insult, but was quick to resent one.

DR. SAMUEL B. WATSON.

Dr. S. B. Watson, of Philadelphia neighborhood, in this county, passed away at his home on the 24th of August, 1895, in his 90th year. He practiced medicine sixty-seven years. The oldest practitioner in the State, venerable in years and in the service of his fellow man.

Dr. Watson was born in York county, S. C., December 17, 1805, and with his father—Robert Watson—moved to Charlotte in early boyhood. He graduated from the Charleston Medical College in 1828, and with little interruption, has practiced his profession until within a few days of his death.

Dr. Watson was a plain, blunt man, simple in all his habits and temperate in all things.

He possessed in a marked degree the qualifications of the true physician. With untiring devotion to his profession and zeal for the relief of the sick and suffering, he faithfully and successfully practiced medicine over a large territory of

DR. SAMUEL BROWN WATSON.

rough country for three score and seven yeats, and many to-day of the fourth and fifth generations of his patrons are ready to rise up and call him blessed. Dr. Watson was possessed with a remarkably retentive memory. He could recall with vividness the diseases and remedies of more than half a century and held tenaciously to many principles and practices in medicines he obtained by personal, practical experience at the bedside. He never compromised the truth, nor became the apologist of error. He had the candor to tell his most intimate friends their faults. But few persons have approached so near the centenarian in years with so few blemishes in his character considered either as a professional man, or as a Christian; and we doubt not that at the last summons from the Great Physician to come up higher, he received the welcome plaudit: "Well done good and faithful servant, enter thou into the joys of thy Lord."

REV. DR. T. H. PRITCHARD.

One of the most devoted and conscientious pastors that was ever in Charlotte. His father was a mechanic, and worked at his trade here for many years before the Civil War. The doctor was loved by all the people of the city; particularly by the children. He could be grave and sedate as occasion demanded, or be jovial at the festive board, and always the favorite with boys. He was immensely popular. He appeared as much at ease in his neighbor's pulpit as in his own; so that wherever a guest, he had a royal welcome. He died in Wilmington, and when the train bearing his remains arrived in Charlotte, the people turned out to do him honor without regard to denomination. On May 24, 1896, the last sad tribute of respect was paid to the deceased. The First Baptist church was exquisitely draped, and flowers—the symbol of the Resurrection—were in profusion.

Dr. Taylor, president of Wake Forest College, was the first to lay his tribute of affection as it found vent in words, on the bier of his life-long friend. He expressed gratitude for the man as he was; for the triumph of his life and death. "He was a many-sided man," said he, "and a man who would have been a gentleman even if he had not been a Christian; as it was, he was a Christian gentleman. He was a man who never outgrew the child, nor child-like simplicity. He was genial, sweet and pure. A current of humor flowed continuously from his heart, and a remarkable thing about it was that it was always pure. I never heard him tell anything that could not be said before the most modest woman. He was one of the most useful men in the South. The State owes him a debt of gratitude it can never pay for the campaign he made in the cause of education when president of Wake Forest College. I thank God for his life work and his victory."

Dr. Preston followed Dr. Taylor, and spoke simply and yet tenderly and beautifully of the deceased. He said: "It is given to few to have such a funeral as this. Perhaps many of you will never see such another. I will not refer to the great deeds of Dr. Pritchard, but to one peculiar something about him which always struck me as forcible, and that was the large number of warm personal friends he had. Had such a wide and loving heart, and expressed his affection so genuinely. What would have seemed insincere in others was perfectly genuine and correct in Dr. Pritchard. No man ever had more friends, and that is the highest tribute that can be paid. I come with a special message and tribute from the First Presbyterian church to lay on his bier, for he was a child of our own Sunday School. He used often to say to me with a twinkle in his eye, "I know the Shorter Catechism, for I learned it under those old trees," pointing to the church yard. Another remarkable thing about this man was his great power of attracting children. He kept young, and made himself so attractive to children that they all loved him and to-day there would be a thousand children in this audience if there was room for them. I want the children to always think of him by the familiar name they called him on the streets. Dr. Preston closed by

R. D. ALEXANDER, ESQ.

urging the members of Tryon Street church to honor the dead pastor by doing what he would have them do.

Rev. Dr. Bowman paid a most feeling tribute to his deceased brother. "A great man," said he, "lies fallen in our midst. He was great in the way the Master was great. We find in this man characteristics which were Christ-like. I am here to bear witness of his faithfulness, of his genial, kind heart and great efficiency. I have had the blessed experience of knowing consolation and comfort from him." May God give us grace to follow him and spend our energies as he did for the glory of God and the good of our fellow men.

Rev. L. C. Hoffman and Rev. Atkins and Rev. Turrentine also took part in the solemn services. Buried in Elmwood.

ROBERT DAVIDSON ALEXANDER.

To write of persons that you have known intimately for one-fourth of a century, it is almost like communing with the dead. Mr. Alexander was the third one of the fourteen children of Wm. B. Alexander, and a grandson of John McKnitt Alexander. The subject of this sketch was born in the old homestead, on the 9th day of August, 1796; was given a common school education that was built upon and improved during his whole life. He was not so fond of the fox chase, deer hunting, and the sports the young men engaged in; but rather would devote his spare moments to reading the New York *Christian Observer,* the *Intelligencer,* the great organ of the Whig party, and kindred literature. He was a well informed man on the great topics of the day, both civil and religious, and was fond of discussing important questions. It always afforded him pleasure to attend church, courts, presbyteries and synods. He was a Justice of the Peace for about forty years. In his day a man was appointed for life, or good behavior, unless he should desire to resign. He did pretty much all the business in his section of the county. For many years he was a member of the county court; emphatically the peoples' court; many were the conveniences, in the first place it cost but a trifle, all small offences could be disposed of. This court could not try civil cases where large amounts were involved; but in criminal cases, except murder and arson and probably some others, they meeted out justice without quams of conscience. Whipping, branding, stocks and pillory were the usual punishments, and the man so punished generally left the state.

He generally kept a fine orchard of all kinds of fruit; also kept enough of bees to furnish all the honey his family would consume.

Mr. Alexander married the youngest daughter of Rev. S. C. Caldwell, Abagail Bain, in 1829. He built a home ten miles from Charlotte, one mile northeast from the old homestead, where John McKnitt lived, and exercised such a healthful influence upon the patriot cause during and after the Revolutionary war. He built up a handsome competency from a well tended farm. Before the days of railroads, when everybody traveled horseback, or in a private conveyance, he was never known to refuse lodging to a traveler. He did not keep a "Hostlery," but took in and entertained people as a Christian duty. He had five children who lived to be grown; the oldest son, Rev. S. C. Alexander, D. D., is now living in Pine Bluff, Ark.; is an evangelist of the Presbyterian Church, has labored in many of the Southern States, and consequently is well known. A sister of his, Agnes, married Dr. W. B. Fewell, of South Carolina; raised an interesting family. She died in 1897, aged 65. She was an excellent Christian woman. Dr. J. B. Alexander practiced medicine in the northern part of Mecklenburg for the third of a century—was a surgeon in the Confederate army —in 1890 moved to Charlotte. In 1858 he married Miss Annie W. Lowrie, of this county. She died February 27, 1893. Bore him six children—but four are now living. Their second daughter was the first woman south of the Potomac that ever graduated in medicine—Dr. Annie L. Alexander.

She is located in Charlotte, and has succeeded equal to expectations. W. D. Alexander, Esq., lives in his father's old residence, and represents his father in his magisterial capacity, is an excellent farmer and wields a good influence in both church and State. His first wife was a daughter of Dr. J. G. M. Ramsay, of Tennessee. She left four children, who are now grown; the daughter married a Mr. Johnston, of Lincoln county; Dr. James R. Alexander has lately moved to Charlotte. The two younger sons, William and Lattimer, are both in Charlotte engaged in profitable work. Both are nice, well behaved young gentlemen. The youngest daughter of R. D. Alexander, Lottie, died soon after her education was completed in 1878.

Mrs. Abagail Bain Alexander was more than an ordinary personage; her parentage, and the exalted positions of her brothers in the legal profession, one, Walter P. Caldwell, of Greensboro, and Septimus Caldwell, of Granda, Miss. Both brothers were great lights in the profession of law; five brothers of no mean ability, as ministers of the Gospel, who early in life moved to the Southwest, where they exercised an influence for good that will extend through many generations. Mrs. Alexander, when married, took her youngest brother, Walter, then a small boy but four or six years old, and raised him as if her own child, his parents being dead. She was first in all cases of sickness or distress; she was welcome in every house where gloom had settled. She was broad in charity to other denominations, particularly to the Methodists. She often worshipped at old Bethasda. The people there were poor and ignorant, and had all confidence in her, and applied to her for help in their spiritual perplexities. This was a mutual pleasure for her to give and they to receive.

The young people were fond of her society; always cheerful and happy, there was a kind of contagion that young folks were fond of.

She was fond of horseback riding, and all her visiting among the sick or well in the neighborhood was on horseback. In the early years of the century all classes rode horseback. Women thought it no hardship to ride six to eight miles to church, and carry a baby on their lap. When the distance was not so great, they would take one also on behind, tied to the mother with a large handkerchief, or with a hank of yarn. The old-fashioned gig was used by the well-to-do classes. In the country many persons walked to church and rested their horses. Mrs. Alexander survived her husband nearly twenty years. In 1889 she entered her rest, being 80 years old. Her childrens' children were old enough and in after years with a full heart, called her blessed.

HON. R. P. WARING.

Capt. Waring was a native Virginian; came of the old English stock that believed it as essential to cultivate the mind as to train the body. His first wife was a daughter of Lewis D. Henry, of Raleigh, N. C. In 1850 he first moved to Charlotte; just before this he obtained license to practice law, and opened a law office here to grow up with the people, and to identify himself with the best interests of the county and State. Smallpox broke out here in 1851, when many people were affected, some died, and terror seized the whole county. The terrible scourge breaking out the next year after Capt. Waring's appearance, has served as a marker in the last half of the Nineteenth century. The disease has not been wanting here for the last six months, and the most nervous people have not lost an hour's sleep on account of the epidemic, it is so mild.

Capt. Waring commenced editing the *Democrat* in June, 1852. He was a success as an editor. If he had put all his time to his paper instead of attempting to run a law office at the same time, his success would have been complete. He was elected county attorney in 1855, and gave universal satisfaction. He was made elector in 1856 on the National Democratic platform for the election of James Buchanan president.

In 1859, he was elected county attorney the second time, which showed how popular he was before the war. He soon resigned his office of county attorney to accept a consulship in the Danish West Indian Islands, which important position he held until war had been declared against the South, when he immediately came home, barely escaping arrest in New York, as he had to come that way to get home, and render an account of his consulship.

When he reached home his country was one vast camp, one side determined to subdue and conquer the South; the South as fully determined to defend that which was achieved by our forefathers in the Eighteenth century. He raised a company, went to the front and fought gallantly for the cause of the South. When the war was over, he came back home and edited the *Times*. He was a bold and fearless writer, criticised the reconstruction plans by which they intended to humiliate our people; he denounced the government they inaugurated as a "military despotism" instead of a republic. For this *crime* (?) he was arrested in the dead hours of the night, carried off to Raleigh, tried by a military court, sentenced to pay a fine of $300.00 within five days, or be imprisoned for six months. This fact and others of a similar nature could be narrated, that were perpetrated on our people six months after the surrender, when we thought the civil courts were enough to take cognizance of the infraction of laws.

The county had every confidence in Capt. Waring, and had him frequently to head the ticket for the Legislature—twice in the House of Commons and four or more times in the Senate. He was a man of ability and unswerving honesty and patriotism.

For a number of years he was judge of the Inferior Court. He held the position until this court was done away with. During the entire time he gave great satisfaction, and the rapid dispatch of business. His services were secured to canvass the county for the contribution, or the taking of stock in the Charlotte and Atlanta Railroad, by Mecklenburg county. The wisdom of building this road has been amply shown by the benefit it has been to the city. In every position that Capt. Waring has occupied, his services have always been endorsed by the people of the county.

ADAM BREVARD DAVIDSON.

Mr. Davidson was well known not only in Mecklenburg county, but all through Western North Carolina as the foremost farmer in this part of the State. He was also well known in South Carolina and Georgia, for his fine cattle, especially for his herd of Devons and Durhams.

Until the war between the States, Mr. Davidson was probably the most wealthy man in the county. When a young man he married a daughter of Mr. John (commonly Jack) Springs, of South Carolina. His father gave him the large and elegant brick dwelling house built by Maj. John Davidson in 1787. Here Mr. A. B. Davidson lived and raised a large family, and accumulated a large estate. He was very liberal in his support of Hopewell church and all benevolent objects. He was always an ardent Whig, was a firm believer in the doctrine of internal improvements; subscribed largely to building railroads, had large amounts in cotton mills in Augusta, Ga., contributed of his wealth to build the A. T. & O. Railroad, and since the war crippled every one so severely, he urged the county to vote $300,000 to build the Atlanta road and rebuild the Statesville road. This road bed was taken up—that is the iron and cross ties—to build the road from Greensboro to Danville, which was deemed a necessity during the war. Mr. Davidson lost by the war, and by security for his *friends,* four-fifths of his estate. He was worth prior to 1865, a half million of dollars. He was a very busy man, as he always looked after his own affairs. He employed overseers on his plantations where everything was raised or made that was used on his farm. Farming was very different fifty years ago from what it is now. Whatever was necessary to feed the stock,

A. B. DAVIDSON, ESQ.

the hands and the family, to clothe and shoe the family, was raised on the farm. Every farmer of any consequence had one of their slaves for a shoemaker, one a carpenter and a blacksmith, a woman for a weaver. So nothing was to buy but salt, sugar, coffee, molasses, etc. Store bills amounted to but little, and when bread and meat had to be bought, it was looked for in the county. A doctor's bill could not well be avoided; but the doctors in those days had some conscience, and were as successful then as fifty years later.

Mr. Davidson did not have the advantage that his younger brothers had in the way of education; but he had a large amount of common sense, listened to what other people expressed, then drew his own conclusions and was rarely wrong.

Some twenty years before he died, he became thoroughly disgusted with free labor. He moved to Charlotte and quit the farm. He owned quite an interest in city property, and confined himself to improving his property here and rented the farms not given to his children. Before he died his noted old home, "Rural Hill," was burned; the old homestead and surroundings were not kept in the repair of forty years ago; the old place is much changed, and in fact bears but a faint resemblance to what it was when Mr. Davidson looked over some three thousand acres of land, and slaves enough to keep it in splendid repair, and have the large pastures filled with mares and colts, and the finest of cattle, sheep and swine. Our old civilization has been swept away, and we are living under the new order of things.

Mr. Davidson's mother was Sally Brevard, a daughter of Adam Brevard, who was a brother of Dr. Ephraim Brevard, the draftsman of the Declaration of Independence. A story is told that one morning after a hard rain, Maj. John Davidson called his son Jacky (who in after years was the father of Mr. A. B. Davidson), and told him: "While the ground is too wet to plow, go and get your horse saddled and get yourself dressed and go over to Adam Brevard's and court Sally; I think she will make you a good wife.

Now you have no time to fool about it; the ground will be dry enough to plow by to-morrow." Jacky went like a dutiful son, and Sally acquiesced in the proposition. They lived a long time, led a useful life and raised a large family of children. The subject of this sketch being the eldest, he was born March 19, 1808, and died July 4, 1896.

In the long ago it was not uncommon for families to have private burying grounds before churches were so numerous, or rather before any were built. Maj. John Davidson had a private plat a little west of the front of his house, probably started before the one at Hopewell church. Nearly the whole of the Davidson family are entombed there. Maj. Davidson's sister, Mary, who married John Price, is buried at Baker's graveyard, about five miles towards Beattie's Ford. It is overgrown with large trees of many varieties. Some old stones, grey rock, covered with moss, render the letters unintelligible. The old resting place is now forgotten by all save a few who live near it. Two desolate places for so important personages to occupy, Maj. John Davidson, a signer of the Declaration of Independence, at one place, and his sister at another.

PATRICK HARTY.

Patrick Harty and wife came from Ireland to America in the year 1820. They crossed the Atlantic ocean in a sailing vessel and landed at Charleston, South Carolina, where they stayed but a short time, when he was induced to move into the up country. The neighborhood is now, as then known, as Coddle Creek, where there is a church by that name. He worked there at his trade—brick mason and plasterer. He did not stay there long as work was more plentiful in Mecklenburg, so he moved his family to Charlotte and worked around through the county.

The people in the eastern part of the county, in Clear Creek Township, employed Mr. Harty to build Philadelphia church. It is a fine structure for that period. The people of that section were skillful and industrious farmers, therefore they put up a building in keeping with their ability. Mr. Harty never put up a shoddy job. Mecklenburg county employed him, as an expert, to look after the building of the court house on West Trade street, in 1845; but the county has disposed of it for a new one that is better and more up-to-date, on South Tryon street. Mr. Harty became thoroughly identified with our people. He raised and educated his children here at home, three boys and four girls, all useful citizens. His son William, for a number of years, clerked for various merchants. In 1846 he clerked for Henderson & Smith, at Davidson College. He was a popular salesman and efficient in his work. Mr. John Harty was a carriage maker in the town, did excellent work. For a long time his shop was on the corner of College and Trade. This was before the cotton market was developed, when corn and wheat was grown up to Harty's shops. Harty owned the lands contiguous to his shop, and was at that time considered of little value only as farm lands.

Mr. Harty made vehicles upon honor. If he sold a buggy and harness, he would warrant it to stand three years, but he would charge from $150 to $200. His buggies were known to last, with ordinary care, from ten to fifteen years; but in those days they were not in every day use.

Mr. Harty was at one time in partnership with Mr. Charles Wilson. They were the principal carriage makers in all this section of country. James Harty began clerking in a store while a mere boy. He proved an expert in this line of business, and he followed it until he could operate a store of his own. He probably had the first china store in the city. He married a daughter of Dr. Frank Ross, and raised an interesting family. He is one of the old landmarks of the town. He has hosts of friends, and is often appealed to for information relating to events that occurred fifty or more years ago.

THE CAMPBELL FAMILY OF MECKLENBURG.

Duglas Campbell came from Scotland in 1720, and settled in Pennsylvania, where he had many descendants. It is not known in what year Alexander Campbell came to this county, but it is certain that he came prior to 1775. He entered a large tract of land south of Hickory Grove church. Alexander Wallis now lives on a part of it, six or seven miles east of Charlotte. Alexander Campbell had two sons, John and Isaac, and one daughter, who moved West. Isaac Campbell was born in 1780, and died in 1854. He was twice married, his first wife being Catharine Orr. She died before she reached middle life, in 1820. Isaac Campbell's second wife—whom he married twenty years after the death of his first—was a Miss Johnston, who was the mother of our countyman, Mr. Joe Lee Campbell, of Clear Creek Township. John Campbell had quite a large family—John, Frank, Mark, Henry, Robert and Joab, and two daughters, Abigail marrying a Mr. Taylor, and Dorcas married a Smith, the mother of ex-Sheriff Smith.

Isaac Campbell's first wife—Catherine Orr—had a daughter, Lydia Campbell, who was the mother of our venerable friend and fine soldier, Julius P. Alexander, in the Confederate army. Frank Campbell was a most efficient elder in Hopewell church. In the early part of the century the Campbell's were among the most active supporters of the church at Sugar Creek, bore an active part in all educational enterprises, and whatever would tend to build the interests of the county.

W. F. PHIFER.

WILLIAM FULENWIDER PHIFER was a prominent citizen of Charlotte, from 1850 until his death, 30th December, 1882. He was born in Cabarrus county February 15, 1809, and was a descendant of Martin Phifer, who came from Berne, Switzerland, and was a member of the Provencial

W. F. PHIFER.

Assembly at New Bern, and is honorably mentioned in the Colonial Records.

MARTIN PHIFER.

Martin Phifer had three sons: John, who was one of the signers of the Mecklenburg Declaration of Independence; Caleb, who represented Cabarrus county almost continuously for many years in the Legislature, and Martin Phifer, who was a Captain of Horse from Mecklenburg county in the Revolutionary Army, and is spoken of by other writers as Colonel Phifer. He had extensive grants of land in Tennessee, upon which some of his descendants still live.

President George Washington, in his Southern tour, stayed over night at Cold Water, the home of Colonel Martin Phifer.

George Phifer was at one time Clerk of the Court of Cabarrus county, and he was the son of Martin Phifer, and the father of the subject of this sketch.

W. F. Phifer, as he signed himself, was a planter, this being the occupation of all his ancestors, though he began life in Cabarrus as a merchant and was associated with the late R. W. Allison, Esq.

He completed his education at Hampden-Sidney College, Va., and his frequent trips to Northern markets, most of the way on horseback, broadened his views and observation.

He was first married to Sarah, daughter of Colonel Robert Smith, who died, leaving one daughter, Sarah Smith Phifer, who married John L. Morehead, Esq.

He then became associated with his brothers, and moved to Alabama, and engaged in cotton planting for several years. On the 10th of April, 1849, he married Mary Martha White, daughter of W. E. White, Esq., of Fort Mill, S. C., and soon thereafter he brought back his slaves and farming equipments, and settled not far from where his life began. He revolutionized the cultivation of cotton in this section of the country.

Near and in Charlotte he purchased a tract of land known as the Lucky estate, and other lands, and predicted, in spite of the jeers of his friends, a great future for this town, and said he, "In later years there will be houses and streets where my plantation now lies, for," he continued, "the prospect for a city is better than any I saw at Atlanta, on my horseback trips to Alabama."

The house now owned by Mr. Wm. Holt he built, and most of the brick was hauled from Cabarrus county. This house was prominently situated in a five-acre square, bounded by Tryon street and College street, Twelfth street and College avenue, afterwards called Phifer avenue, by the Board of Aldermen, in his honor. "I will not live," Mr. Phifer said, "to enjoy much of the refreshing shade, yet I will plant trees and others may enjoy them." And these beautiful oaks stand now as a monument of his thoughtfulness.

He donated half of the land upon which now stands the Presbyterian College for Women, and for this he was given a complimentary share of stock in the school, and this stock was afterwards donated by his heirs to the present corporation.

He had great love for order and the beautiful, and employed a landscape gardener to beautify his yard and lay off the walks, and in this yard are found the most beautiful of the native trees. The color effect of the foliage of the Autumn was taken into consideration.

He disliked crooked lines and gave his land to straighten a street on his neighbor's side. The regularity of that part of the city known as Mechanicsville, is in striking contrast to some other parts of the city.

At the beginning of the Civil War, he was a man of considerable fortune, which he had amassed in farming; and, be it said to his praise, almost every slave he owned remained with him for the first two years of their freedom and always spoke of him with love and respect.

He was always a Democrat in politics, and was an enthusiastic Southerner. Though too old for service in the war, his home was always open to the hungry soldiers, who in the latter part of the war filed in almost daily to have their wants supplied. Mr. Phifer was a man of generous impulses and was loyal to his friends.

Mr. Green Caldwell was superintendent of the United States Mint, and one Sunday the Charlotte Grays captured the Mint. This caused much comment by the people, as they went to church. This came near being very disastrous to Mr. Phifer, for when the war closed, he was sued by the Government, as Mr. Caldwell's bondsman, and judgment was obtained for $25,000.00. However, through the aid of powerful friends, a relief bill was procured through Congress. Otherwise the remnant of his estate would have been swept away.

General Beauregard had his headquarters (and many of his staff were with him) for more than a month at his house, and though there was much confusion incident to the turmoils of war, yet neither he nor his wife ever complained, but accepted the situation gracefully and did all in their power to make the time agreeable for the warriors, and often the music of the evening was hushed to hear read some dispatch foreshadowing the fall of the Confederacy.

The headquarters of the army moved to Greensboro, and President Davis came to Charlotte and Mr. George A. Trenholm and wife became the guests of Mr. and Mrs. Phifer.

The last full meeting of the Confederate Cabinet (and, in the recollection of the writer, all were present) was held in the West room up stairs in the house now owned by Mr. Wm. Holt.

The cause of its meeting there was the fact that Mr. Trenholm, the Secretary of the Treasury, was ill and confined to bed. Mr. Trenholm tendered his resignation, which was accepted. President Davis then moved south and another meeting was held near Fort Mill, S. C., under an old sassafras tree, in front of the old home place of W. E. White, Esq., (the father of Mrs. Phifer), and which Captain S. E.

White, a brother, declares that this was the last Confederate Cabinet meeting.

By the second marriage of Mr. Phifer, to Mary Martha White, there are seven living children. Sons, William White, Robert Smith, George Martin and Edward White. Daughters, Mrs. M. C. Quinn, Miss Cordelia White and Mrs. Wm. G. Durant.—*Contributed by W. W. Phifer.*

COL. ZEB. MORRIS.

COL. ZEBULON MORRIS was born April 23, 1789, and died May 1, 1872. He was the youngest son of William Morris and Elizabeth Ford Morris, the daughter of John Ford, Esq., one of the signers of the Mecklenburg Declaration of Independence. He was born, lived and died on the same plantation, a part of the old Ford estate, ten miles east of Charlotte, on the Lawyers' Road. He was married to Martha Rea, the daughter of the Hon. John Rea, January 13, 1814. He was a remarkable man in a great many respects, as gentle and amiable as a woman and as bold and fearless as a lion. As deputy sheriff of this county, on one occasion he arrested a desperado, who swore that he would kill the first man who attempted to arrest him. Col. Morris handed his pistol to a man who had accompanied him and advanced unarmed on the desperado, who threw down his gun and said, "Zeb Morris, you are the only man who could have arrested me alive."

Col. Morris owned a great many slaves, to whom he was very kind, and they showed their attachment to him by remaining on his plantation after the surrender. He owned about 1,500 acres of land, was a lover of fine horses and a most graceful rider. In fact, it was a common saying—when anyone rode well—"he sits in the saddle like Zeb Morris."

Below are two obituary notices, one by Rev. R. Z. Johnston and the other by the late Wm. Yates, editor of the *Charlotte Democrat*:

COL. ZEBULON MORRIS.

This man's death will carry sadness and sorrow to many hearts. He was an old man—83 years and 7 days—and it would be difficult to point to another whose death would sadden so many homes in our community. He lived fifty-eight years and three months with the wife of his youth, who survives him at the advanced age of 76 years. He raised a large family, and had 46 grandchildren, 26 of whom are living, and 18 great grand-children, 15 of whom are living. Children and grand-children live in this county and adjoining counties, in easy communication with the old family residence. Great was the lamentation to-day over one so agreeably connected in these dear and tender relationships, when his familiar face was seen for the last time, cold in death, in the spacious family hall, and

> "The knell, the shroud, the mattock, and the grave;
> The deep damp vault, the darkness, and the worm,"

told us how "the fashion of this world passeth away."

That dear old home—the dearest spot on earth to so many loving hearts, the scene of so much pleasure in former days—is dismantled. Though the day has been one of the liveliest of the season, even the beautiful lawn around the mansion and the venerable oaks that shade the old spring, and the orchards, seemed to put on mourning, and the birds seemed to sing

> "How vain are all things here below,
> How false and yet how fair!
> Each pleasure has its poison too,
> And every sweet a snare."

Col. Morris lived to look upon strange faces in familiar places, and to feel like a lonely representative of a former generation. That venerable, faithful and useful man, and his life-long family physician, in whose arms he may almost be said to have fallen asleep, Dr. Samuel Watson, and a few others, whose locks are white and whose infirmities are multiplied, are all that remain to tell us of better days. O how can those who knew him afford to give him up!

> "Our dearest joys, and nearest friends,
> The partners of our blood,
> How they divide our wavering minds,
> And leave but half for God!"

He was a successful man; though living on thin land, nothing ever went lean and hungry about him. Constant in his friendship, liberal to the poor, just in his dealings, true to his engagements, kind to his children and servants, tender in his feelings, and generous with his hospitality, he was a gentleman always and everywhere. His piety was unassuming, but deep, and the Philadelphia Church has buried a constant and substantial supporter.

The 1st day of May, 1872, will long be a melancholy day to pastor and people. "Cast thy burden upon the Lord, and He shall sustain thee." May this promise moderate the sorrows of the mourners in this melancholy event, till "they that weep be as though they wept not;" and "God shall wipe away all tears from their eyes; and there shall be no more death, neither sorrow, nor crying, neither shall there be any pain." R. Z. J.

DIED.

In this county, on the 1st instant, after a short illness, Col. Zebulon Morris, in the 83rd year of his age. Up to within a few weeks of his death Col. Morris was a man of extraordinary physical and mental ability. He raised a large number of children, men and women of respectability and worth, and lived to see them all settled in life, and his grandchildren and great-grand-children starting out in the journey of this world's trials and crosses. Col. Zeb Morris was no ordinary man, as the writer of this paragraph knows. He was faithful and true as a man and friend, as an old-line Democrat and patriot, and as a consistent member of the Presbyterian Church, always a firm friend of the right and an enemy of wrong doing in any shape. He leaves a large number of relatives and friends in this county to mourn the death of a true man and a good citizen. Mecklenburg

GEN. WM. H. NEAL.

county has, indeed, lost a devoted husband of 55 years loving intercourse. Peace to the good old man's ashes.

EDITOR DEMOCRAT.

GEN. WM. H. NEAL.

GEN. WILLIAM H. NEAL was born in the extreme southern part of Mecklenburg county, near the Catawba river, in the year 1799, and died in the year 1889. He died at his residence within a few miles of the place of his birth. Gen. Neal was married in 1819 to Miss Hannah G. Alexander, and from this marriage were born the following children, namely:

Samuel Wallace Neal, now deceased, who lived and died in Indian Territory; Dr. Thomas C. Neal, who was a well known physician of Mecklenburg county and who died in 1901; Susan Emily Neal, who married the late Rev. Walter W. Pharr, and who is now living in Charlotte; Mary Adeline Neal, who married the late Capt. M. H. Peoples, who is now dead; Nancy Elvira Neal, who married the late Robert W. McDowell and is now deceased; W. B. Neal, now deceased; Louisa A. Neal, who married the late Rev. J. B. Watt, and is now living in Steele Creek township; and Preston A. Neal, who is now living in Rock Hill, S. C.

Gen. Neal's first wife died a number of years before his death, and he afterwards married Mrs. Martha D. Williamson, who survived him, but there were no children born of this marriage. Gen. Neal was always one of the leading and prominent citizens of Mecklenburg county.

For many years he was a general of the old Ante-Bellum Militia, and it was in this way that he acquired the title by which he was always known. He was a County Commissioner for a number of years and always took an active interest in public affairs. He was one of the very first in this State to engage in the cotton manufacturing business and for a number of years before the war he successfully operated a cotton mill on the Catawba river near his home.

He was a devoted member of Steele Creek Presbyterian Church, and always took an especial pride in his church.

As soon as he reached manhood he married and built him a home on a tract of land adjoining his birthplace, and it was here that he spent all the years of his long and useful life. He was always interested in anything pertaining to machinery and during his whole life was engaged in operating a mill of some kind or other; before and during the war operating a cotton factory and a flour mill, and after the war operating a flour mill.

In an unostentatious manner he spent his life and he was a man of highest character, standing and integrity in his county and community.

THE GARRISON FAMILY.

JOSEPH GARRISON was the progenitor of all of the name in the county. He came from Pennsylvania in the latter part of the Eighteenth century. He entered a large amount of land in Mallard Creek section, and divided it out among the early settlers, in order to have neighbors.

Mr. Garrison built the first bridge over Mallard creek, between Mallard Creek church and Back Creek church. The descendants show a piece of his old family Bible, probably two hundred years old. His children were David, Joshua, John, Arthur, James, Jane, and Sarah. None of these left issue, except James, who died at 65, in the year 1854. His daughter, Viney, married George Monteeth, and then moved West. Sarah married James Robinson and died in the eastern part of the county.

W. Manson Garrison married and moved to West Tennessee; L. S. Garrison died young, and left one child; B. H. Garrison married Mary Ann Hunter, daughter of Robert Hunter, had eight children—some of whom were in the Confederate Army. He is now in good health, but in his 90th year. Has been an active magistrate until recently;

MR. BRAWLEY OATES.

has always been an active supporter of good government, of both church and schools.

Samuel A. Garrison, his brothr, has led a peaceful life, raised an excellent family, and has always patronized the best schools, and, like all the family, helped build up the interests of the county. He was twice married, both times to a Hunter, and raised eleven children, all good citizens. He is now in his 84th year.

W. G. Garrison also is still living, in the 82nd year, hale and hearty. He has four children living, all useful citizens.

David B. Garrison, the youngest of the family, lost his leg in Virginia, where so many were killed and wounded contending for our rights. Has three children now living, and do much to make his last years pleasant. The Garrisons were good people, very much like the descendants of the early settlers of the county. Mecklenburg county was fortunate indeed in the class of her early pioneers.

BRAWLEY OATES.

Mr. Oates was a native of Cleveland county, was the son of good people, but not embarrassed with wealth. He probably came to Mecklenburg about 1830 or 1832.

In 1836 Mr. Oates was elected clerk of the County Court and served continuously till 1842. Charles T. Alexander succeeded him for the place till 1845, when Mr. Oates won the position back again and held the office till 1854. His health had now become very feeble from a pulmonary effection, which rendered him unable to attend to the duties of the office. He moved to Florida and the climate agreeing with his weak lungs so well, that he attended to his farm for eighteen years, enjoying a pretty fair state of health. Mr. Oates was a native of Cleveland county; he moved to Charlotte while quite a young man. He courted and won Miss Lilly Lowrie, a daughter of Judge Lowrie. A farmer's son of Cleveland county won a bride from one of the most aristocratic families of Mecklenburg. This was before the advent of railroads, and Mr. Oates wanted to take his wife over to Cleveland county to visit his people. They were traveling in a gig, and just beyond the Catawba river at Beattie's Ford, their gig gave way and Mr. Oates had to go to a house close by for assistance. During his absence, a party of her acquaintances returning from Catawba Springs, were astonished to meet Miss Lilly alone in the big road, and asked what it meant. She replied that "she had married Brawley last evening, and was just going up to see old Oates and family." They had a jolly time on the highway.

They had two daughters and one son. Margaret married Mr. Charles E. Spratt, a courtly gentleman who is spending the evening of his days with his daughter, Mrs. VanLandingham, in the city. It is said that he and his wife were the most handsome couple that ever lived in Charlotte. Mrs. Mary Eliza Agnew moved to Florida and soon passed away. The son, Dr. David Oates, served through the war of 1861-'65, and moved to Alabama, where he lives in single blessedness.

DR. DAVID R. DUNLAP.

Rev. Alexander Craighead had one daughter, Rachel, who married Rev. David Caldwell, of Guilford county, and one daughter, Jane, who married Mr. Dunlap, who lived in Anson county, who were the parents of Dr. David R. Dunlap, of Charlotte, N. C. He came to Mecklenburg in the first years of the Nineteenth century. He was armed and equipped for the practice of his profession, and made quite a reputation; was often called in consultation with the celebrated Dr. Charles Harris, of Cabarrus county, whose fame as a surgeon was co-extensive with State. Dr. Dunlap was at one time called to see a patient down in Clear Creek. When he got there he was informed Dr. Harris had been to see him a few days previous, and tapped the patient for dropsy, and inserted a goose quill, roughened at

DR. DAVID R. DUNLAP.

both ends, so it would not slip in or out. The man was evidently not good pay. He practiced medicine for a long time, probably forty years; he retired before 1850. He was clerk and master of the Court of Equity for a great many years. His daughter and his nephew, S. J. Lowrie, did all of his writing for fifteen years before his death, which occurred in 1865. He was very efficient in his office, keeping all his papers in the best of order. He was three times married. First he married a Jenkins from Anson county, and she lived but a short time, had one son and died. The doctor in the goodness of his heart, took for his second wife a sister of his first. This being contrary to the rules of the Presbyterian Church at that time, they cast him out. He then joined the Methodist Church, and became the pioneer leader of Methodism in Mecklenburg county. He engaged in a correspondence with his former friends and kinsfolk, who were Presbyterians, that was not commendable on either side. About this time Dr. D. T. Caldwell had a son to die. He and Dr. Dunlap had not been on speaking terms for years, and Dr. Dunlap came to visit him in his affliction. Dr. Caldwell met him at the door, both shed tears of reconciliation, forgot the past, and were the best of friends in all their future life.

Dr. Dunlap having lost his second wife, turned his attention to a daughter of Judge Lowrie, Miss Polly, and was accepted. Together they entertained their host of friends, watched after the interests of their church; their house was the stopping place for all the ministers in passing to and from their conferences. In that day the Methodist church was emphatically nursed on horseback; and it is also remembered that if their ministers were not well paid, they were well fed, and their horse was well cared for. It was a common saying fifty or seventy years ago, "As fat as a Methodist preacher's horse," when talking of animals in fine condition.

The last Mrs. Dunlap had but one child, a daughter. She grew up to be a very handsome woman, and what is better, of brilliant intellect. She, like father, was devotedly attached to the Methodist church. She married Dr. Edmund Jones, of Morganton, but he did not live long, and she returned to her father's house. She continued with her father till 1858, when she contracted a second marriage with Col. T. H. Brem, a most excellent gentleman and large merchant of the city. Dr. Dunlap went to live with his daughter, Mrs. Brem, where he spent the evening of his days. He died in the 84th year of his age in 1865, honored and loved by all the town and many hundreds in the county. His daughter soon followed, and his son, Hamilton, who lived in Alabama, have joined him in the spirit land. Mecklenburg has never had a better citizen than Dr. David R. Dunlap; nor one who contributed more by precept and example, to teach morality and a pure Christianity. A cheerful disposition was as ever present with him, as his shadow when the sun was shining. After having practiced medicine for a great many years, passed safely through many epidemics, he was attacked with ordinary whooping cough when 70 years old. He is said to have whooped as clear as a child of ten. It is strange that he was always proof against the disease when often exposed to it, and yielded to its attacking power when he thought he was immune. But it left no bad effects behind.

REV. W. W. PHARR, D. D.

It might be said with propriety that he was a native of this county. He was born in Cabarrus county, an off-shoot of Mecklenburg, in the year 1813, and died in 1886. He received the most of his early education in the neighborhood, but graduated at the University of North Carolina. He early entered the ministry of the Presbyterian Church, and labored faithfully for the Master during a long life. He was gladly received wherever he went, both in the churches and private families. He did not preach sectarianism, but the Gospel of Christ. He was particularly

DR. W. W. PHARR.

loved by the poor; he sympathized with them in all their anxieties, distresses and fears; his visits to their houses in sickness always brought sunshine and brushed their tears away. He was equally as welcome at a marriage, jovial and gay with innocent amusement, he enjoyed the hilarious assemblage of young persons. He was a great advocate of good schools, and worked for their success. It has been said that preachers, as a general rule, were fine students, but not practical in the affairs of life. Not so with Dr. Pharr. Davidson College owes much of its prosperity to the guiding hand of this benevolent minister while president of the Board of Trustees. He served several churches at different times in his life, and always acceptably. In his early life he was pastor of Bethpage, and then of Poplar Tent, for several years at Statesville. Then called by Presbytery to heal a breach in Ramah, which was of political origin in reconstruction days. Probably no other man could have smoothed the fires of discord that had commenced in Ramah. "Blessed are the peacemakers."

Dr. Pharr was blessed not only in his labors in the church, as hundreds now living in the bounds of Mallard Creek church would gladly testify, but he was blest in his family. His first wife was a daughter of John R. Alexander, one of the best women in the world, who left three children who are an ornament to society and valuable to the county. The last wife was a daughter of Gen. W. H. Neal, who was a very prominent man in the affairs of the county, as well as the church.

Both sons and daughters, four in all, are among our best people, and take a good stand in both church and State. His widow, in feeble health, is blessed by her children and friends. Rev. Dr. Pharr was eminently fitted for the times in which he lived. He spoke extemporaneously, and looked earnestly in the faces of his hearers and always quit before his audience became weary. He made it a rule to shake hands, if possible, with every one at his church every Sunday. In this way he could know the health of his congregation. In his day the people had two services each day, and a bountiful repast spread in a good shade. To this dinner each mother expected Mr. Pharr to dine with them, so as not to be partial he would make the circuit of all the spreads. He was a man for the times, and was well known in the county. His remains rest in Mallard Creek burying ground, close by the remains of his kinsman, Rev. Walter Smiley Pharr, who was his predecessor at both Ramah and Mallard Creek. The people were devoted to the name of Pharr. Some fifty years ago when Rev. W. S. Pharr was the pastor, he invited his son, Rev. S. C. Pharr, D. D., who was a very talented man and given to using much poetry in his sermons, to assist him with the communion then approaching; as was the custom then to hold service out of doors, the young man arose in the stand to preach the morning sermon, and as he gave out his text, the old man who was sitting behind him, pulled his coat tail, intimating that he wanted to speak to him. He at once turned around when his father said to him: "Now Samuel, my son, we must have no rhyming to-day." It was too solemn an occasion for poetry to be allowed a place in the wonderful display of God's love.

DR. W. A. ARDREY.

Dr. William A. Ardrey was born in York District, South Carolina, on the 19th day of April, 1798. His parents, William and Mary Ardrey, sailed for America upon the first vessel leaving the shores of old Ireland after the Declaration of Independence was proclaimed at Philadelphia by Great Britain's erstwhile colonies.

The vessel landed at Charleston, South Carolina, and this young couple made their way to the up-country of South Carolina, and settled in York county, within a few miles of the present town of Yorkville. There they erected the frontierman's cabin and with brave hearts for the hardships of the present and bright hopes in the fortunes of the future, they established their home and cast their lot with the new

DR. WM. ARDREY.

republic. To them were born six sons and daughters. William A. Ardrey, the subject of this sketch, was the youngest son. His mother died in his infancy and he was reared by an elder sister—Miriam, whose training may have developed in her ward a sturdiness of character that the mother's tenderness may not.

With strong intellectual inheritance and with lofty and manly aspirations, he obtained a classical education against all the hindrances and difficulties of the times. After completing his academic course, he entered upon the study of medicine, and when he had finished his lectures and received his medical degree, he located for the practice of his profession on the border line between the counties of Mecklenburg and Lancaster, in the States of North and South Carolina, respectively, his home being on the North Carolina side.

He married Mrs. Lydia L. Cureton, who was a daughter of Capt. John Potts, of Mecklenburg county, and a granddaughter of Mrs. Gen. Graham.

With clear head, sound judgment and genial manners, he practiced medicine for many years, over an area of twenty miles, embracing portions of Union and Mecklenburg counties in North Carolina, and York and Lancaster, in South Carolina.

With a high appreciation of the usefulness and dignity of his profession, he gave medical education and opportunity to quite a number of deserving young men.

In politics, Dr. Ardrey was an old line Whig. Having attended a Kentucky University in the zenith of the fame of Henry Clay, he imbibed and assimilated much of the tenets and doctrines of that brilliant statesman, and continued in that faith as long as there was a Whig candidate to espouse or a Whig ticket to vote. Although his party was in a hopeless minority in Mecklenburg county and there was no chance to win, yet, feeling that its principles were to be counted above success, he was several times induced to make the race, as the Whig nominee, for the State Legislature.

He was a zealous patriot, and was generally the master of ceremonies, or a favorite speaker, at all the Fourth of July or like celebrations and demonstrations in lower Mecklenburg.

He was a man keenly alive to everything that indicated progress and advancement in the life of his country. He was especially active in the agitation in behalf of railroads, and with Judge Osborne and other prominent men of the county canvassed the county in the interest of its first railroad running from Columbia to Charlotte, and the first railroad in this section of the country.

He had been reared in the faith of the Associate Reformed Presbyterian Church, but in the mature and ripened convictions of later years, he joined the Methodist Church, and helped to build and establish Harrison church, in lower Providence township, near the South Carolina line, which is perhaps, the oldest Methodist church in Mecklenburg county. He served his church with all that earnestness and faithfulness that he had devoted to suffering humanity in his profession. He accepted and adorned all the lay offices within her gift. Until disabled by physical affliction, he dedicated to her cause, without stint and with a whole heart, his time, his talents and his means. For many years he maintained on his plantation a Sunday School for the systematic teaching of the Scriptures to his slaves, towards whom he was, at all times, a kind and merciful master.

It was the home and social and Christian life of this busy physician that marked in him the highest consummation of the virtues of a true gentleman.

He died in the year 1861, leaving seven children who, true to the teachings of their worthy sire, have borne well their part in all the calls of the highest citizenship, both in Church and State.

Captain James P. Ardrey gave up his life upon the battlefields of Virginia. His other sons are Captain W. E.

Ardrey, of Providence township; Mr. J. W. Ardrey, of Fort Mill, S. C., and the late Dr. J. A. Ardrey, of Pineville.

His surviving daughters are Mrs. Mary J. Bell, widow of the late Robt. C. Bell, of Providence township; Mrs. Margaret R. Potts, widow of Captain J. G. Potts, and Mrs. S. H. Elliott, all of Mecklenburg county.

DR. CHARLES HARRIS.

When we come by Poplar Tent, one of the original seven churches that were first organized in this part of North Carolina, and formerly in Mecklenburg county, we pass the place of Dr. Charles Harris, who was a surgeon in the Revolutionary war. He lived for many years after Independence was gained, to heal the sick, and perform the surgery that was needed in a radius of more than one hundred miles. He was offered the chair of Surgery in the University of Pennsylvania, but declined the flattering offer to render his services to neighbors and friends with whom he worked to build up the civilization at home, where his labors were appreciated. His manners were rough, like the times in which he lived. An anecdote or two will show him as to his actions better than words.

He attended Mrs. Alcorn, a very poor Irish widow, for a bad case of white swelling. A few months after she got well, the doctor was passing her house when she ran out calling, "Doctor, stop a minute." "What do you want?" he enquired. "I want to give you this web of cloth for attending me." The doctor replied: "Take that cloth and clothe your ragged children. I am going to Hugh Torrance's and Robbin Davidson's, and I will make them pay your bill."

He was sent for to go to Morganton to see a young lady who had dislocation of her jaw. The family thought she had lockjaw and was dying. Dr. Harris wrapped his thumbs with her handkerchief and told her, "Damn you, don't you bite me!" She was instantly relieved.

The descendants of Dr. Harris were prominent characters in Cabarrus county (cut off of Mecklenburg several years after the Revolutionary war), were among the best educated people in the State, and were worthy citizens.

His son, William Shakespeare Harris, was one of the special escort who met Gen. LaFayette at the Virginia line, and escorted him through the State in 1824. His posterity were as true to the Southern cause in 1861-'65 as their forefathers were patriotic in 1775-'81. In the same section were grown up the "Black Boys," who intercepted a load of gun powder between Charlotte and Salisbury, blew up the powder, and escaped. This was in 1777. This whole country was ripe for revolution. In Poplar Tent churchyard is the grave of Rev. Hezekiah J. Balch, a minister of the Gospel, who was a signer of the Declaration of Independence of May 20, 1775. He, with many others, had listened to and accepted the teachings of Mr. Craighead. Here also lived, labored and died Rev. John Robbinson, D. D., whose kindred and descendants occupy this section, and have always maintained a high standard of piety and good citizenship. The family of Flyns, who occupied such position in both Church and State one hundred years ago, are no longer residents of our county. Only the graves of the older set alone, are here to remind us that such people lived once in the county; and their history not having been written, it is unknown to the generation now extant.

SKETCH OF GEN. D. H. HILL—TAKEN FROM "THE NEWS."

The Confederate soldiers all over the State will bow their heads in grief over the announcement that Lieut. Gen. D. H. Hill is no more. He died in this city at 4:30 Tuesday afternoon, in the 68th year of his age.

Gen. Hill was followed through the war mainly by North Carolinians; hundreds who stood with him where shot and shell flew thickest, live in Charlotte. Gen. Hill led our people in war and lived with them in peace, and all that per-

GEN. D. H. HILL.

tains to the history of the dead warrior will be read with mournful interest. Gen. Hill's life was an eventful one. He was born in York county, S. C., in 1821, and graduated from West Point when only 20 years old. He served in the war with Mexico, and was successfully brevetted as Captain and Major for gallant and meritorious conduct at Contreras and Chapultepec, and received at Churiebusco a sword of honor from his native State. He resigned his commission in 1849, and became successively professor in Washington College, Va., (1849 to 1854) and in Davidson College, N. C. He was professor in Davidson College in 1854 and 1859, and then took the superintendency of the North Carolina Military Institute, which position he held until the breaking out of the war between the States.

Gen. Hill was among the first to enter the field of war, and his career as a Confederate soldier is preserved "in records that defy the tooth of time." He took a prominent part in the battle of Big Bethel, and led successfully in the following engagements: Williamsburg, Va., Seven Pines or Fair Oaks, Mechanicsville, Gaines' Mill, Cold Harbor, Malvern Hill, South Mountain, or Boonsboro, Sharpsburg and Fredericksburg. After this latter battle, General Hill was transferred to the seat of war in the West. His reputation was gained in the battle of South Mountain. He held the mountain pass at Boonsboro against the whole of McClellan's army from early dawn until the afternoon, when Longstreet and Hood came to his relief. The fighting at this point was terrific.

When all was lost to the Confederacy, Gen. Hill returned to Charlotte to help our people build up their broken fortunes. He was known for years after the war as "the unreconstructed." Here he published a magazine entitled "The Land We Love," volumes of which are tenderly preserved in Southern homes. Gen. Hill's best work while in Charlotte was done on his weekly paper, *The Southern Home*. He was a writer of great vigor and the *Home* was a power in the land. Gen. Hill left Charlotte in 1876 to accept the presidency of the University of Arkansas. He filled that position until 1885, and in 1887 he was elected president of the State Agricultural College at Milledgeville, Ga. A few months ago, feeling his health declining, he came to North Carolina in the hope of recuperating. He continued to decline, however, and in a few weeks sent his resignation to the trustees of the college at Milledgeville. The resignation was accepted only after it had been tendered emphatically the second time. Gen. Hill's last days were peaceful and quiet, and his death was that of a Christian, resigned. hopeful, confident in winning the last great victory over death.

Gen. Hill was a brother-in-law to Stonewall Jackson. He was married to Miss Isabella Morrison, oldest daughter of the late Dr. R. H. Morrison, in November, 1848. Mrs. Gen. Hill and several children are still living. Gen. Hill's body was buried in the old graveyard at Davidson College, where four of his children were buried.

BREM, JOHNSTON AND ALEXANDER.

This trio of business men at one time or another merchandised in Charlotte, and at various times were partners. Col. T. H. Brem was raised near Beattie's Ford, working in his father's store. When a young man he moved to town, and formed a partnership with Mr. S. P. Alexander. They kept a general assortment store for a number of years. They were very prosperous. In 1851 the epidemic of smallpox was of such an alarming character as to drive everybody from town. Brem & Alexander moved their store up on the Statesville road to Col. B. W. Alexander's, nine miles from Charlotte. The disease lasted six or eight months, when they moved back to town. At this time they made a trade with Mr. J. R. Alexander for his son T. Lafayette Alexander, for three years, agreeing to pay him fifty dollars and his board for the first year, one hundred for the second, and one hundred and fifty for the third. After the first month, Mr. Brem was anxious to cancel the trade; said he could not teach him; but when he was forced to keep him, Lafayette learned so fast and took so much interest in the store, that Brem & Alexander said that they found a treasure in their clerk. When the three years were out, they raised his salary to five hundred dollars, and soon took him in as a partner, which position he held until the war pushed all her men to the field. Col. Wm. Johnston took Mr. S. P. Alexander's place in the early fifties. But his time was taken up so entirely with the C. & C. R. R., that he withdrew from the store. Col. Wm. Johnston made one of the finest railroad managers during the war that was in the Confederacy. Col. T. H. Brem got up an artillery company, with six cannon, well equipped with both men and horses. The county was proud of her artillery company.

Mr. S. P. Alexander, after withdrawing from his partners in the dry goods business, confined himself to the business of dealing in securities. At this he was very successful, accumulating a large fortune. He was never married; he was a liberal subscriber to all church work during his life time; was very liberal in his contributions to Sharon church; gave largely to build the fine temple the people now worship in. In his recent bequests he remembered his church, and many of his kindred. He was a grand-son of Hezekiah Alexander, one of the famous signers of the Declaration of Independence. He loved his church and his kinfolks. He always went to bed at 9 o'clock, no matter how entertaining a party he may be associated with. Regular hours was part of his religion. He lived to be an old man; he was respected by all who knew him; he made confidants of but few, but was a fast friend of those whom he thought worthy of friendship. He died at the end of the Nineteenth century. He lived in the best period of the world's history.

Mr. T. Lafayette Alexander, another of the firm, was a descendant of a signer, J. McKnitt Alexander, a brother of Hezekiah, passed away in the year 1897. He, too, accumulated a handsome competence to leave his children and did many good deeds that his neighbors knew naught of. He was a son of John R. Alexander, one of the most energetic men the county ever produced. He was a firm believer in education, and did more to keep up a first-class school in his section of the county than any other person. He was violently opposed to the war between the States; appeared to see the termination from the beginning. He saw with a prophetic glance the South crushed, and our people bankrupt, who were not killed in the war. Yet, with his feelings wrought up to a dangerous tension, he gave his three sons to the cause of the South. It is needless to say that his worst forebodings came literally true. He was a true patriot, accepted the terms of peace accorded us, never ceased to blame the Democratic party, yet voted that ticket, as he said there was no place elsewhere for a white man to go

The writer once saw Capt. John Walker, as he was called "the wheelhorse of Democracy," meet Mr. Alexander, who had been all his life a bitter Whig, and said to him, "I never expected to see the day when you and I would vote the same ticket." Mr. Alexander replied, "No, and I'll be danged if I would do it now if I could help myself."

DR. J. P. M'COMBS.

The name of Dr. Parks McCombs has been a household word for the last thirty-five years. A student of Dr. P. C. Caldwell, the people took him up to fill the vacancy left by his preceptor. Dr. McCombs came on the stage of life's drama just in the nick of time to meet a great responsibility. The war between the States was just ushered in, and none were more ardent in espousing the cause of the South, or better armed and equipped for performing his duty than Dr. McCombs. When the war was over, and all of our property destroyed, no money in circulation in the South, we scarcely knew which way to turn; it was even difficult to obtain breadstuffs, Dr. McCombs, like the patriot he was, attended the poor people without the hope of reward. Our

DR. ROBERT GIBBON.

people were blessed with rich harvests, and soon we were on our feet again. He did a large and lucrative practice up to the time of his death in 1902. He was a fine surgeon, and was often called to the country, ten to twenty miles, to perform a capital or difficult operation. Dr. McCombs was firmly of the opinion that Mecklenburg county "was the land of gold." He opened several mines, bought and sold for a pastime. If he had not been wedded to his profession, he would have been an expert miner. During the war with Spain he went over to Cuba to visit the troops from Mecklenburg and other places. Although his health was then feeble, his attachment for the military service was strong. From causes unknown to any one, he put off taking a partner until the last year of his life. He married a Miss Guion, a grand-daughter of his old preceptor, Dr. P. C. Caldwell, who was a trained nurse; and well did she fill the place while her husband lingered on the border land.

DR. ROBERT GIBBON.

The eminent subject of this sketch was born in Philadelphia in the year 1823. He was educated in Tennessee and graduated at Yale, and studied medicine at the Jefferson College of Pennsylvania, graduated in 1846. He practiced medicine in Charlotte about the middle of the Nineteenth century, and had for his confreres Drs. D. T. Caldwell, P. C. Caldwell, J. M. Happoldt, McIlwain, J. M. Miller, C. J. Fox, and others. When the great Civil War came on, Dr. Gibbon was among the first to offer his services to the Confederacy as a surgeon. He was assigned to duty with the Twenty-eighth North Carolina Troops, and stationed at Wilmington. In March, 1862, the regiment was ordered to Kinston to report to Gen. L. O'B. Branch, immediately after the battle at New Bern. He then became senior surgeon of the brigade. It was a common saying in this brigade and in this division, that Dr. Gibbon was one of the finest operators in the army. He served through the war with Capt. Nick Gibbon as commissary of his regiment; and his brother John, a Major-General in the Federal army. They were frequently engaged in the same battle, but never met while the war lasted. When peace was declared, he resumed his practice in Charlotte with all of his former energy and usefulness. He married soon after the war Miss Mary Rodgers, of Charleston, S. C., and was blessed with sons Robert and John, who grew up to follow in their father's footsteps—they both studied medicine and both have made for themselves an enviable reputation of fine surgeons, Dr. Robert here in Charlotte, and Dr. John in Philadelphia. Dr. Gibbon was twice married; the last was Miss Corina M. Harris, who survives him. He attained a ripe old age, did a vast amount of work for suffering humanity, lived a well spent life, but in the evening of his life, when the shadows grew long, his health gave way, and without any suffering he gradually fell asleep in the year 1900.

ADAM TODD AND FAMILY.

The early history of this interesting family has become somewhat clouded in its earlier years. But few families can trace an accurate account of their migrations in the mother country, and establish a correct account of their meanderings before they built a home in this country. It is certain that they came here before the Revolutionary war. It is in their family history that John Todd was born the night that Lord Cornwallis came to Charlotte. This being a night of sore distress, the date can hardly be forgotten. Adam Todd had a son Adam who was the father of our worthy townsman, Ale Todd, who met with so serious an accident as to lose both legs in railroad service. His wife was a daughter of Allen Cruse.

James Todd, who was born in the latter part of the Eighteenth century, married Enie Hutchison and raised one son, John, and three daughters; but two are now living. John William Todd married Sarah McCord. Lawson Todd, son of Hugh Todd, married Mary McGinn. Cynthia Todd married Absolum Holdbrooks. They and their children moved to York county, South Carolina. John William Todd is an elder in Paw Creek church. He is now an old man, has been faithful in all things, is spoken well of by all his neighbors. Harvey Todd, the father of Mrs. Alexander (the mother of the druggist, S. L. Alexander), and her sister, Mrs. Cynthia Alexander, died at 81 years. Both of his sons-in-law died in the service of the Confederacy. They were a long-lived family. Some of the older ones were over 100 years. They were a quiet, inoffensive people, strictly attending to their own business. Did all their own work; could make their own plows, harrows and do their own repairing of all kinds, even blacksmithing, shoemaking and the women making all the clothes the family wore. They furnished a full quota of true men to the Confederate army. Sixteen men by the name of Todd went from Paw Creek, and it is reasonable to suppose that as many more whose mothers were Todds, and sent brave sons by another name. Truly Mecklenburg feels proud to have such yeomanry to defend the good name of our county. It was fortunate for our county that our earliest immigrants were among the best people in the world; and the later generations have given abundant proof that blood will tell.

The Central Hotel.

A half century ago, or at somewhat earlier date, a place of entertainment was usually called a tavern, at which place the wants of man and beast could be satisfied. Many men tried at different times to play the part of "Boniface," but very few kept the position long enough to become acquainted with the traveling public, or make an enviable reputation among those who traveled on horseback. Hiram Sloan, from Iredell county, was "mine host" in 1844; but the business did not prove lucrative, and he turned his attention to the farm, which he did know how to manage, so it would be a success. Stokes Norman was induced to try his hand at "catering to the public," but from some cause unknown to the writer, he only kept the tavern one year. He continued to reside in the town and in the county until his course was run. He was a warm, genial friend, particularly to boys and young men. He and Dr. P. C. Caldwell were close friends, and spent much time together.

In 1846 Mr. J. A. Sadler moved to Charlotte and took charge of the tavern. He called it "Sadler's Hotel." He was immensely popular and was known far and near as a "prince of hotel keepers." He was a man of most elegant manners, all of his politeness was natural, merely indicative of the man. The hotel when he took charge was an old frame concern, but poorly constructed for the purpose; but he managed to keep a well-filled house. Maj. Sadler came from South Carolina about the year 1844, and lived at the place of John Hannah Orr's. After 1852 he quit the hotel and retired to private life till the war came on between the States, and notwithstanding he was over age, he volunteered as a staff officer. He was a commissary, and from his training in a hotel, it goes without saying he made an excellent officer. In the year 1853-'54 the hotel was built and furnished anew, and was run by H. B. Williams for a short time; then by W. W. Elms for a while; then by William Moore from New Bern, till the storm of war was over.

MAJ. JENNINGS B. KERR.

The Charlotte Hotel.

The century was young and many of the habits and customs of that day and time are now obsolete, but many of the old men yet living remember the day and the jovial face of the proprietor, Maj. Jennings B. Kerr. He was a natural "wag" and was well suited to play "mine host." In his jocular moods he would tell how he had outlived a dozen rivals. He owned his house, which he called in the early time "The Carolina Inn." His house was well patronized, was very popular with the county people. Persons who were in the habit of partaking of his board could tell what he was going to have for dinner a week in the future. A favorite dish that he never failed to have for dinner was "chicken pie," cooked in a large, yellow queensware dish. Everything was clean and neat about his table, and good behavior in the dining room he would have or eject the disturber of the peace. He raised a most worthy family, two sons, the elder was a lawyer—he volunteered in the Seventh Regiment, North Carolina Troops. Capt. Wm. Kerr, he was severely wounded in the battles around Richmond in 1862. He was killed at Chancellorsville May 3, 1863, where Mecklenburg lost many brave men. He had another son, Rev. David Kerr, preached in Arkansas, was a member of the Associate Reformed Presbyterian Church. He died when quite young. His oldest daughter married Mr. Sloan, of Greensboro. His second daughter, Miss Nannie, married Hon. J. L. Brown, one of the most worthy men of the town. His youngest daughter married Capt. F. S. DeWolf, was mayor of the town, and moved to Seattle, in Washington, on the Pacific Slope. A good family, but have all passed away. Good people can be raised in hotel life. Maj. Sadler left one son in Charlotte, who stands high as an express manager. Every one speaks of him in high terms. Mr. Ab. Elliott married a daughter who is among our best women. Mr. T. D. Gillespie was one of the most popular men of the day, married another, and has left a son who is an efficient accountant and bookkeeper. The other daughters married men of equal worth, and have moved to other parts.

GEN. RUFUS BARRINGER.

Rufus Barringer, of Cabarrus and Mecklenburg.

Rufus Barringer was often head to say, "I believe in but three institutions, the Family, the Church, and the State," and under these heads this sketch will be written.

As to Family, reference is made to a letter of his to Dr. Kemp Battle, written in the spirit of the true American. He says: "So far as I have been able to find, the Barringers, of Germany, laid no claim to noble rank or descent; but I do find that my grandfather, John Paul Barringer, of Wurtenburg, was a man of heroic mould and ever a good man through a long and eventful life."

Rufus Barringer was a firm believer in heredity. Since it is always interesting to note family characteristics, we return to the founder of the Barringer family in North Carolina, John Paul (or Paulus) Barringer. He was born in Wurtenburg June 4, 1721, arrived in Philadelphia September 20, 1743, on the good ship Phœnix, Capt. Wm. Wilson, last from Rotterdam. He married in Pennsylvania Ann Eliza Iseman, and after several years (about 1750) they with their children, Catherine and John, and several fellow countrymen, joined in the exodus to the Piedmont region of North Carolina, where they settled on the fertile lands of Dutch Buffalo, then Anson county, afterwards Mecklenburg, and now Cabarrus, thus living in three counties without moving.

The desolation of the country during the seven years war, added to the desire of being land-owners, is said to have caused this immigration from Wurtenburg.

John Paul's love of family was shown by his sending to the "Old Country" for father, mother, brothers and sisters. The aged parents were buried at sea, but two brothers and three sisters came. George settled at Gold Hill. Mathias married Miss Burhart, settled in Lincoln, and was killed by the Indians in Catawba, where a monument was erected to him in 1891. The sisters were: Catherine married to Christian Overshine, Dolly married to Nicholas Cook, and Elizabeth or Anna Maria, married to Christian Barnhardt. Their descendants are scattered over the South and West, and show the same strong characteristics in Family, Church, and State.

In 1777, John Paul Barringer married his second wife, Catherine, daughter of Caleb Blackwelder and Polly Decker, and raised a large family.

John Paul was of note and influence in his community. He was captain of Queen's Militia, member of Committee of Safety, and was with James Hogg, of Orange, appointed by unanimous consent of the Halifax convention of 1776, Justice of the Peace. He and his brother-in-law, Caleb Phifer, were the first representatives of Cabarrus in the Legislature. It is said that the separation of Cabarrus from Mecklenburg was due to the indignation of John Paul and German friends, at his being ridiculed for giving orders to his company in German or Pennsylvania Dutch. The county was named for Stephen Cabarrus, who aided them to get the act through the Legislature.

John Paul and his father-in-law, Caleb Blackwelder, too old for service, led in defence of the settlement against the Tories, who destroyed crops and carried away slaves. Finally the Fanning gang raided across the Yadkin, destroyed everything and taking these two men prisoners, carried them to Camden. Old Mrs. Blackwelder, nothing daunted, followed them on horseback and ministered to their wants as well as to those of other prisoners, even to the Britishers. Smallpox was raging there and unfortunately, she communicated the disease to her young grandson Paul, who always bore the marks of it. The husband and father were eventually released through her influence and that of a man named Levinstein. The Tory most obnoxious to that neighborhood was named Hagar and was finally run off. Hagar's mill was confiscated by Tom Polk and came into the possession of the Barringer family.

In religion, John Paul was Lutheran and deeply devotional, though neither sectarian nor fanatic. He used daily a large Luther Bible (date 1747) which is still owned by the family. These German Lutherans, like the Presbyterians, ever had church and school house side by side. He gave a large body of land to the church, was active in church building, president of the council and was made referee in all church disputes. The "Yellow Meeting House" was built at his expense and the congregation voted him a raised seat of honor, moving it to the new church of St. John's when rebuilt. He is said to have lived well after the manner of his day, and "they say" he exchanged a barrel of kraut with the Italian miner, Rivafinoli, for a barrel of imported wine.

Gov. Tryon visited him during his tour in 1768, and was highly gratified with his entertainment. He died January 1, 1807, and was buried at St. John's church. His wife, Catherine, lived till October 29, 1847, aged 92.

GEN. PAUL BARRINGER.

The oldest son of John Paul Barringer and Catherine Blackwelder was born in 1778, on Dutch Buffalo, then in Mecklenburg, now Cabarrus. He was both merchant and farmer.

His father had never mastered the English language, but he gave his children the best advantages of the times and directed his executor to have his minor children educated in the Protestant faith. Realizing the disadvantages he had labored under he sent his sons to Chapel Hill, and his daughters to the best schools. Besides his own children, he helped many other young men to get a start in life.

His wife was Elizabeth Brandon, daughter of Matthew Brandon and Jean Armstrong, of Rowan. Her family were the Lockes, Brandons and Armstrongs. The records show that many patriotic soldiers were furnished by them during the Revolution. They were married February 21, 1805. Their children were Daniel Moreau Barringer, member of Congress, minister to Spain, aid to Gov. Clark during the Civil War; Paul Barringer, of Mississippi; Rev. William Barringer, of Greensboro; Gen. Rufus Barringer, of Charlotte; Maj. Victor C. Barringer, First North Carolina Cavalry, and Judge of International Court of Appeals in Egypt from 1874 to 1894; Margaret married John Boyd, then Andrew Grier; Mary married Charles Harris, M. D.; Elizabeth, Edwin Harris, and Catherine, William G. Means.

Like his father, Paul Barringer was a devoted patriot. He was an old line Whig and bitterly opposed to nullification at its first inception, as shown in circulars published in a political contest with Charles Fisher in 1832, and in newspaper records of public meetings of the day. He was often prominent as president of the day on the 4th of July and 20th of May anniversaries. He was a firm believer in the authenticity of the Mecklenburg Declaration and seems to have brought up his sons in the same faith. *The Western Carolinian* of May 24, 1839, mentions the orator of the day, D. M. Barringer, and Wm. Barringer was on the Committee of Invitation. Rufus Barringer's journal for May, 1844, refers to a "grand celebration" at which he was present in Charlotte. Cabarrus was, in 1775, a part of Mecklenburg, and many of the "signers" were from that section of the county. August 22, 1842, we find that Gen. Paul Barringer presides at a meeting to present to the Assembly a memorial for the incorporation of the Mecklenburg Memorial Association.

During the War of 1812, December 23, Paul Barringer was commissioned by Gov. Hawkins Brigadier-General of the Eleventh Regiment, North Carolina Troops. He was a member of the House for Cabarrus for ten consecutive terms (1806 to 1815), and of the State Senate in 1822.

In religion he and his wife were devoted members of the

Lutheran Church and both lie buried in that church yard at Concord.

RUFUS BARRINGER.

Rufus Barringer, fourth son of Paul Barringer and Elizabeth Brandon, was born at Poplar Grove, Cabarrus county, December 2, 1821.

He was prepared for college by R. I. McDowell at Sugar Creek Academy and graduated at Chapel Hill in 1842. He read law with his brother, D. M. Barringer, and then under Judge Pearson, practicing in Cabarrus and neighboring counties. He, like his father, was Whig in politics. He was a member of the House of Commons in 1848, and of the State Senate in 1849, and was a Bell and Everett elector in 1860. Like his father, he was strongly opposed to secession and predicted that it would result in long and bloody war. Seeing that war was inevitable, he warned the Legislature to arm the State and prepare for the support of troops, himself volunteering *for the war* and meaning it.

His great-grandfather, Caleb Blackwelder, gave six sons to his country during the Revolution. His grand-father, John Paul Barringer, suffered from the Tories; his uncle, John Barringer, was captain of a company; his father volunteered for the war of 1812, and his maternal ancestors were active in defence of the country. Nothing less could be expected of Rufus Barringer than that at the fall of Sumter, he should respond to the call of his country and volunteer for her defence. He enlisted for the war in the Cabarrus Rangers April 19, 1861, and was chosen captain of the company, which became Company F, First North Carolina Cavalry, Ninth State Troops. His commission bears date of May 16, 1861. Under fine drilling and through the excellent discipline of Robert Ransom, its first Colonel, this regiment became the best in the Confederate service. Under Hampton and Fitzhugh Lee, its history was glorious in every campaign.

In an old paper there is found an item headed "Won't Go to Congress." "While others are trying to get out of the army by being elected to Congress, Maj. Rufus Barringer refuses to go to Congress to remain with the army. Maj. Barringer is right, for the country needs all able-bodied men in the field. We copy his letter.

'ORANGE COURT HOUSE, VA., Oct. 17, 1863.

" 'I have recently received numerous solicitations to become a candidate for Congress in the Eighth District. These solicitations I have uniformly declined. Within the last few days I have learned that many of my friends still propose voting for me, whether a candidate or not. Whilst I am deeply grateful to all who have thus manifested an interest in my behalf and propose giving me this testimonial of their confidence, I deem it due alike to them and to myself to state, that for many reasons I much prefer my name should not be thus used.

" 'I entered the army from a sense of duty alone, counting the cost and knowing the sacrifices.

" 'Our great object is not yet obtained and I do not consider it consistent with my obligations here to accept any civil or political office during the war. I think it better for those in service to stand by their colors whilst those at home should all unite in a cordial and earnest support of the authorities in feeding, clothing and otherwise sustaining the gallant men (and their families) who are fighting not only for our rights, but for the safety of our homes and firesides. My chief desire is to see all party bickerings allayed. The army is not faint-hearted and will nobly perform its duty to the country.

" 'If croakers, grumblers and growlers who torment themselves and all around them with imaginary evils, could only lay aside their fears. If hoarders, speculators and money makers could only be educated to forget their selfish ends for a season. If conscripts, skulkers and deserters could only be got to their commands and all come up to the work like patriots and men, the army, by the blessing of God, would soon secure us victory and peace. Oh! that those men would reflect upon the error of their way and open their hearts to the call of their bleeding country. My prayers are that all dissentions amongst us in North Carolina may be healed and that headed by our sworn and chosen leaders, President Davis and Governor Vance, the party, appealing alike to our duty, our honor, our interest and our safety would now consecrate themselves to their country.'"

Among his most prized treasures were letters of commendation from R. E. Lee, Hampton and Fitz. Lee to the "Old First." He was promoted Major August 26, 1863; Lieutenant-Colonel October 17, 1863, and Brigadier-General June, 1864, his brigade consisting of the First, Second, Third and Fifth Regiments. Gen. Barringer was in seventy-six actions and was thrice wounded most severely at Brandy Station. He was conspicuous at the battles of Willis' Church, Brandy Station, Auburn Mills, Buckland Races, where he led the charge, and Davis' Farm, where he commanded. He commanded a division at Reams' Station. His brigade was distinguished at Chamberlain Run, the last decided Confederate victory, where it forded a stream one hundred yards wide, saddle girth deep, under a galling fire, and drove back a division of Federal cavalry, March 31, 1865. On April 3rd, at Namozine Church, he was taken prisoner by a party of "Jesse Scouts" disguised as Confederates. (Among the scouts were Col. Young and Capt. Rowland.) He was taken to City Point with Gens. Ewell and Custis Lee. Lincoln in Congress had desked with his elder brother, D. M. Barringer, and he asked for an interview, stating that he had "never before met a live Confederate general in full uniform." His party was sent to the old capitol prison and after Lincoln's death, transferred to Fort Delaware, remaining in confinement until August 5, 1865.

"His courage, efficiency and military services won him a

place alongside of the foremost cavalry leaders of the day." But he cared for no honors which he could not share with "the brave and self-sacrificing private of North Carolina, the glory of the Confederate Army," as he was wont to say, and he was ever anxious that justice should be given them in history. On one of his last days he pleaded with an honored Confederate captain to write of the brave deeds of his regiment, but was answered, "No, General; I have been thirty years trying to forget the war." This met with the response, "You are wrong, all wrong; it is due to yourself, as to them, that history give them the honor to which they are entitled by their bravery and self-sacrifice."

His whole heart was in the honor of his State in war and in peace. He was eager to have the true record published, but he himself felt unequal to any part of the work. Finally, in November, 1894, Judge Clark plead with him, saying: "You are very busy; only busy men have the energy and talent for the work. Your record as a soldier satisfies me you will not decline this part of duty. I respectfully request that you write the history of the Ninth Regiment, N. C. S. T. (First Cavalry). Please acknowledge your acceptance of this assignment to duty, the last which the Confederate soldier can ask of you." Though on his sick bed, he called for notes, clippings, rosters, etc., and as a labor of love, wrote the article for the Regimental History, dictating to his wife, but correcting the proofs himself.

As Gen. Barringer said, he "staked all and lost all" by the war. He then resumed the practice of law, removed to Charlotte in 1866 and formed partnership with Judge James Osborne, giving the closest attention to business and making his client's interest his own.

He disliked litigation and used his influence with his clients for compromise. For object lesson to this effect, he kept hanging in his office a print of two farmers quarreling over a cow; one had the cow by the tail and the other had her by the horns, while the lawyer sat quietly on his stool getting all the milk. I copy from his journal January,

1844, his first court: "I had one case of some importance. We agreed to leave it to arbitration. I got my client off remarkably well. He had been sued for $300, but the plaintiff did not get a cent. I got a fee of $5.00." Seeing that he put his whole soul into the case of his client, one asked him how he felt when he lost a case. "I do the best that is in me for my client, and then accept the consequences." Just so he had done with the result of the war.

Being convinced that it was wisest for the South to accept the reconstruction acts of 1867, he allied himself with the Republican party, and though very sensitive to the opinions of his fellow men, he was tenacious of his principles and no amount of ridicule or opposition could make him swerve from what he considered the part of duty. But "during the most violent and bitter struggle in the State, political difference detracted nothing in the public estimation from the substantial worth of his personal character." And when in 1875, the State Convention was held to amend the Constitution, he was elected as a Republican from the Democratic county of Mecklenburg; and in 1880, though defeated for Lieutenant-Governor, he went far ahead of his party in his own county.

In 1884, Gen. Barringer retired from the active practice of law and devoted himself to his farming interests and to literary pursuits.

He was much interested in general education, made it a point of paying tuition for some needy boy or girl, and was largely influential in establishing the graded school in Charlotte in 1874, advocating an industrial feature in connection with it. He was also a warm advocate for the Agricultural and Mechanical College, and was numbered among the first trustees. He was for years trustee of Davidson College. He and Dr. Hutchison and Col. Myers were for a number of years trustees of the Biddle University, which was included in the home mission work of the Northern Presbyterian Board. He was greatly interested in watching the result of educating the colored man.

One who was intimately associated said: "The one thing about Gen. Barringer that struck me above all others, was his love for his fellow men. He was a man of broad ana true thought. We had never had any conversation, but what he spoke of the different classes and how to better their conditions.

"He was always thinking of how to better conditions, and was filled with a high sense of duty. His thoughts went out beyond himself.

"Another thing that impressed me about Gen. Barringer was, that while I never knew him in perfect health, he never grew old.

"He sympathized with the thoughts and schemes of every man. All schemes ecclesiastical and social, he entered into with zeal and interest. He was largely influential in the establishment of the library in Charlotte, and of the Historical Society, contributing freely to both."

I quote from another that knew him well: "Gen. Barringer was a remarkable man in many respects. He was one of the most liberal and generous citizens Charlotte had. His hand was always in his pocket to give to any good cause and his gifts were munificent. He was eminently a just man and was business to the core. He required the last farthing promised or agreed to be paid, not for money's sake, but for the sake of the agreement, and yet the next moment would give freely to some good cause."

He was a student and devoted much time to political economy. He had great faith in the "power of the press," and frequently wrote for the papers on various subjects. He was progressive in his ideas beyond the times.

Besides the history of the First North Carolina Cavalry, he published a pamphlet for the Historical Society on "The North Carolina Railroad," one on "The Battle of Ramsour's Mill," and a series of "Sketches on the Old Dutch Side." These brought him letters from all over the South and West.

One of a large family, happy in each other, he followed in the footsteps of his parents, ruling well his household, in a firmness of love, believing with Ruskin, "There is a something in a good man's home which cannot be renewed in every tenement that rises on its ruin." A young woman who had been much in his home, said: "When alone in the great crowds of New York battling with poverty, it has rested and comforted me to think of his home and to know that there are such men in the world."

Gen. Barringer was married three times. His first wife was Eugenia, daughter of Dr. Robt. Hall Morrison. To them were born two children, Anna, who died at maturity, and Paul Brandon Barringer, now of the University of Virginia, with a large family of his own.

The second wife was Rosalie Chunn, of Asheville, who had one son, Rufus Barringer. In 1870 Gen. Barringer married Margaret Long, of Hillsboro, who, with her son, Osmond Long Barringer, lives at the home place in Charlotte.

He was a man who lived not only in the present, but in the future, and on the approach of the three score and ten allotted to man, he felt that the world's work were better done by more active men.

Though not shirking any evident duty, he resigned formally from responsibilities as school trustee, bank director, church elder, etc.

In 1894, he felt his health declining and with his usual methodical care and forethought, he "set his house in order," arranged his papers and affairs, and instructed his agent, so that no confusion might arise on account of his death. To the end his mind was clear and strong. He read and kept up with current events in the daily papers to the day of his death, February 3, 1895. He bade his family "Farewell," folded his hands and fell asleep.

Though liberal to all denominations, Gen. Barringer was in faith strongly Calvinistic.

He said: "When a young man and about to connect myself with the church, I resolved to take no man's word, and to search the Scriptures for myself. This I did and to my mind, the Presbyterian doctrine was plainly set forth in every chapter. I have never seen cause to change my belief or to be troubled by any new doctrine."

He passed through deep waters, but said: "Through it all God sustained me."

On one of his last days, he said to his pastor: "If you can unfold to me any new truth of that better land, do so."

The reply was: "I cannot; all I say is, we shall be satisfied when we awake in His likeness." To this he calmly answered: "It is enough."—*Contributed.*

ZEBULON B. VANCE.

The Great Commoner, Z. B. Vance.

To ignore the name of Senator Vance in the history of Mecklenburg, is to leave unrecorded a name of a man "who was not born for a day, but for all time." In the year 1866 Gov. Vance became a citizen of this county, and remained a citizen of the county, and always came here to vote, up to the time of his death, which occurred April 14, 1894.

"Zebulon Baird Vance was born in Buncombe county, North Carolina, May 13, 1830; was educated at Washington College, Tenn., and at the University of North Carolina studied law; was admitted to the bar in January, 1852, and was elected county attorney for Buncombe county the same year; was a member of the State House of Commons in 1854; was a Representative from North Carolina in the Thirty-fifth and Thirty-sixth Congresses; entered the Confederate army as captain in May, 1861, and was made colonel in August, 1861; was elected Governor of North Carolina in August, 1862, and re-elected in August, 1864; was elected to the United States Senate in November, 1870, but was refused admission and resigned in January, 1872; was elected Governor of North Carolina for the third time in 1876, and in January, 1878, was elected to the United States Senate; was re-elected in 1885, was again re-elected in 1891, and died at his residence in Washington April 14, 1894."

His paternal and maternal ancestors both were revolutionary patriots. The "Vance Homestead" was a large frame building of the "olden time" with broad stone chimneys, indicative of comfort and hospitality. It stood near the French Broad river and in the midst of the Blue Ridge mountains. Now the house has been taken down and only a few stones remain to mark the site where it once stood. It is a place of beauty.

In front of it the river is smooth and placid as a lake; above and below it dashes and roars into a mountain torrent, and you almost hear the echoes of the ocean. Around it the great mountains tower like giants, and their dark forests are mirrored in the deep, blue bosom of the stream. On this scene, amid sublimity and beauty, Vance first beheld the light of heaven. From this beautiful river, from these sublime mountains, from neighboring scenes, all bristling with heroic and patriotic recollections, he received his first impressions. These were the books from which he learned the lessons that were to be the foundations of his illustrious career. He was the son of the mountains, and I rarely looked on him without being reminded of them.

At the University, Vance remained two years and pursued a selected course of studies, and soon made a name for genius, wit and oratory. He was a special favorite of President Swain, who for so many years had exerted a powerful influence in elevating and directing the youth of the South and made all of us who came under it better citizens and better men. Young Vance was extremely popular with the students and also with the people of the village of Chapel Hill. Even then reports came from the University of his brilliant wit, his striking originality and his high promise.

He served one session in the State Legislature, and there gave unmistakable earnest of the illustrious life before him. He was elected to the House of Representatives in the Thirty-fifth and Thirty-sixth Congresses and took distinguished position in that assembly, which has been the lists of so many statesmen. In 1861, upon the adjournment of Congress, he returned home, and seeing that war was inevitable, raised a company of volunteers, marched to Virginia and soon afterwards was elected colonel of the Twenty-sixth Regiment, North Carolina Infantry, a regiment justly distinguished for the largest loss of killed and wounded during the war of any regiment, either North or South.

He had always been opposed to the secession of the Southern States, did everything possible to avert it, and was one of the very last Southern men to declare his love and devotion to the Union. In the battle of New Bern, N. C., in March, 1862, Col. Vance was conspicuous for courage and coolness, and received the highest commendation for his soldierly conduct on that field. In August of that year he was elected Governor of the State, and received the almost unanimous vote of the soldiers. In 1864 he was re-elected Governor by a very large majority, and held the executive office until the occupation of Raleigh by Gen. Sherman in April, 1865. As the executive of North Carolina his administration was signally distinguished by great ability, vigor and energy, by ardent and constant fidelity to the Southern Cause, and by wise foresight and prudent husbandry of all the resources of the State. He was in every sense governor of the State. From the day on which he entered upon the duties of the office until the hour when he laid it down, his commanding genius asserted his competence for the great responsibilities of the position, and his administration deserved and received the unbounded confidence, support, and approbation of all the patriotic people of North Carolina.

He called to his councils the wisest, the best, the most trusted men in the State of all shades of patriotic sentiment. He inspired the people with renewed love for the struggle; he united the discordant elements among us; he animated the despondent; he tolerated the conscientious lovers of peace; he rebuked the timid; he brought back to life the spirit of our revolutionary patriots; he gave new hope to the army; he aroused the pride of the State; he strengthened all its means, and prepared for war to the end. Well may he have been designated as the "Great war Governor of the South." These acts of his administration are justly entitled to be ranked as historic. First, the organization of a fleet of vessels to sail from Wilmington, N. C., to Europe, with cargoes of cotton and return with supplies for the soldiers and essential necessaries for the people. This supreme enterprise was eminently successful. For months and years the Advance and other vessels, commanded by skillful officers, well manned and adequately equipped, went like seabirds across the ocean to Europe, laden with the great staples of the South, and returning with stores of needed supplies, triumphantly eluding the blockading squadron, and sailed with colors flying up the Cape Fear to Wilmington. The soldiers were clothed and fed, cards and spinning wheels, sewing and knitting needles were furnished to our noble women, machinery for looms, surgical instruments, medicines, books and seeds, were all brought home to a suffering people. The history of the war does not present an example of greater wisdom and success.

Second: In 1864 and 1865, when the resources of the South were absolutely exhausted, when our noble armies were reduced and hemmed in on every side, ragged, hungry and almost without ammunition; when starvation and famine confronted every threshold in the South, and a morsel of bread was the daily subsistence of a family; in that dark and dreadful hour Gov. Vance first appealed to the Government at Richmond, and finding it perfectly helpless to give any relief, summoned his Council of State and by almost superhuman efforts prevailed upon the destitute people of North Carolina to divide their last meal and their pitiful clothing with the suffering Union prisoners at Salisbury. Humanity, chivalry, piety, I invoke from you a purer, better, holier example of Christian charity in war.

Third: During his administration as Governor in North Carolina, although war was flagrant, though camps covered the fields, though soldiers were conscripted by thousands, though cold-hearted men of ample means refused supplies to soldiers with bleeding feet, though the whole militia was armed, though thousands of deserters, refugees from duty, were arrested; though the War Department daily called for more men; though every art and artifice and device was practiced to keep the soldiers from the field; though spies and traitors were detected and seized; though traders in contraband of war were consequently caught *flagrante delicto* and captured; though in all counties in time of war civil authority has been compelled to submit to military necessity and power, yet in North Carolina during the war, the writ of *habeas corpus,* the great writ of liberty, was never for one moment suspended. Immortal history! Worthy of Mecklenburg and the 20th of May, 1775.

In 1876, Gov. Vance was for the third time elected Governor of North Carolina, and his administration was the beginning of a new era for our State. The millions of fraudulent bonds that were passed and recognized by the State Legislature, were promptly scaled down to what they yielded the State. Our legislative hall had been filled with our former slaves, scalawags and men of uncertain places to dwell. All these things of a bad smelling odor, that proved so detrimental to our State were driven away by the great tribunal of our State. From this time onward North Carolina has taken on new life.

In 1878 he was elected to the Senate, and until he died, remained a member of that body, having been elected four times as a Senator. His record in the Senate is part of the Nation's history. He vigilantly defended the rights, honor, and interests of the Southern States, not from sectional passion or prejudice, but because it was his duty as a patriot to every State and to the Union. He was bold, brave, open, candid, and without reserve. He desired all the world to know his opinions and positions, and never hesitated to avow them.

His heart, every moment, was in North Carolina. His devotion to the State and the people was unbounded; his solicitude for her welfare, his deep anxiety in all that concerned her, and his ever readiness to make every sacrifice in her behalf was daily manifested in all his words and actions. Senator Vance was an uncommon orator. He spoke with great power. His style was brief, clear, and strong; his statements were accurate and definite; his arguments compact and forcible; his illustrations unsurpassed in their fitness; his wit and humor were the ever waiting and ready hand-maids to his reasoning, and always subordinated to the higher purposes of his speech. They were torch-bearers, ever bringing fresh light. He always instructed, always interested, always entertained, and never wearied or fatigued an audience, and knew when to conclude. The Senate always heard him with pleasure, and the galleries hung upon his lips, and with bended bodies and with outstretched necks would catch his every word as it fell. He rarely, if ever, spoke without bringing down applause. His wit was as inexhaustible as it was exquisite. His humor was overflowing, fresh, sparkling like bubbling drops of wine in a goblet; but he husbanded these rare resources of speech with admirable skill, and never displayed them for ostentation. They were weapons of offense and defense, and were always kept sharp and bright and ready for use. He was master of irony and sarcasm, but there was no malice, no hatred in his swift and true arrows. Mortal wounds were often given, but the shafts were never poisoned. It was the strength of the bow and the skill of the archer that sent the steel through the heart of its victim. But strength, force, clearness, brevity, honesty of conviction, truth, passion, good judgment were the qualities that made his speech powerful and effective. He believed what he said. He knew it was true, he felt its force himself, his heart was in his words, he was ready to put place, honor, life itself upon the issue. This was the secret of his popularity, fame and success as a speaker.

He studied his speeches with the greatest care, deliberated, meditated upon them constantly, arranged the order of his topics with consummate discretion, introduced authorities from history, and very often from sacred history, presented some popular faith as an anchor to his ship, and concluded with a sincere appeal to the patriotic impulses of the people. No speaker ever resorted to the bayonet more frequently. He did not skirmish; he marched into the battle, charged the centre of the lines, and never failed to draw blood of the enemy. Sometimes he was supreme in manner, in words, in thought, in pathos. He possessed the thunderbolts, but, like Jove, he never trifled with them; he only invoked them when gigantic perils confronted his cause.

In 1876, upon his third nomination for Governor, speaking to an immense audience in the State House Square at Raleigh, he held up both hands in the light of the sun and, with solemn invocation to Almighty God, declared that they were white and stainless; that not one cent of corrupt money had ever touched their palms. The effect was electric; the statement was conviction and conclusion. The argument was unanswerable. It was great nature's action. It was eloquence, it was truth.

Senator Vance's integrity and uprightness in public and in private life were absolute; they were unimpeached and unimpeachable—he was honest. It was his priceless inheritance which he leaves to his family, his friends, his country. He was an honest man. Calumny fell harmless at his feet; the light dissipated every cloud and he lived continuously in its broad rays; his breast-plate, his shield, his armor was the light, the truth. There was no darkness, no mystery, no shadow upon his bright standard. His compeers will all remember the loss of his eye in the winter of 1889. How touching it was—a sacrifice, an offering on the altar of his country. For no victim was ever more tightly bound to the stake than he was to his duty here. How bravely, how patiently, how cheerfully, how manfully he bore the dreadful loss. But the light, the glorious light of a warm heart, a noble nature, a good conscience, an innocent memory, was never obscured to him.

In his long, tedious illness no complaint, no murmurs escaped his calm and cheerful lips. He was composed, firm, brave, constant, hopeful to the last. His love of country was unabated, his friendship unchanged, his devotion to duty unrelaxed. His philosophy was serene, his brow was cloudless, his spirit, his temper, his great mind, all were superior to his sufferings.

His great soul illuminated the physical wreck and ruin around it, and shone out with clearer lustre amid disease and decay. Truly he was a most wonderful man. His last thoughts, his dying words, his expiring prayers, were for his country, for liberty and the people. A great patriot, a noble citizen, a good man, it is impossible not to remember, to admire, to love him. No man among the living or the dead ever so possessed and held the hearts of North Carolina's people. In their confidence, their affection, their devotion, and their gratitude he stood unapproachable—without a peer. When he spoke to them they listened to him with faith, with admiration, with rapture and exultant joy. His name was ever upon their lips. His pictures were in almost every household. Their children by hundreds bore his beloved name, and his words of wit and wisdom were repeated by every tongue.

What Tell was to Switzerland, what Bruce was to Scotland, what William of Orange was to Holland—I had almost said what Moses was to Israel—Vance was to North Carolina. I can give you but a faint idea of the deep, fervid, exalted sentiment which our people cherished for their great tribune. His thoughts, his feeling, his words were theirs. He was their shepherd, their champion, their friend, their guide, blood of their blood, great, good, noble, true, human like they were in all respects, no better, but wiser, abler, with higher knowledge and profounder learning. Nor was this unsurpassed devotion unreasonable or without just foundation. For more than the third of a century, for upwards of thirty years, in peace or in war, in prosperity and in adversity, in joy or in sorrow, he had stood by them like a brother—a defender, a preserver, a deliverer. He was their martyr and had suffered for their acts. He was their shield and had protected them from evil and from peril. He had been with them and their sons and brothers on the march—by the campfires, in the burning light of battle; beside the wounded and dying; in their darkest hours amid hunger and cold, and famine and pestilence, with watchful care had brought them comfort and shelter and protection. They remembered the gray jackets, the warm blankets, the good shoes, the timely food, the blessed medicines, which his sympathy and provision had brought them. In defeat, and in tumult, amid ruin, humiliation and the loss of all they had, he had been their adviser, he had guided them through the wilderness of their woes and brought them safely back to their right and all their hopes. He had been to them like the north star to the storm-tossed and despairing mariner. He had been greater than Ulysses to the Greeks. He had preserved their priceless honor, and saved their homes, and was the defender of their liberties. He was their benefactor. Every object around them reminded them of his care, every memory recalled, every thought suggested his usefulness and their gratitude.

The light from their school house spoke of his services to their education. The very sight of their graves brought back to their hearts his tender devotion to their sons; and the papers and the wires with the rising of almost every sun bore to their pure bosoms the news of his success, his triumphs and his honors. They were proud of him; they admired him—they loved him. These, these were the foundations, the solid foundations of his place in their minds and in their hearts. From the wind-beaten and storm-bleached Cape Hatteras to the dark blue mountain tops that divide North Carolina and Tennessee, there is not a spot from which the name of Vance is not echoed with honor and love. But his influence and his fame were not confined within State lines.

In New England the sons of the brave Puritans admired his love of liberty, his independence of thought, his freedom of speech, his contempt for pretensions and his abhorrence of deceit. The hardy miners in the far West and on the Pacific hills felt his friendship and were grateful for his services. Virginia loved him as the vindicator of her imperiled rights and honor. From the farms and fields and firesides of the husbandmen of the republic there came to him the greeting of friends, for he was always the advocate of low taxes and equal rights and privileges to all men. From all the South he was looked upon as the representative of their sorrow and the example of their honor; and all over the civilized world the people of Israel—"the scattered nation"—everywhere bowed with uncovered heads to the brave man who had rendered his noble testimony and tribute to the virtues of their race. Even the officers, the sentinels and watchmen over him in the old capitol prison, in which he was confined on the alleged and wrongful charge that he had violated the laws of war, were spell-bound by his genial spirit and became his devoted friends up to the hour of his death. His genius, his ability, his humanity, his long continued public service, his great physical suffering, a martyrdom to his duty, the sorcery of his wit, the magic of his humor and the courage of his convictions had attracted the universal sympathy and admiration of the American people.

In this brief summary is embraced a great life. County attorney, member of the State House of Commons, Representative in two Congresses, Captain and Colonel in the Southern army; three times elected Governor of his State, and four times elected to the Senate of the United States. What a record and what a combination. A great statesman, a good soldier, a rare scholar, a successful lawyer, an orator of surpassing power and eloquence, a man popular and beloved as few men have ever been. Great in peace and great in war, equal to every fortune, superior to adversity and greater still, superior in prosperity. Successful in everything which he attempted, eminent in every field in which he appeared, and fitted for every effort which he undertook. He was master of political science, and distinguished in scholarship and literature. His political speeches were models of popular oratory and his literary addresses were compositions of chaste excellence. He wrote an electric editorial and drafted a legislative bill with equal clearness and brevity. His pen and his tongue were of equal quality. He used both with equal power. He wrote much; he spoke more. Everything emanating from him wore his own likeness. He borrowed from no man. He imitated no man and no man could imitate. He was unique, original, wonderful, incomprehensible unless he was a genius with faculties and powers of extraordinary and exceptional character. His temper was admirable, calm, well-balanced, serene. He cared less for trifles than any man I ever knew. He brushed them away as a lion shakes the dust from his mane. In this respect he was a giant. He was like Sampson, breaking the frail withes that bound his limbs. He was never confused, rarely impatient, seldom nervous, never weak. He was merciful in the extreme. Suffering touched him to the quick. He was compassion itself to distress. He was as tender as a gentle woman to the young, the weak, the feeble. He was full of charity to all men, charitable to human frailty in every shape and form and phase. He had deep, powerful impulses, strong and passionate resentments—in the heat of conflict he was inexorable, but his generosity, his magnanimity, his sense of justice was deeper and stronger and better than the few passing passions of his proud nature. To his family and friends he was all tenderness and indulgence. His great heart always beat in duty, with sympathy, with the highest chivalry to woman.

> " The man that lays his hand upon a woman,
>   Save in the way of kindness, is a wretch,
>   Whom 't were great flattery to name a coward,"

was always upon his lips.

He was ambitious, very ambitious, but with him ambition was a virtue. He aspired to be great that he might be useful, to do good, to improve and to benefit and to help mankind. His was not the ambition of pride and arrogance and of power. It was the ambition of benevolence and philanthropy, the ambition to elevate, to lift up, to bless humanity.

From early manhood he has possessed a respectable competence. At no time did he ever suffer penury. He husbanded with great care his resources and was prudent, frugal, thoughtful in his expenditures, but he never turned a deaf ear to pity or to sorrow. He was not avoricious; he had no love for money, and was never rich in gold, silver, and precious stones or lands, but he was opulent in the confidence and affections of the people. His great wealth was invested in the attachments, the friendships, the faith, the devotions of his fellow men; that priceless wealth of love of the heart, of the soul, which no money can purchase. In many respects he was very remarkable. In one he was singularly so. He never affected superiority to human frailty. He claimed no immunity from our imperfection. He realized that all of us were subject to the same conditions, and he regarded and practiced humanity as a cardinal virtue and duty.

Senator Vance was happy in his married life. In his early manhood he was married to Miss Harriet Newell Espey, of North Carolina. She was a woman of high intellectual endowments, of uncommon moral force, of exemplary piety and exercised a great influence for good over her devoted husband, which lasted during his life. Their union was blessed with four sons, who survived their parents. His second wife was Mrs. Florence Steel Martin, of Kentucky, a lady of brilliant intellect, of rare grace and refinement, who adorned his life and shed lustre and joy on his home; and after his course was finished, he fell asleep in her arms. He loved the Bible as he loved no other book. All of his reverence was for his God. He lived a patriot and philanthropist, and he died a Christian. This is the sum of duty and honor. He has gone. His massive and majestic form, his full, flowing white locks, his playful, twinkling eye, his calm home-like face, his indescribable voice have left us forever. He still lives in our hearts. The great Mirabeau, in his dying moments, asked for music and for flowers, and for perfumes to cheer and brighten his mortal eclipse. Vance died blessed with the fragrance of sweetest affections, consecrated by the holiest love, embalmed in the tears and sorrows of a noble people. The last sounds that struck his ear were the echoes of their applauses and gratitude, and his eyes closed with the light of Christian promise beaming upon his soul.

On the night of the 16th of April, his remains were borne towards the mountains of the State he loved so well. The night was beautiful; the white stars shed forth their hallowed radiance upon earth and sky. The serenity was lovely. The whole heavens almost seem a happy reunion of the constellations. With the first light of day the people, singly, in groups, in companies, in crowds, in multitudes, met us everywhere along the way—both sexes, all ages, all races, all classes and all conditions. Their sorrow was like the gathering clouds in morning, ready to drop every moment in showers. We carried him to the State House in Raleigh, the scene of his greatest trials and grandest triumphs; the heart of the State melted over her dead son. Her brightest jewel had been taken away. We left Raleigh in the evening, and passing over the Neuse, over the Yadkin, over the Catawba, up to the summit of the Blue Ridge, we placed the urn with its noble dust on the brow of his own mountain, the mountain he loved so well. There he sleeps in peace and honor. On that exalted spot the willow and the cypress, emblems of sorrow and mourning, cannot grow, but the bay and the laurel, the trees of fame, will there flourish and bloom in perpetual beauty and glory. There will his great spirit like an eternal sentinel of liberty and truth keep watch over his people. It would have been one of the supreme joys of my life to have done justice to the life and the character of this great and good man, to have enshrined his memory in eloquence like his own. But whatever may have been the faults of these words, I have spoken from a heart full of sorrow for his death, and throbbing with admiration and pride for his virtues."—*Eulogy by Senator Ransom, the colleague of Senator Vance in the United States Senate.*

Calvin Eli Grier.

Calvin Eli Grier was born in Steele Creek Township on the 30th of December, 1845. He was the son of Col. William M. Grier, a man closely identified with the history of this county. His mother was, before her marriage, Miss Feriba Edwards, a daughter of Stouton Edwards, of York county, S. C.

Steele Creek has been noted for its good schools and its interest in education, and in the academy near his father's home Calvin Grier studied until his fourteenth year. As a boy he early displayed a wonderful versatility, and those who were his companions at school tell of his progress in his studies and of the early age at which he read the Latin classics.

In common with all the children raised in Steele Creek, a center of Presbyterianism, he was early trained to study the shorter Catechism. His father, a ruling elder in the Associate Reformed Presbyterian Church, taught him to perfectly ask and answer every question in the Catechism before he was four years old.

In 1859, General, then Major D. H. Hill, founded his Military Institute in Charlotte, and to this Calvin Grier was sent as soon as the school was opened. At that time he was only fourteen, but he was a thorough student and the reports he received were most excellent ones.

On the breaking out of hostilities between the North and the South, Gen. Hill closed his school. Many of the cadets were made officers and others hastened to offer their services to the Confederacy.

Calvin Grier, though not fifteen years of age, enlisted in the Ranalesburg Rifles, a company then formed largely of Steele Creek men, and of which A. A. Erwin was captain. It seemed most appropriate that he should enlist in this company, for Col. Grier, with true Southern generosity, had contributed largely of his means in equipping this company, and so liberal was he to it during the war that some of the men referred to him as the "Father of the Ranalesburg Rifles."

Young Grier remained with the company for one year, but at the end of that time was sent home on account of his extreme youth. But brave and ambitious, he could not bear to remain at home inactive while his companions were dying in defence of the South, so in 1862 he enlisted again, this time in Graham's Battery, which had been organized in Charlotte. He served with this battery but a short while, being transferred to his first command, where he remained till the close of the war.

When the conflict was over, though only 19 years of age, Capt. Grier was acting Adjutant-General of Scales' Brigade, and had made a wonderful record for courage and daring. During the war he was seven times wounded, being shot through and through the body on two occasions, once at Barnett's Ford and again at Reams' Station.

At the close of the war, Calvin Grier returned home to find his circumstances terribly altered. In place of wealth, he had poverty, and instead of vigorous, young manhood, he had a wrecked constitution, the result of the wounds from which he suffered all his life.

With a heroism as great as that he displayed in battle, he took up his round of duties on his father's farm. In 1866 he began the study of law. All day he would plow on the farm and at night he would remain up late reading his law books. Once a week he came to Charlotte and recited to Osborne and Barringer.

In spite of the obstacles with which he had to contend he made such rapid strides in his studies that at the end of a year he stood his examination and received his license to practice law.

In 1868 he moved to Charlotte and began the practice of his profession. He formed a partnership with Capt. Armistead Burwell, but in about a year decided to locate in Dallas.

In 1872 he returned to Steele Creek, broken down in

health, but in 1876 he moved back to Charlotte, where he made his home until the time of his death. For a number of years he was the law partner of Judge W. P. Bynum, and for some time he was solicitor of the Inferior Court of Mecklenburg county.

In 1878 he was married to Miss Addie Ramseur, of Lincolnton, a sister of the gallant Major-General, Stephen D. Ramseur.

In 1889, on the 1st of May, Capt. Grier died and was buried in Steele Creek cemetery, where rest his father, grand-father and great-grand-father.

Nothing can be more appropriate than to quote what his friend, Mr. F. B. McDowell, says of him in his article on Steele Creek: "As I write of another the pen falters. He was so young, so generous, so gifted. His life, too, was so pathetic, and his existence seemed to end almost before it fairly began. If the war called some from the portals of the grave, it took others almost from the cradle. A mere stripling boy went forth as a volunteer. Intrepid as a Hampden, as daring as a Ney, he was twice shot through the body upon the enemy's breastworks, within touch of his guns. He brought back from the field painful wounds and a wrecked constitution; but with all his suffering he was an admirable companion and a natural leader and adviser of men; and no young man in this section and of this generation left a deeper impress of admiration and sympathy upon those who knew him best, than Calvin E. Grier."—*Contributed by Miss Feriba Grier.*

Matthew Wallace and His Family.

The people of Mecklenburg probably know less of this family than any family of equal mental ability that ever lived in the county. Matthew Wallace came from Western Pennsylvania a young man, and married a Miss Young, daughter of Joseph Young, who with his brother William, emigrated from the north of Ireland to Pennsylvania; after remaining in Pennsylvania one year, removed to Mecklenburg, North Carolina, in or about the year 1765. Mr. Matthew Wallace lived and died a close neighbor to old Mr. Andrew Henderson (on the creek a short distance above the mill). He had eight children, viz.: Kesiah, Minty, Harriet, Eveline, Rufus, Pinkney, Joseph and Newton. Harriet married James P. Henderson. They raised three sons, Philo, Matthew (who died when a boy), and Thomas—none ever married. The two daughters married. Martha married E. L. Burney and Lilly married J. C. Caldwell, of Winsboro, S. C. Minty married David Henderson, and had two children. C. A. Henderson, M. D., who died (childless) a few years ago in Greenville, S. C. He had been married twice, but left no issue. Margaret married Dr. Frank McRee. They had but one living child, who married Mr. J. G. Shannonhouse, of Charlotte. Eveline married Samuel M. Moore, and but one child reached adult age—John W. Moore. Rufus Wallace studied medicine, practiced in Charlotte, was a brilliant young man, never married, and died young.

Matthew Wallace was a prominent man in the county in his day; was a surveyor of land, which at that time brought him prominently before the people. He was also a magistrate for a long time, and chairman of the old County Court. He at one time sentenced a man to stand in the stocks for two hours. The sheriff told the worshipful court the stocks were not in fix to hold him. The chairman replied: "Fasten him in the crack of the fence, and do it at once." The order was promptly obeyed. He was said to have been the prime mover in having the court house removed from the public square to West Trade street, as Mr. Alex. McAulay was the prime mover to have the new court house built on the site of Queen's Museum, on South Tryon street.

Mr. Wallace and his children are buried in the old graveyard at Sugar Creek church.

Mr. Matthew Wallace's wife must have been a remarkably brainy woman. At this late day it is impossible to get an insight into her mental capacity; but it is beyond question that the Young family were equal to if not superior to the Wallaces. Her three daughters who lived to be grown and married, were far beyond mediocracy. James P. Henderson's children were all exceedingly bright, and very handsome. Philo was quite a poet, was a gifted writer, had been graduated at the University of North Carolina. A younger brother, "Tom," as he was called by every one, took the first honor at Davidson, and then at Cambridge; was a great reader of books, never entered a profession; joined the Confederate army in 1861, went through the war as a private, when there were few men in Lee's army, would compare with him in scholarship. He made a good soldier; came home and kept books for a mercantile house. David Henderson's son and daughter were observed by the community as a head and shoulder above the compeers in intellectual attainments. The same was observed in Samuel Moore's children. His daughter Lizzie's praises were in the mouth of all who knew her. She died when budding into womanhood. John W. Moore was deemed worthy to represent the county in the Legislature of the State. The name of Wallace—of that family at least—is now obsolete; but collateral branches, carrying the same blood, are still inhabitants of Mecklenburg.

Captain John Randolph Erwin.

The subject of this sketch was born on the 1st day of August, 1838, in Bethesda township, York county, S. C. He was a son of William L. and Annie Williamson Erwin, who belonged to the old Scotch-Irish families who emigrated to this country before the Revolution.

Capt. Erwin was raised on a farm, and was educated in the old field schools, except two sessions spent at an academy in Ebenezer, S. C.

In 1851 William Erwin moved to Mecklenburg county, North Carolina, locating at Ranalesburg, Steele' Creek Township, and from that time Mecklenburg was Capt. Erwin's home.

In the fall of 1856 he entered the general merchandise store of Fisher, Burroughs & Co., of Charlotte, and remained with that firm until the winter of 1859. Then he decided to improve his fortunes by going West, so he went to Texas with a party trading on the Rio Grande. He remained there until South Carolina passed the ordinance of secession, when he sacrificed his business and returned to his home. He volunteered as a private in the Ranalesburg Rifles, but his popularity soon won for him the position of First Lieutenant of his company. Soon after organization this company was ordered to the camp of instruction at Raleigh, and was at the capital when North Carolina seceded on May 20, 1861. The company was then ordered to Garysburg, N. C., where he was made adjutant of the post by Col. W. D. Pender. Here it was that the Third, afterwards the Thirteenth Regiment of North Carolina Volunteers, was organized, and Capt. Erwin was selected as Major of the regiment. Owing to the absence of his captain, who had been wounded, and to the earnest entreaties of his men, he declined this honor and remained with the company.

The company was sent from Garysburg to Suffolk, Va.,

and from there to Todd's Point, on the James river, where they spent the summer. In the fall the company was sent on detached duty to Ragged Island, opposite Newport News, and was in camp there and witnessed the naval engagement of 1861 in which the warships Cumberland and Congress were destroyed. In the spring of 1862 the regiment was ordered to the peninsula near Yorktown, to hold in check the advance of Gen. McClellan.

In April of that year he was elected captain of a cavalry company, organized in Charlotte by Maj. M. N. Hart.

After equipping and drilling his company at the old fair grounds at Charlotte, Capt. Erwin was ordered to join Evan's Battalion at Kinston, N. C. In the winter of 1862 the battalion was ordered to Garysburg, where the Fifth Cavalry Regiment was formed; this regiment was sent to Virginia in 1863, and took part in the memorable campaign of Gettysburg. When the regiment went to Virginia Capt. Erwin was left at Garysburg with typhoid fever, and did not rejoin his men until they returned to Culpepper Court House, where the famous North Carolina brigade, composed of the First, Second, Third and Fifth Cavalry, was organized. This brigade was commanded by the gallant Gordon until his death in front of the breast works near Richmond in 1864, when Gen. Rufus Barringer took charge of the brigade. In this command Capt. Erwin served till the close of the war, taking part in all the battles in which his regiment was engaged. At the bloody battle of Chamberlain Run his colonel, McNeil, and Lieut.-Col. Shaw were both killed, and Maj. Galloway being sick, the command of the regiment devolved on him to the close of the war. He did not surrender his regiment, but marched it back to North Carolina, and in Charlotte he received from John C. Breckenridge, Secretary of War, an order to disband his company.

After the war Capt. Erwin again entered the mercantile field as a clerk for Taylor & Duncan, which position he held for two years. On the 5th of June, 1867, he was married to

Miss Jennie, a daughter of Maj. Z. A. Grier, of Steele Creek. In January, 1868, Capt. Erwin moved to Steele Creek and began the life of a farmer. In January, 1873, he returned to Charlotte and accepted a position with W. H. Houston, a wholesale grocery merchant. In May, 1873, Capt. Erwin was elected city marshal, or chief of police, which office he held until April, 1875, when he was appointed by D. Schenck, judge of this district, clerk of the Superior Court of Mecklenburg county, in which capacity he served for twelve years.

Upon his retirement the following tribute was paid him by Col. H. C. Jones, at the close of Capt. Erwin's last court:

"I desire to call your honor's attention to the fact that the term of office of our much esteemed clerk, Capt. Erwin, is about to close. It has been many years since he entered upon the duties of his office, and in all that time he has discharged them so efficiently, with so much fidelity to the important trust committed to him, with such patience and industry, with such kindness and courtesy to the members of the bar, that I know I speak their sentiments when I say we part from him with feelings of affectionate regret. He came to the position entirely without experience and without any acquaintance with the business that his office devolved upon him, but he devoted himself to the task with such patient industry that he soon became, what I now pronounce him, one of the best—if not the very best—clerks within the limits of this State."

In May, 1878, Capt. Erwin's wife died, and on the 11th of December, 1879, he was married to Miss Sallie, daughter of Col. William M. Grier, of Steele Creek, and a sister of Calvin E. Grier, a prominent lawyer of Charlotte, who died in 1889.

After leaving the clerk's office, he retired to his farm in Steele Creek, where he had made large investments in a milling plant.

In 1888 he was elected chairman of the Finance Committee of the county, which position he held until 1892, when he was elected a member of the State Legislature. Although his first experience as a law-maker, he at once took a prominent position and was the chairman or a member of several committees.

In August, 1893, he accepted a position as private secretary to Congressman S. B. Alexander, and spent two years in the City of Washington. In 1895 he moved back to Charlotte and in the same year was made chairman of the Board of County Commissioners. During his administration and through his influence, the first iron bridges were erected for the county of Mecklenburg. He was also chairman of the committee which had in charge the building of the Mecklenburg county court house.

On the 19th of March, 1901, while seated in the court house in Charlotte, he died very suddenly, and was laid to rest in the old cemetery at Steele Creek.

During the war he had made an enviable record as a soldier, and to all who knew him his name was a synonym for honor and uprightness.—*Contributed by Miss F. Grier.*

Hon. James W. Osborne.

This section is headed by one of the greatest men the country has ever produced, and no better eulogy can be pronounced than the following, written by Gen. D. H. Hill:

"The nations of the earth, the most distinguished in history, for prowess in the field, wisdom in legislation, progress in science and art, purity of taste in polite literature, and refinement in the social circle, are precisely those which have most cherished the memory of their heroes, statesmen, scholars and patriots. It has been well said that the land that erects no monuments to its illustrious dead, will soon cease to produce men worthy of a place in history. To neglect departed greatness is to degrade living eminence.

"The Bible, with its wonderful adaptation to the wants of our race, sanctions cherishing tender recollections of the saints of the Lord. 'The righteous shall be in everlasting remembrance.' 'The memory of the just is blessed.' Here we have a prophecy and a command, both involving a high obligation and a glorious privilege—to keep fresh and green in the minds of men the memory of those who died in the full hope of a blessed immortality."

And thus the friends of the late Hon. J. W. Osborne feel that in attempting a tribute to his exalted worth, they are discharging a sad but gracious duty. It is meet that we should revere the memory of a man of mighty intellect, of profound scholarship, and of matchless eloquence, who brought all of his rare and varied gifts and accomplishments and laid them as an humble offering at the foot of the cross. There remains nothing now of his manly person and noble mein, of his vast learning and attainments, but

> " The knell, the shroud, the coffin and the grave,
> The deep, damp vault; the darkness and the worm."

His simple faith in Christ was worth a thousand-fold more than all his talents and acquirements, and the lesson of his life comes home to every bosom, "With all your gettings, get understanding." We can now think with grateful satisfaction that those great powers of mind, which were our pride and astonishment on earth, are ever expanding in knowledge, ever getting new revelations of Divine love and ever attaining new degrees of holiness. The saddest sight on our afflicted earth is that of a man of great gifts, culture and refinement, living out of Christ and deliberately choosing to spend his eternity with the coarse, the brutal and the depraved. With heartfelt gratitude, we adore that distinguished love which made our illustrious countryman choose that good part which shall not be taken away. Judge Osborne was born in Salisbury, N. C., on the 25th of December, 1811, and died in Charlotte on the 11th day of August, 1869, so that he hardly passed the meridian of life, and until a short time before his death, "His eye was not dim, nor his natural force abated." He was a graduate of our State University at Chapel Hill. He was always an earnest student, devoted especially to the sciences.

The extent and variety of his reading was truly marvelous. There was scarcely a subject he had not looked into, if indeed he had not mastered it. Few clergymen outside of our theological seminaries were so well read in theology. He said on one occasion that there was a charm about the study of theology that no other reading possessed for him, and he devoured huge volumes of theologic lore with the most eager relish. Fluency of speech was a natural gift with Judge Osborne, and this, combined with his vast acquaintance with books, made his language the very choicest Anglo-Saxon. His warm-hearted, genial, pleasant manner, and bright, kindly face added a charm to the whole, which was absolute. He had no equal as a conversationalist, and his intimate friends can never forget the grace and fascination of his address. And so his ready command of the best words, his learning, his enthusiasm, his sonorous voice and graceful delivery, made him one of the very first orators in the land. The magic spell thrown around Judge

Osborne in the social circle and on the hustings was his imperturbable good temper, and that proceeded from his large-hearted humanity, his sincere and unaffected love for his race. He had a kind word and a pleasant smile for everybody, simply because he loved mankind. He needed not a veil of charity to cover their crimes and frailties; in his own simple guilelessness he did not know their faults. Those who had known him for thirty and forty years, say that they never saw him angry. He had not an enemy among the people with whom he lived since early manhood. The most remarkable thing in the career of this great man was the hold he had upon the hearts of men of every creed and party, although in his official capacity he had often been opposed to the interests and wishes of the many.

He was admitted to the bar in Charlotte in the year 1833. He took a high stand in his profession at the very outset and maintained it while he lived. This was not due merely to his genius, his learning, and his eloquence, but in a large degree to his unselfish and sympathetic nature, which made him adopt his client's cause as his own and identify himself thoroughly with the interest, the views and feelings of the client. He was twice elector for the State at large, first in the Clay campaign and then in the contest between Seymour and Grant. He was appointed by President Fillmore superintendent of the United States Mint at Charlotte, which he held for four years. He was chosen by Gov. Ellis to fill a vacant judgeship in 1859, and the General Assembly confirmed the selection November 26, 1860. But it is as the Christian gentleman, we love to think of our illustrious statesman. He was sincerely and unaffectedly devout; a lover of God and man. We who were in the belt of the late total eclipse of the sun, observed a black spot projected on the lower limb of the sun. Gradually, the dark shadow crept higher and higher. The cattle came lowing home. The bewildered fowls of the air sought their roosts. The black spot crept higher and higher, until darkness covered the sky, with here and there a star sending forth a ghastly and unnatural light. Then the sun, like a mighty giant, threw off the black mantle and came forth in all his strength, beauty and majesty, rejoicing our hearts with some glorious beams that had been hid for a time. And thus, as our friend was a star of the first magnitude, we contemplate his death as a temporary eclipse, and believed that when the shadows of earth have passed away, the brilliant intellect that dazzled us below, will shine out with renewed effulgence above.

REV. JOHN HUNTER.

Of this worthy pioneer have descended a number of ministers of the Associated Reformed Presbyterian Church.

Rev. John Hunter was the son of Thomas Hunter, a godly and pious man. He first saw the light in Mecklenburg county, N. C., November 13, 1814. Graduating at Jefferson, Pa., September, 1841, license was granted by the First Presbytery April 17, 1843. His first pastorate was over Back Creek, Prosperity and Gilead, this county, being solemnly ordained and installed July 24, 1844. For three years beginning in 1855, he served a colony mostly of Mecklenburgers in Alleghany county, N. C. In September, 1858, he began his ministry at Sardis and was formerly installed January 11, 1859.

His ministry was very successful. To the west in 1874, Ebenezer was built, now self-suppporting and ministered unto by the able and judicious Dr. G. R. White.

On the east in 1886, Thyatira was erected. In this new and incompleted building occurred his death stroke and last effort to preach. In March, 1886, after singing and prayer, Luther, infant of Annie and E. B. Williams, was baptized. His text, I Cor., 13:13, was given out, but after proceeding a few minutes, his voice faltered and ran lower. As he seemed to be falling, his son, Dr. L. W. Hunter, and others eased him down. Being partially paralized, he succeeded in making them understand he wanted the 23rd Psalm sung. This was the first service in Thyatira, and his last effort to preach—a dedication of sacrifice. He lingered for some four years ripening for that heaven to which he had so often directed sorrowing hearts and fell asleep in Jesus May 16, 1890. He was thrice married. First to Miss Isabella H. Peoples July 18, 1843. His second marriage was to Mrs. Martha Simonton Bell December 10, 1861. A third marriage was contracted with Miss Mary Ann McDill October 9, 1866. Rev. John Hunter had much of the spirit of John Knox, fearless, with the courage of his convictions, conscientious and scrupulously upright in his dealings, popular as a preacher and loyal to his church, he lived respected and trusted and died devout, men carried his mortal remains to the grave and made great lamentations over him.

THE HUNTER FAMILY.

Rev. William May Hunter, son of R. B. and Rebecca W. Hunter, was born February 1, 1850; sought the ministry from inclination; took a full course, literary and theological, at Due West, S. C. Dr. W M. Grier gave him a diploma July 10, 1872, the First Presbytery license September 8, 1874, and the same court ordaination in the chapel, Charlotte, N. C., October 19, 1875. The first three years were spent in Charlotte, reinforced with a judicious help meet and prudent wife September 11, 1877, one year was spent in Georgia; ten years in Iredell county, N. C., as pastor of Stirling and Elk Shoal; ten more years in Mecklenburg as pastor of Prosperity and in the faculty of the Huntersville High School, and also Gilead. He now is stated supply of Lebanon, Monroe county, West Virginia.

Robert Boston Hunter, lately gone to his reward, July 17, 1902, aged 83 years, 11 months and 8 days, wedded January 9, 1845, to Rebecca Wilson Jones, a woman of tireless energy and devoted piety. They climbed in fortune and favor, zeal for the church and devotion to their children. One characteristic of R. B. Hunter was his choice of good company. He abhorred the low and the base. To his hospitable home he welcomed piety and intelligence. Another was his tireless industry. If he prospered, it was the reward of toil and foresight. He and his devoted wife were exceedingly zealous that their children be trained in hand, mind and heart for life. The poor did not stretch out their hands to him in vain, the wives of soldiers in the Civil War were the special objects of his favor.—*Contributed by Rev. W. M. Hunter.*

[The first of the large Hunter family that came to this country, that is to Mecklenburg county, was about 1760. Like all others, they followed farming, and were not different from other people. They have made wonderful strides in education in the last fifty years. They are a quiet, law-abiding people. Prosperity is one of their oldest churches.—EDITOR.]

The Descendants of Some of the Famous Men Who Fought in the Revolutionary War.

"BLACK BILLY" ALEXANDER.

Daniel Alexander, son of "Black Billy," was a man of wonderful energy. He was a farmer of more than ordinary capacity; but was unfortunate financially, having large amounts of security debts to pay. While a young man he courted and married Miss Susan Shelby. He then lived within the bounds of Sugar Creek. He had three sons, viz., Mark, Frank and Winslow; they also had three daughters. Isabella married, first, Mr. Charles Moss, to whom she bore one son (who now lives in Charlotte), and soon afterwards he died, leaving her a blooming young widow. She was very pretty, and was much courted. She married her second husband, Mr. Joab Smith, with whom she lived pleasantly for many years. Their children—some of whom live in Charlotte, Mrs. M. F. Kirby, is a worthy descendant. Margaret married Mr. M. D. Johnston, who was a professor of Mathematics at Davidson College. He was a man of fine learning and eminent piety. They left a small family. Mr. D. A. Johnston, two miles east of the city, is a worthy representative of that excellent family. Martha, the youngest of the family, married John T. Harry, in 1853, and moved West. She had but one child—a daughter—and died.

Of the boys we know but little. Winslow moved West, lived in Chattanooga, Tenn., Memphis, and back to Asheville, keeping a hotel. He married Margaret Alexander from near Rocky River. He had two sons, the eldest, Charles Carrol, was probably the brightest young man ever graduated at Davidson up to his time, 1853. He died young in Florida. Col. Winslow Alexander moved back to Charlotte in the early sixties. His daughter Laura married Capt. W. B. Taylor, at present city tax collector. They have raised a family that the city is proud of. Mrs. Taylor finished her course about a year ago, and left her husband surrounded with grown children and a multitude of friends. Mark Alexander moved West and left no son or daughter to keep his name in remembrance. Franklin married a Miss Gilmer, a sister of the well-known Drs. James and Samuel Gilmer. They left three boys and two girls. One of the sons died a short time ago; one lives in Alabama, and one, R. B. Alexander, lives in Charlotte. Mr. Daniel Alexander once engaged in cultivating the morus multicaulus, to feed silk worms; he had a large orchard planted west of Church street. From 1838 to 1845, it was quite fashionable to engage in silk culture. But no glowing reports were ever put out after 1845. About this time he moved to Davidson College and kept a large boarding house—students principally, his price being six dollars per month—and he made money at it. This was in 1850-54. These were good people, and were valuable citizens. Four miles north of Charlotte Isaac Alexander's widow lived in 1846, where a Miss Chamberlain taught a large female school for several years, with great satisfaction; but she married a merchant of Charlotte, Mr. R. C. Carson, a Christian gentleman. The widow, Anabella, married old "Uncle" Dan Alexander, who had become a widower, and they too soon passed away.

THE HENDERSON FAMILY.

In or about the year 1750, Kearns Henderson and Elizabeth Robinson, who were married in Lancaster county, Pennsylvania, November 14, 1749 (copied from marriage certificate) moved to this section ten or twelve years before Mecklenburg county was established. It is presumed that farming was the principal pursuit. They had three sons, but no daughters are mentioned. Andrew grew up with those stern, prominent features that were characteristic of the times in which they lived. Andrew, it is strange to say, also married, like his father, Elizabeth Robinson. They were of no relation; it was a mere coincidence. This was in 1780. They were blessed with two sons and seven daughters. They reached a ripe age, and filled a good position in church, as well as citizens of the country. Their daughters were as follows: Mary married William Alexander. He was known as "Blind Billy" Alexander. They had one son, Harvey, who never married; two daughters, who were twins, Teressa married Wm. B. Alexander, and Clarissa married Harper Kerns. Both had families. Nancy, Margaret, Elizabeth, Griswold, never married, but continued at the old homestead till death. Jane married Birch Cheshire, and left two sons. Harriet married John R. Alexander. She was certainly one of the most devotedly pious women that our country possessed. Their family was noted for energy and good deeds. Their daughter Amanda, a very bright, pretty and highly accomplished young woman, was wooed and won by Rev. W. W. Pharr, D. D., a most excellent and learned minister. He had the happy faculty of healing ugly breaches in a congregation, or in a community. He might have been called the Peacemaker of the Church. He was very popular as a man and as a preacher.

They left two sons and one daughter. The oldest son, John R. Pharr, is in the state of single blessedness; is successful in business, and lives with and takes care of his aged step-mother. Dr. William W. Pharr is engaged in practicing medicine at Newells. He married a daughter of Mr. Elam Queery, and has quite an interesting family. The daughter, Miss Mary, married Rev. Mr. Arrowood, and is living now in South Carolina. Their daughter Elizabeth, married Dr. Watson Rankin, of Cabarrus county. They both have passed away a number of years ago. Their children are scattered in various sections of other counties and States; but are in a prosperous condition. Miss Nannie married a Mr. Stewart, of Florida, who soon died, and his widow spends much of her time here but still holds her farm in Florida. Miss Sophia married Mr. John Sample, of Memphis, Tenn. Both soon died without offspring.

Capt. A. H. Alexander moved to Florida in 1866, where he still resides. He is now up in seventy years, his health is poor and has but a few years left. T. LaFayette Alexander was long a resident of Charlotte, was a most successful merchant. He was a kind, good man, and did much for his kin who were not so well off. He left one daughter and two sons. Capt. Francis Alexander gave his life for the independence of the South, and for the rights of the States. He was killed the 17th of June, 1864, near Petersburg.

Rev. W. W. Pharr's second wife—who was a daughter of General Neal, of Steele Creek—had two sons and two daughters, who are fit representatives of their worthy parents. Mr. James Pharr is a merchant of standing, and is held in high esteem in both Church and State. Mr. Neal Pharr chose the legal profession, which brings him a handsome revenue, and he promises to occupy an honorable position in the county.

Kairns Harvey Henderson never married, but let a quiet, useful life.

David Robinson Henderson lived five miles north of Charlotte, cultivated a farm, was successful in all his ventures. He had also a farm on both sides of the Catawba; also one in Alabama. This one he visited on horseback once or twice a year. He married Peggy Alexander, daughter of Wm. B. Alexander. In his frequent visits from home, lasting some times two or three months, he would leave everything pertaining to the farm in the hands of his wife. She was indeed an "help meet." They raised four sons and one daughter. The daughter, Jane, married E. C. Davidson, of the Hopewell neighborhood, where Mrs. Davidson still lives. She has three sons, two of whom are physicians, and one a farmer; one daughter, Mary, married Arthur Parks in Iredell county. Miss Sadie, "heart whole and fancy free," enjoys life as a typewriter in Charlotte. Wm. Bane Henderson graduated at Davidson College, and moved to Alabama. Andrew R. Henderson was a thorough-going farmer, raised elegant crops, but was too confident of his friends meeting heir obligations. Being security for them, they left him to pay their debts. He married a Miss Rutlidge, and raised an interesting family just over the Catawba river in Gaston county. Mr. A. R. Henderson died in the spring of 1902. Dr. J. Mc. Henderson was a prominent practitioner of medicine seven miles north of Charlotte. He was well known in the northern part of the county. He married a Miss Simnerell. Dr. Henderson died a few years after the Civil War.

Dr. Simmerel Henderson, his son, is single, lives at the homestead with his mother and sisters, does a large practice and enjoys life. His elder brother, Pink Henderson, married a Miss Dowd, and lives near Croft. A good farmer, a member of the County Commissioners, and is altogether a useful man in his community.

Mr. J. Harvey Henderson, the youngest son of David R. Henderson, lived at the homestead, married a daughter of Batt Irwin, Esq. He had four children, three sons and one daughter. Harvey H. lost his wife probably twenty-five years ago. He moved to Charlotte fifteen years ago. His boys are in business here and are doing well. Mr. Henderson died in 1901. His daughter, Miss Ella, lives with her brothers.

The daughters of Dr. J. Mc. Henderson, one, Margaret, married Dr. John R. Irwin, who has recently moved to Charlotte. He is one of the foremost physicians in the city, has a very interesting family. He is giving his children every possible advantage in a good education. Another daughter married Dr. Elmore Wilson, of Catawba. They hold the traits of their ancestors, provided well for their children. The three who are single are engaged in teaching.

Doctor Kairns Henderson married and had two sons, David and James P. Henderson. Devid Henderson lived six miles north of Charlotte on the Statesville road. He was a good farmer, and operated a small tanyard. He first married a Wallace. She bore him two children. They were uncommonly bright. They lived to be about 60 years.

old. His second wife was a daughter of Isaac Henderson—a third cousin of his. There was eight children by the second wife. His son Charles lives in the old homestead. James P. Henderson lived near Derita. He, too, married a Wallace; most intelligent family, and bore wonderfully smart children. They had two sons and two daughters. Philo was a graduate of the University of North Carolina. He was the recognized poet of the county.

Mr. Henderson moved to Davidson College in the forties, and continued there until the war. His daughters married off, Philo was dead, his wife was dead, Tom was in the army. He married the second time. In a little while death claimed all but the daughters.

Another of these brilliant women married Mr. Samuel Moose. The branch of the Wallaces were remarkable for their intellectual capacity. Dr. Thomas Henderson was one of the earliest physicians that ever practiced in the county. He lived in Charlotte and married the widow Baldwin, whoever she might have been. In those early days the great strife was to push forward, to gain our independence, establish our government, make laws to regulate the affairs of State, only to look forward and forget that which was past; until much of our unwritten history has passed into a state of oblivion. No wonder we do not know who the widow Baldwin could have been, or who her first husband was. We do not know that Dr. Henderson and (Mrs. Baldwin) his wife ever had but one son. Mr. Isaac Henderson (he always looked lonesome) married a McRea. They lived on the Beattie's Ford Road, four miles northwest of Charlotte. They lived handsomely, an excellent house for the time, owned quite a number of slaves, and everything around them to render the family happy and contented. He had one son, David, who also had one son, Dr. James Henderson, who died a few years since. The great majority of this family of Hendersons left their ashes to Sugar Creek burying ground. They lived peaceably together, in the same congregation; and it is meet they should sleep in the same enclosure till the last trump shall sound.

WILLIAM BROWN.

In the northern part of the county, east of Huntersville, in Ramah congregation, Mr. William Brown settled, entering 600 acres of land, prior to the Revolutionary War. In the last one hundred years the land has been cut up and divided into many parcels, but is still owned by the descendants of the Brown family.

It is the plain, common people that constitute the backbone of a country. They thought it was their Christian duty to enter the patriot army and contend for the independence of America. In the war between the States, those who were young enough as well as those who were old enough, did not hesitate to fight for the rights of the South; and no man who bears the name of Brown has any apology to offer for taking sides with the South in the terrific struggle which lasted from 1861 to 1865.

THE BEARD FAMILY.

In about the year 1770, the Beard family came to this country from Ireland. John, Samuel and William Beard lived where John Beard the second afterwards lived, near the Statesville road, fourteen miles north of Charlotte. William alone was married before he emigrated; but his wife died before he reached the promised land. He married a second time in South Carolina. From her appearance when she was old, she must have been a woman of more than ordinary mental calibre. Mr. and Mrs. Beard raised one daughter and six sons. She married Milton Osborne, a man of fine parts, agreeable manners, an excellent farmer. He left a worthy family to perpetuate his name. The oldest son, John Beard, married Camelia McRaven. They lived at the old homestead, raised a large family, the girls married well; one son was killed in the Confederate army, and the others moved West. William married Francis Brown; they were clever people; he had two sons in the Confederate army. His son Joseph gave his life for the Confederate cause, and J. C. Beard was not seriously hurt and is still living, with a prospect of several more years, with his wife and daughters to cheer his old age. Robert Beard lived on the east side of the Statesville road. He was an excellent farmer, had everything in abundance, and was particular about his stock. He was never known to have a poor horse. He married Polly Knox. The whole Knox family were passionately fond of dancing, but there was no impropriety by carrying the amusement to excess. They also gave a son to the Confederate army. This was a time when a patriot would give his all to defend his home. J. F. M. Beard escaped as few battles as any man in the army. He never complained, but was ready for duty always, and frequently stood picket duty every other night towards the close of the war. But he still lives, and his host of friends wish him a happy evening to a well spent life. He married Catherine Alexander, a daughter of Ezekiel Alexander. They have a happy family and are ranked with our best people. Samuel married Sabrian Hale, in Tennessee, and spent but a few years in North Carolina. James married a Miss Humphreys. He worked a tanyard for many years, and moved to Marion. Richard lived on the east side of the Statesville road, lead a peaceful life, and was highly esteemed in all the relations of life. He, too, married a Miss Humphreys, of Tennessee. They raised a nice family, who are among our best citizens. The old grand-mother was fortunate to find a home to end her last days in the family of her son, where every want was gratified. They were good people, held to the Associate Reformed Presbyterians. The older set, both men and women, have long since passed away.

DANIEL M'CAULAY.

Mr. Daniel McCaulay, who lived in the same neighborhood, lived about the same time. His son Hugh, a compeer of the Beards, was a noted surveyor; had a family of eight children—Daniel, Hugh, Alexander and John were all in the Confederate army; Daniel and Hugh died in service; Alexander and John are still living. They are all very intelligent, and useful citizens. The women were very smart—poetically inclined. Like the Beards, they were "seceders."

J. M. HAPPOLDT, M. D.

J. M. Happoldt came to Charlotte previous to 1840. He was well equipped for practicing his profession, did his share of the work, was a fluent conversationalist. At one time he became the victim of typhoid fever. He lay for several weeks, was desperately ill, and was attended by Drs. Caldwell and Harris. They would devote their personal attention to nursing him, giving him medicine, food, and what he needed. At this time ready-made coffins were unheard of. Each neighborhood had a skilled workman, generally a cabinet maker, who made all the coffins needed. Charlotte was not a whit behind other places, and old Archie Miles—the cabinet maker—was always ready to build the last house for any one who had been a good citizen. In fact he was anxious to accommodate, as times were dull and he did not like to lose a job. It was his custom to inquire very often if such and such a one was better or not, until it was a standing joke. Every morning during the extreme illness of Dr. Happoldt, Archie Miles would be seen wending his way along the street to make the usual enquiry, and return disappointed. So one day he rested well, and Dr. Pink Caldwell set up that night, and towards daylight the blinds were closed and the bed curtains were drawn to shut out the rays of light, so that his slumber should not be disturbed, Dr. Caldwell quietly withdrew. Just as he stepped on the pavement, who should he see but his friend Archie coming —buttoning his clothes as he trotted briskly up the street, calling in a loud whisper, "Dr. Caldwell, Dr. Caldwell, how is Dr. Happoldt?" "Well, Archie," Dr. Caldwell answered, "Our poor friend has gone, after a long struggle." The coffin-maker no longer hesitated, but at once mounted the steps, threw the door open, entered the supposed death chamber, opened wide the window shutters, drew the curtains to one side, and placed his thumb on one end of the measuring tape on his forehead, and began unwheeling the tape, when the supposed corps was awakened and asked: "What in the hell are you doing?" Archie looked like he had seen a ghost, and got out of the house quicker than he went in. It is needless to say that the patient's recovery was hastened by the undertaker's misadventure.

WM. W. ELMS.

Wm. W. Elms, as a citizen, deserves more than a passing notice. He was born in the southern part of the county, not far from the South Carolina line. He came to Charlotte in 1829, and clerked for Mr. John Irwin for several years. Then the firm name was Irwin & Elms. Then after several years he dissolved copartnership with Irwin and moved from Irwin's corner to a house now occupied by Mr. Frank Andrews, and had the following clerks, viz.: A. H. Martin, Billy Owens, Washington Blair, Ed. Moss, James Harty, and others as needed. S. Nye Hutchison and Jasper Stowe at one time helped Mr. Elms in the dry goods trade.

In 1848, the firm name changed to Elms & Logan Martin, when Columbus Irwin clerked for them. And, afterwards, it was W. W. Elms alone. He was very popular as a merchant and did an enormous business. After 1852, when the Charlotte & Columbia Railroad was finished here, Mr. Elms was the principal cotton buyer in the market. He built several elegant houses, and did much to improve the town. He was the leading spirit in building the Lincolnton

Plank Road that brought much produce to market. These roads soon fell into decay, but they served a good purpose in giving an example what good roads were worth, and after the people saw the practical working, they did not stop until Mecklenburg had the best roads in all the country.

COL. J. Y. BRYCE.

J. Y. Bryce came to Charlotte when quite a young man, from South Carolina, having been raised in Columbia, and belonged to a family who associated with the Barnwells, Rhetts, Hamptons, DeSeasure and all that class of people who gave the State her reputation for chivalry that she sustained for so many years.

Col. Bryce engaged in the mercantile business, in which he was successful. He married a daughter of Dr. L. G. Jones, took an active part in building up all the interests of the town. He could not help but advocate the right of secession, and when the time came for action instead of talk, he was not slow in going to the front. He was very painfully wounded, from which he never fully recovered. Soon after the war he went to New York and speculated in cotton when the price was high, and amassed a large fortune. After he returned to Charlotte, he was plied by a number of persons to join them in various speculations. He steered clear of the sharpers for a while, but finally yielded and was soon spoiled of his entire fortune. He engaged in working the marl beds in the eastern part of the State, it did not take well with the farmers, and although he worked it faithfully for several years, it proved a failure. After this his health declined rapidly and he died in 1897. His family moved soon away. He was liked by all with whom he came in contact.

CHARLES ELMS SPRATT.

In 1842 Charlotte was still a village, although it was more than half a century old. At this date Mr. Spratt came to

Charlotte, a young man of more than ordinary appearance, of good family, and of fine physique—born and educated below where the town of Pineville now stands. He came here in 1842 to clerk for Moss, Springs & Co. This proved a pleasant firm to work for, but in three years he formed a partnership with R. F. Davidson at Irwin's corner, under the style of Davidson & Spratt. This venture lasted only eighteen months, when he sold out to W. W. Elms, and went to New York. He there clerked in a woolen house, but after one year he returned to Charlotte, and in 1849 bought out Elms, where Mr. Frank Andrews now has a sewing machine store, and formed a partnership with Dr. John Allison, under the name of Spratt & Allison. This house kept the finest goods in the town, was patronized by wealthy people in the surrounding counties. The firm continued for three years, when Mr. Spratt sold out to Allison & Daniel, and joined with W. W. Elms in the grocery business and buying cotcon. Mr. Spratt was married in 1850 to Miss Margaret, daughter of Brawley Oates, probably the most handsome couple ever married in Charlotte. Brilliant intellect as well as beauty of feature appears to be handed down in the family, like an interesting heirloom.

ISAAC ALEXANDER, COMMONLY CALLED "CLERK ISAAC."

This is one of the oldest families of Mecklenburg county. For a great many years he was clerk of the Court, which was then as now, a most important position, and consequently none but the best men in the county were capable of filling. He lived about four miles from town; had his office at home, where he carried all papers belonging to the Court and the county. He had a certain day on which he would meet the people, and during court week, he was at the court house every day. His daughters assisted him much in writing. He lived between Sugar Creek and Providence. He was a regular worshipper at Sugar Creek, and was buried there in the second grave yard, south side of the big road leading to Charlotte. He was born in 1798. He married a sister of David Reese. How particular the people were to keep their posterity on a high plain, never to go backwards, but if possible keep up the strain, or improve it. He died at a good old age, 74. His sister, Elmira Alexander, married John Rankin, from Guilford county. They lived west of Sugar Creek two miles. They were good people and valuable members of society. They afterwards moved on the same place where the old clerk spent his days of toil and pleasure. She and her husband were married on the night the "stars fell" in 1833. They, too, have passed away, and their son, William Rankin, now holds forth on the same place that his grandfather occupied. He has a wife and daughters that remind you so much of the earlier settlers.

Charles T. Alexander, a worthy son of Clerk Isaac Alexander, lived on the same place, but in another house, having built a new one. He never married, was very popular with the young ladies, loved their company, and in return was visited by them. A young peoples' club was not complete without him.

As an elder, he often attended church courts. He was regarded by all as a good Christian man. He died at 72 years of age.

HON. JAMES A. DUNN.

Back in 1840, Hon. James A. Dunn was one of the most influential men in the county in all his several relations of life. After Union county was cut off from Mecklenburg in 1845, Col. Dunn lived in Union county. He served this county for several terms in the State Legislature with great acceptability. He was the leader of everything that tended to help the masses; was always active in educational enterprises, and what was for the best of the county. He was a large farmer, and did his work well. He was a neighbor to Dr. Ardrey, just across the creek, and attended Providence Church, and at last found a resting place in the graveyard, where he had been a worshipper during his life; also his three wives rest here with him. His first wife was Miss ———————————————— His second wife was the widow Ingraham—Miss Walkup. His third wife was the widow Stitt. He was a happy man, and did much good in his lifetime. Something more than a half century ago he passed away, but has left a memory behind him that is cherished by those who would have their works to follow them.

JOAB ORR.

Joab Orr, who lived in the same neighborhood, was also noted in his day, but it was in another direction. He was noted for his skill in playing the fiddle. This appears to have been his chief delight, and to see that the dancers kept step to the music.

Joab Orr had three beautiful daughters, naturally smart, and if living in the civilization of the present day, and had the advantages of education that are enjoyed now, they would have been leaders of the fashionable world, as their father was the leader of music, especially on the violin. They lived at the place now known as the Henigan place, south of Little Sugar Creek, where President Polk is said to have been born. This section of the country was noted for the staunch patriots furnished the American army from 1775 to 1781. It is an elegant body of land, well watered, and owned by the best of citizens, most generally descendants of those who cultivated these lands "when we lived under the king."

Pineville, two miles from the South Carolina line, was marked off as a railroad station on the Charlotte & Columbia road, is quite a depot for distribution of farmers' supplies, a cotton factory, stores, etc. It is a central point for that section of the county, and among the many good people who live and have lived around here, I will mention the name of Alexander. Many of that name lived within five miles, all connected and all were good people. I can go back sixty years and can truthfully say that I have never heard of one of the name who was guilty of a mean or dishonorable action of any kind.

Many Men Who Sustained a Splendid Reputation as Ministers of the Gospel in the Various Years of the Nineteenth Century.

REV. JOHN MCK. WILSON, D. D.

A man whose boyhood was spent amidst the impressive events and influences of the Revolution, and gained a name not to be forgotten, was Rev. John McKamie Wilson, D. D. He was born six miles east of Charlotte in the bounds of Sugar Creek, of which church his widowed mother was a member. With Mrs. Wilson, Mrs. Jackson and her son Andrew, found a refuge, and for a time a home, when the families of Waxhaw, on the borders of South Carolina, were flying from the ravages of the enemy. The sons of these widows, John and Andrew, worked and played together and, together with their mothers, attended the preaching of Rev. Joseph Alexander, then pastor of Sugar Creek. John never dreamed that he was running, wrestling and working with a boy that was to be President of the United States; nor did Andrew, when measuring strength and speed with John, think how difficult it would be to measure the height of usefulness to which his young playmate was destined to reach; nor the vast influences which he was to set in operation for good.

John McKamie Wilson was born in 1769. At the age of 12 years be began his classical education at Liberty Hall, at Charlotte, then under the management of Dr. Henderson. His literary training was completed at Hampden-Sidney, Va., where he graduated with distinction. Having fully and heartily consecrated himself to Christ, he devoted his life to the ministry. His theological training and preparation was received under Rev. James Hall, D. D., of Iredell county. He was licensed by the Presbytery of Orange in 1793, and was sent out to do missionary work in the lower part of the State. His next field of labor was in Burke county, where he remained until 1801. His ministry was very fruitful in elevating the standard of piety, organizing new churches and building up those which had been previously planted in that county.

While living in Burke he married Miss Mary Erwin, whose father was Alexander Erwin, of that county, in whom he found the intelligence, piety and sweetness of disposition which made her a great blessing to her husband for more than thirty years. He was called from Quaker Meadow to Rocky River and Philadelphia churches in 1801, where he spent the strength of his vigorous manhood and the declining years of his life. About the year 1812 he, at the earnest request of many, opened a classical school about one mile from his house, and for twelve years that congregation and many others, enjoyed the advantages of one of the most flourishing and successfully managed academies in all the country. During those years twenty-five of his students entered the ministry, and many others were prepared for position of public trust. As a minister and teacher of youth, he was eminently wise in management. He died July 30, 1831. Among those who entered the ministry from that school may be named Dr. Cyrus Johnston, at one time pastor of Providence and Sharon, and who died in Charlotte, the pastor of the First Church; R. H. Morrison, D. D., Henry N. Pharr, and Alexander Wilson.

REV. JOHN ROBINSON.

Rev. John Robinson was born in Sugar Creek congregation in 1768. Like his friend Dr. Wilson, he was born in troublous times, when it seemed that society was to be torn up by the roots, and the civilization of that period to be utterly destroyed, and the people forced into subjection to the tyranny of England. He was too young to enter the patriot army, but when twelve or fifteen years old, was at school at Queen's Museum, under the special care of Dr.

Henderson, who was an instructor in 1780. The most of his ministerial life was spent at Poplar Tent. He had a large field to operate in, and allowed no part to suffer for want of his attention. He took an active part in the great revivals of 1802, 1803, 1804, 1805 and 1806.

On one occasion as he came home from church, he was passing a man driving a wagon. When the wagoner, judging him to be a minister, began blackguarding, and cursing him, whereupon he alighted from his horse, took off his coat and carefully laid down, and addressed his coat, "Now Parson Robinson, you lie there till I whip this man." He was so deliberate in his preparation the wagoner begged his pardon, and promised never to insult another preacher when attending to his own business.

He was a native of Mecklenburg, and like Dr. Wilson, moved just over the county line, hence we have no apologies to offer, for they belonged to us. After living the full measure of his days, he died December 15, 1843.

REV. SAMUEL C. CALDWELL.

Rev. Samuel Craig Caldwell was a son of Dr. David Caldwell, of Guilford, who was a noted Patriot in the Revolutionary war. His mother was a daughter of Alexander Craighead, whose body lies buried three miles east of Charlotte, in the first graveyard of Sugar Creek church. Mr. Caldwell's first charge was Hopewell and Sugar Creek, installed in 1792. In 1806 he moved to Sugar Creek and tendered his resignation of his services at Hopewell, devoted his time to Sugar Creek, Mallard Creek, Paw Creek, and Charlotte. The last three were not organized when he began preaching; but afterwards he organized Mallard Creek and Paw Creek. The latter has changed its name to Caldwell. Mr. Caldwell taught a large classical school at Sugar Creek, and also taught a theological school. He was a busy man.

It was at his school that young Wallis, a nephew of Mr.

Caldwell's first wife (both he and Mr. Wallis married daughters of John McKnitt Alexander), delivered his speech on "The 20th of May, 1775, the Declaration of Independence in Charlotte was Declared." This speech was delivered in 1809, when there was still living several of the signers and more than a score of those who participated in the War of Independence. If he had made a mistake about dates, surely it would have been corrected on the spot, when it was spoken in the presence of a large crowd, two of the sons-in-law of Mr. Alexander being present, and it is more than probable that the old secretary himself was present, for this was eight years before his death, and he lived but eight miles away.

Mr. Caldwell raised seven sons and two daughters— two by his first wife, Jane Bain, a daughter of John McKnitt Alexander, and Dr. D. Thomas Caldwell, who lived a useful life to both Church and State. He practiced medicine for many years, and raised a worthy family. But three of his children survive. Baxter runs the farm successfully, is an ex-Confederate, is proud of his war record, is a bachelor; his sister, Miss Alice, lives with him. They live happily in the congregation of Sugar Creek, close to the graves of his ancestors, and near the tomb of Alexander Craighead.

Another daughter still living is Mrs. Sarah Jane, who married George Donald, of Greensboro. She is a woman of deep piety, and well versed in the literature of the day.

By the second wife Rev. S. C. Caldwell was blessed with nine children, in addition to the two by the first marriage— the daughter having married Rev. Walter Smiley Pharr, who spent the most of his life preaching at Ramah and Mallard Creek. He had one son, the Rev. S. C. Pharr, D. D., who was a very popular preacher. He had a most wonderful flow of language, and was regarded far beyond the ordinary.

Five of the sons by the last or Lindsay wife, were ministers; but one served a church in Mecklenburg, Rev. J. M. M.

Caldwell. He preached for a number of years at Sugar Creek. In 1845 he moved to Rome, Ga., served the church there very acceptably, and taught a female school for many years. He had three sons to enter the ministry. Harper Caldwell moved to Mississippi in 1845. He, too, had three sons to enter the ministry. Walter P. Caldwell, a lawyer of Greensboro, had but one son, Robert Ernest, and he is one of the most eminent divines in North Carolina. His daughter by the Lindsay wife, Abigail Bain, married Robert D. Alexander, Esq. They raised five children, the eldest of whom, Rev. Dr. S. C. Alexander, now of Pine Bluff, Ark., has been a minister for more than fifty years. It is wonderful how many have followed in the path marked out by their progenitor—Rev. Alexander Craighead. Mr. Craghead was an early settler in our county, in 1758, and was regarded as a wise teacher, both in religion and resistance to British tyranny.

Rev. Mr. S. C. Caldwell, who preached so long at Sugar Creek, left a lasting impression on the community for good. For fifty years after his death, which occurred in 1829, people lived who talked freely about his manners and ways. He left a lasting impress "upon the sands of time" that will continue to exercise a wholesome influence in Mecklenburg county long after his hearers and associates are forgotten. The peculiarities and idiosyncrasies of the fathers are certainly transmitted to the sons through many generations, or to use a more homely phrase, "preaching appears to run in the family."

REV. JOHN WILLIAMSON.

Rev. John Williamson went to Hopewell as pastor in 1818, and gave great satisfaction for twenty-four years, when death closed his pastorate in 1842. He was popular as a man, a pastor, and a preacher. His wife was a Doby, and filled the bill of what a preacher's wife should be. She was in deed a helpmeet to her husband. She, too, passed away two years later. Hopewell church yard was a fitting place to lay them away. Mr. Williamson is the first and only minister that has ever found a sepulcher in Hopewell cemetery. The eldest daughter, Sarah Ann, married Rev. A. H. Caldwell, and at once moved to Mississippi, with the younger children, where their lives were spent in doing good. Mrs. Caldwell is still living, in reach of her family, and is abundantly supplied with this world's goods, and has the pleasure of knowing that three of her sons are regularly ordained ministers. Mecklenburg has probably sent out to other States more men who afterwards entered the learned professions than any other county in the State.

REV. SAMUEL WILLIAMSON, D. D.

Mr. Williamson was a native of South Carolina, graduated at the University of South Carolina, with the first honors of the institution. In 1837 he was elected a professor at Davidson College, which position he held for several years, and the office of President becoming vacant, Mr. Williamson was elected president of the college. He was a man of very brilliant attainments. He was said to have been one of the finest Latin scholars in the State; a preacher of very great power. He was an off-hand speaker, never taken unawares; he was never at a loss in debate. He had the best stored mind with useful knowledge of any man of his day. He was universally loved by the students. He resigned his position as head of the faculty in 1852, and moved to his farm in Hopewell, that was formerly owned by his brother, Rev. John Williamson, and there he continued to reside till 1856, when he removed to Arkansas. His eldest son, James, studied law and in 1861 went into the Confederate army; was promoted to the rank of Colonel, lost a leg and remained a cripple the remainder of his life. Our county was proud to welcome the Williamsons, and very sorry to lose them.

REV. R. H. LAFFERTY.

Rev. R. H. Lafferty came to North Carolina about 1845, and took charge of Sugar Creek soon after Rev. J. M. M. Caldwell resigned. He married a daughter of Mr. Wilson Parks. He **was** a very earnest preacher, and gave very general satisfaction. He ministered to this congregation for a number of years, in fact he never moved until his death, about the year 1867.

REV. JAMES WALLIS.

Rev. James Wallis was licensed about 1790, and he, too, married a daughter of John McKnitt Alexander, and located at Providence, some thirty years after the "Seven Churches" were built. He continued with this charge many years, until his work was done. He and his wife both were buried in Providence graveyard. Their children moved west, and entered the race of life within the new State, opening their doors to emigrants as the century advanced.

A. W. MILLER.

Dr. A. W. Miller, former pastor of the First Presbyterian church of this city, no writer can do full justice to him. He was a great preacher, no one can deny this. His preaching was characterized by sound doctrine, earnestness and no compromise. It was the writer's privilege to be a member of his flock, and to hear him preach for years, hence can judge somewhat of his power. His delivery was different from what we are accustomed to hear now. He used manuscript almost entirely, but quite effectively; occasionally he would preach without any manuscript, and these sermons were delivered with great power. Some one spoke to him in regard to two sermons he preached on a certain Sunday, one with manuscript, and one without, saying to him that he liked the sermon without the manuscript best. Dr. Mil-

DR. A. W. MILLER.

ler intimated by his reply that this was because of inattention, saying it took two weeks to prepare the sermon delivered from manuscript, and the other he had not even given any study, the text having come into his mind just before the service began. He never preached a sermon that did not contain food for thought; he declared the whole law and spared not. I do not think I ever heard him try to modify the obvious meaning of any text of Scripture. He preached from the texts of the Bible as they were written.

The church of which he was the pastor is still reaping the benefits of his noble work, conspicuous in its contributions to the support of the Gospel, and the integrity and steadfastness of many of the older members. Notwithstanding his devotion to his calling, and the arduous duties incident thereto, he took a lively interest in the history of his country, particularly the Mecklenburg Declaration of Independence. He always would preach an appropriate sermon on these occasions, attesting in no uncertain sound his belief in the genuineness of the claim. While abroad he visited London and searched the archives for evidence bearing upon this important event, and ascertained that very important evidence had been abstracted from the files. He continued his search, and found in Charleston evidence convincing him that the claim was true. He secured the file containing this information and brought it to Charlotte and exhibited it to the public at the Y. M. C. A. hall in this city.

It was he who encouraged the erection of a monument to the memory of Rev. Alex. Craighead, a noted Presbyterian minister, who was prominent in the times that tried men's souls. Some persons regarded this great man as stern and unapproachable; this was a mistaken idea. He was just the opposite, being easily approached, and as full of humor as the average man. The same could be said of him as was said of a learned judge: "He could leave the bench and get down on the floor with the children." I have seen him do this at my own house, and he seemed to enjoy the sport as much as the children.

Every one respected him and had great confidence in his piety. He had some peculiarities, as other men; had a peculiar way of putting some things. I remember of hearing him in a sermon on one occasion speaking of consistency of professed Christians. He said "that a man who had an orthodox heart, should have orthodox feet." He was unmistakably a great and good man. His life and work may be summed up in the words (which were the last uttered by him) engraved upon a tablet erected to his memory by the ladies of his church: "I have fought a good fight; I have finished my course; I have kept the Faith." We can truthfully say of him:

"Servant of God well done;
　Rest from thy loved employ;
The battle fought, the victory won,
　Enter thy master's joy.

"The pains of death are past,
　Labor and sorrow cease,
And life's long warfare closed at last,
　His soul is found in peace.

"Soldier of Christ, well done;
　Praise be thy new employ;
And while eternal ages run,
　Rest in thy Saviour's joy."

—Contributed by J. A. Elliott.

Two Church Sessions Act as a Unit.

Hopewell and Sugar Creek churches form a union, in which government of both are under the rule of a joint session. The spiritual welfare was the highest aim of both bodies. During the time of Rev. S. C. Caldwell's ministration of Hopewell and Sugar Creek churches, beginning in 1793, the pressure was very great, as at that time infidelity was felt wherever it could make itself felt. On May 15, 1793, the sessions of Sugar Creek and Hopewell had a full meeting at the house of Elder Robinson, about midway between the churches, and entered into a number of resolutions as laws for the government of both churches.

"NORTH CAROLINA,
"Mecklenburg County, May 5, 1793.

"We, the Sessions of Sugar Creek and Hopewell congregations, having two separate and distinct churches, sessions and other officers for the peace, convenience, and well-ordering of each society, and all happily united under their present pastor, Samuel C. Caldwell, yet need much mutual help from each other in regard of our own weakness and mutual dependence, and also in regard to our enemies from without.

"Therefore, in order to make our union the more permanent, and to strengthen each others' hands in the bonds of unity and Christian friendship, have, this 15th day of May, 1793, met in a social manner, at the house of Mons. Robinson. Present: Robert Robinson, Sr., Hezekiah Alexander, Wm. Alexander, James Robinson, Isaac Alexander, Thomas Alexander, and Elijah Alexander, elders in Sugar Creek; John McKnitt Alexander, Robert Crocket, James Meek, James Henry, Wm. Henderson, and Ezekiel Alexander, elders in Hopewell, who, after discussing generally several topics, proceeded to choose Hezekiah Alexander chairman, and John McKnitt Alexander clerk, and do agree to the following resolves and rules which we, each for himself, promise to observe."

Then follow five resolutions respecting the management of the congregations, as it regards the support of their ministers, inculcating punctuality and precision; and also respecting a division of the Presbytery of Orange into two Presbyteries.

Then follow eight permanent laws and general rules for each session. The first concerns the manner of bringing charges against a member of the church; that it shall be written and signed by the complainant, and that previous to trial all mild means shall be used to settle the matter.

2. "As a church judicature, we will not intermeddle with what belongs to the civil magistrate, either as an officer of State, or a minister of justice among the citizens. The line between the Church and State being so fine, we know not how to draw it, therefore we leave it to Christian prudence and longer experience to determine."

The other resolutions are all found in the Confession of Faith, in their spirit, in the rules given for the management of a single session, with this exception, that it was determined that in this joint session "a quorum to do business shall not be less than a moderator and three elders," and that in matters of discipline there shall be "no *non liquet* votes permitted."

We can readily infer that no precedent of this nature had ever taken place either in this country or in Europe; but the obstacles to the growth of religion were so great that extraordinary rules had to be adopted to guide with discretion, a church recently planted, that was surrounded with the demoralizing influences of war. But the people were fortunate indeed to have men in their double session who had most skillfully and successfully declared independence and made it good, although it was the wonder of the world.

This union of the sessions was productive of most happy consequences to the two congregations, particularly during the struggle with French infidelity, and had the effect to preserve the spirit of Presbyterianism and sound principles, and free religion.

The elders were jealous of any intermingling of Church and State, even in the proceedings of sessions, and endeavored to keep both civil and religious freedom, entirely separating political and ecclesiastical proceedings as completely as possible.

All the difficulty probably arose from the fact that some of the elders were magistrates, and they feared lest, in the public estimation, or their own action, the two offices might be blended in their exercise. This was an age that required a great deal of vigilance on both the part of the State and Church, to prevent atheism from sapping the foundation of the Church, and anarchy from destroying our political freedom, we contended for under the form of Republicanism.

Methodists in the County.

At the beginning of the Nineteenth century, Methodism had no start in Mecklenburg county. In fact it was scarcely heard of in America. John Wesley, the father of Methodism, was born in 1703 and died in 1791. He was born in England, was not satisfied with the Episcopal Church, made what he thought were needed reforms in the Church of England, and was made sport of, the higher classes calling the new sect "Methodists." Their first two churches —one in Ferrel Town—in the extreme western part of Mallard Creek Township, called "Bethesda," now rotted down. The other is in Providence Township, named "Harrison" church. They were built about 1815. They began with the poorest people, that class above all others who would feel the need of a Saviour. The number of adherents soon doubled and trebled their start; but unfortunately, education at that time was at a low ebb. In and about 1825 and 1835, those in charge of the churches would allow almost any one to preach. In this way the church was brought into disrepute, and many things were permitted that if they had been better educated would not have wrought so much evil, and held back the Church in its onward march. By 1850 their ministry was much better prepared for the work they were engaged in. Camp meetings were very common at that time. At almost every church you would see log cabins in rows around the arbor, or church; and at some places there would be two rows of tents or cabins. These meetings would last from one to two weeks, and I would say here that camp meetings were not confined solely to the Methodists, but Baptists, and especially Presbyterians, held these meetings in the early years of the century. People would attend these meetings in covered wagons, going from fifty to one hundred miles.

The whole face, or appearance of the country has been

changed during the last hundred years, not only physically and intellectually, but theologically. When Methodists were firmly in the saddle, we had in earnest, "The Gospel on horseback." It should be added that a Methodist preacher was never known to ride a poor horse; he would always look after the welfare of his horse. This travel from one church to another, afforded him the only time he ever got to prepare his sermons; but then he had the advantage of using the same sermon at every church in his circuit. In the rapid march of time, the mile posts are plainly marked in Mecklenburg by the advancement of Methodism. We have seen its advent in the back woods of Mecklenburg in the early years of the Nineteenth century, we have witnessed its phenomenal growth, and before the close of the century in which it started on the race, it came to the goal, neck and neck with those who were far in the lead at the start. The Methodists are far behind some others in beautiful houses of worship, and schools for the education of their boys and girls; but judging the future by the past, the time is rapidly hastening when they will have schools rivaling Greensboro and other places.

Dr. David R. Dunlap and his brother-in-law, Brawley Oates, were the first men of learning and influence in Charlotte or in the county who espoused the claims set forth by Wesley, and followed by thousands since Dunlap and Oates have fallen asleep. They were not only active men in the Church, but took an active part in the affairs of the county. Their houses were known to all the ministers in this section of the State; they all had a standing invitation to make their houses their home when traveling from church to church, while on their circuit visiting their several charges.

To show the want of thorough education in the ministry of the Methodist Church, an anecdote of how preaching was carried on at old Bethesda, in Ferrel Town, about 1845, is related. There was a local Methodist preacher living near there by the name of Harvey Montgomery, a most worthy and estimable gentleman, a man of a fairly good education, but a slow talker. On the Sunday alluded to he was in the pulpit with Kinchin Howell sitting by his side. Howell was grossly ignorant of letters, could not even read, but was proficient in prayer, and was particularly fond of "exhorting." When the time arrived for preaching to begin, Mr. Montgomery went through the preliminary services and gave out his text. When the congregation was surprised to see Mr. Howell jump up and push Mr. Montgomery to one side saying, Harvey, you do the reading and let me do the 'spounding," and the service was concluded in the usual way, in perfect harmony, and all appeared pleased.

Education has done more for this branch of the Church during the last fifty years than any other creed or form of belief. In the first years of the century, infidelity was in the front rank, and had for those who espoused its cause many of the brightest minds in the whole country; but as camp meetings became common, and revivals were held in many places and Christians of every name participated in the protracted meetings, and there was wonderful manifestations of the divine power exhibited everywhere, the infidels were converted, or fled the country, taking their literature with them. The leading ministers will compare favorably with any other denomination; and all are working harmoniously together for the general good of our fellowmen, and the advancement of the Kingdom of Jesus Christ.

HARRISON METHODIST EPISCOPAL CHURCH, SOUTH.

Harrison Methodist Episcopal Church, South, is located on the extreme southern border of Mecklenburg county, North Carolina, and near the South Carolina line, on the waters of Clemb's branch, in South Carolina, and McAlpin's creek, in North Carolina, on the public road from Charlotte to Lancaster. It was organized in the latter part of the Eighteenth century, in the South Carolina Conference, which was organized in the year 1785. This church was built of hewn logs and knotched up in the old-fashioned way, covered with oak boards and the cracks between the logs filled in with clay mortar. The church was about forty feet long and thirty feet wide, with pulpit in one end and a large batten door in the other, with seats made of split slabs, as there were no saw mills in the country then. Harrison was the first Methodist church in Mecklenburg county, and one of the first in North Carolina; and, as church records were unknown in those days, little of the early history of the church has been preserved, but early in the Nineteenth century its membership consisted of only a few families.

As they were familiarly known by all that knew them, old uncle James Davis Johnathan and Daniel Mills were the founders and supporters of the church. Uncle Johnny was the licensed exhorter and Uncle Daniel the class leader, and in the absence of the preacher they would hold services, and as the circuit then embraced several counties, they only had preaching once a month by the pastor in charge. As the Presbyterian Church pre-occupied and held full possession of this country and Providence church had been organized in 1765, and every family that was able to have horses and vehicles attended Providence, and only those who were too poor to have these conveyances attended Harrison, the old log meeting house, as it was then called, and the new methods of Methodism were regarded scornfully, and the best of society were ashamed to be seen at Harrison. But in 1847, the South Carolina Conference appointed to the Charlotte circuit two very able preachers, Claudius H. Pritchard and William M. Barringer, the latter was a brother of the Hons. Victor, Monroe and Gen. Rufus Barringer, of North Carolina. In August of that year they held a great revival of religion at the Harrison log meeting house. The interest grew and the congregations became so large that it became necessary to erect a stand and a brush arbor in the grove. Services were held day and night for several weeks and the whole country for miles around was aroused on the subject of religion as it never had been before, scores were converted and joined the church and from the time of that meeting Methodism began to grow and became more respectable in the community and embraced many of the best and wealthiest families. Some of the members who joined them with their families were Capts. James B. Robinson, William Gaylor Stitt, Dr. Wm. A. Ardrey, Messrs. James H. Davis, Samuel A. Davis, James Monroe Davis, George D. Beckham, James R. Cunningham, Lee Patterson, Nicholas Davidson, John O. Moore, Robert Cunningham, James Patterson, Dr. John S. Porter and Mrs. Mansion and many others, a few of whom are yet living.

As a result of that meeting and the decayed and dilapidated condition of the old church which was then considered unsafe to have service in, in 1848 money began to be raised for the purpose of building a new church. A building committee was elected, of which Dr. Ardrey was chairman, the contracts were awarded to James Davis, of Union county. The new church was completed, paid for and then was dedicated by Rev. Jacob Hill, and is still standing and is the present house of worship. The building of this church was an epoch in the history of Methodism not only in this community, but in the M. E. Church at large, as the General Conference of 1844 passed resolutions reprimanding Bishop Andrew for marrying into a slave holding family, and informing him that his services would not be acceptable in some sections of the country. Owing to that controversy, the Southern delegates withdrew and in 1845 the Methodist Episcopal Church, South, was formed with Bishops Soule and Andrew at its head. The agitation of these vexed questions of slavery had not only disturbed the social and political quietude of our country, but it was threatening the life of all of our religious institutions, and it engulfed us into a civil war from 1860 to 1865. For undaunted courage and true heroism the world has never seen nor recorded its equal. This war forever settled the question of slavery in Church and State, but the Northern and Southern Churches have never been reunited. Harrison church, like all the other Southern churches, since the war has experienced many trials and changes to become adapted to the new and altered conditions of the country. Several churches have grown out from this original organization. Its first branch was Hebron M. E. Church, between Pineville and Charlotte. This church was built about the year 1850. Its founders were David P. Lee, Sampson Wolfe, John Campbell, and others. The next branch was the Pineville M. E. Church, which is located in a town of that name on the Charlotte, Columbia and Augusta Railroad. This church to-day stands as a monument to the late Samuel Younts, his sons John A. and W. S. Younts, and the late Dr. J. A. Ardrey. This church was founded about 1870. The third branch was Marvin M. E. Church; in Union county, a nice little brick building erected by a few good and devoted Christian men, in 1875. Its founders were Lloyd K. Rone, John W. Squires, T. J. Ezzell and Job Crane. And the last branch was Pleasant Hill, in Lancaster county, South Carolina, in 1880, founded by D. C. Wolfe, John Wolfe, John Davidson, James O. Bales, Lee Patterson, Solomon Harris and his sons.

The old church was transferred to the North Carolina Conference in 1889, when the State line was made the Conference line. It still has about the usual number of members and now, in 1902, money is subscribed and the erection of a new and modern church is begun. The building committee is W. E. Ardrey, chairman; W. E. Cunningham, secretary; John N. Harris, treasurer; James A. Kerr, H. N. Patterson, W. F. McGinn and James P. Ardrey, and we hope to complete the building by the end of this year, 1902.

In 1815 the Sugar Creek circuit of the Methodist Episcopal Church was composed of the following churches:

Harrison Meeting House, Bethel, Mt. Moriah, Rogers, Roses, McCorcles, Mayhews, Christenberrys, Martins, Charlotte, Chalk Level, Cithcoats, Hyatira, Wallases, Newhope, Howells. The presiding elder was Rev. Daniel Asbury; the preacher in charge was Rev. W. B. Barnett.

This circuit was then in the South Carolina Conference.

In 1818 the first Quarterly Conference was held at Harrison on March 14th. Rev. Jesse Richardson was presiding elder, and Rev. Reuben Tucker pastor. Rev. Jacob Hill was pastor in 1821.

Harrison has furnished the following ministers: Rev. W. S. Rone, Presiding Elder in the North Carolina Conference; Rev. R. S. Howie, of the Western North Carolina Conference; Rev. John Loyd Howie, of the Congregational Church; Rev. W. B. Lee, missionary to Brazil; Rev. John Davis, of the South Carolina Conference; Rev. John Owen, of the South Carolina Conference.

Roman Catholic Church.

The first start of the Roman Catholic Church in Charlotte was in 1836. Four years before this the Presbyterian Church was organized, which was the first Church organized in the town, more than fifty years after the people of Mecklenburg had declared themselves free from British rule. It is strange that religion should have been so tardy in making its power felt, after so much toil and suffering to establish our independence here in this town.

In 1836, Rev. Father McGinnis came here as a missionary, and secured a house to live in and taught school in one room, had one room for a church in which he held worship. He and his sister also lived there. The house, a frame building, stood on the lot now owned and occupied by Dr. John R. Irwin. He was said to have been a fine scholar and a good teacher. The family of Nolands, the Hartys, John Rouche and others from the surrounding country attended church here. Mr. McGinnis only stayed one or two years, after which service was held by missionaries, as it was convenient for one to come, until a church was built in 1851. The corner stone was laid by Rev. J. J. O'Connell, D. D. The church was built by Patrick Harty and Ed. Lonergan. Henry Severs carried the brick. The church was small, like the congregation, but in the last fifty years the membership has increased so rapidly, the old church has been torn away, and a handsome structure fills its place, keeping pace with the growing city, and the increasing congregation. The present large and handsome church was built in 1890. Many of the best citizens of the town now hold their membership there. Fifty years has made wonderful changes in Charlotte, and in nothing do we see it more than in the magnificent temples of worship that arise in the various wards, to point passers by to a lasting habitation in the world to come.

The Associate Reformed Presbyterians.

In Mecklenburg county this body of Christians were not very numerous one hundred years ago. Only in certain sections of the county were they sufficiently numerous to have a house of worship. About 1795 Gilead church, and Steele Creek—to distinguish it from the Presbyterian church—it was called "Little Steele Creek." It is more than probable these were the two first churches by that denomination. The building of Gilead church was first intended to be at Baker's Grave Yard, about one and a half miles north of the church. This old burying place was used long before any church was built. The Rev. John Thompson, a Presbyterian minister, and his son-in-law, —. —. Baker, were the first persons to be buried there. Also Maj. John Davidson's sister, Mary, who married a Mr. Price, and many of her descendants. The church (Gilead) was built fifteen miles from Charlotte, on the Beattie's Ford Road, on the spot once occupied by a fort, to protect the early settlers' cattle and horses from roving bands of Indians. Miss Nilley Torrance, who died more than fifty years ago, said that she had often seen the fort when hunting her father's cattle and horses. She lived with her sister Jane, who married Andrew Barry, a son of the patriot, Richard Barry. Their offspring still occupy the old homestead; but how much of interest, especially of the people who once lived in this section, has passed away unhonored and unsung, not even noted down that it might be made known to the children, in the shape of legends or fairy tales, to preserve the local civilization of the Eighteenth century.

Rev. James McKnight was probably the most noted man, and the hardest worked preacher of the Associated Reformed Presbyterian Church. Rev. John Boyce was the first pastor of Gilead. He was in charge of Coddle Creek, Prosperity, Gilead and Hopewell, in South Carolina. He could not have given more than one-fourth of his time to either one of his several charges. He could not have continued here more than five years, as he died March 18, 1793, and was buried at Hopewell, in South Carolina. The second pastor of Gilead was Rev. James McKnight. He had charge of Gilead, Coddle Creek, and Prosperity; installed in 1797. He continued to serve these churches for many years and ended his course September 17, 1831. He was a most remarkable preacher. Two sermons a day was his ordinary rule. Beginning by 10 o'clock, and giving a short interval for refreshments, he would preach some times until it was so dark he would call for candles to read and sing the last Psalm. The stars would be shining brightly before the people would reach home, if they had but two or three miles to go. It was common for them to provide themselves with pine torches to light them home.

Rev. John Hunter, a man of great ability, immensely popular with the people, and was always heard gladly by the common people. He had a peculiar intonation of voice that always held the attention of his audience. He was installed at Gilead in 1844 for half his time, and at Prosperity. After several years he was transferred to Sardis, and remained there till he had run his course. At Gilead he was a welcome visitor, and loved by all his people.

Rev. Alexander Ranson, D. D., was one of the ablest men in the ministry of any church. He was pastor of Gilead and Prosperity for eighteen or twenty years. His neighbors and those who knew him best, thought he was one of the best men living in the world. Rev. R. T. Taylor served Prosperity and Gilead after Mr. Hunter, for about ten years; and he was followed by Dr. Ranson, who served the churches with great acceptability. The two churches paid him a very small pittance. His wife was exceedingly delicate, but when able, would teach school. Dr. Ranson had many warm friends who contributed much to render the last years of his life bright and pleasant, although his bodily pain was very great. A son and daughter soon followed him to the spirit world. The instruction given by such a man, we will expect to hear from as it flows on down the stream of time. Much of the good being done all through the upper end of Mecklenburg is due to the godly life of Dr. Alexander Ranson.

Rev. J. T. Chalmers, who died several years ago, preached at Little Steele Creek and accomplished a great deal of good. In a previous place an account of that part of the county is given, and will not be rehearsed here.

His son, Rev. Dr. J. C. Chalmers, was a man of feeble physical frame, but of a giant intellect. He began preaching in South Carolina, but in after years became pastor of the First Church in Charlotte. He continued pastor of the First Church until 1900, when his health became too feeble, when he went to Mexico hoping to regain his health. But his work appeared to be done. He arrived home about 1902, and gradually sank to rest in the spring of the same year.

Rev. J. G. McLaughlin is probably the oldest minister in the State—active minister. He is 83. He has been relieved of the burden of Back Creek church, and only preaches when he feels able. He has been pastor of the Church for many years, and will remain with the people while life lasts. A few years ago he was sorely tried in the furnace of affliction. He lost his wife and three grown children in one season with fever. It looked as if he was to be tried as Job; but he had many friends that proved to be friends in deed. He is still cheerful as the years go by, knowing that he has to wait but a little while longer. All the churches of this denomination are in a prosperous condition. For the last hundred years they have been very cautious to have all their ministry educated men. That being an absolute necessity to preserve the honorable standing of the Church, not only in Mecklenburg, but throughout the country. And it will not be amiss to say their ministry of to-day are in the van with the leaders of any other denomination.

As many things in this county are dated before or after the war, we will say this denomination had no foothold in

Charlotte in ante-bellum times. Probably Maj. Jennings B. Kerr's family was the only "seceders" in the town.

Where the Queen City Hotel now stands was the first church they ever had. It would seat probably 200 people, ten years ago. Now they have two most elegant churches, with two of the best preachers in the city. They are now reaching out, lengthening their cords and strengthening their stakes.

In the last half of the Nineteenth century there has been a wonderful growth in all denominations. This was to be expected, as the population came from various quarters, and brought the seeds of their religion with them, as there are few people but who are more or less biased in their religious views.

The Lutheran Church.

There was no Lutheran Church or minister in Mecklenburg county prior to 1850. There was but few, if any, German emigrants that ever stopped in this county. Nearly all stopped in Rowan, Cabarrus and Catawba counties. These counties were largely settled with Dutch, consequently they have a large following of Lutherans. In 1885 a large and elegant Lutheran church (St. Mark's) was completed. For several years it was served by Rev. W. S. Bowman, D. D., who came from Charleston, S. C. He was a very learned man, of great piety, and was much esteemed by all the good people of the city, without regard to race or denomination. His health became too feeble to perform the duties of pastor, tendered his resignation and in a short time was gathered to his fathers at a ripe old age.

In the year 1898 the services of Rev. R. C. Holland, D. D., was secured. He gives very general satisfaction to his people, and is popular with the combined ministry of the city.

The Baptist Denomination.

The Baptist denomination was almost wholly unknown in the county fifty years ago. They started with only two or three families in the town, and scarcely a half dozen in the county. They have grown to occupy at least the third or fourth place in point of numbers in the city. Their leading ministers are the peers of any in the county. The Rev. A. L. Stough, D. D., of Pineville, was chaplain of the Thirty-seventh Regiment, N. C. T., in the late Civil War. He did not hesitate to do his duty, whether in hospital or field, without favor or affection. He is now becoming an old man, has labored many years in the Master's vineyard, and is still hale and hearty, and looks as if he would be able for much service for several years to come.

I am aware that it is not considered good taste to criticise the living, but as the name of the author is always obtainable, I hope no one will deny me the pleasure of bearing testimony to the patriotism of those who sacrificed the pleasures of home for the hardships and privations of a soldier's life in the tented field. Chaplain Stough deserved well of his brother Christians. He labored in camp, denouncing wickedness in high places, without the fear of officers before his eyes. I have seen him passing among the wounded at the field hospital, carrying two canteens, one containing water and the other whiskey, administering to the urgent calls of the wounded and dying Confederate soldiers. At all hours of the day and night could this be seen.

Rev. A. L. Stough deserves a monument to preserve his devotion to the welfare of the Confederate soldier. His good name will ever remain green with all classes of Christians, with whom he has come in contact.

In another place Dr. Pritchard has been spoken of as the boys' friend. He was the mainstay of the Baptist Church for many years; but he served his day, and has gone up higher, as the student passes from the Academy to the University. The Baptist churches of the city are ably served by men entirely devoted to the cause of Christ. The increase of the numbers of membership has been phenomenal, and requires a continual lengthening of cords and strengthening of stakes to provide room to accommodate all who come. We are pleased to note the fact that all denominations are getting closer together than they have ever been before. Is it not a sign of the coming of the millenium?

Rock Springs Burying Ground.

Rock Springs burying ground is in the eastern part of the county. There is no data by which any one can tell when the first grave was dug in this quiet and secluded spot. From what we know of the early history of the county, Rocky River and Sugar Creek were the first churches established in the county; but we have undoubted evidence that there were places of burying the dead several years before any church was built. And it may be so here. At any rate, there is no church nearer than Philadelphia, and it is at least one and a half miles distant. Whether the people thought a church would be built in the distant future, we have no way of telling. But in those early days the people thought it no hardship to ride ten to twenty miles to attend church, and to enquire after the welfare of their friends and kindred. Here we find a city of almost forgotten dead. A few tombstones are standing of as beautiful marble as we now see in well-kept cemeteries. Others are of very dark stone, but well polished. Some are soap-stone, and some look as if they had been plank, and handsomely dressed; while some graves look as if an ordinary stone had been placed at either end. But very few have been buried in the last seventy-five years. The graveyard is on the northwest side of the road leading from Mint Hill to the Stanly corner, Marven, Albemarle, etc. It has been enclosed with a rock wall. It is now nearly flat, can be walked over anywhere. There was one acre of ground enclosed, and looks as if it was all used up. There was a ditch four or six feet wide, and probably as deep, around the four sides; the wall was inside the ditch. There are but few large trees among the tombs, but full of small growth.

Some of the names and dates we found are given:

Maj. James Harris, born Dec. 25, 1772, died Sept. 7,

1811; Samuel L. Harris, born 1767, died 1798; Mary Harris, born July 14, 1749, aged 73.

Catherine Maxwell, born 1774, died 1825.

Elizabeth Wilson, born in the year 1800, died in 1832.

Adam Alexander (one of the signers of the Declaration), died Nov. 13, 1798, aged 70 years and 7 months; Mary, his wife, died Nov. 26, 1813, aged 78 years, 3 months.

Robert Queery, died Aug. 25, 1827, aged 64 years.

Samuel Harris, died 1825, aged 83; Margaret Harris, died 1782, aged 58; Jane Harris, died 1797, aged 42. (One wide tombstone.)

Wm. Morris, died 1804, aged 59.

Elizabeth Morris, born 1750, died 1821.

Hannah Moore, died 1821, aged 58.

Elizabeth Moore, died 1811, aged 18.

Elizabeth Rabb, died 1792, aged 40.

Andrew Rodgers, died 1792, aged 25.

Elizabeth Wilson, died 1802.

No person now living can tell us of the hundreds who sleep in this almost forgotten spot. Was there no historian near this silent city to hand down to the future, that generations yet unborn may know what manner of people preceded them, or are we to lose the labors of all those who preceded us on account of not keeping record? We are truly a people who make history, but we have been too negligent about preserving it. Others come in and rob us of a well-earned fame in many things we have been remiss in not asserting our rights.

Sugar Creek Church.

Near the gate of Sugar Creek's second graveyard, south of the road, is to be seen the stone that marks the grave of Rev. Samuel C. Caldwell, a grand-son of Alexander Craighead, whose ashes rest in the first cemetery, who died sixty years before Mr. Caldwell finished his course.

The spot which he selected, and where they made his grave, was just beneath that part of the old log house where the communion table was spread (in that day had long tables that extended clear across the church, with suitable benches, so that communicants could sit around the table to partake of the feast; when one table was served they would give way to others, until all were served), from which he had so often dispensed the emblems of Christ crucified; where he took the vows of ordination, and where he knelt, when by prayers and laying on of the hands of the Presbytery, he was set apart to the work of the ministry. Though the war for liberty and independence had ended in glorious triumph several years before the beginning of Mr. Caldwell's ministry, yet it was followed by another conflict, involving far more sacred principles and interests than those which had been so heroically defended. Following that seven years' war came in like a flood, the rise and rapid spread, over many parts of the country, and particularly over Mecklenburg county, the proud waters of French infidelity; threatening the liberty of those whom the truths of the Gospel make free. Caldwell and Wallis, of Providence, were found in the thickest of the fight with this foe, in their respective congregations. Reared in times which tried men's souls and developed some of the grandest characters, both these men proved themselves worthy sons of their noble ancestors, and worthy defenders of the precious truths of the Gospel. An infidel club had been organized for the purpose of propagating their philosophy, which called in question everything connected with the Bible and its claims upon the human reason and conscience. The burning question discussed on all occasions was, whether the Bible or reason should be the guide of human conscience. This discussion was often hot and gave rise to bitter contests.

The society above mentioned gathered its members from Sugar Creek, Providence and Steele Creek, and met at a point somewhere between those three settlements. They had a library well supplied with works written in defense of infidel views of religion and morality. This society embraced men of wealth and talent.

Wallis, then pastor of Providence and Steele Creek, and Caldwell, of Sugar Creek, met these enemies of the Christian religion with fearless and unflinching fidelity. Wallis prepared a pamphlet of marked ability, and well adapted to meet the demands of truth and righteousness, which was widely circulated.

So while Sugar Creek was found in the front ranks of those who rose up to defend human rights and liberty, through her Caldwell, and Wallis, born and reared in her bounds, she was found equally faithful and efficient in defending the liberty of the sons of God. The forces of infidelity seems to have met their final and almost complete overthrow in the great revival of 1802. An incident connected with that infidel club was related to me by an old uncle, who removed away from Providence to Tennessee about 1803, and who was then a full grown man, and a subject of the saving work of the revival.

One of the members of the club of infidels was taken seriously ill, and it soon became evident that his end was near. His infidel friends were about his bed, and much concerned lest the man should abandon his infidelity in the hour of death. They encouraged him to hold to his philosophy, repeating the exhortation, "Stick to it." But the foundation of sand was giving way before the poor soul, and at last he replied: "It is hard to stick when there is nothing to stick to." And now, where that soul-destroying form of error attempted to overthrow the religion of the Christ, are found temples of truth, where the riches of Jesus are proclaimed every Sabbath, but scarcely a vestige remains of the influence of the infidel club. Now and then we may hear of one of their old books which have survived, hidden away under the dust of years, a forgotten, worthless, worm-eaten thing.

Though it has been the privilege of the writer to spend nearly all his life in Mecklenburg county, and work for the Master in many of its many churches, he has never, except in one instance, found any attempt to circulate the writings of infidels, whose works were found in that old library. The method by which it was sent abroad was as unusual as it was effective. And though it may at first be surprising when stated, that it was an elder in the Presbyterian Church who was found scattering those infidel teachings, yet the opinion is ventured that the orthodox of all Mecklenburg orthodoxy will approve his work. The good brother caught at this business, had by some means got possession of one of those pernicious books, and being one of the most marked shots in the county, he conceived the idea of pasting a number of the leaves together sufficient to make the thickness required. He would then take his wad-cutter and, driving it down through the book, supply himself for a day's tramp after birds. And by night there was much scattering of infidel sentiments and feathers.

The building which occupied a part of the graveyard, in which Caldwell was buried, was the second house built by the congregation. It was a plain, substantial log house. In order to secure room for the large numbers who came to worship there, the house was made of two lengths of logs, joined together at the middle by a crib of short logs, so put together as to form a recess on the inside and a jutting out of several feet from the main side wall. In this house the congregation convened until some time towards the latter part of his ministry, when the third house was erected, a brick structure, a little north of the second house, and on the same side of the road.

ABRAHAM ALEXANDER.

Towards the middle of the yard, near two large trees, is the grave of Abraham Alexander, the chairman of the famous Mecklenburg Convention of 1775. On his unpretending tombstone is found the inscription: "Abraham Alexander, died April 23, 1786, aged 68 years. 'Let me die the death of the righteous, and let my last end be like His.'" He was a marked character and influence, both in Church and State, as manifested by the prominent positions in which he was placed by his fellow men. He was a prominent magistrate, an officer which meant more in that day than in the present time. He lived long enough after the Declaration of Independence, in Charlotte, to see its lofty principles triumphantly maintained, and its solemn determinations executed. His son, Joab, took his place as an elder of the church and magistrate of the county. He has but one great-grandson in this county, Mr. J. P. Alexander, now an elder in the Second Presbyterian Church, of Charlotte.

WILLIAM ALEXANDER.

Another man of that day, William Alexander, is worthy of mention as a man of courage, who could be trusted as a leader of men. He was known by the name of "Black Billy," given to distinguish him from many other Alexanders in the same and surrounding neighborhoods. The Regulators, an organization of citizens, formed, under the provocations and impositions of the governor, were giving him trouble. The Governor had ordered out the militia of the western counties to join the command of Gen. Waddell. He was ordered to wait at Salisbury for the military to gather, and was delaying his march to join the Governor until a supply of ammunition should reach him. The wagons

which were bringing powder had reached a point near where
Concord now stands, on their way from Charlotte, and encamped for the night. A plan was at once formed for the
destruction of the powder. Nine men of Rocky River (the
descendants of some of those men are now living in that
congregation) and William Alexander, of Sugar Creek, as
their leader, bound themselves by an oath to stand together
in the undertaking and to keep each other's part in it a secret,
blacked their faces and disguised themselves as Indians and
about daybreak captured the convoy. The band permitted
the drivers and their teams and the guard to go unharmed,
and then made a pile of the powder on the ground, laid a
train for some distance and set fire to it.

Steele Creek Church.

This is one of the remarkable seven churches that were organized in Mecklenburg county, or rather the place was agreed upon, and worship conducted by the early settlers for a number of years before a temple was built and dedicated to the worship of God. In this early period when the people were few and lived far apart, the roads frequently impassible in the winter season, all their undertakings were necessarily slow of progress. But they acted wisely in securing eligible locations for the different churches. Sugar Creek, near the centre; Rocky River, in the east; Poplar Tent towards the north; Centre, northwest; Hopewell, ten miles north of the centre; Providence, to the south; Steele Creek to the west. This last was like her sisters, had a surrounding population of the best people in the world. Originally the lands around Steele Creek were fertile and valuable. Away from the water courses the lands were covered with tall grass and the wild pea vine; was indeed a prairie, beautiful in its loveliness, undisturbed save only by the foot of the Red men, the deer and the buffalo, and the smaller animals and variety of birds, which gave the appearance of Eden's beauteous bowers as described by Milton. The inhabitants were characterized for their industry, patriotism, morality and love of fair play; they were also noted for their love and reverence for truth and religion. Rev. Hugh McAden, Rev. Elihu Spencer, and Rev. Robert McMordie at different times visited this church as missionaries, as occasion would permit. This was the only kind of ministerial service any of the churches had for several years.

As a place of worship, we can readily see the people were accustomed to assemble at this point, near where the church now stands, but a house of worship was not erected till the year 1762.

In the year 1706 was organized the first Presbytery in

America, consisting of seven ministers and their churches, and this continued the only advisory and governing body till 1717. The Church by this time had so increased it was considered best to sub-divide it into three other Presbyteries, which were to constitute a Synod, which should meet once a year. For several years after Steele Creek Church was organized, it had to be watched over and guarded by missionaries and supplies wherever they could be obtained. It will be remembered that when Rev. Alexander Craighead ended his successful labors in March, 1766, he was the solitary minister between the Yadkin and the Catawba. From this time there was no settled minister, for some years, south of the Yadkin.

Steele Creek's first pastor was Rev. Robert Henry, from Donegal Presbytery. He lived but a few months and he was removed by death. The first bench of ruling elders we have any account of, in 1767, were William Barnett, Walter Davis, Robert Irwin, Hugh Parks, David Freeman, Joseph Swann, Zaccheus Wilson, and Andrew McNeely. For ten years their appears to be a lapse of service, at any rate of ministerial service. But little service of a regular character was enjoyed until after the war of independence. There is no portion of the State whose early record presents a more glowing page of patriotism and valor than Mecklenburg, of which Steele Creek is a component part. It is not boasting too much to say it is in Mecklenburg we find the birthplace of American liberty. On the 20th of May, 1775, two of the signers of the Declaration of Independence, Col. Robert Irwin and Zaccheus Wilson, were elders in Steele Creek Church. Of the twenty-seven members who composed that convention, nine were known to have been elders, and one a minister of the Gospel, Rev. Hezekiah J. Balch. Col. Irwin was a busy man in all the conventions held during the war, and from 1778 to 1800, he served as a member of the Legislature from Mecklenburg county.

Debating societies, formed for political purposes, were common in those days. One of these societies was formed as near as possible in a central position between Sugar Creek, Steele Creek and Providence. It proved to be more for the interest of infidelity than for politics. The battle between the crown and the people had been fought, and the people were victorious. During this long night of darkness the enemy had come in and sown the tares. Infidelity with a brazen front, was defiant, and threatened like an avalanche to overrun the whole country; to extinguish the best hopes of man—yes, threatened the annihilation of the Church, and the ruin of her Lord's authority. The question was debated, "What should govern conscience, philosophy, or the Bible?" At this time the authority of the Bible underwent a sifting discussion, such as Carolina had never seen, and may never see again. About this time a most wonderful revival spread all over the country. At this time all bad and uncharitable feeling subsided, and Methodists, Episcopalians, Presbyterians and Baptists all worshipped together. These were wonderful meetings. The Holy Spirit did not respect the denominational names by which they were called.

In 1795, Concord Presbytery was set off from Orange, and this county remained in Concord for seventy-five years, but is now in Mecklenburg Presbytery. In 1778 Rev. James McRee was elected pastor, and gave general satisfaction. During his term as pastor, the church building was enlarged, as the congregation had increased in numbers, and at that day was considered very elegant. Mr. McRee did much to introduce Watt's Hymns and Psalms instead of Rouse's version. All who held to only Rouse's version of the Psalms were called "seceders."

Rev. Mr. McRee was born in Iredell county, N. C., in 1752, near where Centre church was afterwards built. At this period all this territory belonged to Anson county. He preached at Steele Creek about twenty years. He said: "Often I have ridden in the morning to Bethel (in S. C.), Providence, Sugar Creek, and Hopewell and preached (two sermons), and returned home in the evening of the same day." He preached at Centre for many years, and wound up his course at his son's-in-law, Col. Davidson, in Buncombe county, in the 88th year of his age. He deserved well of his country.

In 1772-'74 Rev. William Blackstock came from Ireland and was ordained by the Associate Reformed Presbytery of the Carolinas, and in 1794 he organized a church called "Lower Steele Creek," eight miles below the first Steele Creek church. The following persons were elected elders, viz.: James Grier, James Harris, James Fox, William Ferguson and Alexander Scott. Mr. Blackstock was elected pastor, and served a few years. Messrs. Dixon and McMillan were the first Associate ministers who came to this county. Mr. McMillan was soon dismissed for indulging too freely in the intoxicating bowl. Afterwards came Revs. Moore, Crie, White and Pringle. They each preached at Lower Steele Creek, and neighboring churches. The early ministers had a vast amount of work to do, and received but little sympathy, or remuneration of any other kind, except a self-consciousness of having done their duty; but they have accomplished wonders for the Church.

It must not be concluded that all the people of the county, or of Steele Creek were Christians—that none were reprobates; for this would lead people to believe that the former times were better than at a later day. Human nature is the same now as it was in the days of the American revolution. Infidelity was ten fold more rampant a century ago in Mecklenburg, than it is to-day; it is unpopular now, and the leaders of thought as, of fashion, do not consider it politic to advocate that which would bring reproach upon society. This part of Mecklenburg—about 1832—became so infected with intemperance, infidelity and universalism, that a large part of Steele Creek and the adjoining country ceased to attend church. And soon followed a fearful deluge of sickness, and many deaths, frequently requiring three and four funerals in a day. This spread a dark pall over the people, and made them think, "Were they being punished for their unbelief?" This falling away of so many from the ordinances of the church, and the moving away of so many on account of sickness, was a sore and heavy trial for the Church. The sickness or bad state of health kept up with more or less severity for several years. The pastor, Rev. Mr. Watson, seemed to suffer the same as his people, and his health became so enfeebled that he resigned in 1840. Notwithstanding this heavy scourge, Steele Creek has been greatly blessed, including Lower Steele Creek and Pleasant Hill. They increased in population, were patriotic, believed in education, and were a church loving people. Steele Creek was organized as a place of worship one hundred and forty years ago; and as compared with other sections, she has a right to be proud of her people. In her first settlement and patriotic impulses to move forward in establishing independence; and to prove a good citizenship by promptly sending forward her contingent of brave men to repel the enemy in 1812 to 1814, when the New England States not only refused troops, but threatened to secede from the union if the war was not immediately stopped. Again, in 1846, aided in furnishing her quota of men to fill up the cavalry company commanded by Capts. E. C. Davidson and J. K. Harrison, for service in Mexico. Our people are emphatically a peace loving people, but by no means will they suffer wrong with impunity, as was abundantly shown in the war between the States.

Many bright names could be mentioned as having taken a noble part in the early history of Mecklenburg, either in aiding to achieve independence, or in maintaining a republican form of government. The people well understood the necessity of having the ruling class well qualified by education, and equally as necessary that the common people should enjoy the blessing of education.

Providence Church.

In looking over the list of early settlers of that portion of the State that was laid off as Mecklenburg county, in that portion bordering on South Carolina, and afterwards called Providence, I find that Henry Downs moved from Pennsylvania to this section about the year 1760. He was elected Captain of Militia for Providence District, or "beat." He was also made an elder in Providence church, which church was built and organized in 1762. He was also appointed a civil officer, or a Justice of the Peace. He was one of the signers of the Declaration of Independence on the 20th of May, 1775, in Charlotte. Mr. Downs was now getting too old for military service; but his son Thomas was young and active, and entered the service with alacrity. He was with Gen. Gates in South Carolina in the battle of Camden, then as bushwhackers hanging on the flanks of Cornwallis' army, as he came towards Charlotte; and assisted in giving the British a warm reception around the old log court house that stood in the public square, and on the Salisbury road for five miles. Tarlton must have suffered severely to get and to hold what he captured around Charlotte, or he would not have called the place "A Hornet's Nest." The Downs family still own and occupy two hundred acres of the original grant that was issued by George the IV. Many of these old places are handed down from sire to son for several generations.

George McKee emigrated to this section with the first settlers of the county. He was a pillar of both Church and State in those early years, being an elder in Providence, and also a Justice of the Peace. When the republic was young, many civil cases as well as criminal, were adjudicated by a Justice of the Peace.

Rev. James Wallace was the first pastor of Providence church. For a number of years after the first church was built, it was occupied by transient preachers, or by temporary supplies, especially in the country one hundred to two hundred miles from the sea coast. The law of custom had decided that the destruction of manuscripts that had been left by religiously disposed persons was a part of preparation for death, as solemn and indispensable as the making the last will and testament. So very little of the records of thoughts of these men have been preserved from destruction. And the unfortunate burning of some houses, leaves the present generation in wondering ignorance of the trials, and energy, and principles of those brave and good men. The grave of but one minister can only be found in Providence burying ground for the first century of the church's existence. When you enter this "old city of the dead," you see the names of some of the leading men who planted the Gospel and civil liberty in the wilderness of the Western world. Among the chiseled names of Stitt, Potts, McKee, Rea, Patterson, McCullock, and Matthews, the oldest of which bears date of 1764. The Rev. James Wallace, who served the church from 1792 to 1819. A lengthy pastorate for that period. Settlements in this part of the county were made about the same time as those in Hopewell, Sugar Creek and Rocky River, and were the same kind of people. Mr. Wallace married a daughter of John McKnitt Alexander, who labored with him in the ministry, and proved a help indeed. Both were buried by the side of those they labored with for more than a quarter of a century in much love and harmony.

In this section the good people were in the habit of assembling in a grove, near where the present church now stands, for several years to hold divine worship. After a while they built a log "meeting house" where stated worship was held, and in 1765 the church was organized and has continued ever since to be the central point in all this section of the county. The leading spirits of these early days were Andrew Rea, Archibald Crocket, Joshua Ramsay, and Aaron Howie. Such men as these encountered and bushwhacked

Cornwallis' army as he marched through Providence, causing severe hardships to the people.

The annoyance of the people—the non-combatants—were put to, the malicious destruction of property, private concerns, taking away the comforts and often the necessities of life, was very trying to the patriotism and patience of all who loved the cause of liberty. But I am glad to say that but few "took protection" in all the bounds of Mecklenburg. In 1802 a great religious revival swept over this country as a storm, in which Mr. Wallis took an active part. This revival lasted for several years, and it is hoped forever downed the miserable infidelity that had its origin in the French revolution during the last decade of the Eighteenth century. The following agreement between the churches of Clear Creek (now called Philadelphia), has been preserved by Mr. William Queary.

"WHEREAS, The representatives of both congregations doth unanimously agree among themselves, in the name of both the aforesaid congregations, to stand and abide by each other from time to time through all difficulties, in order to obtain the labors of a gospel minister, that is to say, the one-half of his labors to one congregation, and the other to the other. And for a true and sincere union for the truth of the aforesaid articles, the representation of both congregations hath hereunto subscribed their names, January 27, 1770.

"New Providence: John Ramsay, James Linn, John Hagens, James Houston, Andrew Reah, James Draffen, James Johnston, James Teate, Thomas Black, Robert Stewart.

"Clear Creek: Adam Alexander, Matthew Stewart, John Queary, Michael Leggett, John Ford."

Five years later two of the men who signed this agreement signed the Declaration of Independence in Charlotte, May 20, 1775, Adam Alexander and John Queary, which shows that they were public-spirited men, patriotic and determined in whatever business they engaged.

John Stitt died about sixty years ago, and was an elder and influential man, and was a leading citizen in the neighborhood. We mention a few of the most prominent, as it would take too much room to mention all the good and true men that are worthy of being placed high up in the niche of fame. A few others have a right to be noticed ere we close this chapter. Col. Solomon Reid was an important man, that both Church and State thought well of and the four from this muster beat who had the moral courage to sign the immortal Declaration of Independence, with their compeers, Henry Downs, Neil Morrison, Robert Harris, and John Queary.

Richard Peoples, elder in Sardis church, but a citizen of Providence, was a merchant and postmaster of Hemphill's Store. He was a large slave holder and a successful farmer. His son Richard now owns his father's farm. He was a true Confederate, and served throughout the war in Brem's Battery, afterwards Graham's, and then Williams'.

Flowers Now and One Hundred Years Ago.

Times and customs have ever been subject to change, but never until the last thirty years did fashion levy upon flowers—the prototype of immortality—to adorn the hymeneal altar, or grace the sacred desk, or strew above the bier of loved ones, or scatter immortelles over the graves of patriots. It is well that the Nineteenth century—the last third of the century—inaugurated this beautiful custom that typifies the immortality that awaits us in the life beyond the grave.

Fifty years or less have elapsed since any one save a botanist, knew anything of flowers, what they represented, or what their language was. It was a rare thing that any kind was met with save the wild flower that was indigenous to our fields and woods; the time had not come to cultivate them for their beauty and their fragrance. The Nineteenth century was two-thirds gone before a bouquet of roses did honor to the sacred desk while the minister proclaimed the beautiful parables as exemplified by the Saviour in his sermons. Two-thirds of the century was gone before the church or the private parlor was decorated with rich and rare flowers where the blushing bride was made an help meet for the man of her choice. And last but not least, they are the sweet emblems of the morning of the resurrection, when those who are considered worthy to join the grand caravan, rise to meet the Lord in the air.

In 1894, when Senator Vance returned from Florida and there was a large political meeting being held in the Auditorium between Tryon and Church, on Sixth street, the entire audience commenced shouting for Gov. Vance—men and women standing up, waving flags and hats and handkerchiefs, and throwing flowers and wreaths and boquets around him till he was nearly covered. The crowd cheered and called for him until he was helped upon the stage, and he was so choked with emotion that he could not speak for several minutes. At last he said: "My friends, I am glad to see you; my physicians have forbidden me to speak, so you must excuse me." Almost a wagon load of flowers were thrown around him. Here the flowers spoke a silent language more powerful than words. They foreshadowed his approaching dissolution of body and spirit, and the eternal joys of the Easter awakening that will bloom till cycles cease to run. It was a happy thought to lift the exquisite floral offering from its long sleep of inactivity, to its place of honor and fragrance. Flowers add much to the pleasures of country life, where books and papers are not so easily procured. Nothing we can contribute to the sick is so cheery as a handsome bouquet, freshly plucked from one's own garden of well-attended roses and flowers.

The Old Four-Horse Stage.

It is now impossible to say when the line of stages was first put on the road communicating between the North and South by the way of Charlotte. It was in the first years of the Nineteenth century, or it may be at an earlier period, but as far back as 1830, the stage coach was looked for with a great deal of solicitude, particularly for the mail. It carried but few passengers, as the ordinary charge was ten cents a mile, and it would be much cheaper to go on horseback. Letter postage was 25 cents, and Newspapers also cost high; but at that time but few papers were taken, and letters were only written when under the greatest stress of circumstances. A person going on a long journey to another State several hundred miles, would frequently have a quantity of letters to carry for his friends, and for those who were kind enough to entertain him at night as he passed along. The stage had the contract for carrying the mails, and gave the best attention, or served the government first; that is, would deliver the mail first, and then the passengers. Seventy years ago the stage delivered the mail here every other day, and that was the only mail expected. A weekly mail was carried horse-back to Statesville, which was considered quite an honor to be waited on so frequently.

In the olden time when the stage coach was the most expeditious mode of traveling, and the most rapid way to transmit the mail, as a precursor to let the people know of the approach of the United States mail, a long, tin horn, probably five feet long, was carried by the driver (and the driver was always a fearless white man) who practiced blowing it until he was an expert in winding his blast until the sound was eagerly listened for by those who anticipated its coming. When the roads were good, a very good speed was attained. They usually kept a relay of horses every ten of fifteen miles, and a man was employed to care for the horses and have them harnessed ready for the exchange. The drivers were so expert with the whip they could pick a buck fly from the ears of the front team, and not touch the horse. In the western part of the State, and still farther west, it became necessary to arm the driver to protect his passengers and any valuables he might be transporting. An efficient mode of arming the driver was to furnish him with a double-barrel shot gun, cut off short so it could be carried in the pants leg, with a hole cut in the bottom of his boot, so when ordered by the bandit to "throw up his hands," he could throw up his foot and down the robber when not expecting it. In the olden times the occupation of the stage driver was anything else than a sinecure.

Lee Dunlap Kills James Gleason.

In October, 1868, an election was held in Charlotte, when a political dispute arose between Lee Dunlap, colored, and Charley Elms. Very ugly words were used, and Elms threatened to shoot Dunlap, whereupon Dunlap cursed him and pulled his shirt front open and dared him to shoot. Elms turned off from the negro and Mr. James Gleason remonstrated with him, when the negro shot and killed him. He was at once put in jail. There was still a large force of Federal soldiers camped around town that was a threat that had a strong tendency to keep the negroes in a state of insubordination, and made them exceedingly impudent. After keeping Dunlap in jail for a month or two, the Federal commander sent him to Raleigh to be tried by the Federal District Court—so said. The noted Tim Lee was sheriff of Wake, and he kept Dunlap for several months as his waiting boy, and in the course of six months he went to Ohio without a trial, and has never returned.

S. A. Harris was Mayor of the town at the surrender, and was removed by Gov. Holden, Dr. H. M. Pritchard appointed, then Mr. Bizel, then F. M. Ahrens. These appear to have held the office but a short while.

In January, 1866, S. A. Harris was elected and held the office till Maj. C. Dowd was elected in January, 1869. During Dowd's term of office the Board of Aldermen discontinued burying in the old cemetery. The new one was marked off, lots were sold, and some persons moved their dead to the new cemetery.

The manufactories of the city were: Rock Island Woolen Mills, John Wilkes' Foundry and Machine Shop, Tatum, Sykes & Company's steam work shop, J. Trotter's carriage shop, Barnhardt & Company's steam work shop, Tiddy & McCoy's marble cutting works, F. A. McNinch's marble cutting works, Charles Wilson's carriage shop, A. H. Creswell's carriage shop, and Robert Shaw & Son's saddle and harness shop. Groot, Kuck & Co. were at this time operating a distillery in Charlotte.

The list of lawyers then was an able one, not so numerous as we have now, but the names of some will last through all time: Burwell & Grier, F. S. DeWolfe, S. W. Davis, W. F. Davidson, Hutchison & Brown, R. D. Osborne, Jones & Johnston, S. P. Smith, W. M. Shipp, Vance & Dowd, J. H. Wilson and R. P. Waring. Almost the entire list was composed of men who followed the Confederate flag, and now desired to assist in building up the wreck of our beloved State. There were 171 merchants and tradesmen of all kinds then doing business in the town. At this time there were sixteen gold mines in operation in Mecklenburg county. This was only four years after the most destructive war that was ever waged against the Anglo-Saxon race, when everything of value had been destroyed, and a conquering army flushed with victory were watching our every move to heap indignities upon us and make us feel the bitterness of defeat.

But time heals wounds that were grievous and hard to be borne, and rankled in great bitterness. Our country was left poor indeed; not a dollar was left even for those who had been in the most affluent circumstances. But our Southern people went to work with a will that reminds us of the days when we snatched victory from seeming defeat. For seven years after the surrender not a public school was taught in North Carolina.

The educational facilities of the city were limited to the Charlotte Female Institute, Mecklenburg Female College, Male Academy by Rev. R. H. Griffith, St. Peter's School, Rev. B. S. Bronson, and Biddle Institute for the colored race. This last was endowed by money from the North, and since then money has been spent lavishly, and most elegant buildings and equipments have been furnished, so that no institution for the education of the colored race can be found in all the Southern States that can surpass Biddle in appointments for the purpose intended, viz.: a university for the education of the young men of the negro race.

There was but one national bank in the town at that time, the First National, of which R. Y. McAden was president and M. P. Pegram cashier. A. G. Brenizer was cashier of the City Bank of Charlotte, and C. N. G. Butt teller. Thos. W. Dewey was president of the Bank of Mecklenburg, F. H. Dewey cashier. These banks furnished all the money needed to do the business of the town.

For the times and circumstances of the country, the town was pretty well off in railroad facilities. The North Carolina Central, Columbia and South Carolina, the Lincoln or Western Division of the Carolina Central, and the Statesville Railroad. These seemed to give us plenty of outlet for the amount of trade. They afterward grew as greater facilities were called for. The first railroad to enter the town was the Charlotte & Columbia Railroad, in 1852. Then the North Carolina Central Railroad from Goldsboro to Charlotte in 1856. Then the Carolina Central from Wilmington, by Charlotte to Lincolnton and up into the mountains after the war. The Atlantic, Tennessee & Ohio Railroad, commonly called the Statesville Railroad, was built in 1860-61. In 1864 it was taken up to finish out the road from Greensboro to Danville. It was vital to the welfare of the Army of Northern Virginia that we should have two great lines by which we could feed and supply the great army that upheld the Southern Confederacy. This road was afterwards rebuilt, in about 1874. In about the same period the county voted $200,000 to build the road to Atlanta, Ga.; also $100,000 to reconstruct and equip the Statesville road. These roads have done much for the county and town.

Mint Erected to Accommodate Those Engaged in Mining.

In 1830-'35 considerable attention was paid to mining, especially to gold mining. All through this section of the State and adjoining States there was a feverish desire to find a rich gold mine. It was not uncommon to find chunks of gold; some persons keeping the beautiful lumps to prop the door of the house open, and carelessly handled, not knowing what it was worth.

It was now thought advisable to have a mint here at home, and not have to travel long distances to have the precious metals coined, as the only way to get to Philadelphia was horseback, by wagon or stage. Fifty miles a day was considered good traveling, and not more than half the year could this speed be attained. In 1836 the United States Mint was built. Mr. John H. Caldwell made the brick and delivered them, when the internal appliances were furnished by the Government, and work was commenced and carried on regularly up to the time of the Civil War. Since then it has only been used as an assay office.

During the first term of Mr. Cleveland's administration the remainder of the lot was used for governmental building —a Federal court room and postoffice. The balance of the lot has been beautified by being used as a city park, a place of recreation, musical entertainments and amusements for children.

The Town Pump.

One of the oldest works of the town, and that impressed itself upon the memory of all who saw it, or I should say them, was the public pump that stood on Tryon street, opposite the Charlotte Hotel, and opposite the *News* office. They furnished water for every one in need in the town, and for all teams passing through the town. When they were dug, or who walled them, or who made the pumps and put them in, we can only guess it was a large-hearted individual, moved by the authority of the town. No doubt the town was governed as wisely then as now, but probably the conveniences were not so numerous. In the days of the pumps the streets were not macadamized, or the sidewalks curbed and paved, or not even planked; but in dry weather the streets were firm, and in wet weather mud was plentiful everywhere. Every one had a door mat of shucks to wipe the shoes on after they had been to the iron scraper, which was fastened to the end of the lower step. These pumps were removed and the wells filled up when the court house was torn away from Independence Square. But another pump stood in front of the court house on West Trade street, at the edge of the pavement, not in the middle of the street as the first ones did. No doubt they served a good purpose for a long time, but they proved an eye sore till they were removed. The town is so located as to be midway between two creeks that run parallel for several miles before forming a junction, and Sugar Creek furnishes an abundant supply of water, but when the city doubles its present size, a large supply will have to be obtained, which can easily be obtained from the Catawba river. A fall of sufficient amount can be obtained from Mountain Island, about seventeen miles west of the town.

Public Works in Charlotte Fifty Years Ago.

At this period no improvements of streets were indulged in further than working the big roads to keep them passable for wagons and horseback riding. But few houses stood on North Tryon beyond the county jail, corner of Tryon and Sixth street. At this time the jail was regarded as a fine structure, probably the finest house in the town, and served as the county prison till the days of reconstruction were over, when a new one was built on a much larger scale, and in a more retired part of the town. South Tryon street did not extend below where the Catholic church now stands, and but few houses filled the vacancies up to Boyd's Hotel, which stood on the south corner of fourth and Tryon. The female academy stood on the square where J. H. Carson now resides. It was burned down about this time, and this square was used for a great barbecue at the celebration which was held in 1852 at the completion of the Charlotte and Columbia Railroad. The completion of this road made quite an epoch in the history of Charlotte and the surrounding country.

About three years before this a barbecue was held in the large grove owned by Dr. D. R. Dunlap, now owned by C. Lee Hunter, Esq. A large concourse of people were in attendance, and Hon. Joseph H. Wilson and Hon. J. W. Osborne were the principal speakers. Strange as it may appear, yet it is nevertheless true, the Whigs believed in internal improvements, and the Democrats opposed anything of the kind. Whigs and Democrats had no confidence in each other, and party spirit ran so high that the sons of one party would not marry a daughter of the other. Dr. Dunlap and Peter Brown, between C and D streets, were supposed to live out in the country. T. J. Holton's printing office (where the Charlotte *Whig* was published) was on the east corner of College and Trade, and but few buildings up to the square. Leroy Springs built up his corner where Jordan's drug store now is in 1830, which was the most handsome store in town. He had a large cellar door to his basement, which was left open, and which proved a dangerous trap for anything that did not have its eyes the way it was moving.

Capt. Samuel Lowrie was drilling a cavalry company in the streets on a general muster day, when his horse became unmanageable and backed down into the cellar with his rider. The crowd became silent and awe struck, feeling sure that both the captain and his fiery steed were killed, but the suspense lasted but a moment, when Capt. Lowrie rode out with spurs to his horse, when the crowd gave a deafening yell of approbation of the fine horsemanship displayed, which Capt. Lowrie received him with his hat in his hand, and returned a most graceful bow.

In 1860 Charlotte town was about 3,000. A directory was issued that year, and is presumed to be correct. It was then said that Charlotte was a growing city, that it was located about the centre of the great mineral wealth of the State. The United States government established a branch mint here in 1837 for the accommodation of the mining interests of the State, and other States where it was more convenient than Philadelphia. This has proved a benefit, incidentally, to the town.

It is said in a directory gotten out in 1869, that in the State there was 200 mines and forty cotton factories, employing $3,000,000. That is not a bad record for that day, but it looks small when compared with the cotton manufacturing industry at the present time in Charlotte alone, when with the new mills, there will be 150,000 spindles, 2,000 looms, 5,000 operatives, a yearly pay roll in wages of $1,000,000 and a valuation of $7,000,000 on the manufactured products.

At this time the city contained a population of 6,000 people, and an abundant supply of newspapers, three daily papers, viz.: the *Charlotte Observer,* the *Carolina Times,* edited by Hon. R. P. Waring; the *Courier-Bulletin*, by E. H. Britton, editor. Gen. D. H. Hill was then publishing *The Land We Love*, and Mr. W. J. Yates was editor of the *Western Democrat*.

It is sad to know that every practicing physician who was living in Charlotte at that time is dead. The wheels of time never stop for the convenience of man, nor for the tides in the revolutions of a nation. J. M. Miller, C. J. Fox, Robert Gibbon, W. W. and R. K. Gregory, J. P. McCombs, J. B. Jones, S. F. Bratton, P. P. Medlin, L. G. Jones, J. C. Neel are a complete list of those who were actively engaged in the practice of medicine in 1869. None of them reached a very great age.

Maj. C. Dowd was comparatively a stranger, recently had come to Charlotte, but the people prevailed on him to accept the mayoralty of the town. It was a difficult place to fill, while Yankee soldiers often made the laws and superintended their execution. It is a difficult matter to present the truth of history so that the people of this generation will believe what the good men and women had to endure. But in 1869 we got a Board of Aldermen that will reflect credit upon the good people of the town. The list is as follows: J. A. Young, Jonas Rudisill, J. A. Earnshaw, A. W. Gray, R. McDonald, H. G. Springs, S. W. Davis, John Treloar, A. H. Creswell, William Maxwell, James Harty and J. Y. Bryce. At this time we began to fill the town offices with high-toned men who would act honestly and deal out justice between man and man. Capt. A. Burwell was town clerk and treasurer; J. J. Sims constable, and Charles Elms cotton weigher and inspector. And the police consisted of the following good men: L. A. Blackwelder, chief; Thomas Harkey, Joe Orr, G. W. McManus, W. B. Taylor, Robt. Howie, M. Harkey, Mike Healey, S. M. Jamison. These will be remembered as good and efficient officers. And as the most of the county officials resided in the town, we give the names of those who held the reins of government in the last days of reconstruction: Col. E. A. Osborne, clerk of the Superior

Court; W. P. Little, coroner; Capt. R. M. Oates, chairman, S. W. Reid, R. R. King, R. L. Detmond and Thomas L. Vail, County Commissioners; F. M. Ross, Register of Deeds; R. M. White, Sheriff; W. P. Bynum, Solicitor Ninth Judicial District; S. E. Belk, Treasurer.

The people now began to breathe easier, but still they had to be very careful how they expressed themselves and how they acted. The "Red Strings" took notice of every word that an ex-Confederate uttered, and all over the South commenced burning barns and gin-houses, that gave rise to the "Ku Klux Klan," which was all that saved the South from a worse fate than befell San Domingo. In the language of the Alabama poet—

> " As it is I can't tell you, in numbers sublime,
> The things that I know of in prose or in rhyme;
> But I'll swear that we had just a hell of a time,
> Enduring the days of reconstruction."

Changes in Mecklenburg in the Last Century.

One hundred years ago our grand-fathers were the active men in all branches of progress. The wealthy people all lived in the country. They never thought of riding in a carriage or gig. Buggies were not then made, but every man kept a first-class horse. A horse that had a good walk, trot or gallop was always in demand. The fancy gaits that we now see had not been developed—like "single-footing," was not common until recent years. The best of houses were on the plantation. Until the last fifty years it was difficult to get suitable lumber. The first steam saw mill in the county was after 1850. Then the county commenced improving her dwellings—building frame instead of brick. In the eastern part of the county, where building rock could be easily obtained, rock houses were built before the Revolutionary war. The century was well advanced before many fine houses were built in Charlotte. The great bulk of the improvements that have been made in the city, has principally been done since 1880. Since then many new streets have been opened and macadamized. The old military academy has been turned into a graded school; a new building on Ninth street was put up for the same purpose, both schools barely furnishing sufficient room for all who will accept free tuition. There are two first-class private schools for boys in the First and Fourth wards.

A system of street cars was started by horses, but it was soon found inadequate for the city, and electric cars soon took their place and yield a handsome revenue, running in all parts of the city, with a bright prospect in the near future of the track being extended to the Catawba river. But a few years ago our people were moved with wonder and amazement at every new discovery that was brought to their attention. Now in this second year of the Twentieth century they think as a matter of course something will be gotten ready to meet any emergency that may arise. We have as yet nothing that is perfected to take the place of the hand hoe to thin the cotton to a stand, to dress it up for rapid growth. Nor have we yet succeeded with a machine to gather the cotton when it matures. But the inventive genius of our people is ever on the lookout for anything to save labor, or cheapen the cost of production. The railroads of the country, and the public roads of the county call for hands and machinery; so do the great plants of the various foundries, and other large works employing hundreds of laborers. So that a constant stream from other sections is necessary, in order to supply the demand for labor. The number of cotton mills now running in the county makes farm labor very scarce. Twenty-five years ago a great improvement began on county homes, but now we see this is stopped and the land owners are moving to the city and railroad stations; if not to work in shops or factories, to get where they will get the advantage of better schools. This is a fast age.

Sixty years ago, or in the early part of the century we did not look for a radical change, and it did not come. But when the times were ripe for railroads to be built, we heard the iron horse in every direction. Steam has wrought a great revolution in the last fifty years in Mecklenburg county. It is now used in the place of human labor. In all places that formerly required muscle, now we see machinery, as if thinking how to do the bidding of its master.

One of the great changes we see in Charlotte is "the get up and push" of all the trades people. The mighty push to pick up the floating dollar seems to be the chief aim of life. A generation or two ago, the women took a delight in showing each other their fine handiwork. They knit most beautiful hoods and shawls; stockings that would now be the envy of those who only dress in store clothes. All the clothing was made at home, except wedding outfits, or for extra occasions. All the foot wear was home made; the material was carded, spun, and knit; the clothes for the entire family, white and black, was all done or supervised at home. Fifty years ago the women always took their work with them when they went visiting. They would either spend the day or go immediately after dinner. Until the last twenty-five years everybody ate dinner at 12 o'clock. Persons who were able to afford it, always carried a nurse along to care for the baby. If they wished to go several miles, and the roads were bad, they generally put in two or three days. In a visit of that length, all the neighborhood news was pretty well ventilated. In our churches at this time, it was customary to hold communion twice a year, when it was thought best to have one or more preachers to assist in the service. The meeting would begin on Thursday and continue till Monday evening. It always was a solemn time. Tokens were given to each communicant on Friday or Saturday to prevent any one from sitting down to the Lord's table who were unworthy; and the tokens were collected on Sunday while the sacrament was being administered. The long tables that extended across the church with low benches to sit on, have all passed away, and the present plan has been adopted.

Healthfulness of Mecklenburg.

We have no data to go by for the first hundred years of Mecklenburg's history; but from the sparseness of population of the first century, we can safely say it was a rare thing for an epidemic to appear in her confines. Ordinary chills and fevers, pneumonia, pleurisy, typhoid fever, rheumatism with the contagious diseases peculiar to childhood, have been common to all parts of our country. But severe epidemics have left marks of their ravages only in the last sixty years.

In 1845 an epidemic of erysipelas raged with great violence through the county. One-fourth of those attacked died. It commenced with a chill, lasting from two to four or six hours, followed with high febrile excitement, with diptheritic exhudation in the throat and fauces. The head was frequently swollen to the size of a half bushel measure, the act of swallowing much hindered, if not rendered impossible, and the eyes entirely closed, and the entire body emitting an odor very similar to gangrene or mortification. Whether it was an epidemic, or when started it became contagious, it is now uncertain. The first case in the county was a man by the name of Fizell, a Kentucky hog drover. He stopped over night with a steam doctor by the names of Jas. Clark. In the night he had a violent chill, followed by a high fever, for which Dr. Clark bled him. In a few hours he sent for Dr. M. W. Alexander, who found a violent attack of erysipelas, which began where the lancet opened the vein of the arm and spread rapidly. Dr. Alexander said, "He should not have been bled. as it would hasten the disease to a fatal termination." Mr. Fizell replied, "Don't blame him, Doctor, for the poor damned fool had no better sense." The case ended fatally, and Dr. Alexander was the next victim. The doctor was very popular, and an immense crowd attended his funeral and the disease spread with wonderful rapidity. Vast numbers died in the upper part of the county.

Some sections the burials ranged from one to six per day, and this in a sparsely settled country was putting the death rate very heavy. It was difficult in some families to have the sick cared for, and often but few to attend a funeral. A panic was among the people, and the sick were much neglected, and there was considerable suffering; but after two or three months the plague was stayed. In this epidemic the whites were the principal sufferers, although the blacks had the disease, not one-fourth the number of them were affected by it, yet it proved fatal to a considerable extent.

In the years 1853, 1854, 1855 and 1856, we had an epidemic of dysentery that was very fatal. It was said that Dr. ——— lost one thousand cases in the county during the scourge, which lasted four seasons. It was emphatically a summer disease; no special cause was assigned, but hot weather and eating fruits. Fifty years ago but little attention was paid to the cause of disease, but the symptoms were combatted as they should arise. Microbes did not then exist, or at least had not been discovered. The deadly miasma that arose from the swamps and low grounds was virilent enough of itself to produce chills and fever, without the aid of mosquitoes.

Whether this malaria generated in our creek bottoms and swamps could have given rise to dysentery, as the people believed it made chills and fevers, is still a disputed question, but it is a fact admitted by all, that it was a very fatal disease. Typhoid fever was more common in former years than of late. In ante bellum days, the negro was specially liable to the disease, but for the last third of the Nineteenth century, he is almost exempt from it, and has taken on consumption, which is more fatal in its consequences.

Snow on the 15th of April, 1849.

Everything in the way of vegetables was well advanced in the spring of 1849. The farmers were ready to give corn its first plowing when the snow came. It fell very gently, no crust on top. It was so piled up in the apple blossoms that they looked like snow balls. All vegetation was killed, no fruit that was in bloom escaped being killed. The great crop of Mecklenburg "blackberries" alone escaped of all our fruits. The tender shoots on the forest trees, with all the herbs and grasses were nipped "with one fell swoop" of the devouring king. It was not till mid-summer that the trees made a respectable shade, or the cattle could make a tolerable living in the range at large. The snow was about five inches deep, and got in his accustomed work the middle of April with as much efficiency as in earlier months. On May 18 and 20, 1875, the frost was so heavy that the wheat all fell down, corn and cotton was badly killed, and vegetation in general was badly set back. Our seasons have changed very much in the last fifty years, our springs have become later. We formerly planted cotton the first of April, now it is frequently the tenth of May before cotton is planted. The falls are noticed to linger in the lap of summer, and the vegetation remains green until the middle of October.

Aurora Borealis as Seen in October, 1865.

A most wonderful electrical display, which disturbed the serenity of many of the people of Mecklenburg, who witnessed the gorgeous display in the after part of the night. Mr. E. A. McAuley was asked by two deserters from the Confederate States Army the next morning after the occurrence, if he could explain the phenomena. He said, "Yes, it was the devil uncapping hell to take in all deserters of the Confederate Cause."

"Stars Fell" in the Fall of 1833.

One of the most remarkable events that ever occurred in the history of the State, or of America, was the wonderful fall of meteors in 1833. It was not in a single county or a State, but its appearance was in all parts of America. Without noise or trumpet or any disturbance in the elements, little blazing balls of light, like shooting stars, commenced falling soon after dark, and kept on till daybreak. The most of the meteors would fall three or four feet from the ground and the blaze would then go out, and leave no residue. It was a most beautiful sight; not burning or setting fire to anything, simply a blazing ball of gas. Many very ignorant people, in their fright, thought judgment day was at hand. It soon passed from the imaginations of the masses, and was only remembered as a great display of electricity, or as an eclipse of the sun.

The Passing of an Aerolite From West to East.

Probably in the year 1846, or thereabouts, in the summer time, in the afternoon of a warm, clear day, a very large areolite passed over Alexandriana Academy, making a roaring noise louder than that made by a train of cars. It was going in an easterly direction, emitting sparks by the thousands as it rushed on in its course, gradually approaching the ground, till it fell in the southeastern part of Cabarrus county. The teacher in the academy when he heard the roaring, called to the pupils "to run quick, that the house was on fire." Fortunately there was no damage done to the house, for it did not fall in less than twenty miles, where it was afterwards discovered. Its weight was several tons. Pieces of it was carried off and placed in cabinets of minerals. It was spoken of for a long time, and was supposed by many of the common people to be a piece of some disrupted planet; that this block came to earth, and here met an obstacle that it could not pass.

Earthquake Shocks in 1886.

On the last night of August, in 1886, the people of Mecklenburg were shaken up, and many of them alarmed at the convulsions of nature. Some few persons who had a clear conscience and a good digestion, slept on as peacefully as an infant. The first came about 10 o'clock, probably one-third of the people in Mecklenburg were asleep, and many of those who had done a hard day's work, did not awake. But on the farms the negroes were badly frightened; they called their nearest neighbors to come to their relief; some prayed aloud with great earnestness; others thought some enemy was trying to pull down their house, and they were defending their premises with rifles, pistols, shot guns, or anything they could get hold of. Cries of distress and fear could be heard on all sides, that were truly distressing. A large family who lived in a large house, some of the members had retired, and the father had partaken too freely of his cups to be reasoned with, when the family all got safely out of the house, begged the father to get up and come out of the house, that judgment day had come. Immediately the firm answer came back, "Go back to your beds you fools you, don't you know judgment day is not coming in the night?" How many people will leave home when great fear comes upon them; they are hunting sympathy, or protection. In a negro church near Huntersville, the house was crowded when the first shock was felt, but the preacher partially quieted the alarm, saying, "If that is some mischievous persons doing that, they will be afraid to do it again; but if it's the Lord, look out." Just at the instant the house was shaken more violently than before, when the negroes poured out the doors and windows, and over the heads of those who did not move fast enough—it was a panic. A religious awakening was started among both whites and blacks; but, like all revivals that spring from fear, it soon passed away.

August 31, 1886, was the date of the great earthquake of the century. Its centre was near Charleston, S. C. Probably its centre was in the Atlantic ocean near Charleston. The damage to buildings and railroads was very great. The ground in many places near the coast was sunken several feet and in other places was raised, making it appear in waves. It cost hundreds of thousands of dollars to repair the damages to buildings and railroads. In the up-country but comparatively little damage was done to buildings, except that brick buildings were cracked and rendered unsafe. A perfect pandemonium of fear and alarm ran riot over the country. The people were not educated in the behavior of earthquakes, and not one out of fifty persons knew what it was. Of course fright and fear filled the hearts of most persons who had no knowledge of such phenomena. In every direction in the country you could hear cries of dirtress—one person called to another to come to them. The lamps setting about in the houses were shaken so violently that they were taken from the mantle or table and put on the floor.

Many persons who paid no attention to religion were persuaded through fear that they needed assistance from a higher power. Loud prayers and strong crying was heard in many places, and many joined the Church.

A friend of mine coming home from Church in the upper part of this county, said when he heard the rumbling noise that accompanied the earthquake, he immediately got off the track of the railroad, thinking it was the train coming. Others saw electric balls of fire flashing along the track. I had two little boys, 15 years old, sleeping out in my office, who ran into my dwelling house after the first shock, and I asked them "what the dog was barking at so furiously." They said, "Somebody's horses and wagon went by the office like a whirlwind." This noise was from southeast to northwest; such appeared to be the course of the cesmic disturbance. These shocks were continued for several days, at intervals of a few moments to several hours. This is a fair statement of what took place in one hundred miles of Charlotte. But the nearer you approch to Charleston, or the centre of the disturbance, the greater was the destruction of property, many houses were rendered unsafe, and some were shaken down.

Progress.

The olden times have passed away, and their associations have in a great measure been forgotten with their plans of education, when it was thought that boys were alone worthy of an education—at least of a high class, that would fit them for the most exalted positions in the State. That filling the place of maid—of all work, was the highest round on the ladder of fame that a girl was capable of filling, unless she was born under a "lucky star." The aristocracy of one hundred years ago was handed down from royalty, and cropped out in generations after leaving a government that was run by the best of the land. That was far superior to a rule of money bags, which now controls in this country. For more than a quarter of a century millionaires have bought seats of Senators with enormous wealth, and had no other claim to patriotism. But we are happy to know that in our county no office has ever been obtained through barter or fraud, nor in the State of North Carolina.

In the first sixty years of the Nineteenth century, not a single millionaire could be found in North Carolina; since then a few men have crept up to the much desired mark, and as they ascended the giddy height, probably one hundred were forced on the downward scale. The two extremes of riches and poverty meet here in Mecklenburg, but we have very few of either class in our more than fifty thousand population. Our county is now progressing in a most satisfactory manner; our modes of agriculture have kept pace with the improvements of the age; it is now not necessary to sow the wheat, oats and rye by hand; drop corn, peas and other things by hand, but everything is worked by machinery.

In the early years of the century almost every one lived in the country, and continued to live on the farm till 1850. The evolution of Southern hospitality was not interfered with in any form until we were robbed of our liberty and denied the right of managing our private affairs as a free people were accustomed to do for one hundred years. The people of Mecklenburg were noted for their hospitality, and would never take advantage of a neighbor's necessity. It was rare and uncommon for a friend or neighbor to charge another interest for the loan of money for a few months, or a year; he would simply say, "I loaned my neighbor or friend for accommodation; I don't keep money for speculation." Simply to be wealthy did not give a passport into select society; a clean moral character would have to be accepted. The public roads were regarded good in dry weather, and exceedingly bad in wet weather. Fifty years ago to haul produce to market was a job to be dreaded. To Cheraw, in South Carolina, was then our nearest market, generally taking about eight or ten days; or a trip to Charleston, consuming three weeks, and to Philadelphia, six to eight weeks. Roads in that early period were poorly worked, just so that they would "pass muster."

The first agricultural fair ever held in Mecklenburg was in the year 1846. It is not known to what extent it was advertised, but it must have been very limited from the number of persons who attended, and the articles on exhibition. The first fair was held in the back room and the back yard of H. B. & L. S. Williams' store, which was located at the corner of the Second ward, where is now kept the Carolina Clothing Company.

The middle of the afternoon of that momentous November day, a few of the county's best farmers congregated in the rear of H. B. & L. S. Williams emporium to talk of what the foremost county of the State could do, and what the county proposed to do. They did not despise the day of small things. The people were looking forward when the day should come that agriculture would eclipse all that had been done, or dreamed it was possible to do. But in justice to the people of the county and to those outside her borders, it is fit and proper that an account of the fair—probably the first in the State—certainly the first in Mecklenburg county.

There were no marshals appointed for the occasion; there may have been a president and secretary, but no one appeared to be in command. Maj. Ben. Morrow did the most of the talking. He invited the crowd into the back room of the store where we examined seven or eight of the largest turnips that ever grew in the county. These were thoroughly examined, and pronounced most excellent. There was nothing else in the room intended for exhibition, we were asked out in the yard to pass judgment on a horse colt and a mule colt—one year old the next spring, their tails and main perfectly matted with cockleburs—next was a very fine Durham bull, belonging to Maj. John Caldwell. This constituted the first fair. Col. B. W. Alexander urged its repetition with greater effort. It has grown to respectability in the last fifty years.

Gentlemen and Ladies Before the Civil War.

A complete revolution in manners and habits, in the civilization of the middle of the last century—all is changed.

Gentlemen as a rule, attended to their own business. Some large farmers who were not willing, or for any cause were unable, employed an overseer who attended to the affairs of the farm by direction of the owner. In many cases the proprietor owned several farms or plantations, with a number of slaves to each farm, and in those cases the proprietor oversaw the different overseers. Of course these are or were rare cases. There were not more than a dozen very rich men in the county, and probably not more than that many who were very poor. In our county poor house there were not more than half a dozen, who had to be cared for by the hand of charity. The great multitude of our people lived in easy circumstances; they lived plainly, were industrious, paid for what they purchased, raised what they needed to eat, and what they wore. Almost every family had their own loom, wheel and cards for every two females of the family, white and black. Sewing thread was also spun, doubled and twisted on the spinning wheel at home. Only for very fine goods was spool thread bought. Flax thread, of different colors was brought on by the merchants in hanks of four cuts each, which the good housewife would wind into balls, being more convenient for sewing. For home made thread, there was always kept in reach a ball or cake of beeswax to wax the thread, and keep it from getting in knots, or "kinking." The civilization of fifty years ago and now, is very different.

Negro women spent all their time when not employed in making or gathering the crops in spinning and weaving cloth to make their clothes, or bedding, or clothes for members of the white family. Four to six cuts was regarded a day's work, either winter or summer. For a web of fine cloth an expert weaver was employed; usually that would weave from four to six yards a day, if they had an extra hand to "fill the quills." Anything like plain shirting, they could weave ten to twelve yards per day. They were not taxed very heavily with work when they had children to see after; on the whole their life was a happy one, fifty years ago.

It was different in many places from what it was here; it was common in this country where a man owned a half dozen or more negro men, for him to have one a blacksmith, or a carpenter, a tanner or a shoemaker; it may be they would not be fine workmen, but abundantly capable of doing the farm repairs that were constantly being needed. In other counties, especially south of here, they were not learned a trade, but every effort was made to increase their output of cotton.

There was nothing fifty years ago of the "codfish aristocracy," built on a money basis; but if a man's character was good, he was freely admitted into the best society. But let him once get down by an ill-timed stroke of policy, or overreach his neighbor in a money transaction, or change the mark of his neighbor's stock, or be strongly suspected of an underhanded trick, he lost his standing instantly; and as a rule he never regained his former standing. It was do right, or move, or else be under the ban forever.

Fifty years ago the party lines were so tightly drawn, that men in opposing parties—Whigs and Democrats—were loth to mingle together freely socially. They frequently spoke of each other "as a very clever man, but he is such a Democrat, or he is such a Whig." In fact it was carried so far that a gentleman of good standing in the Democratic party would not pay his address to a young lady whose parents were as invenerate Whigs, and vice versa. A half century ago the better classes of society were very particular with whom they associated; that is they would not allow their daughters to go riding, or attend social parties or in any way to be thrown together with people of a lower caste. Money, or wealth did not give admittance to the circles of worth and merit. This did not extend to our common schools or churches, except where there was guilt, criminal guilt. Fifty years ago the leveling principle was not tolerated; but where worth was found, it was always recognized. About 1856 the bars were let down, or rather thrown away, in admitting free suffrage to the voters of North Carolina, permitting every one to vote for Senator, the landed interest of the State was confided to the non-property holders (the land holders being in the minority), here was opened the Pandora's box that put in operation the leveling process that destroyed the old time aristocracy of the State, and admitted all classes, disreputable characters as well, to the highest privileges in the State. Party lines and the party lash had a wonderful influence for good or evil, and was only tempered by falling into the hands of good men.

Sixty years ago female education had made wonderful progress. Academies, colleges and boarding schools for young women and girls were taking a prominent place in the State, and especially in Mecklenburg county. In 1835 an excellent school was taught in Charlotte by Mrs. S. Nye Hutchison, with whom Miss Sarah Davidson was associated as music teacher. In the forties a Presbyterian minister by the name of Freeman had charge of the school. Then in or about 1847, the Rev. Cyrus Johnston took charge of the Female Academy and taught a large school till he died in 1853. Mr. A. J. Leavenworth, a minister, taught and preached in Charlotte early in the thirties, for several years and afterwards moved to Petersburg, Va., where he ran a school for a number of years. Rev. J. M. M. Caldwell and wife taught successfully a fine school in Sugar Creek neighborhood three miles from Charlotte, till he removed to Rome, Ga., in 1845. Another school was then gotten up at Claremont, near Sugar Creek church, taught by Misses Chamberley and Gould. These were Northern ladies and gave fine satisfaction. A fine school for young ladies was taught at the residence of J. R. Alexander, half way between Charlotte and Davidson College, by the daughter of Mr. Alexander, who married Rev. W. W. Pharr, D. D. Now there may have been other female schools in the county, the names of which I do not now recall. Did any other county in the State do as well towards educating the girls in either town or country? As a rule only those who belonged to the wealthy class enjoyed the advantages of education in the early days of the Nineteenth century.

Education in Mecklenburg has been on the increase all the time since the first school was taught in the county. It was slow progress to build up the schools from their crude starting point—the little log cabin, with weight poles to hold the rough boards in their place; dirt floor, wooden chimney, lined with rock; split logs for benches, a log cut out of the side of the house to admit light to the writing desk, made by boring a hole and putting in a large pin to lay a plank on to hold the copybook, or paper.

This completes the furniture of the school house one hundred years ago, except the master's chair, and a handful of hickories. This is not an inviting picture, but it is a true one. No wonder our State has led all her sisters in ignorance of books. But the tide is now turned; and if we can prophesy from the buildings now going up, the schools now under way, the money being spent, we will soon be as far ahead of our neighbors as we have been behind. In our town we have two colleges for girls that but a few years ago might have been taken for palaces. Our graded schools will accommodate two thousand children, with all the paraphrenalia that is necessary for a school of the highest order. The trustees have had an eye to secure the best teachers, and none are retained who do not fill the bill in every particular. The school for the negroes is equally efficient, and has the same trustees to see that each teacher is capable and does his or her work in an admirable manner. Other schools in the town, which are private, are well patronized and their boys enter with praise whichever college they elect to attend. Charlotte is well off for schools for either sex.

One of the results of the great war between the States from 1861 to 1865, was to rob the people of their property, bearing heaviest upon the women of our country, forcing them into channels of trade to which they nor their mothers were used in former times. New fields of industry have been opened up to girls and women, that prior to 1870 were never thought of. In all departments of mercantile life women are now an important factor. There is now scarcely a store or place of business in our thriving city, but what a young lady presides over the apartment suited for female work. Hundreds of ladies, even of the best families, fill the short hand and typewriter's place in the cotton stores, in the offices where machinery of all kinds is kept; in fact they are everywhere that work is to be done that she is suited for. All professional men now have a typewriter, especially lawyers, if their business will allow or can afford it. Probably they will work for less than a man, or it may be that they are more efficient. It is surely not simply a "fad," but renders them more independent.

Quite a number of young women have become nurses in hospitals where they are doing a most excellent work. This has also developed since 1870. The first Southern woman to enter the medical profession was from Mecklenburg county. Dr. Annie L. Alexander graduated in Philadelphia in 1884, has been a successful practitioner ever since, and has led the way in this new venture in all the Southern States where many have since followed, and are meeting with success in their new calling.

The time was in the early part of the century when an education was almost impossible for a woman in humble circumstances to attain. Then but few attained positions above that of helping about the house, taking care of the young children, raising chickens, milking the cows and making butter, or working in the fields. In the early years of the century, it was more than fashionable for young people to marry; it was natural, and it was the rule and not the exception to raise large families. From twelve to sixteen children was by no means uncommon. And the Psalmist was often quoted where he said, "Hapy is the man who has his quiver full of them." In that age the people lived plainly; the hours of the day and night were kept separate, the day for work and the night for sleep and rest. They raised on the farm what they wanted to eat, and spun their clothing at home. It was considered quite an accomplishment for the mistress of a household to be an expert in cutting and fitting a dress, a man's coat, vest and pants. This was an accomplishment to be proud of. If a man should be so unfortunate as to marry a woman who knew nothing about having the family clothed and fed, and the house furnishings attended to, with a growing family of children to provide for, he was to be pitied indeed. Such cases were rare, but not unknown. Newspapers were scarce at this period, and the dime novel was unheard of, and the light, trashy reading of the present day was undreamed of. Hence no time was idled reading unprofitable works.

Patrol in Slavery.

Many changes have taken place in the last forty years, mostly for the betterment of our people. About the year 1740 people began to move from the older settled portions of the country to find new homes in the various sections of the county. From the time the first emigrants began to seek homes in the wilds of this part of the country—before the county was laid off—the negro came along as part of the emigrants' family, with no one to interfere or put mischief in his head; but was taught the rudiments of religion with the skill of cultivating the soil. That was a time when one section did not envy another, but stood ready to lend a helping hand against a native foe, and a few years later to combine against the tyranny of England.

The climate and soil of Mecklenburg were suitable and were eminently fitted for slave labor to be profitable. In one hundred years the increase in numbers was very great, notwithstanding large numbers were moved South and West, as the citizens sought more fertile lands, as the markets of the world were opened up to king cotton. It soon became the custom to sell all the bad negroes; in fact, the good people of a neighborhood would not tolerate a bad character at home, either man or woman. One who was smart and given to crime, had a most pernicious effect on those with whom he came in contact; hence he was promptly sold out of the State. It was to prevent negroes from holding meetings at night and on Sundays for planning mischief, that our county courts organized the patrol to keep the negroes from congregating at places unbeknown to their masters. They were permitted to go to the church of their choice, and were not interfered with. If they wanted to visit any of their friends at night or Sunday, they could easily get a pass, which would insure them safety from the patrol. The last twenty-five years of their servitude, the patrols were very vigilantly engaged in looking after the interests of the South. In about 1845 it was no unusual thing for Northern school teachers— both men and women—to come down South to teach school, and frequently hold secret meetings with the negroes, doing a great deal of harm to our system of labor, and as abolitionists, rendering the negroes dissatisfied with their lot. This was the prime cause of appointing a patrol, and in justification of the good name of the people of Mecklenburg, one raid of the patrol will be given:

One afternoon in the autumn of 1845, Capt. Caleb Hunter, who lived in Prosperity neighborhood, received a letter from Capt. Johnston, of Paw Creek, requesting him to bring his contingent of police or patrol, and make a visit in Paw Creek, according to agreement. On Sunday evening about sun down, Capt. Hunter, James Alexander, David Allen, Henry Hunter, Columbus Corum, with probably two or three more, started for the appointed place in Paw Creek. When the place was reached, Capt. Johnston was in his yard awaiting their arrival. The two captains conferred together as to their expected gain, and what should be done with it, if found. A ride of two miles more brought them to the place. Silently they approached the negro house. They requested the door to be opened, and a light was quickly made, when Mr. Allen espied a very fair skinned man lying very cozily in bed with his "Dulcinia del Tobosa." Mr. Allen took him by the collar, and as he led him out, he whispered, "I am a white man; I am a white man." His captor pretended not to hear him, when he spoke louder and said, "I am Mr. Cook, the school teacher." With this Mr. Allen gave him a slap on the face and said, "You lying scoundrel, you are trying to pass yourself off for Mr. Cook. Mr. Cook is a gentleman and would not be caught in a negro house; draw your shirt; we will learn you not to try to pass yourself for Mr. Cook, you trifling mulatto." Here the captain spoke up and ordered him to be given thirty-nine lashes on account of his impudence. The law was soon satisfied, and the miscegenationist no longer tolerated in the county. Such characters were frequently found as camp follower in the wake of the Yankee army, sowing the seeds of disaffection and anarchy and all the ills that follow where license is encouraged, both by precept and example, and where law and order are ignored.

The system of patrolling where judicially carried out, was an important factor in preventing trouble with both negroes and whites. Mean white men always made mean negroes; hence the necessity for a patrol to make each race know their position in society. It seems to have been natural for the negro to steal, but if he did not get encouragement from the low order of the white race, he would not be noted for his proficiency in the pilfering art. In ante-bellum times when a negro was strongly suspected of trading with a white man, their maneuvers were closely watched by the patrol, and when caught, the negro was whipped and the white man heavily fined, or punished by whipping, stocks, or imprisonment. These were ante-bellum ways of dealing with crime; and it was much more effective than the present, which seems to say "We are sorry to imprison you, but we will be as light as possible." When not interfered with by those who have no interest in their welfare, the negroes were a contented and happy people. They seldom appeared in our courts, only in the gravest of crimes, and then they were the dupes of unprincipled white men. Well-bahaved negroes had the respect of the good people wherever known; but bad and disreputable white men were equally despised by both white and colored persons. As a general rule negroes hated "poor white trash," and when spoken to by them, gave unmistakable evidence that they considered them their inferiors. Anything that the master or mistress trusted to the care of a negro was as safe as if deposited in the vaults of a bank. They were remarkably true to each other, except in cases where there had been a quarrel, or a falling out. They would never give away one of their color.

It was a noted fact that they would submit to the lash rather than tell on each other, even in arson and murder. There is as much difference in the breed of negroes as in the breed of white people. Some are very tractable and docile, others are morose and vicious. A patrol will be needed for many years to come.

Roster of the Twenty-One Companies Furnished by Mecklenburg County, N. C., in the War of 1861-65.

To preserve a correct list of all Confederate troops furnished by Mecklenburg county, N. C., it was moved by Capt. John R. Irwin, in the camp of United Confederate Veterans, while holding a reunion at Sharon church, August 31, 1894, that Dr. J. B. Alexander be appointed to make a Roster of all Confederate troops from Mecklenburg county, and have the same published at his earliest convenience. The resolution was adopted without a dissenting voice.

S. H. HILTON, *Lieut. Com'dcr.*
D. G. MAXWELL, *Adjut. and Sec.*

It should be preserved as important in the history of Mecklenburg county, that in 1860, at the general election for governor, the vote stood: For John W. Ellis, 1,274; for John Pool, 757; total, 2,031. Soldiers sent to the C. S. A. by Mecklenburg county, 2,713. Were not the people terribly in earnest? The number killed, wounded and died in the service, was beyond a parallel. The patriotism our people are noted for was handed down from sire to son, from 1775 to 1861. Those who were patriots in the first revolution, propagated in every instance patriots in the second. Blood will tell.

Key to Abbreviations.—w, wounded; k, killed; w. c., wounded and captured; d, died.

334   HISTORY OF

ROSTER.

Company B, First, or Bethel, Regiment. (Six Months Men.)

Officers.

L. S. Williams, captain, cm. April 18th, '61, Mecklenburg Co.
W. A. Owens, captian,R.
W. A. Owens, 1st lieutenant, cm. April 18th, '61, Mecklenburg Co.
P., Major of 34th Regt. and Lieut. Regt., K.
Robt. Brice, 1st lieut., (Eluled).
W. P. Hill, 2nd lieut.
T. D. Gillespie, 3rd lieut.

Non-Commissioned Officers.

T. D. Gillespie, 1st sergeant.
J. H. Wyatt, 2nd sergeant.
J. B. French, 4th sergeant
R. B. Davis, 1st corporal.
J. J. Alexander, 2nd corporal.
W. M. Mattheus, Jr. 3rd corporal.
A. M. Rhym, 4th corporal.
Phillips, 1st sergeant.
Black Davis, corporal.
Julius Alexander, sergeant,
Minor Saddler, druggist.

Privates.

Anderson, C.
Alexander, J. L.
Alexander, M. E.
Alexander, F. T.
Barnett, William.
Bond, Newton.
Boone, J. B. T.
Black, Josiah.
Bourdeaux, A. J.
Biggart, W. S.
Crawford, R. R.
Crowel', E. M.
Caldwell, R. B.
Caldwell, J. E.
Cannedy, Robt.
Davis, J. G. A.
Davis, R. A. G.
Davidson, J. F.
Dorsett, J. F.
Dyer, W. G.
Eagle, A.
Eagle, John.
Frazier, M. L.
Frazier, John.
Fredrick, J. R.
Fullenweider, H.

Fanygen, M. L.
Gray, H. N.
Gray, R. F.
Grier, S. A.
Graham, S. R.
Gillett, J. H.
Griffin, J. H.
Hunter, J. H.
Hollingsworth, B.
Harris, W. L.
Howell, S. A.
Hilton, S. H.
Henderson, W. M.
Howell, E. M.
Jacobs, G. W.
Jones, Milton.
Jaswa, L. R.
Kesiah, Wm.
Kerr, Wm. J.
Landler. Orminer.
Lee, J. M.
McGinnis, R. C.
Lowrie. J. B., k at Gettysburg.
Muny, T. N.
McDonald, Allen.
McCorkle, R. B.
Mosley, M.
Means, W. N. M.
Meholers, John.
Nichols, J. S.
Norment, A. A.
Oates, Jas. H.
Oates, Coowy.
Orr, S. H.
Price, R. S.
Paredoc,S.
Phifer, R.
Petts, J. H.
Price, Joseph.
Phelps, H. M.
Query, R. W.
Rose, W. C.
Rieler, G. H.
Rea, W. P.
Rose, W. C.
Rozzell, W. F.
Squires, J. B.
Stowe, John.
Sharpe, R. A.
Shaw, L. W. A.
Sadler, Julius.
Smith, J. Perry.
Steel, M. D.
Sheppard, J. W.
Taylor, J. W.
Torrence, George.
Tovam, Willam.
Tiddy J. F.
Tiddy, R. A.

MECKLENBURG COUNTY. 335

Tate, A. H.
Tate, Henry.
Thompson, R.
Wagner, J. W.
Windle, M. F.
Wiley, W. J.
Williams, W. S.
Williamson, J. W.
Total, 108 men.

Charlotte Grays, Company C, First N. C. (Bethel) Regiment. Enlisted April, 1861.

Officers.

E. A. Ross, Capt. P. Maj. of 11th N. C.
E. B. Cohen, 1st lieut.
T. B. Trotter, 2nd lieut.
C. W. Alexander, 2nd lieut.
C. R. Staley, orderly sergeant.
J. P. Elms, 2nd sergeant, P. lieut., 37th N. C.
J. G. McCorkle, 3rd lieut.
W. G. Berryhill, 4th lieut.
D. L. Bringle, 5th or Ensign.
W. D. Elms, 1st corporal, P. Capt. 37th N. C.
W. B. Taylor, 2nd corporal, P. 2nd Lieut., Co. A, 11th N. C.
Henry Terris, 3rd corporal.
George Wolfe, 4th corporal.
Dr. J. B. Boyd, surgeon.

Privates.

Alexander, M. R.
Alexander, T. A.
Adams, Lindsey.
Andrey, J. P., P. Capt., 49th N. C.
Ardrey, W. E., P. Capt., 30th N. C.
Brown, A. H.
Brown, Wm.
Brown, Wm. J.
Britton, Ed. F.
Behrends, L.
Calder, Wm.
Cathey, J. W.
Caldwell, S. P.
Crawson, J. F.
Cowan, T. B.
Campbell, T. J.
Clendenpen, J. W.
Collins, J. F.
Davis, T. G.
Downs, T. J., P. Lieut., 30th N. C.
Downs, L. W.
Davidson, J. P. A.
Dunn, J. R.
Engel, J.

Earnheardt, J. M.
Ezzell, M. F.
Ezzell, J. A.
Elliott, S. H.
Elliott, J. A.
Flow, R.H.
Flore, James.
Frazier, I. S. A.
Grier, R. H., P. Lieut., 49th N. C.
Grier, J. C. Capt., 49th N. C.
Grier, J. M.
Gibson, J. A.
Glenn, D. P.
Gribble, J. R.
Gray, N.
Gillespie, R. L.
Hall, D. W.
Hill, J. C.
Hill, W. J.
Hill, H. H.
Harrel, W. Lee, P. Capt. A 11th N. C.
Hand, Robt. H. P. Lieut. A 11th N. C.
Howard, R. H.
Howard, Thomas.
Hutchison, Jas. M.
Hutchson, Cynes N.
Holton, Tom F.
Harkey, Tom M.
Holms T. Lindsey.
Haskell Jas T.
Hanser, W. T.
Herron, George T.
Howey, Geo. W.
Harkey, Jacob.
Henderson, L. P.
Isreal, Jack R.
Icehower, Wm. S.
Ingold, E. P.
Johnson, Robt. W.
Houston, Harper C.
Hymans, S.
Katz, Jacob.
Kistler, Wm. H.
Kinsey, Jack A.
Knox J. H.
Keenan, Robt.
Leon, Louis.
Levi, J. C.
Leopold, Jacob.
Moyle, Henry.
McGinn, Tom F.
McKinley, John.
McKeever, Wm.
McDonald, D. Watt.
McDonald, John H.
Monteith, Robt. J.
Montieth, Moses O.
McElroy, Sam'l J.
Norment, Jack.
Norment, Isaac.

Neal, Wm. B.
Neal, L, M.
Neal S. R.
Neal, P. A.
Neely, Thomas W.
Oppenheim, S.
Orr, J. T.
Osborne, John L.
Orman, J. E.
Pettus, Mack.
Phillips, S. A.
Carter, W. R.
Carter, R. A.
Potts, John G. P. Lieut., 49th Rgt.
Patts, Wm. M.
Potts, Lawson A. P. Capt., 37th N. C.
Queny, Calvin M.
Ruddock, Theo. C.
Rea, J. R.
Rea, D. B.
Stone, Wm. D.
Steele. W.
Stowe, Jim M.
Sizer, Wm. E.
Sims, J. Monroe, Q. M. Sergt. 11th N. C.
Springs, Richard A.
Smith, C. Ed.
Smith, S. B.
Smith, M. H.
Smith, W. J. B.
Saville, W. H.
Sample, John W.
Sample, David I.
Saville, James M.
Simpson, Robt. Frank.
Todd, S. E.
Todd, Wm.
Treloan, John W.
Tate, Hugh A.
Watt, Charles B.
Watt B. Frank.
Wingate, C. C.
Wolfe, T. D.
Wolfe, T. J.
Wiley, John.
Total, 143 officers and men.

Company C, First Regiment N. C. Cavalry.

Officers.

J. M. Miller, captian.
M. D. L. McLeod.
R. H. Maxwell, lieut.
J. L. Morrow, lieut., k.
W. B. Field, lieut.
J. F. Johnson, captian.

Non-Commissioned Officers.

M. Steel.
D. S. Hutchison.
J. P. Alexander.
P. C. Harkey.
J. M. Pugh.
R. H. Cambell.
D. K. Orr, w.
J. Lewellyn.
M. L. Davis.
J. B. Stearns.
J. W. Moore.
J. W. Kizziah.
W. T. Bishop.

Privates.

Antrice, J. W.
Antrice, W. M., d.
Archey, J. W.
Anderson, L. D.
Ardrery, J. W.
Blake, S. N.
Barris, E. C.
Burris, J. T.
Breffard, W. J.
Ballard, F. A.
Ballard, J. L.
Boyd, P. L.
Butler, J. T.
Black, T. N.
Barnett, T. E., k.
Calloway, J. C., d.
Cobble, J. D.
Conner, T. A., d.
Cottraim, A. W.
Carroll, J. H.
Craig, M. F.
Cruse, M. C.
Crump, R. H.
Cathey J. W.
Davidson, E. C.
Dulin, J. M., d.
Edleman, T. P.
Edwards, A. J.
Edwards, E., k.
Efird, J. C.
Efird, J. E.
Finley, M. K., w.
Furr, John, d.
Flow, E.
Flow, J. M., w.
Fords, H. H.
Tredermick, W. S., k.
Tredermick, N. P.
Tredermick, J. R.
Gillespie, S. A.
Gaisesen, W. G.
Gillespie, A. M.
Goodsen, H. M.
Graham, J. R.

MECKLENBURG COUNTY.

Hurston, A. W.
Harget, Harrison., d.
Hargett, F. M., d.
Hargett, Osborne.
Hargett, H. M.
Harkey, T. B., d.
Helms, J. A.
Helms, J. W.
Helms, H. M., c.
Hopkins, P.
Hudson, J. H.
Holden, E. M., d.
Hilton, S. H.
Henderson, W. M. F.
Hunter, J. W., w.
Hartis, M. A.
Hartis, A. L.
Holbrook, A.
Johnson, W. P.
Jennings, C. J.
Jordan, B. F.
King, R. R.
Lewis, C. J.
Lewis, J. M.
Morris, G. C.
Martin, Edward.
McCall, J. M.
McCarver, Jas.
McNeely, T. N., w.
McLeod, J. M., w.
McCall, J. A.
McGinnis, John.
McDoughall, M.
McCall, Wm.
McCarver, Alex.
Noles, A. T., d.
Noles, W. A.
Orr, J. A., k.
Orr, J. J., k.
Orr, N. D., w.
Parks, J. L., c.
Potts, T. E.
Potts, C. A.
Pholan, J.
Page, E. M.
Peach, H.
Rea, J. M.
Rea, D. B.
Robson, G. M.
Reenhardt, J. F.
Rea, W. A.
Rea, R. R.
Rea, Robt.
Rea, J. L.
Sparrow, J. S.
Smith, J. W.
Stanis, J. B.
Schneider, G.
Sanders, W. H.
Starns, C. R., c.
Steele, W. G.
Stucker, Christian.
Tye, W. B., deserted.

Tomberlen, E. M., w.
Thompson, J. N., d.
Taylor, A. W.
Taylor, Art. deserted.
Taylor, J. C.
Taylor, J. A.
Taylor, J. M.
Tomlin, J.
Taylor, W. F.
Thompson, R. G.
Underwood, S. M.
VanPelt, J. N.
Vance, J. C., d.
Ualle, P. O
Watson, W. A.
White, J. S.
Wilson, John.
Williamson, J. A.
Werner, L.
Wallace, M. L., k.
Williford, T. F.
Walker, J. B.
Wallace, Wm., k.
Williams, J. M.
Whitaker, H. A., k.
Yandle, W. A.
Yandle, W. H.
Yandle, J. B.
Total, 145; from other counties 56; 8 wounded; killed 9.

Company D, Seventh Regiment.

Officers.

Captain W. L. Davidson.
Captain T. J. Cahill.
Wm. J. Kerr, W. '62, K.'63.
Tim P. Mollay.
Lieutenants, I. E. Brown, J. A. Torrence, B. H. Davidson, Thos. P. Mollay, P. J. Kirby.

Non-Commissioned Officers.

McLure, Jas. M.
James Paul.
LeLain, Al.
Herbert, W. G. W.
Wedlock, W.
Jamison, S. N.
Clark, Jas.
Bundle, Thos.

Privates.

Alexander, Wm., d.
Anderson, Richard.
Ayers, A. G., c. .'62.
Bynum, Rufus. d.
Buglin, Patrick.
Beard, J. H., d.
Bennett, G. W.
Bennett, J. G.
Berry, Jas.

Bolton, G. B.
Brannan, Patrick.
Brinkle, John., w.
Brinkle, Thos.
Burnett, J. S., d. '62
Brown, J. J., w. '63
Eillow, W. H., d. '62.
Brown, Alex.
Biown, Nicholas.
Donovan, Philip.
Donovan, Jeremiah.
Dasinger, Francis.
Dobson, Hiram.
Davidson, J. W.
Davidson, B. W.
Elliott, Wm.
Elmore, J. T., d.
Eller, John.
Edmirton, J. R., k.
Frick, Jacob.
Fogleman, P. L.
Gallagher, Arch, w.
Claywell, J. F., d. '62.
Carricker, Levi d. '62.
Caskill, Tim L.
Cable, Lewis.
Conder, Wiley, k. '63.
Collins, John.
Chancy, John.
Calder, Wm., Sr.
Calder, Wm., Jr.
Cashion, Wm., w.
Cashion, Thomas, k.
Carter, F. B., d.
Gallagher, Jas.
Gleason, Jas. W.
Grady, Jas.
Griffin, Thos.
Goodman, S C.
Graves, A. C.
Grant, R. W.
Hartsell, J. M., w.
Howell, Jas.
Howell, John.
Howell, David. w.
Harris, Francis., k.
Hicks, T. W., w.
Halshouser, A. R.
Hanna, J. M., d.
Humble, David.
Icenhour, P. E.
Jackson, John.
John E. Edward, k.
Jones, David, K.
Jannison, R. J., w.
Johnson, Thos.
Johnson, Rufus.
Jamerson, S. N.
Kurtz, P. K.
Kelley, Lowerence, w.
Kanapum, A. E.
Kirby, Patrick, w.
Kisler, Wm.

Kennedy, Jepe.
Lane, A. D.
Mason, Wiley J.
McConnell, Thos.
McLellan, W. A.
McGarar, Wm. W.
Meredith, Stephen W.
McGuire, John K.
McGinnis, George.
Munsey, John.
Mulson, Robt.
McBean, John.
Mason, W. B.
McConnell, T. A., d.
McConnell, A. M.
Meredith, J.
Newton, Eli.
Newton, Meredith, d.
Newton, John, k.
Nail, Richmond, k.
Nantz, A. E.
Oliver, Calvin.
Plyler, R. C.
Packard, John.
Petit, Jas.
Patterson, J. E., k.
Quinn, Jas.
Rhodes, Wm.
Rafferty, Thos.
Rogers, Jas.
Rogers, J. C.
Reynolds, John.
Riddick, H. L.
Riddick, J. A.
Rolmer, W. C.
Riggins, Robt.
Sullivan, D. C.
Stephens, M.
Spears, Wm. H.
Stewart, Thos. A .
Sherill, N. J.
Seagraves, A. C.
Sanders, G. W., k.
Sheridan, John, w.
Stanning, Wm.
Stroups, David, k.
Spawl, A. B.
Skinner, S. L.
Sullivan, D. C.
Staley, John.
Staly, W. Y.
Towey, Lewis.
Vincent, Jas. B.
Vaker, Wm., w.
Vance, Richard.
Vaughn, H. J.
Weaver, Wm.
Wilson, Lewis.
Woodard, W. L., d.
Williamson, D. J.
Whalon, Roderick, w.
Wilkerson, W.
Wilkerson, J. H.

MECKLENBURG COUNTY. 339

Winecoff, J. T., k.
Washam, J. B., d.

Company C, Tenth Regiment Artillery, N. C. Troops.

Officers.

T. H. Brem captain.
Jos. Graham, captain.
A. B. Williams, captain, w.
Robt. Lowrie, lieut.
W. B. Lewis, lieut.
Abdan Alexander, lieut., w.
T. L. Seigle, lieut., w.
H. A. Albright, lieut.
J. S. Davidson, sergeant.
Dennis Collins, sergeant.
J. L. Hoffman, sergeant.
R. V. Gudger, sergeant.
J. E. Albright, sergeant.
R. P. Chapman, sergeant, w.
J. P. Smith, sergeant.
Moses Blackwelder, corporal, d.
D. M. L. Yont, corporal.
Patrick Lyons, corporal.
Mathero Chapman, corporal,
M. A. Henderson, corporal.
W. W. Shelby, corporal.
W. S. Williams, corporal.
Dan W. McLean, corporal.
I. N. Peoples, sergeant, d.
Jas. W. Murry, bugler.
R. R. Peoples, guidon.
Wm. H. Runfelt.

Privates.

Abernathy, James.
Abernathy, Clem H.
Abernathy, Wm.
Armstrong, Mathews, w.
Baldwin, Alfred.
Beatty, Wm.
Beatty, J. W.
Bridgers, W. B.
Burus, Jas.
Brackett, Wm.
Broadway, Whitson.
Buff, Henry.
Baker, J. B.
Bray, Winfield M.
Cannon, Wm.
Cannon, Fred.
Cannon, Sid.
Cannon, Joseph, d.
Cannon, Francis.
Carroll, Francis C.
Connell, S. C.
Connell, Jas. H.
Chapman, A. H.
Chapman, Wm.
Chapman, Peter.

Cochrane, A. J., d.
Cochrane, David.
Costener, Jacob.
Carter, Jas.
Kanip, John.
Kanip, Henry.
Cannon, Wm. S., c.
Canipe, Hardy.
Causnet, Martin L.
Cathart, John, d.
Crane. Madison C.
Crane, Wm.
Cannell, Jas H.
Chalkley, W. P.
Christenbery, A. B., d.
Doyle, Bernard.
Dunlap, Sam'l N.
Dobbin, Mark H.
David, G. K.
Ellington, Werley P.
Farley, A.
Finley, Hugh.
Fite. Sam'l.
Fite, J. C.
Fite, Robt. D. R.
Fox, W. T.
Yaunt, Sam'l.
Yaunt, D. L.
Yancy, John.
Freeman, Wade.
Freeman, Theodore, k.
Dawns, Robt. R., d.
Fullbright, J. K.
Fullbright, D. B., d.
Fullbright, M., k.
Fullbright, K.
Fite, Sam'l., d.
Flowers, Jessie, deserted.
Fowler, John, deserted.
Goodman, John.
Maxwell, d.
Markcus, d.
Peeler John.
Reding, James.
Wilson. John.
Grigg, B. W.
Grier, W. M.
Grier, Marshal, w. and d.
Grier, C. E.
Heavener, J. J.
Hoover, T. H.
Hoover. J. D.
Hoover, W. G.
Hoover, W. H.
Hoover, T. J.
Howell, Joseph.
Hinkle, J. L.
Hawkins, J. A.
Hawkins, J. P.
Hawkins, Albert.
Herrvell, R.
Hoyle, D. R.
Hunter, R. B.

Johnson, Daniel.
Johnson, R. L.
Johnson, Joseph.
Johnson, David.
Jenkins, Tillman, k.
Jenkins, Aaron.
Jenkins, Sam'l.
Jenkins, Edward.
Kaloram, Thos., w.
Knuipe, Henry.
Knuipe, Peter.
Knuipe, Andrew.
Kerr, J. H.
Kerr, J. B.
Kerr, S. W.
Kerr, R. F.
Lattimer, A. M.
Lane, J. D., killed.
Laughlin, D. P.
Ledford, John.
Lindsey, W. G.
Lamb, Mike, deserted.
Lawler, John, deserted.
Lineburger, J. M.
Lawing, A. W.
Lawing, J. W.
Marrable, W. M.
Meaghim, W. H.
Marshal, Jas. H.
McDuffy, John, k.
McCausland, W. B.
McCorkle, Robt.
McKinney, Sam'l.
Moad, John.
Murphy, Daniel C.
Motz, Mayfield.
Morris, W. C., w.
Needham, Thos., d.
Newton, Robt.
Nantz, R. E.
Nantz, Calvin.
Nantz, R. R.
Carter, Jas. N.
Culer, J. A. J.
Potts, Wm. P.
Potts, Jas. A.
Pool, A. W.
Pool, J. T.
Parker, Wm.
Queen, Joseph.
Queen, Laban.
Roberts, J. W.
Rodden, T. B.
Richards, J. W.
Scott, Nelson.
Seagle, G. W.
Shaw, J. G.
Shaw, Wm.
Shelby, J. M.
Sloan, J. W.
Sloan, Sam'l., k.
Sloan, Robt., d.
Sloan, Robt., w.

Smith, J. A.
Smith, Jacob.
Smith, George.
Smith, W. M.
Stamy, John, d.
Stillwell, Jacob, d.
Stutts, J. J., c.
Stout, S. G.
Summerville, J. W.
Tallent, Daniel.
Terepaugh, J. H.
Todd, Wm.
Towery, A. J.
Towery, Jack, k.
Underwood, J. S.
Underwood, J. O.
Underwood, Jas.
Underwood, Reuben.
Underwood, J. R.
Underwood, David.
Veno, Francis.
Watts, C. L.
Watt, Charles B.
Walls, A. A.
Wallace, Wm.
White, D. W.
White, A. S.
West, Wm. F.
Wilson, John, transferred.
Will, John.
White, Wm.
Delling, Mike.
Cannady, Peter.
John, Weren.
O'Doniho, Mike.
Cotter, John.
Quin, Thos I.
Mahony, Dennis.
Forester, Ned.
Hunt, Robt.
Whalen, Martin.
Hinkle, Jas., k.
Moffitt Eli, d.
Moffitt, Wm., d
Moffitt, Samuel.
Moffitt, Henry.
Blalock, D. O.
McCaffry, Hugh.
Cidny Connell.
Warren John.
Ormsby.
McGilbry, J. A.
Heart, Yergin.
Ingrim, S. A.
Queen Meredith.
Stamie, Wm.
Towy, Jackson.
Towry, I. A.
Tutts, John.
William, Wallace.
McDuffie, W. S.
Armstrong, Mathew.
Veno, George.

MECKLENBURG COUNTY. 341

Hallet, Moses.
Crowley, Jerry.

Company A. Eleventh North Carolina Regiment.

Officers.

E. A. Ross, captain, P. Major, k.
W. L. Hand, 1st lieut., w.
C. W. Alexander, 2nd lieut., retired.
R. H. Hand, lieut., w.
W. B. Taylor, lieut., w.
J. G. McCorkle, O. S., P. lieut., Co, E.
J. S. McElroy, S., w.
R. B. Alexander, S., w.,
J. M. Sims, Q. M. S., c.
T. W. Neely, S., w.
T. C. Ruddock, corporal, c.
W. S. Icehower, corporal, k.
J. R. Gribble, corporal, w.
E. Lewis, corporal, w.

Privates.

Alexander, M. R., w.
McAlexander, M., k.
Alexander, M A., k.
Alexander, J. G., k.
Alexander, W. S.
Alexander, R. C.
Alexander, J. N., w.
Allen, H. W., w.
Allen, C. A.
Allen, L.
Auten, P. S., k.
Barnett, E. L. S.
Barnett, J. F.
Barnett, J. L., k.
Blakely, M. F.
Blakely, J. J., k.
Byrum, James.
Brigman, C. C., w.
Black, J. M.
Black, T. J., w.
Black, Ezekial.
Bigham, J. R., w.
Bigham, J. W., w.
Brown, W. J., P. sergeant, w.
Creasman, J.
Cochrane, J. F.
Campbell, W. H.
Cheshier, M. E.
Duckworth, H. D., w.
Duckworth, J. A.
Deaton, J. C.
Dulin, Daniel, w.
Darnell, Jack, w.
Earnheardt, J. H., k.
Earnhardt, J. M., p. to d. s., w.
Earnheardt, W. C.
Earnheardt, S. O.
Ewing, W. E., w.
Ewing, G. R., w.
Elliott, W. A., k.
Elms, J. P., P. Lt., k.
Flow, R. H., w.
Frazier, I. S. A., w.
Fisher, J. W.
Ford, W. C.
Galoway, J. S., k.
Gray, W. W.
Gibson, J. A.
Glenn, D. P., w.
Glenn, F. C.
Glover, Joshua, w.
Garrison, J. S., k.
Groves, R. H.
Goodrum, W. J., k.
Goodrum, C. H.
Hill, H. H., w.
Hill, Milton.
Hill, Miles, w.
Hovis, Monroe, w.
Hand, A. J.
Henderson, I. S.
Henderson, T. M.
Herron, G. T., w.
Hutchison, J. H., k.
Holms, T. L., k.
Hunter, T. H.
Hunter, M. B.
Hunter, D. P.
Herron, J. M.
Hinson, G. T., k.
Howard, T. M.
Hobbs, F., w.
Harris, W. C.
Harris, N. O., w.
Hutspeth, L.
Johnson, Alfred.
Johnson, T. N., w.
Jenkins, David, w.
Jenkins, Jacob.
Kerns, J. D.
Kenedy, Wm., w.
Knipper, Thos.
King, J. A.
King, C. C., w.
Kinney, B.
Monteith, R. J.
Monteith, H. L. D.
Monteith, M. O., k.
McConnell, J. H., w.
McConnell, J. F., k.
McConnell, T. Y.
McWhirter, J. H., w.
McWhirter, Jas., k.
McGinn, R. F.
McCall, J. A., w.
Montgomery, J. H., P. Lt, w.
McGinnis, S. A., w.
Norment, Isaac, w.
Norment, Jacob.
Neal, G. A., k.

Newell, A, H.
Orr, J. F.
Orr, N. C. N.
Orman, J. E.
Powell, Dan, k.
Pettus, H. M.
Pettus, J. W.
Pettus Stephens.
Paysour, C., w.
Paysour, Peter.
Prim, T. A., k.
Query, R. L.
Query, S. F.
Ruddock, B. W., w.
Ruddock, B. M.
Roberts, Peyton, w.
Rabon, M. B.
Ross, R. A.
Ratchford, E. C.
Stowe, J. M., w.
Stowe, J. C., k.
Simpson, R. F.
Simpson, J. W.
Smith, J. S., k.
Taylor, R. C. C.
Taylor, H. S.
Taylor, J. Q., k.
Thomason, J. C.
Wingate, Angus, k.
Wingate, M.
Wingate, C. C.
Wallace W. A., w.
Williams, S. H.
Wright, Taylor, w.
Withers, B. A., w.
West, J. L.
Wilson, W. M.
Steele, J., k.
Bigham, J. H., w.
Hunter, A. J.

Summary.

Killed, 29; wounded, 43; Company A, 11th W. C. Regt., total in Co., 154.

Company E, Eleventh Regiment N. C. Regiment.

Officers.

Nichols, J. S. A., captain, d.
Kerr, Wm. J., captain.
Clanton, J. B., lieut.
Turner, W. S., lieut.
Means, W. N. S., lieut. k.
Roszzell, W. F., lieut.
Alexander, Jas. F., lieut.

Non-Commissioned Officers.

McDonald, D. W., w.
Means, J. S., d.
Goodman, J. E., k.
McDonald, J. H.
Wilson, R. S., d.
Hunter, A. J., sergt.

Privates.

Abernathy, E. R.
Alexander, Peter.
Auten, S. W.
Ashley, M.
Adams, H. A.
Baker, Aaron,
Baker, Wm. M.
Ballard, Benj.
Bradshaw, J. T.
Beal, Charles, c.
Beal, John, c.
Bird, W. L., w. and pr.
Bass Jas. A., w.
Bass, Buston, c.
Beek, Wm. A.
Baker, Joel M.
Bradly, J. L., c.
Beatty, J. W., c.
Bunier, J., w.
Christy, J. H., k.
Clark, J. A., k.
Cathey, W., w. and pr.
Carmick, J.
Campbell, J. W., c.
Culberson, J. W., c.
Clemmons, R. R.
Denton, John.
Dixon, W. W., k.
Edwards, Sheperd.
Edwards, Marshal, c.
Eller, A.
Eller, S. W.
Finger, John., w.
Grier, T. H.
Garrison, Alex., c.
Hartline, Andrew.
Hartline, Adam.
Harris, C. C.
Holdsllaw R.
Hinton, A. J.
Hollingsworth, J. B.
Hartgrue, W. W., w.
Hartgrue, R. D. S., w. and c.
Hill, J. W., w.
Helms, E. T., k.
Hartline, P., w.
Hartline, D. L., w.
Hartline, G. H., d.
Jamerson, J. W., c.
Jameson, T. J., w.
Jameson, J. W., c.
Johnston, J. H., c.
Kyles, Fielding, c.
Kyles, Wm.
King, G.
Kestler, P. H.
Kyle, John.
Ledwell, David.

MECKLENBURG COUNTY. 343

Lineberger, Marshall.
Lawson, Hudson.
Loften, Martin.
Lambert, Wm.
Lewis, Linsey, w.
Lambert, J. M.
McQuay, S., d.
McQuay, W. H., k.
McLure, C. A., w. and c.
McCorkle, H. P., c.
Mitcha, John, c.
Martin, W., w.
Murdock, W. D.
Miller, J. F.
McLure, J., d.
Madden, G. W.
Munday, O. M.
Mathison, Jas.
Narson, J. G., c.
Null, J. T.
Nesbitt, J. G., d.
Neal, G. A., w. and c.
Ostwald, Francis, c.
Puckett, T. J., w.
Puckett, W. C., w.
Pool, G. S.
Pennix, J. W.
Pennix, J. A.
Reid, J. C., k.
Rives, J. R.
Rhyne, David, c.
Ruis, W. R., w.
Richley, W. L., k.
Rozzell, J. T.
Stone, A.
Stinson, J. B.
Sherrell, W.
Smth, D. J.
Griffin, G., d.
Turner, J. W.
Wilson, J. R.
Walker, B., k.
Walker, L. L., c.
Walker, J. H., c.
Walker, Jas. H.
Wingate, J., w. and c.
Wingate, T., w.
Williamson, E. Y., c.
Younts, R. C., k.
York, G. W., c.

Company H, Eleventh Regiment N. C. Troops.

Officers.

Grier, W. L., captain.
Lowrie, P. J., lieut., d.
Boyce, C. B., d.
Lowrie, J. B., k.
Saville, J. M.
Knox, J. M.
Lowrie, R. B.

Non-Commissioned Officers.

Saville, R. D., w.
Clark, P. M., w.
Caldwell, J. S. P.
Bell, C. E.
Hotchkip, Aug., c
Campbell, Thos., k.
Smith, J. T.

Privates.

Abernathy, Elig.
Ashby, J. T.
Alexander, J. A.
Andrews, E. M.
Ashley, Wm., c.
Bailley, Wm.
Brown, A. M.
Belk, Wm.
Boyd, J. J.
Boyd, J. A.
Boyd, David.
Brown, J. W.
Blair, S. W.
Black, J. B.
Bigart, Jas.
Barns, Robt.
Bryant, Sidney.
Boyce, Hugh.
Blankenship, J. N.
Blankenship, T. G.
Blankenship, S. P.
Caruthers, J. A.
Caruthers, J. B., d.
Chantenberg, C. E., d.
Coffe, B. M., w.
Cooper, J. M., c.
Crowel, E. M.
Campbell, J. C.
Cobb, C A.
Clark, W. A., d.
Carpenter, J. C.
Carpenter, W. B.
Cox, Eli.
Clark, P. M.
Drewry, A. G.
Deggarhart, J. V., c.
Deggarhart, J. L.
Dallarhit, J. D., d.
Dixon, Hugh M, d.
Eltres, J. H., d.
Edwards, J. M., c.
Ellis, Dan, c.
Earnhardt, Geo.
Fite, W. J.
Greer, Z. B., d.
Greer, E. S.
Harris, R. H.
Hall, R. B.
Harris, F. C., w.
Harris, J. C.
Harris, J. H.

Hannel, A. R., k.
Harmon, Levi, c.
Hannon, J. N.
Hays, J. B., c.
Hargett, Aleg.
Herron, J. W.
Hill, C. H.
Humphrey, T. L.
Haron, S. L., c.
Hanna, J. W., c.
Hatchup, A., c.
Hall, N. C.
Henry, J. B.
Henry, B. G.
Hedgepath, Geo.
Harris, Morris.
Holland, Robt.
Hainant, Henry, w.
Hoffman, Miles.
Henderson, W. R.
Ingle, Peter, w.
Johnson, J. W.
King, J. A.
Keenan, Peter.
Key, Albert, w.
Kerr, R. O., d.
Knox, W. H., w. and c.
Kilpatrick, W. F.
Lowrie, R. B.
Madden, J. P.
McQuaig, James.
Mincel, Willis, w.
Morrison, W. T.
McMillan, J. E.
McQuaise, Jas., c.
Marshburn, J. M., w.
Neely, J. J.
Porter, R. C., w.
Price, J. A., d.
Peppen, John.
Russell, J. C.
Rice, J. S.
Rhine, A. M.
Rachelle, J. B.
Reid, W. M.
Rumell, J. C.
Ross, R. A., d.
Smith, J. W.
Smith, T. J.
Smith, John L.
Smith, A. J.
Sloop, Alex.
Snider, J. A., k.
Snead, Frank.
Squire, J. A.
Sanders, Jacob.
Sumney, J. B.
Sumney, George, c.
Scott, R. S.
Turbifield, Jas.
Taggart, J. C.
Thuner, E. A., w.
Thuner, J. T., w.
Watt, C. B.

Wingate, R. J.
Wilkerson, W. H.
Wilkerson, Jno.
Warren, T. W., c.
Walker, P. L., w.
Watters, Allen.
Young, J. H., d.
Total, 137; No. killed 4; wounded 14.

Company B, Thirteenth Regiment N. C. Troops.

Officers.

Erwin, A. A., captain, w.
Robinson, W. W., captain, w.
McLean, J. D., lieut.
Erwin, J. R., lieut.
Thompson, Joe,, lieut., k.
Warren, R. S., lieut., k.
Presley, W. A., lieut.
Alexander, W. S., lieut.
Hart, W. S., lieut., d.
Smith, E., lieut.
Walker, H. J., lieut., w.
Choat, J. M.

Non-Commissioned Officers.

Youngblood, F. C., d.
Erwin, F. L.
Todd, J. W.
Swann, R. L., k.
Knox, J. M., k.
Wingate, Jas. R., k.
Knox, Jas. F., w.

Privates.

Alexander, Oswald.
Alexander, H. C., k.
Alexander, Ossil.
Alexander, O. S. P., k.
Alexander, W. W.
Alexander, M. C.
Alchison, J. C., d.
Adiar, Thos.
Adiar, Wm.
Brown, Jas. W.
Bailes, G.S., d.
Baker, Green C., k.
Baker, J. C.
Bartlette, W. F., w.
Berryhill, J. J.
Berryhill, Jas. L., d.
Blackwelder, A., w.
Bowden, S. D., deserted.
Boyd, Jepe A.
Boyd, John, d.
Boyd, J. G. W., w. and d.
Brimer, Alfred, k.
Brown, C. W., k.
Brown, R. E.
Bryan, T. J.

MECKLENBURG COUNTY. 345

Bigham, M. S.
Beeman, G. C.
Barnett, R. S.
Bartlett, J. H., w.
Clark, A. A., d.
Crawford, Micajah.
Carnthens, J. K.
Cathey, Henry, w.
Choate, A. D., k.
Choate, R. W., w.
Choate, Wm., w.
Clanton, W. D.
Clark, R. F., d.
Crowell, S. W., c.
Darnall, J. J.
Davis, J. C.
Edwards, M. A., w.
Erwin, A. R.
Erwin, J. C., d.
Erwin, J. M., w.
Ellis, Wm.
Frazier, Richard.
Frazier, W. F.
Frazier, Isaac A.
Frazier, J. T.
Frenekin, J. B., d.
Freeman, W. H., w.
Gallant, J. A., w.
Glover, T. M., d.
Grier, E. C.
Grier, S. M., k.
Grier, Thos. M.
Groves, J. R., c.
Garner, Wm.
Hall, W. H.
Heitman, O. B.
Hawkins, J. P.
Hall, W. H., w.
Hawkins, F. A., w.
Hotchkip, S. A.
Hill, W. H.
Jamison, E. A.
Johnston, H. F.
Kerr, John B., w.
Kimball, J. L., k.
Kirkpatrick, J. F., w.
Knox, J. D.
Knox, J. N., k.
Knox, T. N.
Kerr, J .T.
Lee, D. P.
Liberman, C. S., k.
Marks, S. H., w.
Marks, T. H.
McGinn, I. H., w. and c.
McGinn, N. C., w and c.
McGinn, W. A., w.
McGinn, J. N.
McLean, J. L.
McRumb, S. W.
McRumb, S. J. S., k.
Mulwee, J. W.
Morrison, J. E., d.
Moser H. S., k.

Maness, J. A.
McConnell, Jas. H.
Neagle, Jas. H., w. and c.
Nicholson, J. R.
Nevins, J. G., w.
Orr, G. B., k.
Okley, C., w.
Parks, D. K.
Parks, G. L., d.
Porter, S. A.
Prather, E. L., k.
Powell, A. T.
Prag, W. J.
Parker, S. S., d.
Reed, J. W.
Sterling, J. W.
Sheffield, J. M.
Sloan, G. W., w.
Smith, D. H.
Smith, Ed.
Smith, J. W.
Sturgan, C. S , w
Spencer, Clark.
Stowe, R. A.
Torrence, W. B.
Taylor, W. J., w.
Thomburg, F. B., k.
Thomburg, G. J.
Thomburg, H. M.
Thomburg, S. L., d.
Ticer, R. C. S., k.
Tradewice, N. P.
Thompson, W. J.
Todd, J. A. W., d.
Taylor, A. A.
Walker, L. J., w.
White, Wm.
Wilson, J. E., k.
Wingate, N. J., w.
Wolfer, H. F., w.
Wryfield, J. R., w. and d.
Wiley, J. C.
Watt, W. T.
Weaver, G. H.
Total, 152; killed, 20; wounded, 32.

Company K, Thirtieth Regiment N. C. Troops.

Officers.

J. T. Kell, captain, w.
B. F. Morrow, captain.
J. G. Witherspoon, captain, k.
W. E. Ardrey, captain, w.
C. E. Bell, lieut.
N. D. Orr, lieut.
J. T. Downs, lieut., w.

Non-Commissioned Officers.

J. T. Lee, sergt., k.
A. L. DeArmond, w.
A. B. Hood, sergt., k.

J. W. McKinney, corporal.
J. P. Bales, corporal.
H. T. Cotlharp, corporal.
A. J. Dunn, corporal, k.

Privates.
Adkins, W. H., w.
Adams, Wm.
Alexander, S. D., w.
Alexander, T. P.
Alexander, J. L.
Alexander, J. M., k.
Allen, J. W., d.
Anderson, Wm., d.
Baker, J., k.
Bailey, E. D.
Bailey, J. A.
Bailey, Wm.
Bales, E. M., w.
Bales, J. P.
Barnett, R. C., k.
Barefoot, N. G., w.
Bentley, M. W. H.
Bell, N. J.
Black, J. N., k.
Black, J. S., d.
Black, J. H., k.
Black, T. A., d.
Bradston, V. M.
Brewer, J. H.
Bowman, R.
Boyce, S. T.
Brinkley, H.
Bristow, J. C.
Church, Eli.
Church, Martin.
Coffey, A. S.
Crowell, Isreal.
Culp, A. A., w.
Davis, G. W., k.
Downs, W. H.
Dixon, S. L., w.
Duckworth, G. P.
Dunn, Geo., c.
Dunn, A. S.
Dunn, S. W. T., d.
Ezzell, M. F., d.
Gamble, Jas., d.
George, E. P.
George, Prepley, d.
Glover, B. C., w.
Griffin, J. J., w. and d.
Grifith, A. E., k.
Graham, J. W.
Hall, J. F.
Hall, A. G.
Hall, R. B.
Harts, J. H., d.
Harts, W. S., k.
Henderson, W. M., d.
Henderson, W. T., d.
Hood, W. L., w.
Howie, J. H.
Howie, Wm.
Holmes, B., d.
Jennings, G. W., w.
Johnston, D. E.
Johnston, S. A.
Johnston, J. H.
Johnston, G. W.
Kirkpatrick, H. Y., d.
Lee, S. B., d.
Lee, J. A., d.
Lewis, W. H.
Massingale, R. H.
McLean, Thos., w.
McCurry, J. A.
McKinney, R. M.
McMallen, J. H., k.
McQuaig, J.
Miller, D. M., w.
McRea, James, k.
Milton, J. G.
Morris, W. T., d.
Morris, J. T., d.
Myers, James.
Nichols, B. G.
Nelson, J. H.
Orr, T. J.
Patterson, M. S.
Pierce, Orren L.
Pierce, J. M.
Pierce, J. W.
Pierce, J. R., d.
Rayner, L., k.
Ray, J. M., k
Richardson, W. W.
Robinson, W. H., m.
Robinson, J. R., k.
Ross, W. J.
Ross, J. N., k.
Russell, W. D.
Saville, J. C.
Sample, Wm.
Shelby, D. H.
Simmons, —
Smith, W. S.
Smith, S. B., d.
Smith, J. D.
Smith, J. S., w.
Shaw, Alex.
Simpson, M. S.
Simpson, J.
Squires, J. W.
Squires, J. B., k.
Stanford, M. T.
Stancil, A. G.
Steel, A. F., k.
Stephenson, J. R., k.
Tart, Henry.
Tedder, Sid., k.
Thomasson, J. L., k.
Thomas, W. B.
Thompson, L.
Thompson, Lewis.
Thompson, Lee, d.
Thompson, Jas., d.
Trower, T. J.

MECKLENBURG COUNTY. 347

Walston, S. L., d.
Webb, Wm., d.
West, Wm.
Weeks, R. B., k.
Witherspoon, M. T., k.
Wolf, J. N.
Wolf, R. B.
Wolf, G. D., d.
Williams, W. E.
Yeargan. W.
Young, S. T.
Youth, J. A.
Total No. 150; killed 25; wounded 16; died 23.

Company G, Thirty-Fourth Regiment N. C. Troops.

Officers.

W. R. Myers, captain.
G. M. Norment, captain, w.
J. M. Lawing, lieut.
A. A. Cathey, lieut.
A. H. Creswell, lieut.
R. S. Reed, lieut., k.
Jas. C. Todd, captain, w.
J. N. Abernethy, k.

Non-Commissioned Officers.

Lucas, H. C., sergt.
Joe B. McGhee, sergt.
J. L. Todd, ordinance sergt.
J. W. Davenport, corporal, k.
Geo. L. Campbell, corporal, k.
Jas. A. Todd, corporal, k.
T. A. Johnston, w.

Privates.

Alcorn, A. S., w.
Alexander, J. O. D., k.
Abernethy, C. W., w.
Abernethy, J. N., k.
Anderson, C. J., k.
Asbury, J. R., w.
Bain, J. J., d.
Beatty, A. W., w.
Beatty, Samuel, d.
Beatty, John, w.
Bennett, Thos., w.
Berryhill, J. H., w.
Bailliff, Fred, k.
Brotherton, John, w.
Brotherton, Wm.
Burgwyn, Fred.
Bolton, J. C.
Cathey, J. L., w.
Cathey, W. H., d.
Clark, John, k.
Cathey, Wm. A.
Clark, Almirive, k.
Cox, W. C. L., w.
Carpenter, Jas., k.
Downs, Frank.
Duan, T. J., w.
Duglass, S. A.
Elliott, H. W., k.
Etters, P. P., d.
Erving, John.
Faires, G. N., d.
Frazier, I. A.
Garren, Andrew.
Gregg. D. H., d.
Greenhill, Lawson, k.
Hayes, S. L., k.
Hovis, Moses, w.
Hipp, Andrew, d.
Hipp, Pinkney, d.
Hipp, John, d.
Hipp, Wm.
Hipp, J. M.
Hoover, A. B., w.
Hutchison, S. B.
Johnston, D. H., d.
Johnston, F. E., k.
Jarrett, Samuel, k
King, Thos., w.
Lawing, J. S., w.
King, Ezekiel.
Lawing, J. M., d.
Lynch, Robt.
McGee, T. J.
Mills, W. T.
McGhee, J. T., d.
McCord, W. C., w.
Means, G. W., d.
Means, J. K. P., k.
McCall, Jas., w.
McCall, Alex., c.
McGahey, T. C.
Nicholson, John.
Odell, J. C., d.
Odell, G. W., d.
Puckett, J. H., d.
Parks, George, w.
Pickerell, J. H., w.
Phillips, J. J., k.
Proctor, J. A., m.
Rodden, J. J., w.
Reid, Robt. S., w. and d.
Rosick, G. W.
Scott, W. A., k.
Shelby, J. L., k.
Stephens, A. B., d.
Stephens, R. T., w. and d.
Sanford, J. M., k.
Sanford, Jas. O.
Terres, James. w.
Todd, G. F., k.
Todd, G. N., k.
Todd, C. B., w.
Todd, G. C., w.
Todd, J. L., k.
Todd, J. W. S.
Todd, D. S.
Todd, L. N.
Watters, J. G., c.

Winston, C. W.
Total, 100; killed, 26; **wounded, 32.**

Company H, Thirty-Fifth Regiment N. C. Troops.

Maxwell, D. G., captain.
Dixon, H. M., captain.
Davis, J. M., captain.
Alexander, Thos. M., captain, d.
Alexander, J. G., lieut.
Alexander, J. K., w.
Alexander, Leander.
Alexander, C. F.
Alexander, A. P., k.
Alexander, S. W.
Alexander, G. W.
Auten, J. W., d.
Barckley, A. C.
Barckley, H. S.
Brown, J. F.
Brown, J. F., c.
Brown, S. H., w.
Benfield, H. S.
Benfield, J. R.
Blount, J. M.
Blakely, W. J., w.
Blakely, A. C., w.
Burgwyn, W. H. S., lieut.
Benfield, B. E., c.
Baker, J. R., lieut.
Biggers, W. A.
Beaver, J. M.
Chesire, C. M., d.
Cook, R. W., d.
Cook, J. P., k.
Caldwell, G. M., sergt., w.
Caldwell, H. W., k.
Caldwell, J. M., d.
Caldwell, R. N.
Caldwell, D. G., d.
Caldwell, D. P., d.
Caldwell, D. A., lieut.
Campbell, W. H., k.
Cochrane, R. B.
Cochrane, N. R.J., c.
Cochrane, L. J., d.
Campbell, C. M., c.
Cochrane, J. L., sergt.
Cochrane, W. C., sergt., k.
Deaton, L. L., k.
Dulin, D. H., c.
Dulin, John, sergt., k.
Dulin, R. H., d.
Dulin, J. C., d.
Dulin, T. L.
Dulin, Matthias, d.
Dulin, W. W., k.
Davis, W. H.
Dennis, J. T.
Earnhardt, C. D., d.
Earnhardt, S. O.
Farris, M. C., w.
Fesperman, W. M., d.
Foard, J. C., k.
Foard, C. A.
Foard, Henry.
Flow, T. J.
Garrison, R. W., w.
Garrison, C. A., w.
Gibson, J. M., k.
Grier, J. O., w.
Hodges, P. B.
Hodges, C. J.
Hodges, W. G.
Howie, S. E., w.
Hunter, G. S., w.
Hunter, Hugh.
Hunter, A. G., w.
Hunter, J. M.
Hunter, J. M. C., w.
Hunter, Hester, k.
Hunter, J. M. C.
Hunter, R. C., d.
Hunter, S. C., lieut., w.
Hunter, R. H.
Hutchison, J. R., corporal.
Hall, T. M.
Hall, Amriz.
Hooks, Dave.
Hood, J. M.
Hood, W. S., k.
Hood, J. R.
Hucks, D. W.
Hucks, John.
Harris, G. W., k.
Harris, F. R., k.
Herron, Calvin.
Herron, Green, w.
Herron, John.
Houston, G. W., d.
Irwin, G. C., d.
Johnston, J. J.
Jordan, Mc. H.
Kirk, Wm., k.
Kirk, J. C., w.
Keenan, John, w.
Kilough, E. d.
Kerns, T. M. A., d.
McCombs, Jas.
Mason, J. J., w.
Mason, R. C., d.
McCall, C. N.
McCall, D. H.
McCall, R. W., d.
McCall, Josiah F., k.
McGinnis, J. J.
McGinnis, T. M.
McGinnis, J. P.
McLean, H. W., d.
McLure, James.
McLaughlin, W. J., w.
McLaughlin, J. J., w.
McKay, Robt. W., w.
Miller, H. M. W., d.
Miller, J. M., k.
Miller, S. J., d.

MECKLENBURG COUNTY. 349

Montgomery, Leander.
Montgomery, J. P. C., d.
Morris, W. G., sergt., d.
Morris, D. W.
McCorkle, T. J., d.
Maxwell, W. M.
Morrison, S. N.
Morrison, D. M.
Morrison, Marshall.
McCewon, J. M.
Morris, J. C., k.
McConnell, T. M.
Neal, W. B.
Noles, John, k.
Newell, D. S.
Nelson, R. A.
Nelson, T. J.
Osborne, Harvey, d.
Orr, Franklin, d.
Petre, Wm.
Puckett, S. J.
Puckett, J. W., k.
Puckett, F. M.
Pharr, T. F.
Query, Wm. W., d.
Query, Leander, sergt., w.
Query, F. E.
Query, F. N.
Rodgers, J. R., k.
Rogers, T. P.
Rodgers, J. W.
Roday, T. A., d.
Rankin, C. S., k.
Rankin, W. W., w.
Russ, W. A.
Roberts, S. L.
Roberts, W. A., w.
Roberts, J. L., k.
Ramsey, J. F.
Rice, J. W., w.
Rea, James, w.
Stuart, A. H.
Shaffer, J. S., w.
Shaffer, W. H., w.
Solomon, Wm. R.
Solomon, D. A., d.
Stinson, Dave, d.
Thompson, J. W.
Taylor, J. M., d.
Taylor, W. J.
Taylor, W. H.
Tarlton, James D., w.
Wilson, M. A., w.
Wilson, R. L., d.
Wilson, T. J., w.
White, E. F.
White, James. A., lieut., d.
Woodall, Thos., w.
Wallace, A. W., k.
Wilson, M. N., w.
Yandle, M. N.
Total 181· 24 killed; 35 wounded; 5 captured; 33 died.

Company C, Thirty-Seventh Regiment N. C. Troops.

Officers.

J. M. Potts, captain.
O. N. Brown, captain, k.
L. A. Potts, captain, w.
J. D. Brown, captain.
T. A. Wilson, lieut., d.
T. J. Kerns, lieut.
J. S. Johnston, lieut.
J. L. Jetton, lieut.
G. H. Beattie, lieut., k.
J. W. Pettus, lieut., w.
A. P. Torrance, lieut., w.
B. A. Johnston, lieut., k.
W. W. Doherty, lieut., k.
J. R. Gillespie, lieut.
J. B. Alexander, surgeon.
G. M. Wilson, sergt. k.
J. A. Gibbs, sergt., k.
D. H. Fidler, corporal, d.
J. A. Bell, corporal, d.

Privates.

Armstrong, M., w.
Alexander, J. H.
Alexander, D. R., k.
Alexander, T. L.
Alexander, T. R., w.
Alexander, W. D.
Alexander, W., d.
Armor, T. S., w.
Alcorn, T. P., d.
Bell, J. D., d.
Baritt, W. R., d.
Barnett, J. D.
Barnett, J. W.
Beard, Joseph, d.
Beard, J. C., w.
Beard, J. M., k.
Beard, J. F. M.
Black, A. J. L., k.
Black, J. C
Black, W. A., d.
Black, S., d.
Blakely, J. B., d.
Blakely, W. F. M., d.
Blythe, J. W.
Boyler, J. H.
Brady, R. A., d.
Brown, B. F.
Brown, H. W., k.
Brown, J., d.
Britt, John.
Burleyson, Benj., w.
Carrigan, W. F.
Cathey, J. W.
Caldwell, W. W., c.
Carpenter, J., c.
Carpenter, J. C., w.
Cochrane, J. C., w.

Cox, Thomas, d.
Chrestainbury, S. D., w.
Dellinger, W.
Derr, A J., lost a leg.
Deaton, J. Z.
Fesperman, J. C., d.
Gardner, H. T., d.
Gibbs, Jack, d.
Gibson, J. J., d.
Gibson, T. A., w.
Goodrum, Zeb, d.
Goodrum, J. W., c
Gardener, D., k.
Gardener, S. S.
Grier, J. S., k.
Harrison, W. H.
Hastings, W. C.
Henderson, W. F., k.
Hendrix, J. M., w.
Hendrix, W. P., d
Holbrooks, R. S.
Hucks, S. L., w
Hunter, H. C., c. and d.
Hunter, J. F., k.
Hagons, H. M., k.
Hamilton, J. R., k.
Houston, H. L., d.
Houston, J. M.
Howie, A. J., w.
Jenkins, A. B.
Johnston, M. F., d.
Jamison, J. R.
Kelley, A. A., w.
Kerns, J. A., d.
Kerns, T. J.
Knox, S. W., w.
Lentz, R. R.
Little S. S.
Luckey, T. S., d.
Leach, L., d.
McAllister, C., w.
McAuley. H. E., d.
McAuley, A. E.
McCoy, Albert.
McCoy, J. F., k.
McCoy, C. W.
McFadden, John, c.
Miller, R. C., c.
Monteith, R. A., k.
Moore, R. D., d.
McAuley, D. N., d.
Morrison, W. S.
Nantz, C. R., d.
Nantz, D. J., w.
Page, J. F., d.
Puckett, E. M., w.
Reid, J. L., d
Rhyne. J. J., d.
Rodgers, John, d.
Sample, J. W., k.
Sample W. L., k.
Sloan, T. A.
Sloan, T. C.
Stearns, A. L., d.
Stearns, W. R.
Stuart, S. J., w.
Sellers, Eli.
Solomon, D. A., k.
Stroup, C.
Stroup, M., k.
Sample, E. A.
Shaver. M., k.
Shaw, A.
Todd, J. A., k.
Taylor, W. A., d.
Tiffins, M. B.
Torrance, J. A.
Torrance, H. L. W., k.
Torrance, W. W., w.
Tummice, L. G.
Weddington, J. Y.
Wallace, C. S., d.
Warsham, Alex., k.
Warsham, F. M., w.
Warsham, R. R., w.
Warsham, T. L., k.
Warsham, W., d.
White, J. H.
Wiley, J., k.
Williams, C. R., d.
Williams, F. C., d.
Wilson, T. C., d.
Wagstaff, J. R.
Walker, J. C.
Total 149; died 37; wounded 26; killed 27.

Company I, Thirty=Seventh Regiment N. C. Troops.

Officers.

Harrison, J. K., captain.
McCoy, M. A.
Hart, M. N., captain.
Elms, J. I., captain.
Stitt, Wm. M., w.
Elms, W. D., captain, w.
Oats, R. M., quartermaster captain.
Sammond, T. K.
Rupel, E. H.
Price J. G.
Crowell, E. M.
McCoy, J. G.
Yandle, A. F., w.
Wilson, J.
Elms, J. P., c.
Icenhour, H. F., k.
Robinson, D. C., sergt., w.
Reed, J. C., sergt.
Alexander, J. O., corp. & sergt.
Rigler, D. M., lieut., w.
Adams, Lourie, w.

Privates.

Adaholt, M. L., w.

MECKLENBURG COUNTY.   351

Alexander, A. M., c.
Alexander, J. A.
Allen, J. H.
Austin, J. W., k.
Ballard, W. H., d.
Barnhill, J. W.
Bean, J. T.
Black, J. P., k.
Black, S. J.
Blackard, Jas., k.
Blankenship, T. E., k.
Blythe, S. W.
Bridges, W. A., w. and d.
Brown, T. G.
Brown J. K. P., c.
Bruce, Jas., d.
Burns, S. A.
Brines, J. W.
Crowell, E. M.
Carpenter, Levi, c.
Carpenter, Marcus, c.
Cathey B. G., w. and d.
Clark, J. F., c
Clark, J. W., k.
Clark, Jas., k.
Clontz, Ab., k.
Crocker, W. J., w.
Cross, W. D.
Devine, W. G.
Dulin, T. S., w.
Edwards, J. A.
Flanigan, B. F.
Flowe. J. C., w.
Freeman, J. J., d.
Freeman, Mc. C., d.
Fronebarger, John, k.
Gates, M. W.
Gordon, J. P., w.
Gordon, J. R., c.
Gurley, W. D., k.
Hargett, A. J.
Hall, Jas.
Hayes. Elijah, c.
Headly, Wm. L., d.
Henderson, J. W., w.
Henry, Berry.
Henry, Terrell.
Hipp, J. F., w.
Hipp, L. A., w.
Hood, H. C., d.
Hovis, A. J., k.
Hunsucker, J. W., w.
Higgenson, John, w.
Hunter, C. L., k.
Johnston, A. N.
King, G. W.
King, Wm., w.
Harris, N. J.
Haney, E. H.
Hunsucker, Wm., w.
Kissiah, G. W., w.
Kissiah, T. A.
Kissiah, W. M., w.
Kistler, G. H., w

Kaiser, D. W., w.
Kaiser, T. P., c.
Kaiser, Solomon, c.
Kirkley, Thos., d.
Lawring, David.
Lawring, P. W., k.
Looker, J. C.
Lourie, S. J.
McGhee, Isaac.
McCoy, W. L., k.
Manning, Jas.
Manning, J. W., w.
Montgomery, A. F.
Moody, M. D. L.
Mosters, F. A., d.
Maxwell, D. S., w.
McCall, J. C.
McCord, D. L.
McGinn, J. M., w.
Montgomery, Jas.
Mooney, Caleb., w.
Mullis, Coleman, d.
Mason, Robt. G.
Nicholson, J. B., w.
Orr, Joe L., w.
Orr, J. G. A.
Orr, C. M.
Orr, J. L. V., w.
Orr, W. S.
Patterson, Eli., k.
Patterson, J. H., w.
Paysour, Caleb., c.
Phillips, J. A., k.
Rarefield, Frank, c.
Reid, George, d.
Robinson, Jas. A., d.
Robinson, T. C.
Rudisill, Jacob, w.
Rumage, L., d.
Rupel, S. H., d. in p.
Sharp, R. A., w.
Sharp, T. A.
Shaw, D. C., w.
Shoe, Jacob, w. and c.
Simpson, C. L., d.
Simpson, Ira P., c.
Smith, Franklin.
Spears, A. J.
Spears, J. J., k.
Stearns, Brown, k.
Stearns, Dulin,
Stearns, J. M., w. and d.
Stewart, A. A.
Stewart, P. J., c.
Stinson, D. W., d in p.
Targart, J. S., k.
Tally, Mike, d.
Taylor, Chas.
Taylor, Jepe.
Oate, D. W.
Pegram, M. P.
Charles, I. Voorheis.
Tally, John, k.
Todd, R. J.

HISTORY OF

Turner, S. R.
Turner, Wm., d.
Walker, Robt.
Whitley, G. M. D.
Whitley, J. H.
Williamson, G. W., w.
Woodall, W. C., c
Wolf, E. B., k.
Young, A. J., k.
Yandle, A. F., w.
Total 157 men; killed 23; captured, 5; wounded 18; died 16.

Company K, Fifty-Sixth Regiment N. C. Troops.

Officers.

F. R. Alexander, captain, k.
J. F. Mc Neely, captain.
J. A. Wilson, lieut.
J. W. Shepard, lieut.
J. W. Spencer, lieut.
C. M. Payne, lieut.
J. A. Lowrance, lieut.
Alex. Livingston, lieut.

Non-Commissioned Officers.

J. L. Sloan.
J. C. Faucet.
J. T. Hotchkiss.
W. B. Osborne.
J. J. McNeeley, k.
J. H. Williams.

Privates.

Arney, Henry.
Alexander, A. H.
Alexander, J., k.
Alexander, J. Mc., d.
Alexander, M. D., d.
Alexander, R. A.
Alexander, T. C., w.
Allison, James.
Auten, T. J., w.
Barnett, A. G., w.
Barringer, D. A., w.
Bell, J. C.
Benson, R. P., d
Bingham J. M., w.
Black, Wm. M.
Bradly, J. H.
Brawley, R. W., w.
Brown, B. D., w.
Brown, J. M., w.
Brown, W. L., w.
Brown, J. C.
Burkhead, White, d.
Beard, J. O., k.
Carrigan, R. A., d.
Caldwell, M. E., w.
Carrigan, Adam.
Cashion, Frank, w.

Cashion, Jas., w.
Cashion, I. W., w.
Cathcart, J. R., k.
Christianberry, Allison, w.
Christianberry, A. H., d.
Christianberry, Jas.
Christianberry, R. F.
Christianberry, Wm.
Clark, Alex.
Cork, Walter, c. and d.
Craven, W. P.
Cornelius, M. A., w.
Davis, H. W., k.
DeArmond, J. A.
Deweese, Calvin T.
Deweese, G. B., k.
Edwards, G. W., k.
Elms, J. I.
Emerson, M. H.
Faucet, J. C., d.
Fouts, J. M., k.
Garner, Henry.
Heldt, Enoch.
Hill, Jas. R. L.
Hunter, H. S., d.
Hux, John, d.
Hux, W., d.
Jackson, C. H.
Jackson, W. K., d.
Johnston, J. H.
Jones, A. J.
Jordan, Sansom, d.
Kennerly, E. M.
Kennerly, John, c.
Ketchie, Wm.
Kerns, J. F., c. and d.
Lowrance, R. W., d.
Lowrance, L. N.
Lowrance, S. L., w.
Moble, Joel.
Moble, John.
Martin, J. M., d.
Martin, John.
McAuley, J. C.
McConnell, R. A.
McGahey, Jas. A., k.
Miller, W. C.
Moore, Jas. C.
Morgan, Zac., k.
Mowery, Henry.
Nance, J. A., d.
Nelson, W., d.
Osborn, N. B., w.
Oliphant, J. R., k
Reese, D. L.
Shepard, G. T.
Shields, A. C.
Sloan, A. C., d.
Sloan, J. Mc., d.
Sloan, W. E.
Smith, W. T., d.
Sosaman, J. P., c. and w.
Stearns, Henry M.
Sloan, D. F. A., w.

MECKLENBURG COUNTY. 353

Stokes, J. J.
Stough, Rich I.
Strider, John, k
Tepleton, J. E. D.
Templeton, J. M., w.
Templeton, R. D.
Tye, Wm. A.
Vance. W. H., d.
Watts, R. A., d.
Walls, Thos., w. and c.
Worsham, Alfred, w.
Worsham, B. A., d.
Worsham, Richard, d.
Worsham, H. J., w.
Watts, R. F., k.
Williams, J. H., w.
Williams, Rufus.
Total, 121; killed, 13; wounded 25.

Company K, Forty=Second Regiment N. C. Troops.

Officers.

S. B. Alexander, captain.
B. F. Wilson, lieut.
A. M. Rhyne, lieut., d.
Jos. H. Wilson, lieut.

Non-Commissioned Officers.

Thos. Norment.
Wm. Hecks, w. and c.
Wm. Price.
Jas. Keenan, k.
S. W. Talton, w.
W. S. Bynum, c.
Ed. Day, k.
J. H. Staten, d.
Jas. Scott, w
T. C. Dule.
L. Adams.

Privates.

Anderson, W. H. H., w.
Anderson, G. W., d.
Benfield, Dan, w.
Cullet, Ezekiel.
Coots, Jacob, d.
Dulin, W. C., k.
Dulin, W. L.
Foster, J. H., d.
Flowers, R. B.
Gilbert, Harrison.
Gilbert, Jas.
Grub, Absalom, d.
Gaston, J. A.
Griffin, B. F., d.
Hendrix, Grayson, w.
Hendrix, L. J., c.
Hendrix, Sanford, c.
Harman, Paul, w.
Helfer, P. E.
Helms, Hosea, c.
Helms, Enoch, c.
Helms, Gilliam.
Helms, D. B., c.
Helms, Albert.
Helms, John.
Helms, Josiah, c.
Helms, Kennel, c.
Helms, Copeland, w.
Helms, J. L.
Helms, Joshua.
Helms, Eli. W.
Johnston, Mathew, d.
Milton, Francis, w.
Milton, Alex.
Mitchell, Allison.
Makaler, Frank.
Minor, H. J., c.
Norment, Charles, d.
Orrell, Sam'l.
Paul, J. L., w.
Phillips, J. B., d.
Polk, —, k.
Perry, Noah.
Privette, Wesley.
Privette, Wm., k.
Randall, E. D.
Rindal, L. L., c.
Severs, —, k.
Singleton, Henry.
Scott, John, w.
Scott, Leander.
Smith, Alex.
Staner, P. C.
Shoemaker, Lafayette, d.
Smith, John.
Stone, John, w.
Sanring, J. M.
Sharpe, Isaac.
Triplette, J. H.
Walsh, G. B., c.
Walsh, J. H.
Whitley, John.
Total number 82.

Company F, Forty=Ninth Regiment N. C. Troops.

Officers.

Jas. T. Davis, captain, k.
Jas. P. Ardrey, k.
John C. Grier, w.
John W. Barnett, lieut., k.
R. H. Grier, lieut., k.
J. G. Potts, lieut.
S. R. Neal, lieut.
Jas. H. Helms, lieut.
W. T. Barnett, k.
L . M. Neal, k.

Non-Commissioned Officers.

J. A. Elliot.
R. C. Bell.

Wm. L. Mason, w.
J. A. Ezzell.
J. W. Wolf.
Robt. N. Alexander.

Privates.

Alexander, E. E.
Alexander, R. W.
Alexander, J. J., k.
Alexander, T. B., d.
Alexander, W. P., w.
Barnett, W. P.
Allen, A. W.
Ashley, Wm.
Bennett, D. G., w
Brown, J. G.
Brown, W. H.
Coffee, Ben.
Crouthers, T. M., w.
Crane, Job. S.
Crenshaw, John, w.
Culp, John, w.
DeArmond, J. B., w.
Dunn, Jas. R., w.
Elliott, S. H., w.
Farris, J. A., w.
Fields, M. A.
Fincher, J. E., d.
Fincher, O.
Fleniken, L. B.
French, Wm.
Garrison, A., d.
Gordon, A. E.
Griffin, Egbert.
Griffith, I. G.
Griffith, J. W.
Griffith, T. D.
Grier, Laurence.
Hannon, J. J.
Harkey, D. E.
Harkey, J. J.
Harkey, M. L.
Harkey, Wash.
Hartis, J. L.
Hartis, J. S.
Hanfield, Jas. W.
Hennigen, J. E.
Howard, J. M., w.
Hudson, Wilson.
Jamison, Emory.
Johnston, Dan.
Johnston, J. A.
Kenan, D. G.
Kenier, J. R.
Kerr, Jas.
Kerr, Sam'l.
Kirkpatrick, S. A.
McAlister, H. B.
McRaney, Sam'l.
Miller, W. T.
Moore, W. W.
Morris, G. C.
Morris, J. W.
Morris, Wm.

Neel, W. B.
Neely, W. A.
Newell, W. A.
Osborne, J. H., w.
Paxton, S. L.
Phifer, E. M., k.
Pierce, John, k.
Pierce, L. M.
Porter, Robt. A., w.
Porter, S. L.
Porter, Zenas.
Prather, A. R., d.
Prather, S. F.
Previtt, Allen.
Raterree, W. L.
Rea, D. J., w.
Reid, William, k.
Richardson, J. H.
Ross, W. A.
Shaw, J. N.
Smith, E. C.
Smith, Wm. B. J.
Spratt, A. P.
Squires, M. D., w.
Stanford, C. L.
Stephenson, Wm. J., w.
Stitt, Jas. M.
Swan, J. B.
Taylor, Ed. S., w.
Taylor, J. A. R., w.
Tevepaugh, Wm.
Tidwell, W. T. A.
Turner, F. M.
Walker, E. M., w.
Warwick, J. M., w.
Watson, J. A., d.
Watts, J. S.
Watson, J. B.
Weeks, J. L., w.
Whitesides, Wm., w.
Wingate, J. P., w.
Wingate, Wm. C.
Wolf, J. W.
Total 116; killed 5; wounded 23; died 5.

Company B, Fifty-Third Regiment N. C. Troops.

Officers.

J. H. White, captain, k.
S. E. Belk, capt., lost an arm.
J. M. Springs, lieut.
W. M. Matthews, lieut.
M. E. Alexander, lieut.

Non-Commissioned Officers.

R. J. Patterson, w.
S. M. Blair.
R. A. Davis.
A. N. Gray.
W. R. Bailey.

MECKLENBURG COUNTY. 355

R. H. Todd, k.
W. H. Alexander, k.

Privates.

Alexander, J. W., d.
Alexander, Benj. P., d.
Alexander, Benj. C.
Anderson, Wm., d.
Atchison, Wm., c. and w.
Armstrong, Leroy, c.
Barnett, R. S.
Barnett, W. A., k.
Barnett, E. L. S.
Berryhill, W. A., c.
Berryhill, Andrews, w.
Berryhill, Alex.
Barns, S. S., d.
Bruce, G. W.
Burwell, J. B.
Benton, Sam'l., w.
Baker, G. F., w.
Cochrane, J. M.
Cochran, Wm. R.
Cochran, R. C.
Catchcoat, J. H., w.
Capps, John, d.
Caton, Elijah, w. and c.
Caton, Sylv., c. and d.
Clark, W. H.
Clark, W. C.
Clark, A. W.
Collins, John, k.
Campbell, J. P.
Davis, W. A., d.
Demon, Jacob.
Donnell, W. T., w and c.
Engenburn, J.
Eagle, John, w.
Eagle, W. H.
Epps, W. D., k.
Engel, Jonas.
Frazier, J. L.
Fincher, Asa.
Farrices, Z. W.
Frazier, J. C. R.
Grier, J. G., w.
Giles, M. O.
Giles, S. H.
Howie, J. M.
Howie, Sam'l. M., w.
Howie, F. M., w.
Hall, H. L., w.
Hood, R. L., c.
Harry, W. B., w.
Hoover, F. M
Katz, Aaron.
King, P. A., k.
Kirkpatrick, T. A.
Knox, J. S.
Leon, Louis.
Love, D. L.

Marks, S. S., c.
Marks, J. G., w.
Marks, T. E., k.
Marks, W. S.
McGinn, Thos.
McElroy, Jas. W., k.
Mitchell, C. J.
McKinney, Wm.
McKinney, T. A., c.
Merritt, Wm. N., k.
McCrary, Jordan.
Morrison, J. M.
McCombs, A. H., w and c.
Maxwell, P. P., w.
McCrum, A. H., k.
Norment, A. A., k.
Otters, Cooney, c. and d.
Owens, J. Henry, k.
Oates, Jas.
Potts, Jas. H.
Patterson, S. L.
Parks, Miah, c.
Reid, H. K.
Reid, J. F., k.
Robinson, Thomp.
Russell, H. T., c.
Rodden, N. B., w.
Rodden, W. R., k.
Robinson, J. P.
Smith, Lemuel.
Sweat, J. M.
Sample, H. B., c.
Sample, David.
Sample, J. W.
Sample, J. M., c.
Springs, R. A.
Stone, W. D., w. and c.
Sulivan, W. L.
Stewart, W. S., d.
Taylor, J. W., w.
Todd, E. S.
Thomas, Henry.
Trotter, A. G.
Trotter, Thos., d.
Vickers, E. N.
Worthen, Henry, d.
Wilkenson, Neil, k.
Wolfe, C. H.
Winders, P. S., c.
Wilson, L. R., c.
Wilson, J. H., k.
Wilson, S. W., w. and c.
Wilson, J. M.
Wilkerson, R. L.
Williams, Hugh.
Williams, J. W.
Williams, A. L.
Williamson, A. L., c.
Williamson, J. M., c.
White, J. T.
Total, 110; killed, 16; wounded 21; died, 12; captured, 20.

Company E, Fifty-Ninth Regiment N. C. Cavalry.

Officers.

J. Y. Bryce, captain, w.
Robt. Gadd, lieut.
B. H. Sanders, lieut.
Wm. Bryce, lieut.

Non-Commissioned Officers.

J. J. Misenheimer.
J. B. Davis.
J. F. Davidson.
G. F. Vickers, k.
— — Vickers, k
W. H. A. Kluts.
R. Kluts.
M. L. Furr.
Noah Shore.

Privates.

Blackwelder, D. C.
Biggers, Wm.
Biggers, Houston, d.
Biggers, Robt.
Bost, Moses.
Bost, S. C.
Bost, J. K. P.
Beattie, J. O.
Barbon, George.
Barber, Josiah.
Benson, H. A.
Broadstreet, J. R., c.
Browning, J. M., d.
Cline, H. B.
Cline, . D., c.
Carriker, S. C.
Cox, J. D.
Cruse, Peter.
Clay, J. L., c.
Craig, Alex., c.
Davis, W. E.
Doolan, E., k
Eaudy, Paul.
Furr, Mat.
Furr, D. C.
Furr, Allen.
Furr, Darling.
Furr, W. M.
Furr, A. W., d.
Fisher C. A.
File, J. F.
Falls, W. A.
Faggart, D. C.
Foard, E. M.
Floyd, Wm.
Fink, Peter, k.
Griffin, Wesly.
Gatlin, G. W.
Grover. Austin.
Hagler, Jacob.
Hagler, Allen.
Hagler, Nelson.
Hagler, J. A.
Hoffman, J. L.
Hoffman, J. M.
Hartman, H. L.
Howell, W. E.
Hunsucker, N. J.
Johnston, J M., c.
Johnston, G. W.
Johnston, Jacob.
Kiser, G. A.
Kiser, N. D.
Kimmons, R. M.
Lay, J. G.
Linker, Jas.
Linker, W. R.
Linker, Aaron.
Linker, Moses.
Lefter, W. H.
Lay, W. J.
Lay, A. L.
Lay, J. W.
Ledford, C. M.
McCoy, J. R.
McDaniel, E. B., k.
McDaniel, E. A., d.
McEntire, M. L., c.
Misenhemier, J. H,
Moreton, W. R., d.
Moore, Dr. T. J.
Osborne, J. F.
Osborne, Robt., d.
Plyler, F. S.
Pender, J. H.
Perkins, A.
Pace, Young.
Reaves, F. A.
Rice, Moses.
Richards, Wm.
Ray, A. D., c.
Rhyne, C. M.
Rinehart, W. D., c.
Rinehart, Thos.
Starns, John, d.
Starnes, E. W.
Sossaman, D. G.
Sossaman, W. H.
Smith, J. B.
Smith, G. L.
Smith, G. F.
Stranter, Wm.
Stranter, John.
Stranter, T. H.
Stowe, L. P.
Smith, Frank, k.
Smith, L. A.
Thomas, C. W.
Turner, W. D.
Troutman, Geo.
Wallace, J. M.
Wilson, J. M.
Wilson, Wm.
Wallace, J. R.
Williamson, J. M.

MECKLENBURG COUNTY. 357

Williamson, J. B., w.
Total 116; died 6; killed 6; wounded 3; captured 4.

Company B, Forty-Third Regiment N. C. Troops.

Officers.

Robert P. Waring, Captain.
Drury Ringstaff, 1st lieut.
William E. Still, 2nd lieut.
Julius Alexander, 2nd lieut.
Robert T. Burwell, 2nd lieut.

Non-Commissioned Officers.

Drury Lacy, 1st sergt.
Robert B. Corble, 2nd sergt.
S. R. Johnston, 3rd sergt.
J. Harris Hunter, 4th sergt.
R. T. Burwell, 5th sergt.
Henry S. Presson, 1st corporal.
Smiley W. Hunter, 2nd corporal.
Robt. C. McGinness, 3rd corp'l.
Hiram Secrest, 4th corporal, k.

Privates.

Alexander, John M.
Aycock, W. M., k.
Broom, Samron,
Broom, Solomon.
Broom, S. A.
Broom, N. W.
Broom, Calvin, k.
Broom, Wilson.
Broom, A. T.
Barnes, Bryant.
Blackwelder, D. M.
Boyd, Hugh.
Burwell, W. R.
Cochran, W. L., k.
Craft, A. J.
Allen, Dees K.
Fincher, Levi J., w.
Fowler, Moses F.
Fowler, Geo.W., k.
Griffith, J. Henry, k.
Griffith, J. L.
Grier, Paul B., k.
Griffith, Marley.
Griffith, Farrington.
Harrington, Ed. P.
Helms, Asa.
Helms, Josiah, k.
Helms, Noah.
Helms, Elbert, k.
Helms, W. M.
Helms, Alex. L.
Helms, Noah J.
Howell, W. J., k.
Hunter, Mad, k.
Hargrave, Robt. W.
Knight, W. M.
Singleton, Lacy D.
Little, Bryant.
Moore, Pleasant.
McGwirt, David.
McGwirt, H. A.
Mullis, Simon.
Mannis, T. M.
Mannis, A. W.
Price, Josiah G.
Phillips, John.
Presley, John M.
Presley, Caswell.
Parsons, Larkins.
Paxton, William W.
Robinson, M. M.
Bobinson, M. B.
Robinson, Samuel J.
Reams, John W., k.
Rea, W. F.
Stearns, Johnston.
Stearns, Daniel, k.
Stearns, Thos. H.
Stearns, John R., k.
Stacks, Albert.
Steele, Albert, k.
Steele, Thos.
Stegall, Moses.
Stegall, Ambrose.
Stancel, James.
Stout, J. S.
Swift, Geo. W.
Simpson, H. Mc.
Sikes, Geo. G.
Sherrill, William E.
Thornburg, John L.
Wilson, W. A.
Womack, John.
Wilson, J. A.
Wilson, G. J.
Reported killed 20; wounded 1; died 7; but 19 lived to get home; 50 not accounted for.

Company F, Sixty-Third Regiment N. C. Cavalry.

Officers.

John R. Erwin, captain.
J. McWhite, first lieut.
C. S. Gibson, second lieut.
W. J. Wiley, third lieut.
S. A. Grier, first, sergt.
J. R. Kirkpatrick, second sergt.
R. A. Davidson, third sergt.
P. W. Lintz, fourth sergt.
J. H. Henderson, first, corporal.
J. M. Beaver, second corporal.
H. C. Bird, third corporal.
C. B. Palmer, fourth corporal.

Privates.

Armstrong, Larkin.
Armstrong, Mathew.
Alexander, H. L.

Alexander, W. N.
Alexander, J. W.
Alexander, J. S.
Abernathy, W. D.
Andrews, G. W.
Asbury, Eugene.
Adams, James.
Brown, J. C.
Blackwelder, Jas.
Blackwood, Eli.
Burroughs, John.
Brum, C. F.
Bowden, Lewis.
Bigham, Green.
Cochran, J. C.
Cochran, R. E., capt. and q. m.
Caldwell, D. A.
Caldwell, R. B.
Caldwell, J. N.
Caldwell, H. M.
Cahill, John.
Cathey, John.
Coleman, T. P.
Davidson, R. A.
Davis, J. T. A.
Downs, J. T.
Eudy, John.
Erwin, W. R.
Furguson, F. A.
Flenigan, R. G.
Ferrell, J. F. M.
Fisher, J. V.
Fisher, Alfred.
Fisher, Francis.
Fisher, E. L.
Faggot, Dan.
Gibson, D. M.
Griffith, C. F.
Grier, J. H.
Grier, Sam.
Harkey, W. F.
Howie, W. H.
Halobough, J. M.
Hunter, A. B.
Hoover, T. J.
Hovis, F.
Hannon, D. A.
Harris, J. S.
Hinson, M.
Hutchison, C. N.
Hartsell, Wm.
Jamison, J. L.
Jennings, J. H.
Kirkpatrick, W. L.
irkpatrick, J. M.
Kerr, R. D.
Kustler, M. E.
Love, D. L.
Love, J. M.
Lentz, Aaron.
Lindsay, Thos.
Leeper, Jas.
Ludwick, S.
Ludwick, Wm.
Montgomery, R. C.
McCall, J. A.
McElhany, E. A.
McElhany, S. L.
McDonald, J. R.
McDonald, Worth.
Millen, R. A.
McKinzie, Wm.
Means, P. B.
Moore, J. M.
Miller, S.
Minus, J. S.
Nance, W. T.
Nelson, J. M.
Norwood, R. F.
Neagle, J. F.
Prather, W. S.
Quiry, Walter.
Reed, W. H.
Russell, P. J.
Roper, P. H.
Regler, J. R.
Rea, D. B.
Rea, Sam'l.
Smith, D. W.
Smith, A.
Smith, R. T.
Smith, J. B.
Smith, John.
Smith, Wm.
Sloan, W. S.
Shuman, W. H.
Sharp, J. R.
Survis, T. O.
Terris C. E.
Tiser, W. H. G.
Taylor, D. B.
Tate, T. A.
Tate, F. A.
Torrence. C. L.
Wilson, Wm.
Wilson, J. C.
White, R. S.
Weaver, J. A.
Wright, J. C.
Wryfield, Wm.
Wallace, I. N.
Younts, J. A.
Young, J. A.
Casualties not reported.

From Mecklenburg, Not in Companies Raised in County.

Solomon Harkey, Heavy Artillery, Wilmington.
Captain Nic. Gibbon, Com. 28th Regt., N. C. Troops.

Mecklenburg Men Recruited by Capt. N. P. Rankin, of Guilford.

J. L. Adams, orderly sergt.
W. A. Mock.
W. H. Mock, sergt.
John N. Patterson.
Wm. Boils.

Reconstruction Times in Mecklenburg.

With the end of the war came reconstruction. The county of Mecklenburg never saw trouble before or since equal to the anoyance we were made to endure for seven years. Immediately on the disbanding of our armies, the Federal soldiers, six thousand strong, camped in and around Charlotte, to keep our people quiet.

It is hard to keep within the bounds of decorum and tell the plain, unvarnished truth, while this despotism lasted. The people were helpless indeed; their armies disbanded, all arms given up, or at least were called for. Crops were pitched and worked over once before the surrender, but the people had no money to hire labor to work their crops; horses and mules were stolen by Federal soldiers, and some by our former slaves; no redress by process of law. Where a negro man stole a mule and was placed in jail, he was immediately taken out of prison and the owner of the mule notified that any further molesting of the colored man or depriving him of his liberty would meet with speedy punishment.

A freedman's bureau was at once established that took the oversight of all freed men, to see that they got what they thought they were entitled to. But for a "consideration" in the way of a private fee, the captain would grant the employer of negroes permission to use a "persuader" to increase the amount of work gotten out of the freed man. The negroes had never enjoyed freedom before, and if they had not been led astray by unprincipled white men, they would have listened to their best friends, their former masters. They always had looked to them for food, clothing and shelter; and now in their new condition they could see no help only in the Freedman's Bureau. And here they were kicked about by petty tyrants to steal what little they could get out of them.

This bureau encouraged stealing and enmity between the

races all over the country. It was a rare thing for those in authority to urge an idea or plan that would be beneficial to both races; they were not willing for the negroes to be governed by the same code of laws held good for the white race. Probably they would not enrich the negro, but they would not allow the law to be enforced, for their stealing. A case is stated that occurred four miles from town on the Beattie's Ford road that illustrates the matter as it really occurred.

John Henderson—a mulatto—who was a very thrifty man, really more free when a slave than he ever was after he became a freed man. His house was well furnished, he kept a gold watch and a broadcloth suit of clothes. These last items were stolen out of his house by Yankee soldiers. John found them in the possession of a soldier, and complained to the General commanding, who told him to say nothing more about it; that it would not be safe for him (the negro) to have the man arrested. This was a common way of settling things gotten by the slight of hand. Some gentlemen who were tired of this kind of imposition in the eastern part of the county, put blood hounds on the track of a thief or thieves, and tracked a load of bacon to the central part of town, where the officer of the day ordered the dogs to be taken off. It was worse than idle to have resisted. Yes, the bureau encouraged stealing.

It was very annoying for a good citizen of the county to be subpoenaed by a former slave, acting as deputy, to appear at the bureau to answer certain complaints lodged by said freedman. It was worse than foolish to ignore the order. Here you were confronted with negroes, probably some that you had never seen before.

Political speeches were made by shrewd negroes of an inflammatory character that set the freedmen wild. They expected the time to speedily come when they would be the lawmakers of North Carolina. All the leading white men of the State were disfranchised. All who would not take the oath to support the Emancipation Proclamation, setting the negroes free, and giving them the right of suffrage, were prohibited from voting, or exercising the right of suffrage. This exceedingly bitter pill was forced upon us, when we were in this helpless condition. This election, the first after the surrender, was held in 1868. I thought I could vote without fail, as no office in the gift of the State or the United States had ever been entrusted to me. When I approached the election box with a ballot, the chief manager called me to halt, to hold up my right hand, that he would have to swear me, and commenced reading a printed oath of great length, the latter part of which was in these words: "And you further swear that you never carried arms, aided or abetted in the rebellion against the United States." Here I said: "Hold on, 'Squire; that lets me out." It is not to be supposed that one of all the splendid body of soldiers that went from Mecklenburg acted less patriotically. Some scalawags did swallow the oath, but the people believed they were paid for their treachery. On the other hand every negro voted on his own freedom, and his right to the election franchise. The election, like the negro's idea of religious worship, was too good to be done with in one day. The negroes and scalawags had it all their own way; it is true, they had orders how to conduct it. It is true things were done by the orders of Gen. Canby, headquarters in Charleston, S. C.

The election was held for three successive days, carrying the boxes containing the ballots home with them at night for three nights, and then sending the boxes to Charleston for Gen. Canby to count. The whole election machinery in the hands of an irresponsible party, and the enemies of the best people in Mecklenburg county. Truly we were in a horrible condition. No one knew what a day would bring forth.

The first election was about to come off, and the freedmen were exceedingly jubilant, thinking that freedom meant licence, to take whatever they wanted without giving a *quid pro quo*. Any kind of rumors could be heard on the streets, great crowds of negroes could be seen at almost every corner discussing every move that was made. Scarcely any person was cool enough to guide the storm that was brewing. The whites were but indifferently armed. Probably a thousand negro men parading the streets and six thousand Federal soldiers here in camp to take the part of the negroes against the white people of the country. They were in such a high state of frenzy as to only need a match to cause an explosion. A man by the name of Ed. Bizzel was mayor at this time, and had his office in the old frame building on West Trade street nearly opposite the Presbyterian church, where in after years a negro killed an Italian by the name of Mocha. Bizzell strongly sympathized with the turbulent element. He had two or more negroes on the police force, with some very bad white men, who were no better.

The man Bizzell, the mayor at the time—a northern man—was a fit representative of the party that was preying upon what was left of the once glorious county of Mecklenburg. He had a negro wife and family of mulatto children! A chief ruler, where he was not fit to serve. This was called reconstruction.

Capt. F. S. DeWolf, a true Confederate, married a daughter of Maj. J. B. Kerr soon after the war, while the town was infested with Federal troops. Maj. Kerr was lying dangerously ill and his garden—hotel garden—was raided every night by a large squad of soldiers, and Capt. DeWolf asked for a guard to protect the premises from the nightly thieves. One night just after dark he walked out to see after the safety of his garden, and he saw the guard talking to the thieves as hail fellows well met. The captain remonstrated with them, and they cursed him. The captain fired upon them and killed one. He surrendered and was tried by military law and acquitted. But the privates swore vengeance against him, and he had to keep hid for weeks in daylight.

Sergt. Joe Orr, a brave soldier and good man, was living about five miles from town. He was sent in town by his employer on an errand. He hitched his horse—which was a very fine one—to a tree where Mr. Lum Springs now lives, and stepped into a store for a few minutes, and when he came out his horse was gone. While enquiring about his horse, a Yankee sergeant remarked: "If you will give me five dollars, I will find your horse." Mr. Orr promptly gave him the money. The soldier said: "Now get up behind me and we will find your horse and the thief at the liquor shop in the outer edge of town." When they got there, there were both thief and horse in a crowd drinking at the saloon. Mr. Orr commanded the Federal soldier to get off his horse and to give up his property. The Federal immediately dismounted and made for the one-arm sergeant, but he was ready for him and struck the Yankee a blow on the head with a hickory stick that settled him. Orr was immediately arrested, and by the time they got up town to the court house a great crowd had collected and going up stairs in the great throng, Sergeant Orr made his escape, jumped his fine horse and never halted until he reached home, loaded his double-barreled shot gun with buckshot and waited in the front porch all night. But fortunately he was not molested afterwards. The Orr family have proved themselves to be brave men on many fields of battle, and on more than one occasion here in Mecklenburg. John Orr is thought to be by many persons the bravest man in Mecklenburg; but they are all good citizens.

Immediately after the arrival of the Federal troops in Charlotte, they issued an order that no Confederate soldier should be allowed to wear an insignia of rank, a Confederate button. The order was to humiliate the Confederate soldier, and if possible to make "treason odious." The order merely served to fan the coals of hatred and keep alive the spirit of resentment. Nothing was more common for a few days than to see a Yankee cut the buttons from the coat of an ex-Confederate, and immediately see the Federal soldier knocked down. There were some indignities, though trifling in themselves, no worthy man would submit to. The order was countermanded after a few days, when it was seen that the indignity would be resented. Little things that were unworthy of notice could become intolerable owing to the spirit in which they were done.

It was quite common for Federal soldiers to parade the streets in crowds of six to fifteen in a squad, taking up the entire pavement, insulting men or women, compelling them to step off the pavement, and give the right of way to the men dressed in blue. One morning a squad passing up North Tryon met an Alabama ex-Confederate who was well known in the county before the war for his good humor, when treated as a gentleman, but when treated insultingly, he was a devil incarnate. S. L. Carrol was ordered by a squad of blue coats "to *git* off the pavement and let *gentlemen pass.*" Quick as a flash of powder, Carrol struck the spokesman on the side of his head, knocking him senseless. The rest ran off for help, intending to mob the Confederate, but his friends urged him to get away, as he had no chance against their entire force. The little mill created quite a talk in the county for a few days. Nothing ever grew out of it. Mr. Carrol stayed out of town for a while, and it was soon forgotten.

A very unequal tax was put on the people. Whether it was down right robbery or not, we cannot say; but it had the form of coming from the United States Government. The land tax, they claimed, was levied during the war, and it was impossible to collect it. In some counties it was collected and in other counties they never made an effort to collect it. Some persons positively refused to pay it, and no effort was made to collect. In five or ten years, by some means they returned what they pressed from our people. Whether a guilty conscience held before their eyes or their minds the ill-gotten gains, we will never know, but all the same, we were glad to get back what had been stolen without interest.

Whenever a rich prize could be found it was sure to be seized by those in control. If it was not lying around loose, they could quickly issue an order that would take in charge whatever they could see had money—big money—in it. The South was a bonanza for those who ran the despotism for what money was in it. They put a tax on lint cotton of three cents a pound—$3.00 per hundred, $15.00 per bale for 500-pound bale. A farmer who raised ten bales paid a tax of $150.00. We had many farmers in Mecklenburg county who raised five times that amount of cotton, and consequently paid the tax in full.

The cries of the oppressed people were not loud, but they were deep. Many women who were raised tenderly and were accustomd to have every wish gratified, now saw the wolf of want at their doors, now rose up and saw their all taken away, instead of pining about the hard luck, they went to work with a will and forced nature to open her storehouse, and no one starved in our county. But we certainly are under no obligations to the United States Government for favors shown in the days of our humiliation.

In the times of reconstruction one of the most humiliating spectacles we were forced to witness was the order forbidding ministers to perform the functions of their office unless they would take the iron-clad oath, "Declaring that they never aided or abetted in the war of the rebellion." Some of the best men in the world, in this county, for two years never administered the sacrament of the Lord's Supper, administered baptism, or solemnized a marriage till the order was revoked. Some ministers paid no attention to the order, but went right on, virtually defying the commands of Gen. Canby.

The political situation in this county had to be held with an iron hand in the troublous days of reconstruction. It got into some of the churches in the country that did no good to the cause of religion, but wrought much evil. The wonder is it did not do more harm when the people were so stirred in political matters. But it was fortunately arranged that no permanent bad effect resulted. We got rid of some preachers that were more anxious to reap political honors than win souls for Christ.

Within a few months after the Federal soldiers took charge of the town and county, they organized the Loyal

League, a preliminary to the Republican party. All over the county meetings were held at night to encourage negroes to join. A few white men would act with them, but extremely few who were educated, and they were generally ostracised by the good people of the county. Politics absorbed all the attention of every one. It was the negroes and bad whites against the conservative element. It went from bad to worse until the "Ku Klux" was organized for self-protection. The two parties did not go so far in disturbing the peace of the county, as was done in other places. Hence the Ku Klux were not called on so often to regulate the troubles in this county; but they exercised a wholesome authority in the community. A negro, Tom Alexander, who lived just west of Huntersville, thought if he was free he had a right to vote as he pleased; and he voted the conservative ticket, whereupon he was ostracised by all the negroes and his children beaten by other children and called "Democrat niggers." This was carried on till it became more than Tom would bear. He went over to the house of the father of the children who had beaten his, and asked him to correct his children for their bad behavior. He jumped up and seized a hand spike and ordered Tom out of his yard, advancing on him, when Tom shot him dead. The negroes applied to a Justice of the Peace for a warrant for Tom's arrest. The warrant was put in the hands of the worst negro in the county as a deputy officer, who said he was specially instructed to search the houses of Dr. J. B. Alexander and R. B. Hunter, Esq. For two or three days a gang of fifty negroes were scouring the roads and fields in every direction, armed with every conceivable kind of weapon, on foot and horseback. The neighborhood was thoroughly terrorized; that is, the women and children were in danger. They had never witnessed a similar sight before. Mr. James Blythe went to the negro deputy and asked to see his warrant, which he transferred to his own pocket, and dismissed the negroes. It was truly a reign of terror while it lasted; but it was in keeping with the manner of reconstruction. Thirty years have passed, and Tom has not returned. His wife and children still live in Mecklenburg. The white people at large have shown her much sympathy, and her children have done well, and are regarded as good citizens.

Another scheme of robbery practiced by Federal soldiers during their stay in Charlotte, was to hunt up branded horses which Gen. Grant willingly let the Confederate soldiers take to their homes to cultivate a crop with. They would bring them in and demand from ten to thirty dollars for the horse, and if the poor soldier could not raise the cash, it was sold to some one else. So the crop would have to be lost for the want of a horse.

The people were all miserably poor. It was hard to get a start in the race of life. Some farmers had a few bales of cotton laid away for a rainy day; but the order of stealing had become so common it was almost impossible to keep it, and it was in almost as much danger to offer it for sale. The Yankees were as watchful as hawks for anything that they could turn into money. Cotton that was stored in Charlotte stood no better chance of safety.

Col. L. S. Williams had more than five hundred bales in different places, and lost it all but one hundred bales. An expert thief commanded a premium, and truth forbids it to be said that no thief belonged to Mecklenburg county. The whole country was more or less demoralized. One of Gen. Canby's orders that was enforced was that every woman, before she could be lawfully married, would have to take an oath to "support the Constitution of the United States." This was done to humiliate our people, the women who stood firm for the rights of the South and exhibited a patriotism that has never been excelled in the world. This oath had to be administered by a Notary Public or a Magistrate. And as no preacher could take the iron-clad oath, a Justice of the Peace could not only administer the oath, but could perform the martial rites as well. It was also ordered that all negroes living as man and wife, must be married over again, that is, buy new license, which cost them $3.00, even if they were on the down hill of life, and their children had left home to start families of their own. The price of the license had to be paid.

Last Chapter of Mecklenburg History.

We have seen the appearance of Mecklenburg one hundred and fifty years ago, "in good old colonial times when we lived under the king;" when the tall prairie grass and the wild pea vines covered the whole face of the Western part of the State; when the log cabin of the early settler, located down near the spring, always extended a most cordial invitation to the "new comer," who was hunting a home in the land of the deer and the buffalo, with great abundance of smaller game; when the water courses were well stocked with fish, even the spring branches were frolicsome with the horny heads and minnows, up to the fountain head.

Modern utilitarianism will have much to answer for at the shrine of natural beauty of scenery, of the virgin soil of Mecklenburg county. The deep channels of our creeks are now filled up; the timber on our uplands, as well as the creek and river bottoms, has been cleared, and the soil has been carried away by the rains; the meadows have been overflooded, and the sweet grass that formerly fed the cattle and sheep in large heards and flocks, is now only heard of when some old man who was raised on the farm becomes reminiscent. The first half of the last century our people seemed to think we should raise at home all that we needed to eat or wear; that if our people stayed at home, that they had but little need of money, consequently they did not try to have much for market, or at least did not raise much that would have to be hauled by wagon. Some horses, mules, cattle, sheep and turkeys were driven to Charleston to find a market and sometimes to Philadelphia. The first railroad finished to Charlotte was from Columbia, in 1852.

Before this period, that is before railroads were built, but little was consumed on the farm but what was raised there, or manufactured at home.

Until the first half of the Nineteenth century was passed,

all the iron that was used in Mecklenburg came from the iron works in Lincoln county. It was in bars six to ten feet long, about one inch thick and two and a half wide, with a wide expanse at one end, from six inches to a foot in width. This wide piece was to make various sized plows. This required heavy work to hammer it into the shape desired. The blacksmith was truly an artist a hundred years ago. Everything that was wanted or needed, had to be home made, even the nails to build our houses, fix the doors and window shutters, and to nail on the roofs. Fortunately the timber out of which our shingles were made would last indefinitely. It was not uncommon for shingle roofs to last and turn rain for eighty years, and when patched, it would be good for a century. Now what do we see as for building material? Lumber is dried and dressed by machinery, put at your door, all the irons, nails, screws, hinges, locks and bolts are gotten from the hardware stores, in every variety that the most fastidious taste could desire. The old time blacksmith is now a back number, except to shoe horses and repair breaks in vehicles and machinery. The farmers no longer cut their small grain with a scythe and cradle, but they use reapers and binders, which do the work of ten cradles, and save the grain much better. Before 1850 farmers were hard put to have their small grain thrashed out of the straw. The most common way was to have it tramped out with horse or oxen. Some persons beat it out with a flail, and some by turning a wagon upon it, but then it would have to be done out of doors, subject to rain and storm.

In this the revolution has been as great as in the harvest. The thrashing and cleaning and sacking is all done by machinery. All work is done by the saving of labor, the expense is less and the work is more efficiently performed than when done by hand. The first three-fourths of the century only the French burr stones were supposed to be the best of all substances that could be found for making flour; but in these latter years it has been discovered that roller mills give the greatest satisfaction. Iron, or chilled rollers, the porcelain or glass rollers, having a wonderful velocity, makes the most elegant flour on the market. The old water mill that we thought fifty years ago could not be improved upon, is now almost forgotten, and grain mills are now to be found in successful operation at all respectable sized towns, although no creek or river may be in sight. Steam has been the great motive power, but is now giving way to electricity, which in one or two decades will be the great motive power of the world, unless liquid air or some future discovery should take its place.

At the first of the Nineteenth century, or during the first quarter of the century, the people only planted a small "patch" of cotton, just enough for the good women of the home to spin and have woven into cloth for the family. It is not supposed there was a ctoton gin in Mecklenburg county prior to 1825. Prior to this cotton was finger-picked—that is, the seed were picked out by hand. The end of the century has come, and all agricultural work has changed as if the fabled Genii had made a revolution that has made us a new civilization; virtually, "old things have passed away, and all things have become new." Cotton was then in its infancy.

In the closing years of the Nineteenth century, we have seen a wonderful change in the civilization in times in which we live. Instead of the cotton "patch" of one hundred years ago, we have large fields of the fleecy staple, and it has become the principal crop. It used to be the rule on negro quarters for the negro men to gear two horses to the gin and leave a woman and a half-grown boy to gin cotton; they would finish one bale by noon, which the hands would pack while the horses were eating, and gin another bale by night. Two bales in a day fifty years ago was considered a good day's work. Now, in the year 1902, ten to fifteen and even twenty bales a day is not considered as great a day's work as when five bales were done in a day.

It was a question a half a century ago, what is the easiest way to dispose of the cotton seed; we did not know their value then, the oil had not been expressed, no price was fixed; meal was not known then to hold so much nitrogen for making fertilizers of so great value, and for feeding purposes. The seed that we formerly wasted is now worth one-fourth of the entire crop. The cotton crop now holds the balance of power among the crops of the country. There was probably not a cotton factory in the county prior to 1875. Now the county stands first in the number of mills or factories. Our county has been anything else than a laggard in the race of progress.

When a boy going to school it was a common sight to see large flocks of sheep. A half a century ago but few people kept their sheep up in pasture, but let them run at large. Almost every farmer kept from 20 to 80 in a flock. By salting them when they came home, they always knew where to find a "lick."

It was rare sport for school children to witness the leader of a flock to espie another flock approaching, and he knew intuitively that a fight was brewing, for every flock had its ram that would champion the cause of the family. The two belligerents seemed to understand that nothing short of a decisive battle would put a quietus on the approaching leaders. The flocks would take opposite sides, remain quiet, and the rams would step backwards till they were about twenty paces apart, when they would run rapidly together, butting their heads together with a loud noise, frequently both being knocked down. This operation being repeated till one of the two would run. Sometimes their horns would become locked, and they would be found dead, still unclasped. For the last twenty-five years the worthless dogs have made it unprofitable to raise sheep in this county. It is now a lost industry, that children and vagrants may enjoy the pleasure of keeping a pack of dogs.

The common, or the old field schools, did not improve very much till the last quarter of the Nineteenth century. The room in which the school was taught was generally built of logs, with a dirt floor, a log was cut out for a window where a writing desk was made; slabs were used for benches, generally so high that little children could not reach the floor, and a child would be in punishment for days or months at a time. But we are glad to know that a decided improvement in respect to school houses has taken place in the latter days. The pupils are more comfortable, and in a better spirit more in accord with a desire to learn. We now have teachers worthy of the name, to train our children.

In the early part of the century, the rod was considered a necessity—very necessary part of the school furniture. Mr. T. W. Sparrow, who was a most excellent scholar as well as a good teacher, often remarked: "If you will furnish the boy and the book, I will do the whipping." In the last quarter of a century the pendulum has swung too far the other way. A happy medium would probably produce the best results.

Until the last fifty years, or even down to twenty-five years ago, to see a child or a young person wearing spectacles was almost unheard of. Now you hardly see a school room but has one or more pupils with defective vision. In fact we are noted as a people given to wearing eye-glasses. The question is frequently asked, "What is the cause of so much impaired vision?" It can be truthfully said that the vigor of manhood has been impaired to a remarkable extent in the last third of a century. It formerly was not considered excessive for a man to cut and split one hundred rails in a day, or cut one hundred dozen of wheat or oats in a day. Now it takes two men to perform the same amount of labor. "The part of least resistance is the first to give way." The offspring of such enfeebled persons shows degeneracy in different parts of the body, and we might expect as delicate an organ as the eye to be affected more or less seriously.

The negro in slavery time never complained of any defect of vision until old age came on, but now they can sport eye-glasses with as much grace and pride of dress as if they came of a long line of weak eyes.

The thousands of Confederate soldiers with whom we

were associated, scarcely a one needed his eyesight improved forty years ago. But now if we go on a visit to the various asylums in Morganton and Raleigh, we see not only the blind and deaf and dumb, but what is worse, the vast and increasing number of insane. The State has a heavy load. Our new civilization will have much to answer for at the bar of a healthy people.

Dr. Julian J. Chisholm, of Baltimore, told the writer once in treating a lady's eyes, in which he met with only failure, at which he was much mortified, he said to her if he were not sure to the contrary, he would say she was addicted to the use of tobacco. She blushed and said she would have to plead guilty. That may be the cause of many cases of defective eyesight.

In the early years of the Nineteenth century, the price of newspapers was three to five times as high as one hundred years later, and so was the postage on papers and letters, which last was twenty-five cents, which has gradually been reduced to two cents, and a postal card to one cent. There was but one postoffice between Charlotte and Davidson College. That was Alexandriana, the mail on which route was carried once a week—going from Statesville to Charlotte on Friday and back on Saturday. The mail was always light. The postmaster would carry all the Hopewell mail to church the next day and leave it on the table, and every one could get his own mail. All the mail for north Mecklenburg and South Iredell for one week's distribution, was carried in one mail sack—about a peck. But few persons went to the office, nearly every person wrote by some one going in that direction. People in the olden time were very accommodating—more so than now.

Dime novels were then unknown, and it is more than probable there was nothing lost in that respect. Books at that time were scarce and high. There was no room for cheap novels then. Political papers of a high order could be had—that is, weekly papers; but they cost high. Educated gentlemen had pretty fair libraries, but they were few and far between. A cultured gentleman like D. A. Caldwell would have a good library.

For the first 25 years of the Nineteenth Century, newspapers were exceedingly scarce in the State, not to speak of the county. It is more than probable that Charlotte could not boast of a paper prior to 1825. Holton's *North Carolina Whig* was established in 1824. The *Hornet Nest* was published by Badger and Philo Henderson, commencing about 1848. It lasted several years and gave way for the *Western Democrat* in the early fifties, by R. P. Wearing, who ran it successfully until he received a consulate in the Danish West Indies, when Mr. W. J. Yates took charge and made it a splendid success, both as a newspaper and a business enterprise. E. H. Britten began editing the *Bulletin* about 1860. It was kept up till after the war, when bankruptcy overtook the whole country. Gen. Hill published his magazine, *The Land We Love,* for several years, and afterwards the *Southern Home* newspaper, which was very spicy and popular. About the same time the *Observer* was started by Charles R. Jones, which was well edited for a number of years, and wielded considerable influence. This was a big stride forward. The *Bulletin* was the first daily, but the *Observer* was an improvement. Mr. Jones' health gave way and the paper was run by the stockholders as best they could for a few years. Mr. Robert Hayden took charge for some time, but in a year or two abandoned the paper, when the stockholders secured the present editor, Mr. J. P. Caldwell, who has given Mecklenburg the best paper ever published in her bounds. He is associated with D. A. Tompkins in publishing the paper, with a staff of good reporters, and are making a grand success. The *Evening News* is also proving a successful venture, with Mr. W. C. Dowd as editor. It now appears to be one of the fixtures which the city is proud of.

The *Peoples' Paper,* edited by J. P. Sossaman, has been running for several years as a free lance, criticising according to how people do. The virtuous are praised and those

MECKLENBURG COUNTY COURT HOUSE.

who violate the law are condemned. He has a satisfactory circulation.

The *Mill News* is ably edited and reaches many readers. The *Enterprise,* a negro paper, has been issued—not regularly—for a number of years, and is read by the people of that race. The organ of the Presbyterian Church of North Carolina is published here, and has a backing by the Synod of the Presbyterian Church of the State, and it has the best opportunity of any in the State. Our town and county is admirably supplied with the best of religious and political papers, and mill and scientific papers to teach science as applied to manufactures. Charlotte has two medical journals that will compare favorably with any published in any city in America. In the earlier years there was no progress in caring for the sick, but what every family could do in looking after their people. Time has brought many changes, and some for the good of our fellow beings. We now have three hospitals where forty years ago we had only a temporary shelter for soldiers, we now have such pleasant quarters that some of our most refined ladies cheerfully accept a ward in the hospitals to bring their sick.

There are two elegant hospitals in use here for the white people, and one for the colored people. Both have the latest appointments with the most skillful physicians and well-trained nurses. Discoveries in medicine and surgical appliances, and the microscope have all yielded benefits to suffering humanity.

The first railroad in the county, Columbia & Charlotte, was finished in 1852. A big celebration and barbecue with speaking was the order of the day. In 1856 the railroad from Goldsboro to Charlotte was finished. Until this road was finished, the Democratic party was opposed to all internal improvements by State taxation; but they were not opposed to individuals subscribing to public works. The State took no stock in the Charlotte & Columbia railroad. Many Democrats laughed at the idea of building a railroad that would not have more than two *train loads* a year, one in the fall and one in the spring!

The road from Wilmington to Lincolnton and on up the mountains, has been in operation since 1875, or there abouts. The road to Statesville or Taylorsville was put in running order soon after the war, the iron having been taken up to build the road from Greensboro to Danville during the war, as a necessary war measure. In the latter part of the seventh decade—about 1876 or 1877, the road was completed to Atlanta. The county paid $300,000 to build the Atlanta and Statesville roads. The county has made wonderful progress in the last twenty-five years, and has at least doubled her population.

In the last twenty-five years the bicycle has made its appearance, and is in use in all parts of the world. There appears no valid reason why it may not be a fixture to stay. It is now used by both sexes to visit the metropolis, in all sections of the county. The depots and repair shops now indicate their common use, and the price having come down within the reach of all, there is no reason why every one should not ride a wheel, wherever the roads will admit it.

MERCHANTS IN 1850-1900.

A half century ago the stores were dry goods establishments. If a man wished to carry a variety of goods, they were all in one house. H. B. & L. S. Williams kept in the south corner of the public square, now occupied by the Carolina Clothing Company. It was a fair sample of the stores. They carried a general assortment of dry goods, a few sacks of coffee, sugar, molasses, cheese and tea. Loaf sugar, moulded in cone shape, wrapped in blue paper, tied with twine and hung overhead—this was the only kind considered good enough to sweeten "bought" tea. They also had vast quantities of yarn, hung overhead. This was in "bunches," five pounds, ranging from 400, the coarsest, on up to 1,000 or 1,200, the finest. But little or no negro cloth was brought on by merchants. It was all spun and woven at home, both for summer and winter wear. The plain wool hats to wear for every day were made by hatters in every neighborhood. The merchants fifty years ago kept finer goods than they do now. Broadcloth sold—a good article—at $15.00 per yard, and a silk dress equally as high. When the merchants, or any one else wanted to borrow money, they applied to their country friends, where they would not be turned down. When the railroad got to town the merchants multiplied. Ready-made clothing first made its appearance with the advent of Levi Drucker. The Israelites followed close on the coming of the railroads. They have proved amongst our best citizens.

The city has grown so that it would not be recognized as the same place if visited by persons who liveed here a half century ago. Among the active men who took part here fifty years ago we mention Leroy Springs, William Davidson, W. W. Elms, H. B. Williams, John Irwin, David Parks, Sam Harris, Richard Carson, John A. Young, T. H. Brem, and men of a more recent date, who were very active—T. L. Alexander, William Johnston, A. B. Davidson, R. Y. McAden, J. Y. Brice, S. P. Alexander, R. M. Oates and many more. The town was then only a small village, with streets hardly any better than the ordinary big roads. It was common for wagons to stall or mire down in the public square. The streets were not macadamized, or begun to be paved until after the close of the war. Nor were the roads made hardly passable for wagons, in the winter time twenty years ago. Some expert drivers stayed near the creek west of town to drive your load up the fearful Irwin's lane. For fifty cents they would land your load up town.

The chain gang had much to do with the good roads we now have in the county. Much of the road was done over two or three times before a satisfactory highway was constructed. Much money has been spent for the county's good roads, but no one complains of the taxes paid. From the little village we had fifty years ago, we now see the most thriving city in the State, with cotton mills that give employment to thousands of hands, and other kinds of mills and machinery of every description in full blast. The city and its suburbs now numbers over thirty thousand inhabitants, which gives employment to truck farmers and dairymen, who realize a handsome profit, that formerly were engaged in a less profitable business. A general market has been built up for everything raised on the farm, and by the advancement of Mecklenburg, all the surrounding counties have been benefited. Two of the best female colleges in the State are largely patronized, having young ladies from several States in attendance. This is a city of elegant churches of every denomination, well attended—in all at least thirty churches—of elegant structure, besides chapels and temporary places of worship.

THE OLD CEMETERY.

The old cemetery, attached to the First Presbyterian Church, was used for a burying ground since the present site of the town was laid off, or soon afterwards. The old graveyard east of the city was discontinued soon after the town was located. The elder Polks and Barnetts and others whose names have become dim or obliterated, a mile and a half east of the town, have many of their posterity and compeers laid to rest in what is now called "the old cemetery" in Charlotte. For a little over one hundred years this graveyard was the common place of sepulture. When the enclosure (walled in with brick) was filled with the dead, a new burying ground was laid off and inclosed, known as Elmwood, on the northwest side of the city. It is handsomely kept, a beautiful city of the dead. How soon is the old one forgotten! Many patriots of the Revolutionary War are sleeping there—Col. Thomas Polk, Dr. Ephraim Brevard, Gen. George Graham and many others of more than ordinary fame. But such is life. Many of the old graveyards have been woefully neglected, and the private yards in Mecklenburg are no exception. It is only within the last forty years that the civilization of the present has ripened up into flowers, blooming for the blushing bride, and all the holiday attire of schools and appropriately for temples of worship; but especially for those who defended our course in the late war of Constitutional Liberty.

When Governor Vance last appeared before a Charlotte audience, although too feeble to speak, showers of bouquets were thrown around his seat, indicative of the Easter morning that awaited him, when he should have completed his course of incessant labor for his people of North Carolina. Decorating the graves of our dead is a beautiful custom.

Fifty years ago wild game was abundant of every kind. The deer and wild turkey were found in all parts of the county. The red and grey fox could be started with a pack of hounds any morning a chase might be desired. A grey one would lead the pack from two to four hours, and the red would run six to eight hours. When it was known which variety was going to lead, one-half of the pack was held in reserve until Reynard would *lower his brush,* which was a sure token that his race was nearly run. Fox hunting was then considered the gentlemanly sport of the county. If the fox should have partaken of a midnight supper of a pig, a lamb or a goose, he would make a poor run, lasting not more than an hour. The raccoon and opossum were principally hunted at night.

Times have changed and all these species of wild game—save the opossum—have disappeared from the county. The forests have been cleared, and no place is now left to raise their young. The old field rabbit is at home in the broom sedge and briar thickets. The appearance is that the rabbit will alone occupy the places that formerly were occupied by the different varieties that are missing. The birds that forty years ago made the woods alive with their voices, are now all hushed; the coveys of doves, larks, yellowhammers and black birds are nearly all gone; here and there we see a mocking bird and a jay, a cat bird and a thrush; all are gone save the partridge, and it alone is protected by law. The English sparrow now occupies the place of all other birds, but has been but a late importation, and has a pugnacity that well becomes the English, for the Anglo-Saxon will not tolerate a rival.

In this good year 1902, it is well for us to take a look backwards and see what our county population was one hundred years ago, and what it was when the century was finished.

In 1800 it was 10,439, in 1810 it was 14,272, in 1820 it was 16,895, in 1830 it was 20,073, in 1840 it was 18,273, in 1850 it was 13,914, in 1860 it was 17,374, in 1870 it was 24,298, in 1880 it was 34,175, in 1890 it was 42,673, in 1900 it was 55,261.

In the decade from 1845 to 1855, there was a vast emigration. Both before and after these dates the move was very considerable. Large numbers of slaves were sent to raise cotton on the fertile lands of the southwest. By the year 1870 the tide of emigration was turned, and the best element poured into Mecklenburg from all directions. Charlotte and the suburbs has a population now estimated at 35,000. The rapid growth is not of the boom character, but it is solid. She is constantly lengthening her cords and strengthening her stakes, and bids fair to be one of the largest inland cities of our Southland. Why should our city not be an emporium? No city or town has a finer back country to draw from. The county is full of gold and copper and iron ores. One of the three metals can be found on every mile of territory, and in many places in quantities that will pay to work. The company now engaged in extracting the gold from the sands of the Catawba river have certainly got a bonanza that pays the company most handsomely.

Scarcely a farm in the county but what has unmistakable signs of gold, copper or iron. This is an inviting field for an expert, and awaits his coming with much solicitude.

HOW MECKLENBURG HAS SUFFERED.

For the last fifty years this county has offered advantages to the educated classes that other sections of the State have not been able to compete with in all the different branches of learning. Her schools have attracted many learned individuals who have given us of their store of useful knowledge, but they have tried to rob us of our priceless treasure, the Declaration of Independence on the 20th of May, 1775. We have a large population of learned preachers, lawyers and scientific men who deny the truth of those immortal signers, notwithstanding one was a minister of the Gospel and nine others were elders in the Presbyterian Church, and was witnessed by a great number of the best people in all this section of country; two, if not more of the witnesses, were young men who achieved a reputation for patriotism and learning, coextensive with the State, Maj. Gen. Joseph Graham and Rev. Humphrey Hunter. These were conspicuous figures who were present at the meeting of the great committee on the 20th of May, 1775. It is strange that men, not of our State, not of Mecklenburg county, should move here and enjoy the blessings of our county, reap the magnificent rewards as teachers in our schools and colleges, fill pulpits of our churches, occupy exalted places in our courts and legislature, and then deny the chiefest diadem in our crown of liberty and independence. "He who steals my purse steals trash; 'twas mine, 'tis his, and has been slave to thousands; but he who filches from me my good name, robs me of that which enriches him not, but leaves me poor indeed."

North Carolina has been regarded as a "strip of land lying between two States," fit only to furnish material for history, that may garland the brows of her sisters. Virginia and South Carolina have enough to be proud of, and we would be unworthy of our illustrious ancestors if we would tamely submit to such robbery, while we have such abundant proof of all the facts ever claimed, to establish the validity of the memorable declaration put forth on the 20th of May, 1775. Many persons, natives of other States, who have found a home within the bounds of Mecklenburg, are not willing for us to hold that which belongs to us not only by right of inheritance, but by priority of date. Before 1819 not a whisper was heard against Mecklenburg being the birthplace of liberty, but now we see men in every walk of life who have an itching desire to tarnish the honors of Mecklenburg's old heroes, rather than accord the dues to whom they belong. Strangers have shown a strong desire to write a history of the county, but for reasons not given, their works have never seen the light.

APPENDIX.

Extract From Lyman Draper's Notes.

Signers of Mecklenburg Declaration of Independence.

GEN. THOMAS POLK.

The original names of the ancestors of the Polks of Mecklenburg was Muirhead, whence it was changed to Pulloak, then to Pollock—which by obvious transition, assumed its present—as is evident by the will of Magdalen Polk, dated 1723, preserved among the records of the Orphans' Court of Summerset County, Md.

The traditions of the Greeks and Romans were not more quaint and curious as to the origin of their heroes than are those of many of the Scotch-Irish Presbyterians who early migrated to the New World. The Polks have had handed down to them a tradition running in this wise:

On a certain great occasion, a way back in the misty past, a king of Scotland was marching at the head of an immense procession, when a small oak shrub appeared directly in front of his majesty, to which one of the king's attendants, by the name of Muirhead, a man of great physical strength, sprang forward, and with a Herculean effort, tore it up by the roots and bore it out of the way. Such an act of gallantry prompted the king to order a halt, when he knighted Muirhead upon the spot, and changed his name to Pulloak—pull-oak. Another tradition is related of the same person. An enormous size and vicious wild boar inhabited that region, a terror to all who came within his range. A reward was offered by the king to any one who would rid the country of the dreaded monster. Pulloak determined to try it single-handed. Armed only with a bow and arrows, he sallied forth on the dangerous adventure. One version of the story is that when the wild boar discovered his pursuer, he rushed towards the bold hunter, who climbed an oak tree, and from its branches he shot the fierce animal. Another version of the story is that, pursued by the enraged boar, Pulloak sprang through an old church window, the boar after him; but Pulloak instantly darted out of the door and shut it quickly, and managed to close the window, and then quietly returned home. His neighbors were not a little surprised at his safe return. In response to their expressions of astonishment, he effected equal surprise, saying with nonchalance, truly a bit of a pig had the hardihood to run at him, when he seized it by the tail and threw it into the church window, where they might go and satisfy themselves of the fact. At length some of the more courageous of the number sallied forth to see the game of the forester, and were astonished beyond measure when they discovered the "bit of a pig" was none other than the dreaded wild boar for whose taking off the king had offered the large reward. Some of those present argued that Pulloak was more than a Sampson, and must have been imbued with supernatural aid. And as an additional evidence of his fearlessness, he boldly advanced, and shot the enraged animal through one of the windows.

The hero of the exploit, as the tradition goes, kept his own counsel and it was many a long year before he saw fit to divulge the manner of his getting so dangerous a beast into the church alone and single handed. The coat of arms of the Polk family is no doubt derived from the latter tradition— "Polloak, Bar't, Scotch; a boar, passant, pierced by an arrow." Motto: Audacter et strenne—Boldly and readily. The boar is represented with elevated bristles and angered mien, transfixed with an arrow.

To aid in ameliorating the natural turbulence of the Irish character, James I. encouraged a large emigration into Ireland, and among those who settled in that part of Ulster known as Donnegal, was the family of Pollocks. Robert, a son of the elder Pollock, took an active part in the wars against Charles I. and fought side by side with Cromwell against the Royalists, under Rupert. The powder-horn worn by Robert Pollock during the civil wars is now in possession of Col. W. H. Pollock.

Returning home he married Margarette Tasker, the widow of Col. Porter, and heiress of Mo, a beautiful estate near the town of Giffoard; whose father, Col. Porter, a chancellor of Ireland, had been an eminent man in his day.

Robert and Magdaline Pollock reared six sons and two daughters. The father and sons obtained grants of land in Maryland from Lord Baltimore. John Pollock, or Polk—the eldest son—in 1685, settled at a place called Locust Hammock, in Summerset county, on the eastern shore of Maryland. Thither parents and children migrated at an early period, and became prominent and useful settlers in the colony.

John Polk, who first married ———————————— and for his second wife Joanna Knox, died in 1707, leaving two children, William and Nancy.

William, Priscilla, Robert and Thomas Polk, the subject of this sketch, and the eldest of eight children, was born in Summerset county, Maryland, about 1730. His father moved to the neighborhood of Carlisle, Cumberland county, in 1750, then a newly settled region of Pennsylvania, fast filling up with hardy Scotch-Irish emigrants.

Thomas Polk's early educational advantages must have been quite respectable for that day, since he fitted himself for the occupation of surveyor; and on attaining the age of manhood, and learning of the new settlement along the Catawba Valley, since known as Mecklenburg, he directed his course thither, about the commencement of the border trouble of 1754-'55, the Indian outbreak incited by French influence extending from the frontiers of New Hampshire to the back settlements of the Carolinas.

Thomas Spratt is said to have been the first man who moved his family on wheels across the Yadkin, stopping a while on Rocky river, and then settling within the present limits of Charlotte. Thomas Polk, when he arrived at Thomas Spratt's, had only a knapsack on his back and a goodly share of indomitable enterprise. He soon married Susanna Spratt, the daughter of this early settler, and their son, William, who distinguished himself in the Revolutionary war, was born in Mecklenburg county in 1758. During the period of 1756 to 1760, there were some Indian troubles on the Catawba and Yadkin frontiers; and it may well be supposed that Thomas Polk here learned some of those lessons of bravery and leadership which he displayed so creditably during the subsequent years of the Revolutionary war. The characteristics of the pioneer settlers of Mecklenburg are well described by an aged native of that region, whose clear memory reaches back into the close of the last century. They were, he says, strong in body, strong in mind, brave, and patriotic.

They were driven by persecution from Scotland and Ireland, and were called Scotch-Irish.

They were determined to have *liberty* or have *death*. They lived far from market and had few luxuries. Those who could afford it had coffee for breakfast on Sunday morning, before they went to church, but at no other time. Though they lived plainly, they lived abundantly. The land was rich, producing all manner of grain, stock always plenty and always fat. The women were the best of cooks; no negroes then; no cotton, no drunkards, no thieves; no locks on dwellings, corn crib or smokehouses. The hardest time of the year was to harvest their crops. Then all through winter they had little to do but to attend their stock, pay and receive visits. Happy days!

Thomas Polk was originally a surveyor, says Dr. Johnson in his traditions of the revolution in the Southwestern part of North Carolina; his education was not acquired within the classic walls of a college, but partially obtained at intervals from his occupations in hills, valleys and forests of the province.

Then he became universally known and respected, no man

possessing more influence in that part of North Carolina. As early as 1770 he was one of the two representatives of Mecklenburg county in the popular house of the Legislature, and in June, 1772, he was employed by Gov. Martin as surveyor in running the western extension of the boundary line between North and South Carolina. As indicative of the independent spirit of the people in opposing royal encroachments on their rights, the popular house in February, 1773, refused to vote an appropriation of £172 10s. to pay the claim of surveyor for running the line, even though so popular a man of the people, and a former member of the house, as Capt. Polk, contending that the previous Assembly had expressed its sense of injury that accrued to the colony by fixing the line as proposed by the Governor.

At the breaking out of the Revolution, Thomas Polk was the colonel of the militia, and the most popular man in Mecklenburg, and all his influence was exerted in behalf of the popular cause.

It is apparent from Jones' defense of the Revolutionary history of North Carolina, and from the statements of some of the aged men with reference to the Mecklenburg resolves of May 20, 1775, that he had the principal agency in calling the convention of which he was a conspicuous member and popular leader of the people. Foote adds that he was well known and well acquainted in the surrounding counties, a man of great excellence and merited popularity. He was also one of the Mecklenburg members of the Provincial Congress that held sessions at Hillsboro during August and September, 1775, and served on important committees—one to prepare a plan for the regulation of internal peace, order, and safety of the Province. On September 9, 1775, he was appointed by the Provincial Congress colonel of the militia of Mecklenburg, and in November and December following, marched at the head of six companies, aggregating three hundred men, into the Southeastern part of South Carolina to aid in suppressing an outbreak of the Tories in that quarter. Some 300 pounds of powder was supplied by the authorities of

North Carolina for the use of his troops against the insurgents near Ninety-Six. It was a hard service with some fighting. The Tories were subdued and many made prisoners, and in consequence of a heavy snow fall, it was called the snow campaign. This service was all the more creditable since it was to serve a neighboring Province in suppressing a dangerous insurrection, and Col. Richardson, the South Carolina commander, was directed to take Col. Polk's men into the pay of the colony for the expedition, and tender them the thanks of the South Carolina Council of Safety with the assurance that "the service of those good neighbors" would ever be held in grateful remembrance.

In December, while absent on this service, he was appointed colonel of the Second of the two regiments of Minute Men, ordered to be raised in the district of Salisbury, composed of Rowan, Mecklenburg, Tryon and Surry counties. He had been but a brief period returned from South Carolina when he was called to lead his regiment against the Tory Highlanders on the Cape Fear in February, 1776, and reaching Cross Creek, now Fayetteville, received intelligence of the decisive victory of Caswell and Lillington over the insurgents, and returned home.

In April, he was recommended by the Provincial Congress to the command of the Fourth of the six Continental regiments, which the Continental Congress confirmed early in May; and the same month he was ordered with his regiment to join Gen. Moore at Cape Fear. The six Continental regiments finally rendezvoused at Wilmington, from which at least a portion were ordered in June to the defence of Charleston, Polk's regiment being of the number. But a single regiment of the North Carolinians, Clarke's, appears to have had any active part in repelling the enemy from Charleston. This service ended, the North Carolina Continentals seem to have returned to their old camp at Wilmington, and drilled and perfected themselves during the summer and autumn, when they were marched into South Carolina.

In February, 1777, Francis Nash, who had just been promoted to a brigadier, was ordered by the Continental Congress to use his influence in the western part of North Carolina to stimulate the filling up of the Continental regiments, and march the ensuing month to join Gen. Washington.

Major William Lee Davidson, of Polk's regiment, marched with the North Carolina line, but it is not apparent that Col. Polk himself engaged in the service. It is probable that inasmuch as the Continental regiments were deficient in numbers, there were only enough of Polk's to form a major's command.

From this time to the fall of Charleston, in May, 1780, was comparatively a quiet period in North Carolina.

In 1777 Liberty Hall Academy was established in Charlotte on grounds and improvements purchased by Col. Polk, and he was made one of the trustees. Thus were means for public education provided and sustained, until the institution was suspended by the subsequent British invasion of the country. In 1780, Col. Polk had troops at Charlotte guarding the public magazines, which were removed when the enemy approached in September of the same year. He acted as Commissary General of supplies both for the North Carolina troops and the Continentals under Gen. Yates (Lee Paper N. Y. Hist. Society, p. 145), and there was some complaint for inattention to duty on his part in his important office, which he explained upon the ground of scarcity of supplies and necessary attention to his family.

Col. Alexander Martin, a member of the State Board of War, to which Col. Polk was amenable, having visited the army of Mecklenburg, declares in a public letter recorded in the journal of the board, that in his opinion Col. Polk had fulfilled the duties of his office as well as circumstances would admit.

During Cornwallis' occupancy of the country, Col. Polk had necessarily to retire from Charlotte, and his residence became the headquarters of the British general. An original letter written by him at this period to the North Carolina Board of War is in possession of Col. J. H. Wheeler, viz.:

"CAMP YADKIN RIVER, Oct. 11, 1780.

"GENTLEMEN:—I have the pleasure to inform you that on Saturday last the noted Col. Ferguson, with 150 men, fell on King's Mountain; 800 taken prisoners, with 150 stand of arms. Cleveland and Campbell commanded. Glorious affair. In a few days doubt not we shall be in Charlotte, and I will take possession of my house and *his* lordship take the woods.

I am gentlemen, with respect,
Your humble servant,
THOMAS POLK."

How such a man as Col. Polk should have been under a cloud of distrust even for a short time, as Lossing states, is a little marvelous; yet some mischief-making person must have invented a "suspicion that he had accepted of protection from the British," and reported it to Gates, who turned from his late defeat and the recent treachery of Arnold, readily surmised "suspicious circumstances" and ordered Col. Polk to Salisbury to answer for his conduct. So utterly baseless were those cruel suspicions that they were promptly dismissed, and Col. Polk was continued in his double office of Commissary General of provisions for the State of North Carolina and commissary of purchases for the Continental troops. The very first night that Gen. Greene, having succeeded Gates, passed at headquarters early in December, he spent with Col. Polk in studying the resources of the country. and by "the following morning," said Polk to Elkanah Watson, "he better understood them than Gates had done during the whole period of his command." The Mecklenburg region had been the granary of provisions for the Americans for the whole season, and for the British for a short season, the latter demanding heavy supplies; according to Stedman, their Commissary General demanding 100 cattle per day.

The country was, therefore, so much exhausted that Col. Polk, who still acted as commissary from patriotic motives, declared that it could scarcely afford subsistance for a single week. It was with regret that Gen. Greene learned from him that many reasons conspired, rendering it necessary for him to relinquish the office. "I am now too far advanced in years to undergo the task and fatigue of a Commissary General," wrote Polk to Greene on December 10th. On the same day Greene wrote to Col. Wm. R. Davie inviting him to that position, saying "Col. Polk finds the business of subsisting the army too laborious and difficult for him to conduct, and, therefore, has sent in his resignation to the Board of War, but the greatest difficulty with him is, he cannot leave home owing to the peculiar state of his family." Dr. Johnson has presented in his traditions of the Revolution the following letter:

"CAMP CHARLOTTE, Dec. 15, 1780.

"*To Col. Polk*:

SIR:—I find it will be impossible to leave camp as early as I intended, as Col. Kascius has made no report respecting a position upon Pee Dee. I must, therefore, beg you to continue the daily supplies of the army, and keep in readiness three days' provisions beforehand. I have just received some intelligence from Gov. Nash and from Congress which makes me wish to see you.   I am, etc.,

"NATHAN GREENE."

There is proof that Gen. Greene had such unlimited confidence in Col. Polk that he wished to confide in him intelligence that he did not wish to write. Before retiring from service on Gen. Greene's appeal, he exerted himself to procure lumber for the barracks at the new position selected for the army on Hicks' creek nearly opposite Cheraw Hill, on the Pee Dee; to build boats for the transportation of stores;

to collect provisions, and do everything that could be done to enable the new commander to prepare his men for the active duties of the coming campaign.

Gen. Greene's letters evince a high appreciation of Col. Polk's service, and a still higher evidence of his confidence in his skill and patriotism may be found in the fact that upon the fall of the gallant Gen. Davidson, early in February, 1781, Greene appointed Polk to fill the vacancy on the recommendation of the officers of the brigade as the fittest person for the important position among all the many patriotic soldiers of Mecklenburg.

On the receipt of the news of the battle of Guilford, it was thought Cornwallis would retrace his steps by the way of Salisbury and Charlotte, so as to keep open the communication and act in concert with Lord Rowdon at Camden; and as the citizens of that section had already experienced the distress of the presence of the British soldiers, they determined to do their best to keep the enemy at a distance.

Gen. Polk accordingly ordered out the next division of militia liable for duty, with a view of marching to Salisbury to fortify the fords and passes on the Yadkin, but before reaching there intelligence was received that the British were directing their course towards Fayetteville, when Col. Polk dismissed his men and returned.

Gen. Greene re-entered South Carolina in April, taking position before Camden. He called upon North Carolina for a draft of three months' men, when Col. Polk exerted himself to meet the demands of the occasion, and led a considerable force of his countrymen, and joined Greene at Rugeley's Mills shortly after the battle at Hobkirk's Hill, and remained in that border region, watching and checking the British and Tories in both Carolinas, until the expiration of the term of service for which his men had been drafted. This appears to have been Col. Polk's last military service. Gov. Graham well observes that when placed in command as Brigadier General, "in all after, as in prior times, he was regarded as an unwavering patriot."

Gen. Polk now retired to private life, which with his advancing years, he yearned to enjoy. After Rutherford's expedition in the autumn of 1781, in pursuit of a body of Tories under McNeil and other Tory leaders, peace was practically restored in North Carolina.

He owned mills two miles south of Charlotte, and kept a store in the village, and was now enabled to give his undivided time to his private affairs.

Elkanah Watson, in his "Men and Times of the Revolution," who visited Charlotte in 1785, states: "I carried letters to the courteous Gen. Polk, and remained two days at his residence in the delightful society of his charming family."

After the war, when the disbanded soldiers of the North Carolina line received their land warrants in payment for their military services, Gen. Polk purchased many of these warrants and went, early in 1786, with his four sons, armed with their rifles, into the wilderness of Duck River county, in Middle Tennessee, to locate them, Col. Wm. Polk having been chosen in 1793 one of the principal surveyors. Resuming his original profession of surveyor, Gen. Polk selected the finest lands in that rich valley, ran the line, marked them, and secured the titles, notwithstanding the hostility of the Indians. So when he died in 1793, he left a rich inheritance in lands for his children. "He was," says Dr. J. G. Ramsey, "a high-souled cavalier, full of dash and courage; rich, hospitable, and charming." Dr. Johnson relates that several of his children were wild and frolicksome —one bore the sobriquet of "Devil Charley"—; that on one occasion the General was speaking of the boldness of single highway robbery, and declared that no single man would dare make such an attempt on him. The sons all heard it, and Charley resolved to have his fun, even at his father's expense. So when his father was returning on a by-road with a sum of money he had been collecting, the reckless son, disguised, waylaid him in a creek bottom and demanded the instant delivery of his money. The General's first thought was to snatch up his pistols, but Charles was too quick for him, and seeing a pistol, as he supposed, presented at his breast, the father gave up his money and returned home not a little fretted and mortified at the result. Perceiving his depression of spirits, the young men enquired into the cause and offered their aid in any difficulties. He frankly told them he had been robbed of such a sum of money, designating the place. They all expressed surprise, and enquired if he were not armed. He acknowledged that he had his pistols, but had not had time to use them. When they concluded that there must have been several highwaymen banded together to have effected their purpose, he, with increased mortification, confessed that there was but one; but added that he was off his guard, and was taken by surprise. Charles at this point returned the money, acknowledging that he had taken it from him. "What!" exclaimed the General, "Did you endanger your father's life?" "No, sir," said Charles. "What, did you not present a pistol at my breast?" "No, sir," replied the son. "How can you say that?" asked the father. "I assure you, sir, it was only my mother's brass candlestick that I took off from your own mantlepiece."

Of Col. Polk's three daughters, Margaret married Dr. Ephraim Brevard, whose name is so intimately associated with the Mecklenburg Convention and famous resolves of May 20, 1775. She died early and left an only daughter, Margaret Polk, who became the wife of Nathaniel Alexander, a native of Mecklenburg, who graduated at Princeton in 1776, and after studying medicine, entered the army, served in the House of Commons in 1797, in the State Senate in 1801 and 1802, and, while holding a seat in Congress in 1803-'5, he was chosen by the Legislature Governor of the State, serving two years. He died at Charlotte November 8, 1808, at the age of 52 years, leaving no children. Gen. Polk's third daughter married a man named Brown, leaving no issue.

CHAPTER II.

COL. ABRAHAM ALEXANDER.

The Alexanders were very numerous at the time of the Revolution and since in Mecklenburg, and although of the same original Scotch-Irish stock, they were of different degrees of consanguinity. Hezekiah and John McKnitt Alexander were brothers; while Abraham, Adam, Charles and Ezra Alaxander were their cousins. (See Mans. Letters of Dr. J. G. M. Ramsay, October 2, 1875.)

Foote relates that, among Presbyterian emigrations from Scotland to Ireland, to escape persecution for conscience's sake, during the period between 1610 and 1688, there were seven brothers bearing the same name of Alexander.

But their grievances increasing a few years preceding the Revolution of 1688, their ministers imprisoned for holding fasts, the Alexanders resolved to seek quiet and repose in the New World. On the eve of their departure, they sent to Scotland for their old preacher to baptize their children and administer to them the consolations of the Gospel. The faithful and fearless preacher arrived in time to meet the friends on the vessel on which they had embarked, and there held becoming religious services. An armed company now came on board, broke up the meeting and lodged the minister in jail. Towards night an old matron addressed her kinsman: "Men gang ye away tak' our minister out o' the jail, and tak' him, guide soule, wi' us till Ameriky." Her commands had never been disobeyed. Before morning the minister was on board and the vessel had proceeded on its voyage. The minister having no family, cheerfully consented to the arrangement, and with joy and thanksgiving they landed safely on Manhattan. Part of the company remained there, from whom it is related Wm. Alexander, commonly known as Lord Sterling, a Major General of the Revolution, descended. The others took up their abode for a time in New Jersey; then settled in part, perhaps, in Cecil county, Md., and others in Pennsylvania. There they mingled with their countrymen, intermarried, and their descendants in great numbers migrated to the Catawba country, following the great valley of Virginia from Pennsylvania and Maryland. This movement began slowly about 1745, and more rapidly from 1750 onward. Maj. Thomas Alexander and Dan Alexander, both soldiers of the Revolution, were natives of Mecklenburg, the former having been born in 1753, the latter in 1758. Abraham Alexander was among those early emigrants. He was born, apparently, in Cecil county, Md., in 1717, and migrated early to the Catawba country; soon attained a prominent position among the pioneer settlers. He was long a leading magistrate of his county, and the honored chairman of the Inferior Court both before and during the Revolution. With Col. Thomas Polk, he represented Mecklenburg in the Assembly in 1771, and ranked among the leading Whigs of that day. He seemed, however, not to have been ambitious for honor and place, for he declined at the next election to solicit the suffrage of the people. He is next found presiding at the Mecklenburg Convention of May 20, 1775, and was active during the whole period of the Revolution, both as member of the Justice Court and as chairman of the Committee of Safety. He was, in 1777, appointed as one of the original trustees of Liberty Hall Academy, and was for many years an elder in the Presbyterian Church. He died April 28, 1778, in the 69th year of his age, and his widow, Dorcas, survived till May 28th, when she passed away in her 67th year, and her remains rest beside those of her husband in the old Sugar Creek burial ground. They had five sons and one daughter—Abraham, Isaac, Nathaniel, Elias and Joab. Isaac became a distinguished physician, and settled in Camden, S. C., while his brothers spent their days as tillers of the soil. Elizabeth, the sister, became the wife of William Alexander, son of Hezekiah Alexander.

DR. EPHRAIM BREVARD.

The earliest known Brevard was a French Huguenot, leaving his native land on the revocation of the Edict of Nantes, and settling among the Scotch-Irish in the northern part of Ireland, where he formed an acquaintance with a family of McKnitts, in company with whom he sailed for America. Among the McKnitt emigrants was a blooming lassie, who may have had quite as much to do in attracting his attention as the cheap lands and glowing accounts of the New World. A mutual attachment sprang up, which eventuated in marriage. They settled on the waters of Elk River, Cecil county, in the northeastern corner of Maryland, bordering on Pennsylvania. Five sons and one daughter were the issue of this union, of whom John, Robert, Zebulon and their married sister and husband migrated to the Yadkin and Catawba country about 1747, and settled in what was subsequently Rowan, and since Iredell county.

Some years prior to this removal, John Brevard, the elder of the brothers, had married Jane McWhirter, a sister of Dr. Alex McWhirter, of Scotch-Irish extraction, of the adjoining county of New Castle, Delaware; and their fifth child and eldest son, Ephraim, was born in 1744 in Cecil county, Maryland, and was only about three years old when his parents removed to the wilds of North Carolina, settling in what subsequently became Iredell county. While a boy he had the misfortune to lose one of his eyes, and after attending a classical school near his father's residence, he was sent, on the conclusion of the Indian war in 1761, with his cousin, Adlai Osborne, to attend a grammar school in Prince Edward county, Virginia, under William Capples. The young men, with Thomas Reese, entered Princeton college in 1766, graduating in 1768. Reese and Brevard taught school some time in Maryland, which enabled Brevard to put himself under the tuition of Dr. David Ramsay, subsequently so celebrated in civil life during the Revolution and as an historian after the war. After pursuing his medical studies some time in Philadelphia, Dr. Ramsay removed to Somerset county, Maryland. Brevard accompanied him there, and after a due course there, he commenced the practice of his profession in Charlotte. Possessed of more than common abilities, well cultured under the instructions of Dr. Witherspoon, Dr. Ramsay and others, and of prepossessing manners, he at once took a prominent position and exerted a large influence among the Mecklenburg people. He was soon united in marriage with a daughter of Col. Thomas Polk, who died leaving him an only daughter. The distinguished part he acted in the Mecklenburg Convention of May 20, 1775, as a member, the secretary, and the reputed author of the Mecklenburg Declaration of Independence Resolves of May 20, 1775, will cause his name to ever fill an honored place in the record of Western Carolina. Bancroft declares that his name "should be remembered with honor by his countrymen" for having "digested the system which was then adopted and formed in effect a Declaration of Independence, as well as a complete system of government," and Gridsby pronounces him an exalted patriot, and as to the record of the Resolves, that the beauty of their diction, their elegant precision, the wide scope of statesmanship which they exhibit, prove incontestibly that the men who put them forth was worthy of their high trust at the difficult crisis.

In February, 1776, we find him the tutor of the Queen's Museum Academy, with nineteen young men under him, whom he led as their captain in Col. Polk's regiment in an expedition against Scotch Tories on the Cape Fear. How long he continued teaching is not known.

In 1777, when Liberty Hall Academy was organized, he was one of the original trustees, and his name as such is appended to a degree given to John Graham in 1778.

After performing every duty to his people befitting a patriot, he entered the Southern army as a surgeon, and was captured at the surrender of Charleston in May, 1780. There, from long confinement and unwholesome diet, he was taken sick, and when at length set at liberty, he reached the home of his friend, John McKnitt Alexander, where he lingered for several months, his disease baffling the best medical skill— Dr. William Read, Physician General to the Southern army, visiting him from the hospital at Charlotte. He finally breathed his last some time in 1781, at about the age of 37 years, and his remains were buried beside those of his wife in Charlotte on a lot now occupied by the county court house. The particular place of his interment is unknown.

In the language of Dr. Foote, "He thought clearly, felt deeply, wrote well, resisted bravely, and died a martyr to that liberty none loved better and few understood so well." He was a man of undoubted genius and talent. (See MS. Letters of Rev. R. H. King to Dr. J. G. M. Ramsay, April 9, 1823.) His only daughter, on arriving at years of womanhood, married a Dickerson, settled at Camden, S. C., and left one child, a son, James Polk Dickerson, who was Lieutenant Colonel of Butler's regiment of South Carolina Volunteers in the Mexican war; was severely wounded at the siege of Vera Cruz March 11, 1847; recovering from that, he was again badly wounded at Cherubusco on the 20th of August following, and died of his wound three weeks later, greatly regretted by his regiment and the whole army.

COL. ADAM ALEXANDER.

The place of Col. A. Alexander's birth is not certainly known, but he was possibly a native of Cecil county, Maryland, and was born in 1728. He was among the pioneer settlers of Mecklenburg. He married a Miss Shelby. As early as June, 1770, we find him a prominent member of Clear Creek congregation, and the next year he commanded a company under Gen. Waddell to aid in putting down the Regulators, who had taken the law in their own hands in upholding the usurpations and extortions of Gov. Tryon's favorites. That Capt. Alexander was unwilling to shed the blood of his oppressed countrymen is readily seen by the course he and other officers pursued in persuading Waddell to return from their camp on Pott's creek across the Yadkin, both on account of the superiority of the insurgents, and the unwillingness of the men to engage them, while waiting for a convoy of ammunition under a small guard from Charlotte. A party of ten or twelve, under Capt. William Alexander, blackened and disguised, seized the convoy and destroyed the powder, and ever after he was known as "Black Billy" Alexander.

Capt. Adam Alexander, on the day of the 11th of May, immediately after uniting with his brother officers in advising a retreat beyond the Yadkin, went in person and reconnoitered the Regulators, and returning, reported that he had passed along their lines and the footmen appeared to him to extend a quarter of a mile, seven or eight deep, and that the horsemen, 120 yards, twelve or fourteen deep. On the 19th Waddell, with his small force of 250 men, was obliged to retreat from his position, two miles eastward of the Yadkin, to Salisbury, the Regulators having surrounded his party and threatened to cut them to pieces if they offered to join the main army under Tryon. But the principal body of the insurgents had been defeated on the 16th at Alamance, and Tryon marched with his victorious troops to join Waddell, then entrenched near Salisbury, eight miles to the eastward of the Yadkin. Receiving intelligence that the Regulators in the region embracing the present counties of Mecklenburg, Lincoln and Iredell were meditating further hostilities, Gen. Waddell was sent into that quarter with a strong detachment, including the Mecklenburg troops. Early in June, with orders, after he had performed the service assigned him, to disband his troops, meeting with no opposition, he had little to do beside administering the oath of allegiance to the people. Adam Alexander was many years a prominent magistrate and member of the County Court, and on May 20, 1775, was one of the members of the Mecklenburg Convention. In September following, he was appointed Lieutenant Colonel of the Mecklenburg "Minute

Men" under Col. Polk, and served shortly after in one of the Snow Campaigns against the Tories in South Carolina.

When the "Minute Men" of the Salisbury district were, in December, 1775, formed into two groups, he was re-appointed Lieutenant Colonel of the Second regiment under Col. Polk, and marched, in February, 1776, to aid in quelling the insurrection of the Highlanders on the Cape Fear.

In the ensuing April, when Polk was chosen to command one of the Continental regiments, Adam Alexander succeeded him as Colonel of the Mecklenburg regiments. When the Cherokees commencel hostilities early in the summer of 1776, incited thereto by the machinations of the enemy, Col. Alexander led a force to the head of the Catawba, where he served six weeks in protecting the Catawba Valley during the harvest, and went with his regiment under Gen. Rutherford, later in the season, on his expedition against the treacherous Cherokees, destroying their crops and villages.

Dr. Caldwell refers to Col. Alexander when President Washington made his Southern tour in 1792, as "far advanced in life." His death occurred in 1798, at the age of 70 years, lamented by all who knew him. His remains were interred at Rock Springs. Adam Alexander was a man of military genius, remarkably endowed. He was a Presbyterian.

He had four sons—Evan, Isaac, Adam and Charles, and one daughter. She married John Springs. All the Springs of Mecklenburg, a large, wealthy and intelligent connection, are descendants of Col. Alexander.

His son, Evan Alexander, whom he sent to Princeton with the hope that he would enter the ministry, graduated in 1787, became a prominent lawyer in Charlotte; was two years a member of the Legislature, then representative in Congress from 1805 to 1809, and died unmarried October 28th, in the latter year.

Isaac Alexander held various offices of trust in the county, while his brother Charles occupied the old homestead, married a Miss Means, and had several talented sons who died young.

CHAPTER XVII.

GEN. ROBERT IRWIN.

William Irwin was one of the early Scotch-Irish settlers in West Pennsborough, Cumberland county, Pennsylvania, a few miles southeast of Carlisle. His son, Robert, the eighth of thirteen children, was born August 26, 1740, and was reared with few advantages on his native homestead. When his father died, not long prior to May, 1763, the farm of one hundred acres was purchased of the heirs at £15 each, by their elder brother, John Irwin, and with this Robert Irwin commenced life and wended his way to the Steele Creek settlement in Mecklenburg. He was soon after united in marriage with Mary Alexander, daughter of Zebulon Alexander, an early emigrant from Pennsylvania. About the period of 1767, Robert Irwin was one of the first bench of elders of Steele Creek Church. He was one of the members of the Mecklenburg Convention in May, 1775, and thenceforward proved himself one of the active leaders of the Mecklenburg people during the war. It is altogether probable he had seen service during the French and Indian war on the frontier of Pennsylvania, for Col. Armstrong led many a daring force against the Indians during that period from the Carlisle region; and more probably still he was employed against the Regulators in 1771, and on the Snow Campaign near the close of 1775. After having served as a member of the North Carolina Provincial Congress in April and May, 1776, he engaged in Gen. Rutherford's campaign against the Cherokees during the summer and autumn of that year. Returning from this expedition in October, he was rechosen to a seat in the Provincial Congress, which met in November in the double capacity of making laws and forming a new Constitution. On the death of Lieutenant

Colonel Phifer, he succeeded him in 1777 as second in command of the Mecklenburg militia.

Gen. Irwin died at his residence in the Steele Creek settlement, in Mecklenburg county, December 23, 1800, in his 61st year, and was interred in the Steele Creek burial ground, his wife's remains occupying the same grave. On his tombstone is engraved this beautiful and truthful delineation of his character: "Great, noble, generous, good, and brave."

JOHN M'KNITT ALEXANDER.

Little more can be said of Mr. Alexander than has already been indicated. Born in 1733, in Pennsylvania, as stated by Dr. Foote, but according to more reliable information, in the northeastern portion of Cecil county, Maryland, where his father, James Alexander, settled on a tract of land called New Munster, in 1714, where, soon after he married Margaret McKnitt, a sister of John McKnitt, an early emigrant to the southern part of the same county. The father, James Alexander, remained in Maryland, surviving till 1779; but his son, John McKnitt Alexander, who had served an apprenticeship to a tailor, migrated in 1754, when 21 years old, to Mecklenburg county, accompanied by his brother, Hezekiah, and sister, Jemima, and her husband, Maj. Thomas Sharpe, also of Cecil county. In the early days of Mecklenburg, when the deer and buffalo furnished not only viands for the table, but a portion of apparel for the people, a leather-breeches maker was not probably a sufficiently profitable occupation for the enterprising young Marylander; so we soon find him a land surveyor and a large land-holder, surveying and taking lands as far away as Chester District, in South Carolina, forty miles distant. In 1759, he married Jane Bane, from Pennsylvania, of the same Scotch-Irish stock with himself, and settled in the Hopewell congregation. Enterprising, shrewd, and honorable, he prospered in business and became wealthy. Col. Wheeler, in his "Sketches of Mecklenburg Delegates," states that Mr. Alexander was a member of the Provincial Assembly in 1772, while Jones' defence indicates that Martin Phifer and John Davidson were the Mecklenburg representatives at that time. But his was a busy and useful life in the civil time, during the Revolutionary war, long and faithfully serving as a magistrate and member of the County Court; one of the members of the Mecklenburg Convention of May, 1775; the successor of Dr. Brevard as secretary of the Mecklenburg Committee of Safety, and a representative in the Provincial Congress in August and September, 1775. The same year he visited Philadelphia, where he communicated to Dr. Franklin the facts and circumstances of the preceding Mecklenburg Convention, when they were fresh in his memory, who expressed his approbation of their act. In April, 1776, we again find him a member of the Provincial Congress; in the State Senate in 1777, and the same year chosen a trustee of Liberty Hall Academy.

How Mr. Alexander regarded the Red Coats when they invaded the soil of Mecklenburg in the fall of 1780, may best be seen in the notice of Duncan Ochiltree. It was a high compliment to his sterling patriotism that Gen. Davidson, at that period, named his encampment in Mecklenburg "Camp McKnitt Alexander."

When Cornwallis undertook the vain effort of endeavoring to recover the Cowpens prisoners from Morgan, early in 1781, and Gen. Greene exerted himself to thwart his lordship's purpose, Mr. Alexander, though his age would have excused him from exposure, accompanied Greene as a pilot, if not a volunteer aid, and was actively employed in destroying, or sinking, ferry boats on the Yadkin and Dan rivers; and by his zeal in the cause, his intimate knowledge as an old surveyor of the topography of the roads, and people of the county, he was able to afford valuable assistance as counsellor to the American General.

For many years he was a sturdy Presbyterian, an elder in the Church, and a prominent actor in all its public convocations. During the closing five or six years of his life he was nearly blind and very infirm; but his children, grand-children and numerous friends loved and revered him, and united in lamenting his separation from them July 10, 1817, in the 85th year of his age. In the graveyard at Hopewell his remains sleep in peace beside those of his beloved companion. He left two sons, William Bane and Dr. Joseph McKnitt Alexander; and of his five daughters, one, Abigail Bane, was united in marriage to Rev. S. C. Caldwell; another to Rev. James Wallis, and a third to Col. Francis A. Ramsay, father of the worthy historian of Tennessee. As he appeared to D. G. Stinson in 1813, Mr. Alexander was a man of medium size, dark skin, with a good intellectual face, neat and tidy in his dress; he was very dignified, and had the reputation of being a very sensible person. He was quite a politician in his day, of the old Federal school—while his son-in-law, Rev. James Wallis, was a prominent Democratic leader, and was often engaged to deliver political addresses on the Fourth of July occasions.

REV. HEZEKIAH BALCH.

The Balch family was originally from Wales, and the name signifies "proud" in the Welsh language. John Balch is said to have emigrated to New England at an early period from Bridgewater, in Somerset, England, and became possessed of a large property and extensive influence. A great grandson of his, Col. James Balch, migrated directly from his native England, married Anne Goodwine, and settled on Deer Creek, in Harford county, Maryland, where his eldest son, Hezekiah, was born in 1746. His father was a man of highly gifted and cultivated mind, possessing a fine poetical talent, and was the author of some anonymous pieces that had no small celebrity in their day. While his son was yet a youth, the father moved with his family from Maryland and settled in Mecklenburg.

After assisting his father on the farm, young Balch was at length sent to Princeton college, where he graduated in

1766 in the same class with Waightstill Avery, Chief Justice Ellsworth, and the celebrated Luther Martin. He was licensed to preach by the Presbytery of Donnegal in 1767, and in 1769 he was ordained and sent as a missionary to Rocky River and Poplar Tent churches, within the limits of Mecklenburg. He had married (a Miss Sconnel, it is believed) shortly before removing to the county, and settled six miles west of the present town of Concord, on the Beattie's Ford road. It must be conceded that during his brief period of labor, about seven years, he performed a good pioneer work for the Church and State—for the cause of liberty and the cause of education. A member of the Mecklenburg Convention of May, 1775, he not only voted for the noble resolves, but enforced them by his vigorous sense and eloquence. He did what he could for his country and his kind; but, in the summer of 1776, he was called to his reward at the early age of 30 years. He was reputed an elegant and accomplished scholar. He is said to have been a tall, handsome man, with fair hair, which he wore long and curling. He had two or more children. His widow subsequently married a man by the name of McWhorter, a professional teacher, and moved with her and her children to Tennessee, Mrs. McWhorter taking the children as she passed along on her journey to view their father's grave for the last time. All trace of these children has been lost. Mr. Balch had three brothers and several sisters. Two of the former were noted Presbyterian clergyman, Rev. Dr. Steven B. Balch, of Georgetown, and Rev. James Balch, of Kentucky; the third, William Balch, a planter in Georgia. In 1847 means were provided and a suitable monument erected over his grave, for which Rev. J. A. Wallace prepared an appropriate inscription.

HEZEKIAH ALEXANDER.

This member of the numerous Alexander family was a brother of John McKnitt Alexander, and was born in Cecil county, in the northern part of Maryland, in January, 1722. He migrated with his family to the Mecklenburg country in 1754, and was soon assigned a prominent place among the early settlers. He located four or five miles east of Charlotte and in 1764 erected a stone residence on which the date is cut, and is a good house to this day. He was for many years a magistrate and member of the County Court. Foote relates of him that he was "the clearest-headed magistrate in the county," a high compliment. In May, 1775, he served in the Mecklenburg Convention, and in the ensuing September he was chosen a member of the Salisbury District Committee of Safety. In April, 1776, he was appointed paymaster of Col. Thomas Polk's regiment of the Continentals, and the next month he was chosen one of the two members to represent the Salisbury District in the State Council of Safety, on pay of twenty shilling proclamation money for each day's traveling and attendance. He died June 16, 1801.

CHAPTER XVIII.

CAPT. ZACCHEUS WILSON.

The Wilsons were of Scotch-Irish Presbyterian stock, and were among the early settlers of Cumberland county, Pennsylvania, where Zaccheus Wilson was born, probably as early as about 1735 or 1740. When he grew to man's state, he was not "little of statue" as Zaccheus of old—for like nearly all of that numerous connection, his person was of full medium size, rather heavily framed, and possessing great power in the vigor of life. He received but a limited education, and while yet quite young, settled with his parents in the Poplar Tent region, originally a part of Mecklenburg, now Cabarrus county. This was prior to March, 1753. He had a younger sister who married Capt. Stephen Alexander, who survived till the age of 90—the chronicler of her region.

Zaccheus Wilson had three brothers, two of whom were

Robert and David, and three sisters. Reared on the frontier, Zaccheus and his brothers were not the men to have shirked any duty in aiding in the defence of the country. On the Yadkin river, in Rowan county, one Nicholas Ross early settled, marrying Lizzie Conger, daughter of John Conger. There were then many wild horses running in the woods. Having a fine animal of his own, and needing another, Ross went in the spring of the year to the range and selected one that he thought would suit his purpose, and started to run him down and halter him. But in the race, the horse plunged in a hole, turned a complete summersault; fell back on and crushed his pursuer, who left a widow and two little daughters. (MS. Letter of Rev. Nicholson Ross Morgan, a son of the younger of Mr. Ross' daughters. The elder married Matthew Harris, a nephew of Col. Robert and Samuel Harris, of Rocky River.)

Zaccheus Wilson, in his occupation of a surveyor, was sent for to survey and divide the land for the heirs; saw, admired, and married the young widow, and took her to his home in the Steele Creek region.

About 1767, we find him one of the elders of Steele Creek Church. He had a decided love for mathematical studies, which he pursued with little or no instruction, and became one of the best surveyors of his day.

He was a member of the Mecklenburg Convention in May, 1775, and of the Provincial Congress of November, 1776, for making laws and forming a Constitution. The only military service particularly remembered, though much in the army, was as a Captain at King's Mountain, where among plunder taken, was an English surveyor's compass and platting instruments, which were assigned to him in the division, and are yet preserved by one of his descendants. He was a member of the North Carolina Convention of 1788 for the consideration of the Federal Constitution, and he was among the large majority that refused to give it their approval, as wanting in a proper protection of the rights of the people.

When the county of Cabarrus was set off from Mecklenburg, in 1792, Capt. Wilson was a resident of that region, and was chosen county surveyor.

In 1796, Capt. Wilson, having lost his wife, resolved on following his brother, Maj. David Wilson, who had nine years before moved to Sumner county, Tennessee; and just prior to his departure he visited his step-daughter, the mother of the venerable Rev. N. H. Morgan. "The last night he spent with us," says Mr. Morgan, "I slept with him, and about midnight the wolves raised a furious howling around the cow pen. The old gentleman went out and chased them away, and I as a mere lad, remember how I trembled lest he should be devoured." In this migration, beside his two sons, a goodly number of Wilsons and some Alexanders accompanied him. His removal was much regretted by his old friends and neighbors. His education, mostly self-acquired, was quite liberal. He was very popular, a Presbyterian spotless in life, a noble, worthy man, without an equal in his profession as a surveyor. He settled one mile northeast of Gallatin, in Sumner county, twenty-six miles above Nashville, where he followed his profession as long as he was able to do so. He died in 1824.

NEIL MORRISON.

James Morrison, a native of Scotland, early migrated to this county; settled in Philadelphia, where his son, Neil Morrison, was born in 1728. On reaching years of manhood, he engaged in mercantile business in that city, and then married.

A few years before the Revolution, the father and his three sons moved to Mecklenburg and located on Four Mile creek, in Providence settlement, Neil Morrison at this time having a family. James Morrison lived to be an old man, 81 years, and was interred in Providence burial ground. Neil Morrison's abilities soon commanded respect, and he was chosen one of the members of the Mecklenburg Convention in May, 1775. He engaged heartily in the military service, commanding a company on Rutherford's campaign in 1776, against the Cherokee Indians, burning their towns, cutting down their corn and throwing it into the streams.

His other services are not known. He was a Justice of the Peace and a member of the County Court. He died September 13, 1784, at the age of 56 years, and was buried in Providence graveyard. His widow survived him until her 89th year. His son, William Morrison, was early sent to Princeton college, but the war early in 1776 interrupted his studies; so he bought himself a rifle and returned home; entered the service, serving a while on Sullivan's Island. At Gates' defeat in August, 1780, he was wounded by a musket ball, taken prisoner and confined in jail in Camden, whence his mother and sister succeeded in getting him pardoned; then conveying him to Charlotte, where Dr. Henderson extracted the ball and he recovered. He subsequently became a prominent physician, and died in 1806, together with his brothers, Alexander and James, all within a period of three months. Dr. William Morrison was a member of the Legislature in 1796—elected as a Federalist—and his brother, Alexander, in 1801 to 1803, as a Republican. Their sister became the wife of Maj. Thomas Alexander, who served under Davie and Sumter in the Revolution.

RICHARD BARRY.

Of Scotch-Irish descent, Richard Barry was born in Pennsylvania in 1726. He married Anne Price, of Maryland, also of Scotch-Irish descent, and settled many years before the Revolution in the Mecklenburg district, twelve miles northeast of Charlotte, at what is still known as the old Barry tanyard.

Though best known as a member of the Mecklenburg Convention of May, 1775, he performed many other services of a useful character, having served many years as a magistrate and a member of the County Court, and though advanced in life, he set the good example of taking his place among the Mecklenburg troops, when their services were called into requisition. At the age of 55, he fought as valiantly as the younger soldiers in disputing the passage of Cornwallis' army at Cowan's Ford, in February, 1781, when the lamented Davidson was slain, and aided in burying his body by torchlight in the graveyard at Hopewell. Mr. Barry was long a ruling elder in Hopewell Church. The first sermon by a Presbyterian clergyman in that section of the county was preached under the sade of a tree at the side of his house. His death occurred August 21, 1801, in the 75th year of his age.

JOHN FLENNIKIN.

James and John Flennikin, descendants from Scotch-Irish ancestors, were among the early settlers of that race in Pennsylvania. They had nine children, of whom John Flennikin, the subject of this sketch, was the seventh, born in Pennsylvania March 7, 1744. The family early migrated to Mecklenburg, and settled on the waters of McAlpin's creek, in what is now Sharon Township. John Flennikin seems to have had a fair education, but beyond his service as a member of the Mecklenburg Convention of May, 1775, and many years as a magistrate and member of the County Court, we have no record. His life was one mainly of peaceful pursuits. He lived to a good old age, when he was thrown from his horse on his way to church and killed, and his remains mingle with the dust of Providence burial ground. His brother, David Flennikin, served under Col. Irwin and Gen. Sumter at the battle of Hanging Rock, where he was wounded and carried to the hospital at Charlotte. He long enjoyed a pension for the wounds he received in the service, and died April 26th, 1826, in the 78th year of his age, and was buried in Providence graveyard. Both of the brothers left numerous and worthy descendants.

WILLIAM GRAHAM.

But little can be gathered of this delegate to the Mecklenburg Convention of May, 1775. His was a farmer's life, quietly spent in his calling, and he left behind him few evidences of his public career. He was an Irishman and early settled in Mecklenburg county. He was useful in his day, serving, it is believed, in the army. He died at an advanced age in 1820 or 1822, near Davidson College.

MATTHEW M'CLURE.

In the north of Ireland and about 1725, was Matthew McClure born, where he married; then came to America and settled in Mecklenburg about 1751, five miles south of Davidson College. It is an evidence of his worth that he was chosen one of the delegates to the Mecklenbubrg Convention of May, 1775. It is not known that he filled any other public position. His home was a rendezvous for the patriots of his section. In January, 1782, the County Court ordered that no person in Charlotte, or within two miles of the place, should be permitted to sell any spirituous liquors, so long as the hospital was continued in that town, and employed Matthew McClure to take possession of all such contraband liquors for the use of the hospital, or as the commanding officer should direct. Too old himself to enter active service in the field, his sons were much engaged in the army.

JOHN QUEARY.

A native of Scotland, John Queary first migrated to Pennsylvania, and then to Mecklenburg some years before the Revolution. As early as January, 1770, we find Mr. Queary residing in what was called for a time Clear Creek, now Philadelphia, in the bounds of Rocky River, and was an elder in that church.

Of his Revolutionary service, save that he was a member of the Mecklenburg Convention of May, 1775, nothing is known. He is represented as a man of strong and vigorous intellect, and a good scholar, especially in mathematics; accumulating means to a moderate extent, and died at an early period. He is buried in what was once Mecklenburg, now Union county.

EZRA ALEXANDER.

All that can be stated of Mr. Alexander in addition to his having been a delegate to the Mecklenburg Convention of May, 1775, is that he headed a company in June and July, 1780, in Col. W. L. Davidson's command, during the Tory rising at Ramsour's Mill, and in the affair near Calson's Mill with a body of Tories while in pursuit of Bryan's party, and the next month served in Capt. John Brownfield's company of ——————— Regiment at the battle of Hanging Rock. (MS. Letters of Dr. C. L. Hunter, September 21, 1775.) He died in the summer of 1800, at an advanced age.

CHAPTER XIX.

WAIGHTSTILL AVERY.

The Avery family trace a Hungarian origin. Capt. James Avery, of Devonshire, England, came over with Winthrop's company in 1630, only ten years after the May Flower, first settling at Gloucester; then in 1651 at New London, Conn., and shortly after at Groton. From him descended Waightstill Avery, the subject of this sketch, who was born in Groton May 3, 1743. He graduated at Princeton College in 1766, where he remained a tutor for a year. Then removing to Maryland, he studied law for about a year and a half under the direction of Littleton Dennis, where early in 1769 he set out for North Carolina.

Selecting Mecklenburg for his home, he domiciled with

Hezekiah Alexander at the moderate rate of £12 (twelve pounds) per eight months.

In 1771 he was made prisoner by the Regulators at Yadkin Ferry, and carried to their camp in the woods. They gave him a flogging and soon set him at liberty. When the great war came he was prepared to meet it. In such an atmosphere as Mecklenburg, he could only learn to breathe the purest sentiments of patriotism. In the Mecklenburg Convention in May, 1775, he filled an honored place. He was most probably associated with Brevard and Kennon on the committee who reported the memorable Resolves of May 20th, and could scarcely have kept silent in enforcing their adoption by his talents and persuasive powers of eloquence. He was a "shrewd lawyer," said Prof. F. M. Hubbard, "whose integrity, no less than his deliberate wisdom, made his counsels weighty."

Jones, in his "Revolutionary Defence of North Carolina," states that Brevard and Avery, with their classical attainments, with the native talent and enthusiasm of Thomas Polk, produced the Mecklenburg Declaration. He was returned one of the Mecklenburg representatives to the North Carolina Provincial Congress of August and September, 1775, when he was chosen one of the two members for the Salisbury District of Provincial Council of Safety. The Council held two sessions that year, one in October and one in December.

He was dispatched, in behalf of the Council, to purchase from the South Carolina Committee of Safety 2,000 pounds of powder for the use of the Province, and was also appointed one of the committee for the District of Salisbury to purchase materials and to employ proper persons to make and repair guns and bayonets, and purchase guns, lead and flints. In April, 1776, he was appointed chairman of four commissioners by the Provincial Congress to erect salt works and manufacture salt for the use of the public, which proved successful and of great importance.

He was in this year, 1777, appointed one of the trustees of

Liberty Hall Academy at Charlotte, and was also chosen one of the two members to represent Mecklenbubrg in the House of Commons, and served on the committee to revise the whole body of the public laws of the State. On the 12th of January, 1778, he was commissioned Attorney General of the State.

To the last his was the costume of the Revolution—short breeches, long waistcoats, silk stockings and knee buckles— wearing his hair in a cue, and presenting altogether a singular appearance to the younger generation. Absent-mindedness was one of his peculiarities, of which his more intimate friends would take occasion to play off practical jokes at his expense. He was devoted to his friends and strong in his prejudices. He was very fond of his books and newspapers. He died in March, 1821.

COL. WM. KENNON.

The Kennons migrated from England and settled in Virginia about as early as 1660. Richard Kennon, with three associates, obtained a grant from the Colony of 2,827 acres in Henrico county, April 1, 1670, and Elizabeth Kennon, perhaps the widow of Richard, April 24, 1703, secured a grant of 4,000 acres in Henrico. Robert, William and Richard Kennon, Jr., were the sons of this early couple. William Kennon, recorded as "Gentleman," between April 17, 1725, and November, 1750, obtained five grants of land in Henrico, aggregating 4,063, and one tract of 4,000 acres in Prince George county. (MS. Letters of R. A. Brock, Corresponding Secretary Virginia Historical Society, Sept. 13, 1875.)

He was probably there on professional business, and was invited as a matter of courtesy to a seat in the Convention in Charlotte May 20, 1775.

COL. JAMES HARRIS.

According to the late Hon. W. S. Harris, an intelligent chronicler of the family, the Harris connection of Mecklenburg and Cabarrus were of Scotch-Irish stock, natives of Harrisburg, Penn., who emigrated first to Cecil county, Maryland, and in 1740 to North Carolina. The facts are that James Harris, a native of Yorkshire, England, first settled on the Susquehanna in 1719. But Harrisburg was not laid out as a town till sixty-five years after. A grandson of the first settler bore the name of Robert, a family name among the North Carolina Harrises. An immediate descendant of Col. James Harris states that he was a native of Wales, born April 3, 1739, but the probabilities are that he was of Welsh descent, and a native of Pennsylvania. He early settled on Clear Creek, in Mecklenburg county. He proved himself a leader among the people, and was chosen a delegate to the Mecklenburg Convention of May, 1775. In June, 1780, we find him serving as Major of Col. Irwin's regiment, and marched against the Tories at Ramsour's, who were defeated a little before the arrival of the rear under Gen. Rutherford and Col. Irwin. He was subsequently promoted to be Colonel.

In 1785, he was chosen to represent Mecklenburg in the State Senate, a high honor in a region where there were so many able and worthy men. His death occurred September 27, 1797, in the 59th year of his age. He is represented as a very rich man, quiet in his demeanor, provident and successful, and a member of the Presbyterian denomination. Some of his descendants reside in Texas. His younger brother, Samuel Harris, a soldier of the Revolution, lived till he was 80 years old. Another brother, Robert Harris, will receive a special notice.

DAVID REESE.

David Reese, a native of Wales, was among the Protestant emigrants who were induced to settle in Ireland. He was a Presbyterian preacher, and took part in the terrible siege of Londonderry, which lasted eight months on scanty allowance. He subsequently returned to Wales, where his son, David Reese, was born in 1710, and came to America when a lad about 15 years old. He settled in Pennsylvania, where in due time he married Susan Polk, a near relative of Thomas and Ezekiel Polk, where their son, Thomas, was born in 1742, who subsequently became a distinguished clergyman in the Presbyterian Church. About 1750, David Reese emigrated, with his young family, and located in Poplar Tent settlement of the Catawba country.

Well educated for his day, he became a prominent man among the early settlers, and was chosen one of a bench of Poplar Tent Church elders in 1751. Waightstill Avery, in Diary of September, 1767, records: "Went to David Reese's, plotted a piece of land for him," and "wrote a deed for him to his son," which would indicate wealth in the rich land of the country. He is one of the reputed delegates to the Mecklenburg Convention of May, 1775; was long a magistrate and member of the County Court.

Though too old to take the field, he was appointed by the Provincial Congress of April, 1776, with Thomas, to procure, purchase and receive fire arms for the use of the troops of Mecklenburg. He lived to see his country free and happy. His will bears date of February 5, 1787, and was admitted to probate in September following. He must have died not long before the latter date, at the age of about 77 years. His remains lie buried in Poplar Tent burial ground, in an unknown grave.

"He was a born statesman," writes Hon. W. S. Harris, and "one of the best of men." He was commanding in appearance, fine looking, with bright, black eyes.

HENRY DOWNS.

Of Scotch-Irish descent, Henry Downs was born in 1728, probably in Pennsylvania, and early settled in Providence settlement, which subsequently became a part of Mecklenburg.

Of his public career, we only know that he was one of the reputed delegates to the famous Mecklenburg Convention. He lived to see his country free, and to enjoy the blessings of a well-spent life. He died October 8, 1798, at the age of 70 years, and was buried in Providence burial ground, 12 miles south of Charlotte. One correspondent speaks of "Henry Downs of precious memory," indicative of his worthy character, and the good name he left behind him. His sons, Thomas and Samuel Downs, were well known in their day, and their descendants are quite numerous in the Mecklenburg region.

JOHN FOARD.

There was a John Foard in Somerset county, on the eastern shore of Maryland, a Presbyterian elder, as early as 1710, mentioned in the first stories of Foote's Sketches of Virginia. As that region furnished many of the early settlers of Mecklenburg, it is most probable that the John Foard of Mecklenburg was descended from that Maryland Presbyterian family of the same name.

As early as January 27, 1770, he is found among the members of Clear Creek congregation. He is said to have been one of the delegates to the Mecklenburg Convention of May, 1775, and long served as a magistrate and member of the County Court. He served as a private in Col. Charles Polk's Dragoons in the fall of 1781, on the Raft Swamp expedition. His will bears date of April 25, 1798, and he probably died not long after this period. Mr. Harris represents him as a worthy and good man, possessing great courage. He lived and died in that part of Mecklenburg which now forms Union county. There are none of his lineal descendants remaining in the old Mecklenburg region, but a good many kindred bear his name.

CHARLES ALEXANDER.

Of this member of the numerous Alexander family, little is known save that he was one of the reputed delegates to the Mecklenburg Convention of May, 1775. He lived on the line from Waxhaw to Charlotte. He was a gallant and true patriot, and unlike most of his Alexander kindred, he was an unbeliever in the Christian religion. His death took place in 1801. He had a grand-son recently deceased, who was an officer and soldier in the war with Mexico.

ROBERT HARRIS, SR.

In the notice of Col. James Harris, a brother of the subject of this sketch, it was stated that he was descended from Welsh ancestry, and was probably a native of Pennsylvania.

Robert Harris, born about 1741, is also supposed to have been born in that State, and certain it is that the family connection included probably the parents and their sons. James, Robert, Samuel, Charles and Thomas, and an only sister, who became the wife of Rev. Thomas Reese, early migrated to the Catawba Valley. Hon. W. S. Harris, who descended from Charles, fixed the period of their migration in 1740; but it was probably a few years later, else some of the brothers and the sister must have been born in Mecklenburg county. The venerable Rev. N. R. Morgan and lady, the latter a grand-daughter of Robert Harris, thinks he came to North Carolina with the early crowd of emigrants from Pennsylvania or Maryland.

As early as May, 1771, he was chosen an elder of Poplar Tent Church. (The Robert Harris of this sketch should not be confounded with the Col. Robert Harris, of Reed Creek, referred to in Foote's Sketches of North Carolina, page 480.) Rev. Humphrey Hunter included the name of Richard Harris, Sr., among the list of delegates to the Mecklenburg Convention, which the Legislative Committee in the State pamphlet of 1831 adopted in the second organized list of *bona fide* members.

Lossing, in his "Field Books of the Revolution," corrects the apparent error of Richard Harris and substitutes the name of Robert Harris. "It is surprising," writes W. S. Harris, who lived all his life in that region, and one of the best chroniclers in that section of country, "that such an error should have been committed, and the name given as Richard; it is a mistake. I know that the name should have been Robert Harris."

It is due to truth to say that Rev. N. R. Morgan and lady, the latter his grand-daughter, who remembered him personally, state that they never understood that that Robert Harris was one of the famous Mecklenburg delegates.

In view of his services and sufferings, a grant of 5,000 acres of land was donated to him in Tennessee, which was neglected for many years, but finally secured by his descendants, proving of great value to them. He became the possessor of a large body of land around what is now known as Harris' station, on the North Carolina Railroad, in Cabarrus county. The mill he built on Rocky river, the dam of which is solid rock, still stands and continues to be known as Harris' Mill.

CHAPTER XXI.

MAJ. JOHN DAVIDSON.

Robert Davidson and wife, Mary Ramsay, of Dundee, Scotland, became early settlers of Chestnut Level, Lancaster county, Pennsylvania, where their son, John Davidson, was born December 15, 1735. With respectable education, and reared to the occupation of a farmer, and while yet a young man, about 1760, he migrated to the Catawba country, in North Carolina.

Here he was united in marriage with Violet, daughter of Samuel Wilson, and sister to the wife of Ezekiel Polk, and settled on the Catawba near Tool's Ford. Such was his prominence that he was chosen, in conjunction with Capt.

Thomas Polk, to represent Mecklenburg county in the Colonial Legislature in 1773. When such a man as John Davidson states positively that he was one of the members of the famous Mecklenburg Convention of May, 1775, chosen in his captain's company with John McKnitt Alexander as his coadjutor, no one has ever called this claim into question. It should stand as one of the fixed facts of history. How Dr. M. Winslow Alexander, in making up his list of delegates in 1824, should have omitted him, then being a venerable survivor of the Revolution and sustaining the highest character with Gen. Joseph Graham among his honored sons-in-law, and how the Legislative Committee of 1831 should have ignored his claim to that undoubted honor and placed other names of doubtful import in their recognized list of delegates, is not the least of many strange things connected with this Mecklenburg matter. An intelligent gentleman states that his grand-father, Maj. Davidson, rode home the night after the declaration was made, fourteen miles, taking by-paths for fear of being killed by the enemy, when in truth there were no British soldiers within hundreds of miles of Mecklenburg in May, 1775; no Tories, of whom there were few in that region at any time, had shown themselves in hostile array. The Indians were still peaceful on the frontiers and remained so for more than a year later, and no Redcoats trod the soil of Mecklenburg till after Cornwallis' forced himself there in September, 1780.

In September, 1775, he was appointed second Major of Col. Polk's regiment, and doubtless went with the regiment on the Snow Campaign at the close of the year against the Tory insurgents in the region of Ninety-Six, South Carolina. He was promoted to first Major of Mecklenburg militia under Col. Adam Alexander and Lieut. Phifer in April, 1776, and in the spring of that year, then in the summer and fall of the same year, he went on Rutherford's campaign against the Cherokees. No particulars are mentioned of his other services. The remainder of his long life he continued to reside at his old homestead on the Catawba until the death of his wife and marriage of his children, when, in 1824, he went to reside with his daughter, Mrs. W. Lee Davidson, near Davidson College, where he closed his long and useful life January 10, 1832, in the 97th year of his age, and was buried in the family burying ground at his former home, a spot selected by himself, near Tool's Ford, on the Catawba.

COL. EZEKIEL POLK.

Capt. Jack included in his list of those "who appeared to take the lead" in the Mecklenburg movement of May, 1775, Col. Ezekiel Polk, Samuel Martin, William Wilson and Duncan Ochiltree; and Lossing has given the names of the three latter in his enumeration of the delegates. They were all doubtless prominent actors among the people on the interesting occasion. Of William Polk's eight children, a sketch of Col. Thomas Polk, the eldest, has already been given. Ezekiel was the youngest, born in Pennsylvania December 7, 1747. "Pennsylvania born, and Carolina bred," as he himself composed in evidence for his tombstone, would imply that when quite young he followed the fortunes of his brothers to Carolina, and was mostly raised, or bred, as he preferred to term it. Of his youthful days, nothing is remembered.

He early married Mary Wilson, a sister to the wife of Maj. John Davidson. In 1769 he was clerk of the Court of Tryon county—territory from which Lincoln and Rutherford have since been formed.

In 1778, Col. Polk removed into Mecklenburg county, just south of Sugar Creek Church, and eleven miles south of Charlotte, where his son, *James K. Polk, was born. This was a period of quiet in this region, and remained so until Cornwallis' invasion in September, 1780. There was no regular army then, after Gates' defeat, to protect the county. When Cornwallis reached Col. Polk's, on Sugar Creek, in order to save the burning of his home, the destruction of his property, and the suffering of his family, he was forced to

---
*James K. Polk was the son of Samuel Polk, and grandson of Ezekiel Polk.—EDITOR.

take British protection, which merely was understood to protect himself, family and property from molestation, without implying any pledge for sympathy or service.

CHAPTER XXII.

CAPT. JAMES JACK.

The bearer of the Mecklenburg Resolves of May, 1775, to Philadelphia—Capt. James Jack—was of Irish descent, born in Pennsylvania in 1739, whence he removed to North Carolina, and settled in Charlotte eight or ten years before the commencement of the Revolutionary war. He married Margaret Houston, and was long a popular hotel keeper in Charlotte. He took a decided and active part in the Revolutionary war. He probably served under Col. Thomas Polk on the Snow Campaign in 1775. His large acquaintance with the people enabled him to raise a company of men, whom he led forth on Rutherford's Cherokee campaign in 1776. He was with the troops embodied who opposed Cornwallis when he entered Charlotte in September, 1781. Capt. Jack also led his company in Gen. Polk's brigade in April, 1781, joining Gen. Greene at Rugeby's Mills, and serving a three months' tour of duty. The particulars of other services of Capt. Jack are not preserved. It is only known that he was ever ready for service, and was so popular with his company that they induced him not to seek or accept the promotions, which indeed he did not desire. In a certificate extracted by Col. Abraham and Hezekiah Alexander December 24, 1781, it is stated that Capt. Jack had resided several years in Mecklenburg county, was a good and worthy member of society, both civil and religious, and since the beginning of the war, had always conducted himself as a patriot and as an officer in such a manner as to evince his honest zeal and attachment to the cause of his country. The close of the war left him poor. He had freely advanced all he possessed in the great struggle, a portion of it as a loan to North Carolina. His unrequited claims at the time of his death upon North Carolina amounted to £7,446 State currency. In 1783, Capt. Jack removed to Georgia, settling in Wilkes county.

REV. FRANCIS CUMMINGS, D. D.

A child of Irish parentage, Mr. Cummings was born near Shippenburg, Penn., in the spring of 1752. In his 19th year his parents moved to Mecklenburg county, and young Cummings exchanged his former life for the classic halls of the Queen's Museum in Charlotte, where he was an eye witness of the Mecklenburg Convention of May, 1775, concerning which he furnished a certificate, and also gave some account in a published sermon. He graduated at Queen's Museum about 1776, and spent several years teaching. Among his pupils in Bethel, York county, South Carolina, was Andrew Jackson, afterwards President, and William Smith, a United States Senator from South Carolina.

When licensed to preach he occupied various pulpits at Hopewell, Bethel and other places. In 1788, while residing at Bethel, he was chosen by the people of York county a member of the South Carolina Convention for deciding upon the Constitution of the United States. Mr. Cummings was at various periods the pastor of some twenty congregations, some in North Carolina, South Carolina and Georgia, dividing his time between teaching and preaching.

His last sermon was preached January 15, 1832, and three days later he was seized with influenza, which terminated his life at Greensboro, Ga., on the 2d of the ensuing February, in the 80th year of his age. He left behind him a good name and many descendants.

GEN. JOSEPH GRAHAM.

A native of Pennsylvania, Joseph Graham was born October 13, 1759. His widowed mother in 1776 removed with her five children to North Carolina, settling in the vicinity of Charlotte, where Joseph received the most of his education. He was present during the meeting of the famous Mecklenburg Convention, and his reminiscences concerning it are not only the most detailed of any preserved, but the most important in citing facts connected with the Resolves which, when those of May 20th were subsequently discovered, go to substantiate that they were the real and only Resolves adopted by the people of Mecklenburg in May, 1775.

In May, 1778, when 19 years old, he enlisted in the Fourth Regiment of the North Carolina line, and marched into Caswell county, and was subsequently furloughed home; but in August, was ordered to South Carolina, and then to Georgia; was in the battle of Stono, June 20, 1779, and soon after discharged. The next year he was appointed Adjutant of the Mecklenburg regiment, and when the British army, under Lord Cornwallis, invaded the country in September, 1780, he was ordered by Gen. Davidson to take command of such of the inhabitants as should collect in Charlotte on the news of the enemy's approach, who amounted to fifty in number. When the British entered Charlotte September 26th, Maj. Davis and Capt. Graham made a daring resistance, brief, but unavailing. They were compelled to retreat, but resisted as they retired. In one of the enemy's charges, Graham received nine wounds, six from the sabre and three from bullets. His stock buckles probably prevented one of the cuts upon his neck from fatally wounding him. As it was, he ever afterward bore marks of the severity of the blow aimed at his life. Four deep sabre gashes scarred his head and one his side. He was left for dead when the enemy departed, and with difficulty crawled to some water near by, where, slaking his intolerable thirst, he washed his numerous painful wounds as well as he could.

For a time he expected to die unnoticed in this secluded spot, but by night was discovered by kind-hearted people who were in search of their wounded countrymen, and conveyed to a neighboring house of a widow lady. Here he was concealed in an upper room and was attended by the widow and her daughter during the night, expecting he might soon die. Once he slept and breathed so quietly, and was so pale, they thought he was dead. The next day a British officer's wife, with a company of horsemen, visited the widow's house in quest of fresh provisions. By some means she discovered that there was a wounded person in the loft, and pressing the inquiry, learned he was an officer and his wounds severe, and kindly offered to send a British surgeon to dress his wounds as soon as she should reach the camp at Charlotte. Alarmed at his discovery and dreading to fall into the hands of the enemy, he rallied all his powers and caused himself to be placed on horseback the ensuing night and taken to his mother's, and not long after to the hospital. Three balls were taken from his body.

GEN. GEORGE GRAHAM.

Nearly two years the senior of his brother, Joseph, whose career has just been sketched, George Graham was also a native of Pennsylvania, born in 1758, and when some nine years of age was brought to Mecklenburg county by his widowed mother, and educated at the Queen's Museum Academy at Charlotte, and became strongly imbued with the republican principles of the Scotch-Irish of that region. He was one of the party of young patriots who rode from Charlotte to Salisbury early in June, 1775, and arrested Dunn and Boothe, a couple of prominent Tory lawyers who proposed to detain Capt. Jack when on his way to Philadelphia with the Resolves of the Mecklenburg Convention. He was active in harrassing and thwarting the foraging parties of the enemy when Cornwallis lay at Charlotte, and one of the gallant fourteen who dared to attack, October 3, 1780, and actually drove a British foraging party of 450 infantry, 60 cavalry and about 40 wagons, under Maj. Doyle, at McIntire's, seven miles north of Charlotte.

Capt. James Thompson commanded this daring party of

Mecklenburgers. Two hundred yards from McIntire's was a thicket down a spring branch, to which Thompson and his party repaired. A point of rocky ridge, covered with bushes, passed obliquely from the road towards the spring, and within fifty steps of the house, which sheltered them from view. From under this cover Thompson and party deployed into line ten or twelve feet apart, and advanced silently to their intended position. The British were much out of order; some in the barn throwing down oats for the horses, others racing after the pigs, ducks and chickens; a squad was robbing the bee hive, while others were pillaging the dwelling. A sentinel placed on watch, within a few steps of where the Americans were advancing, appeared to be alarmed, though he had not seen them. Capt. Thompson fired the first shot and brought down the sentinel. This being the signal for the attack, each man, as he could get a view, took ready and deliberate aim before he fired at the distance of 60 to 70 steps. In two instances where two happened to aim at the same pillager, when the first fired and the fellow fell, the second had to change his aim and search for another object.

The enemy immediately began to form and fire briskly. None of the Americans had time to load and fire the second time, except Capt. Thompson and Bradley, who were the first to discharge their rifles. The last shot of Thompson's was aimed at the Captain of the party at the barn, 150 steps distant, who died of the wound he received two days afterwards, at the house of Samuel McCombs, in Charlotte. Thompson's party retreated through the thicket, which was nearly parallel to the great road, and only about one-half mile from it. The enemy continued to fire briskly and ceased about the time the Americans were half a mile away.

The main body of the British under Maj. Doyle, who were in the rear, hearing the firing at McIntire's, became alarmed and hurried to the support of their friends. Capt. Thompson's party now loaded their rifles, ascended the creek bottom, deployed, as before, under cover of a high bank parallel with the road, and about 40 rods from it. They had not been long at this station before the enemy's advance, and some wagons, came on. They severally fired, taking deliberate aim, and then retreated down the creek. When the front of the enemy's column arrived near the creek's ford, they formed and commenced a tremendous fire through the low ground, which continued till Thompson's army had retreated near a half mile. The cavalry at the same time divided, one-half passing down each side of the creek. Simultaneous with this movement, six or seven hounds came in full cry on the track of the retreating Americans, and in about three-quarters of a mile came up with them. One of the dogs was shot, and the others seemed to comprehend the situation and made no further noise. The country being thickly covered with undergrowth, Thompson's men escaped unhurt. The British cavalry kept on their flank on the high ground until they reached the plantation of Robert Carr, Sr., where they appeared much enraged, and carried the old gentleman, though 70 years old, a prisoner to Charlotte. Maj. Doyle's party moved on from the ford of the creek and formed a junction with those at McIntire's farm; gathered up eight dead and twelve wounded, put them in their wagons and retreated to Charlotte in great haste. On their arrival they reported that they had found a rebel in every bush after passing seven miles in that direction. The names of those fourteen deserve to be perpetuated in Mecklenburg history, namely: Capt. James Thompson, George Graham, Frank Bradley (killed a few days after by four of Bryan's Tories), James Henry, Thomas and John Dickson, John Long, Robert and John Robinson, George and Hugh Theston, Thomas McClure and Edward and George Shipley. It is believed that during the whole war the enemy did not sustain so great a loss nor meet with so complete a disappointment in his objects by such a mere handful of men. That out of 30 shots fired, 20 should have done execution, is quite a new experience in the history of war, and several of Thompson's men thought that every shot would have told, so deliberate was their aim, had each singled out a different object; but in two or more instances, aiming at the same person. (Gen. Joseph Graham's narrative, in North Carolina University Magazine, March, 1836).

Surname Index.

[Every subject of a biographical sketch in this book has been indexed with the notation "(bio)" before the page number(s) on which the sketch appears.]

ABERNATHY, 339 342 343 358
ABERNETHY, 347
ABRAHAM, 425
ADAHOLT, 350
ADAM, 54
ADAMS, 335 342 346 350 353 358 359
ADIAR, 344
ADKINS, 346
AGNEW, 178
AHRENS, 299
ALBRIGHT, 339
ALCHISON, 344
ALCORN, 96 185 347 349
ALEXANDER, 26 32 34 38-40 44 46 52-56 58-62 64 69-71 78-85 90-93 98 102 104 105 108 116 133 136 143 144 150 153 154 159-162 168 175 177 181 188-190 193 230 237-240 244 249 251 252 255 256 258 261 262 280 284 285 292 293 311 322 325 327 330 333-337 339 341-344 346-355 357 358 367 379 396-398 401-409 411 412 415 416 421 423 425 (bio) 78-85 98 104-106 143 144 159-162 188-190 237 238 248 249

ALEXANDER (continued) 284 285 397 398 401-409 415 421
ALISON, 19
ALLEN, 52 56 330 341 346 351 354 357
ALLISON, 17 169 248 352
ANDERSON, 334 336 337 346 347 353 355
ANDREW, 268
ANDREWS, 16 148 246 248 343 358
ANDREY, 335
ANTRICE, 336
ARCHEY, 336
ARCHIBALD, 112
ARDRERY, 336
ARDREY, 60 142 182-185 268 269 335 345 353 (bio) 182-185
ARMOR, 349
ARMSTRONG, 199 339 340 349 355 357 404
ARNEY, 352
ARNOLD, 392
ARROWOOD, 239
ASBURY, 269 347 358
ASHBY, 343
ASHLEY, 342 343 354
ATCHISON, 355
ATKINS, 159

AUSTIN, 351
AUTEN, 341 342 348 352
AVERY, 32 34 78 79 82 408
   415 416 419 (bio) 415-417
AYCOCK, 357
AYERS, 337
BAILES, 344
BAILEY, 346 354
BAILLEY, 343
BAILLIFF, 347
BAIN, 71 83 255 256 347
BAINE, 59
BAKER, 55 272 339 342 344
   346 348 355
BALCH, 30 32 186 287 407
   408 (bio) 407 408
BALDWIN, 242 339
BALES, 269 346
BALLARD, 336 342 351
BALTIMORE, 387
BANCROFT, 48 400
BANE, 82 405 407
BARBER, 356
BARBON, 356
BARCKLEY, 348
BAREFOOT, 346
BARFLEET, 56
BARITT, 349
BARNES, 56 357
BARNET, 95
BARNETT, 41 50 51 55 70
   269 287 334 336 341 345
   346 349 352-355 380
BARNHARD, 54
BARNHARDT, 198 299
BARNHILL, 55 351
BARNS, 13 53 56 343 355
BARNWELL, 247
BARRETT, 52

BARRINGER, 197 198 200-
   207 223 228 267 352 (bio)
   197-208
BARRIS, 336
BARRY, 10 32 115 117 272
   412 413 (bio) 412 413
BARTLETT, 345
BARTLETTE, 344
BASS, 342
BATES, 148
BATTLE, 197
BAXTER, 55
BEAL, 342
BEAN, 351
BEARD, 243-245 337 349 352
   (bio) 243 244
BEATTIE, 59 349 356
BEATTY, 339 342 347
BEATY, 53 55
BEAUREGARD, 171
BEAVER, 348 357
BECKHAM, 268
BEEK, 342
BEEMAN, 345
BEHRENDS, 335
BELK, 53 56 63 307 343 354
BELL, 185 235 343 345 346
   349 352 353
BENBOW, 53
BENFIELD, 348 353
BENHILL, 55
BENNETT, 337 347 354
BENSON, 352 356
BENTLEY, 346
BENTON, 355/
BERNS, 56
BERRY, 337
BERRYHILL, 335 344 347 355
BIGART, 343

BIGGART, 334
BIGGERS, 54 348 356
BIGHAM, 55 341 342 345 358
BINGHAM, 42 53 352
BIRD, 342 357
BISHOP, 336
BIZEL, 299
BIZZEL, 363
BIZZELL, 120 363
BLACK, 53 54 293 334 336 341 343 346 349 351 352
BLACKARD, 351
BLACKBURN, 55
BLACKSTOCK, 289
BLACKWELDER, 198 199 201 306 339 344 356-358
BLACKWOOD, 59 358
BLACWOOD, 55
BLAIR, 246 343 354
BLAKE, 46 97 336
BLAKELY, 341 348 349
BLALOCK, 340
BLANKENSHIP, 343 351
BLOUNT, 348
BLYTHE, 349 351 367
BOID, 53
BOILS, 359
BOLTON, 338 347
BOND, 334
BOON, 13
BOONE, 334
BOOTH, 117 131
BOOTHE, 428
BOST, 54 356
BOURDEAUX, 334
BOWDEN, 344 358
BOWMAN, 159 276 346
BOYCE, 272 343 346

BOYD, 55 200 304 335 336 343 344 357
BOYLER, 349
BRACKETT, 339
BRADDY, 56
BRADLEY, 429 430
BRADLY, 116 342 352
BRADSHAW, 342
BRADSTON, 346
BRADY, 349
BRANCH, 191
BRANDON, 86 199 201
BRANNAN, 338
BRATTON, 306
BRAWLEY, 352
BRAY, 339
BRECKENRIDGE, 228
BREFFARD, 336
BREM, 180 188 189 294 338 379 (bio) 188-190
BRENIZER, 301
BREVARD, 22 30-32 45 52 76 78 86-89 117 165 166 380 396 399 400 406 416 (bio) 86-90 399-401
BREWER, 346
BRICE, 334 379
BRICKETT, 120
BRIDGERS, 339
BRIDGES, 351
BRIGADE, 143
BRIGMAN, 341
BRIMER, 344
BRINES, 351
BRINGLE, 335
BRINKLE, 338
BRINKLEY, 346
BRISTOW, 346

SURNAME INDEX.

BRITT, 349
BRITTEN, 376
BRITTON, 306 335
BROADSTREET, 356
BROADWAY, 339
BROCK, 417
BRONSON, 300
BROOM, 53 357
BROTHERTON, 347
BROWN, 52 53 144 195 243 244 300 304 335 337 338 341 343 344 348 349 351 352 354 358 396 (bio) 243
BROWNFIELD, 415
BROWNING, 356
BRUCE, 216 351 355
BRUM, 358
BRYAN, 53 344 415 430
BRYANT, 343
BRYCE, 247 306 356 (bio) 247
BUCHANAN, 162
BUFF, 339
BUFORD, 109
BUGLIN, 337
BUNDLE, 337
BUNIER, 342
BURGWYN, 347 348
BURHART, 197
BURKHEAD, 352
BURLEYSON, 349
BURNETT, 338
BURNEY, 225
BURNS, 351
BURRIS, 336
BURROUGHS, 227 358
BURTON, 59
BURUS, 339
BURWELL, 17 60 97 223 300 306 355 357

BUSHBEY, 53
BUTLER, 336 401
BUTT, 301
BUTTON, 56
BYNUM, 224 307 337 353
BYRUM, 341
CABARRUS, 198
CABLE, 338
CAHILL, 337 358
CALDER, 335 338
CALDWELL, 15 52 55 59 60 69-72 76 77 82 83 91 92 97 99 100 116 149 160 161 171 178 179 191 194 225 245 246 254-258 261 281-283 302 322 325 334 335 343 348 349 358 376 403 407 (bio) 71 72 99 100 254-256
CALLOWAY, 336
CALSON, 415
CAMBELL, 336
CAMERON, 53 146
CAMPBELL, 54 168 269 335 341-343 348 355 392 (bio) 168
CANBY, 362 366 368
CANIPE, 339
CANNADY, 340
CANNEDY, 334
CANNELL, 339
CANNON, 339
CAPPS, 355
CARMICK, 342
CARNTHENS, 345
CAROTHERS, 55
CARPENTER, 343 347 349 351
CARR, 430

SURNAME INDEX.

CARRELL, 54
CARRICKER, 338
CARRIGAN, 54 349 352
CARRIHER, 54
CARRIKER, 356
CARROL, 237 365
CARROLL, 13 336 339
CARSON, 13 17 19 55 95 238
    304 379
CARTER, 336 338-340
CARUTHERS, 343
CASHION, 338 352
CASKILL, 338
CASWELL, 32 390
CATCHCOAT, 355
CATHART, 339
CATHCART, 352
CATHEY, 335 336 342 345
    347 349 351 358
CATHY, 83
CATON, 355
CAUSNET, 339
CHAINEY, 56
CHALKLEY, 339
CHALMERS, 274
CHAMBERLAIN, 238
CHAMBERLEY, 325
CHANCY, 338
CHANELS, 55
CHANTENBERG, 343
CHAPLE, 54
CHAPMAN, 339
CHARLES, 351
CHARLES I, King of England
    387
CHARLOTTE, Princess of
    Mecklenburg 68
CHEEK, 53
CHERRY, 56

CHESHIER, 341
CHESHIRE, 239
CHESIRE, 348
CHISHOLM, 375
CHOAT, 344
CHOATE, 345
CHRESTAINBURY, 350
CHRISTENBERY, 339
CHRISTIANBERRY, 352
CHRISTY, 342
CHUNN, 207
CHURCH, 346
CIDNY, 340
CLANTON, 342 345
CLARK, 53 200 204 311 337
    342 343 345 347 351 352
    355
CLARKE, 390
CLAY, 45 46 183 233 356
CLAYWELL, 338
CLEMMONS, 342
CLENDENNEN, 335
CLEVELAND, 302 392
CLICK, 54
CLINE, 356
CLONTZ, 53 351
COBB, 64 154 343
COBBLE, 336
COCHRAN, 54 57 355 357
    358
COCHRANE, 339 341 348 349
    355
COFFE, 343
COFFEE, 354
COFFEY, 346
COHEN, 335
COLEMAN, 358
COLLINS, 335 338 339 355
COLUMBUS, 44

SURNAME INDEX.

CONDER, 338
CONGER, 410
CONNEL, 55
CONNELL, 339
CONNER, 45 55 336
CONNOR, 58
COOK, 13 56 79 198 330 348
COOPER, 62 343
COOTS, 353
CORBLE, 357
CORK, 352
CORNELIUS, 352
CORNWALLIS, 22 80 90 109 110 117 120 131 192 291 293 391 394 406 413 423-425 427 428
CORUM, 330
COSTENER, 339
COSTLEY, 57
COTLHARP, 346
COTTER, 340
COTTRAIM, 336
COUGHRAN, 53
COWAN, 335
COX, 343 347 350 356
CRAFT, 357
CRAGHEAD, 256
CRAIG, 56 336 356
CRAIGHEAD, 25-27 48 49 66-69 84 85 178 186 254-256 259 281 287 (bio) 66-70
CRANE, 269 339 354
CRAVEN, 352
CRAWFORD, 46 51 334 345
CRAWSON, 335
CREASMAN, 341
CRENSHAW, 354
CRESWELL, 299 306 347
CRIE, 289
CROCKER, 351
CROCKET, 261 292
CROMWELL, 387
CROSS, 351
CROUTHERS, 354
CROWEL, 343
CROWELL, 53 56 334 345 346 350 351
CROWLEY, 341
CRUMP, 336
CRUSE, 192 336 356
CULBERSON, 342
CULER, 340
CULLET, 353
CULP, 346 354
CUMMINGS, 426 (bio) 426
CUMMINS, 41
CUNNINGHAM, 52 268 269
CURETON, 183
CUTHBERTSON, 53
DAFTER, 53
DALLARHIT, 343
DANIEL, 248
DARNALL, 345
DARNELL, 53 341
DASINGER, 338
DAVID, 339
DAVIDSON, 11 12 16 19 32 34 40 41 45 59 60 71 73-78 82 83 97 99 100 106 115-118 132 150 164-166 185 240 248 268 269 272 289 290 300 325 334-339 356 357 358 379 391 394 406 413 415 422-424 427 (bio) 73-78 97 132 164-166 422-424

SURNAME INDEX. 439

DAVIE, 39 86 393
DAVIS, 55 59 85 139-142 147 148 171 203 268 270 287 300 306 334-336 345 346 348 352-356 358 427 (bio) 139-142
DAWNS, 339
DAY, 353
DEARMOND, 345 352 354
DEATON, 341 348 350
DECKER, 198
DEGGARHART, 343
DEKALB, 110 111
DELLING, 340
DELLINGER, 350
DEMON, 355
DENNIS, 57 348 415
DENNY, 19
DENTON, 342
DERR, 350
DESEASURE, 247
DETMOND, 307
DEVINE, 351
DEWEESE, 352
DEWEY, 119 301
DEWOLF, 195 363
DEWOLFE, 300
DICKERSON, 401
DICKSON, 430
DINKINS, 55
DIXON, 54 289 342 343 346 348
DOBBIN, 339
DOBSON, 338
DOHERTY, 99 349
DONALD, 71 255
DONNELL, 355
DONOVAN, 338
DOOLAN, 356
DORSETT, 334
DOUGHERTY, 59
DOUGLAS, 58
DOUGLASS, 52
DOVE, 54
DOWD, 60 241 299 300 306 376
DOWNES, 32
DOWNS, 56 291 294 335 345-347 358 419 420 (bio) 419 420
DOWNY, 53
DOYLE, 339 428-430
DRAFFEN, 293
DRAPER, 385
DREWRY, 343
DRUCKER, 379
DUAN, 347
DUCKWORTH, 52 55 341 346
DUGLASS, 347
DULE, 353
DULIN, 154-156 336 341 348 351 353 (bio) 154-156
DUNCAN, 228
DUNLAP, 14 15 136 137 178-180 265 299 304 339 (bio) 178-180
DUNN, 17 55 59 97 117 131 249 250 335 346 354 428 (bio) 249 250
DURANT, 172
DYER, 334
EAGLE, 334 355
EARNHARDT, 341 343 348
EARNHEARDT, 335 341
EARNSHAW, 306
EAUDAY, 356
EDLEMAN, 336
EDMIRTON, 338

SURNAME INDEX.

EDMUNDS, 113
EDWARD, 338
EDWARDS, 336 342 343 345 351 352
EFIRD, 336
EILLOW, 338
ELLER, 338 342
ELLINGTON, 339
ELLIOTT, 52 53 55 185 196 260 335 338 341 347 353 354
ELLIS, 233 333 343 345
ELLSWORTH, 408
ELMORE, 338
ELMS, 16 194 246 248 299 306 335 341 350 352 379 (bio) 246 247
EMERSON, 352
ENGEL, 335 355
ENGENBURN, 355
EPHRAIM, 86
EPPS, 355
ERVING, 347
ERWIN, 53 59 65 106 222 227-229 253 344 345 357 358 (bio) 227-230
ESPEY, 220
ETTERS, 347
ETTRES, 343
EUDY, 358
EVAN, 228
EWELL, 203
EWING, 341
EZZELL, 269 335 346 354
FAGGART, 356
FAGGOT, 358
FAIRES, 347
FALLS, 134 356
FANNING, 198

FANYGEN, 334
FARLEY, 339
FARR, 52
FARRA, 55
FARRIS, 348 354
FAT, 53
FAUCET, 352
FERELAND, 54
FERGUSON, 289 392
FERRELL, 56 358
FERRET, 53
FESPERMAN, 348 350
FEWELL, 160
FIDLER, 349
FIELD, 336
FIELDS, 354
FILE, 356
FILLMORE, 233
FINCHER, 354 357
FINGER, 342
FINK, 54 356
FINLEY, 336 339
FINOLA, 120
FINSHER, 56
FISHER, 56 111 200 227 341 356 358
FITE, 339 343
FIZELL, 311
FLANIGAN, 53 351
FLEMMING, 54
FLENIGAN, 53 358
FLENIKEN, 354
FLENNIKEN, 32
FLENNIKIN, 413 (bio) 413
FLORE, 335
FLOW, 53 335 336 341 348
FLOWE, 351
FLOWERS, 56 339 353
FLOYD, 356

FLYNS, 186
FOARD, 55 348 356 420 (bio) 420
FOBES, 54
FOGLEMAN, 338
FOOTE, 90 397 401 405 409 420
FORD, 32 61 172 293 341
FORDS, 336
FORESTER, 340
FORSYTHE, 56
FOSTER, 353
FOUTS, 352
FOWLER, 339 357
FOX, 13 16 59 191 289 306 339
FRANKLIN, 44 406
FRAZIER, 334 335 341 345 347 355
FREDRICK, 334
FREEMAN, 56 287 325 339 345 351
FRENCH, 334 354
FRENEKIN, 345
FREW, 70
FRICK, 338
FRONEBARGER, 351
FULLBRIGHT, 339
FULLENWELDER, 334
FULLER, 57
FURGUSON, 358
FURMAN, 13
FURR, 336 356
GADD, 356
GAISESEN, 336
GALLAGHER, 338
GALLANT, 345
GALLOWAY, 228
GALOWAY, 341

GAMBLE, 346
GARDENER, 350
GARDNER, 350
GARNER, 55 345 352
GARREN, 347
GARRESTON, 53
GARRETSON, 54
GARRISON, 177 341 342 348 354 (bio) 176 177
GASTON, 353
GATES, 110 291 351 392 412
GATLIN, 356
GAUGUS, 54
GAYLER, 54
GEORGE, 346 King of ? 85
GIBBON, 16 191 192 306 359 (bio) 191 192
GIBBS, 349 350
GIBONY, 52
GIBSON, 335 341 348 350 357 358
GILBERT, 353
GILES, 61 355
GILLESPIE, 83 196 334-336 349
GILLETT, 334
GILMER, 238
GILMORE, 54
GIVENS, 54 110
GLEASON, 299 338
GLENN, 335 341
GLOVER, 341 345 346
GOFORTH, 55
GOODLUCK, 121
GOODMAN, 54 338 339 342
GOODNIGHT, 54
GOODRUM, 341 350
GOODSEN, 336
GOODWINE, 407

GORDON, 228 351 354
GOULD, 325
GRADY, 54 338
GRAHAM, 32 39 40 44 51 53
    58 59 62 70 76 86 117 131
    148 183 223 294 334 336
    339 346 380 383 394 400
    423 426-428 430 431 (bio)
    131 132 414 426-431
GRANT, 233 338 368
GRAVES, 338
GRAY, 17 56 306 334 335 341
    354
GREENE, 392-394 406 425
GREENHILL, 347
GREER, 343
GREGG, 347
GREGGS, 53
GREGORY, 306
GRIBBLE, 335 341
GRIDSBY, 400
GRIER, 59 60 62 142 145 200
    222-224 229 230 235 289
    300 334 335 339 342 343
    345 348 350 353-355 357
    358 (bio) 222-224
GRIFFIN, 334 338 343 346
    353 354 356
GRIFFITH, 62 300 354 357
    358
GRIFITH, 346
GRIGG, 339
GROOT, 300
GROVER, 356
GROVES, 341 345
GRUB, 353
GUDGER, 339
GUION, 191
GURLEY, 351

HAGAR, 198
HAGENS, 293
HAGLER, 356
HAGONS, 350
HAIL, 345
HAINANT, 344
HALE, 244
HALL, 54 91 108 109 113 135
    252 335 343-346 348 351
    355
HALLET, 341
HALOBOUGH, 358
HALSHOUSER, 338
HAMBLETON, 56
HAMILTON, 54 350
HAMMONS, 53
HAMPTON, 59 112 201 203
    247
HANCOCK, 39
HAND, 335 341
HANEY, 351
HANFIELD, 354
HANLEY, 56
HANNA, 338 344
HANNEL, 344
HANNON, 344 354 358
HANSER, 335
HANSON, 56
HAPPOLDT, 191 245 246 (bio)
    245 246
HARBESON, 56
HARGET, 337
HARGETT, 56 337 344 351
HARGRAVE, 357
HARKEY, 56 306 335-337 354
    358 359
HARMAN, 353
HARMON, 344
HARON, 344

HARREL, 335
HARRINGTON, 357
HARRIS, 15 32 52 54 58 59 61 64 83 105 106 108 139 144 145 153 178 185 186 192 200 245 269 279 280 289 294 299 334 338 341-344 348 351 358 379 410 418-422 (bio) 185 186 418 421 422
HARRISON, 52 55 56 59 99 100 118 290 350
HARRY, 237 355
HART, 53 228 344 350
HARTE, 59
HARTGRUE, 342
HARTIS, 337 354
HARTLINE, 342
HARTLY, 55
HARTMAN, 356
HARTS, 346
HARTSELL, 338 358
HARTY, 166 167 246 271 306 (bio) 166 167
HASKELL, 335
HASTINGS, 350
HATCHUP, 344
HAWKINS, 55 200 339 345
HAYDEN, 376
HAYES, 347 351
HAYNE, 74
HAYS, 344
HEADLY, 351
HEALEY, 306
HEART, 340
HEAVENER, 339
HECKS, 353
HEDGEPATH, 344
HEITMAN, 345
HELDT, 352
HELFER, 353
HELMER, 56
HELMES, 56
HELMS, 337 342 353 357
HEMPHILL, 294
HENDERSON, 44 53 55 58 59 70 83 98 121 167 225 226 238-242 252-254 261 334 335 337 339 341 344 346 350 351 357 361 376 412 (bio) 238-243
HENDRIX, 350 353
HENLEY, 54
HENNIGEN, 354
HENRY, 11 39 73 162 261 344 351 430
HERBERT, 337
HERRON, 335 341 344 348
HERRVELL, 339
HEWES, 32
HICKS, 338 393
HIGGENSON, 351
HILL, 20 186-188 222 231 268 270 306 334 335 341 342 344 345 352 376 (bio) 186-188
HILTON, 333 334 337
HINKLE, 339 340
HINSON, 341 358
HINTON, 342
HIPP, 347 351
HOBBS, 341
HODGE, 56
HODGES, 348
HOFFMAN, 159 339 344 356
HOGG, 198
HOLBROOK, 337
HOLBROOKS, 54 350

HOLDBROOKS, 193
HOLDEN, 53 299 337
HOLDSLLAW, 342
HOLLAND, 276 344
HOLLINGSWORTH, 334 342
HOLMES, 53 346
HOLMS, 335 341
HOLT, 170 171
HOLTON, 304 335
HOOD, 52 57 187 345 346 348 351 355
HOOKER, 53
HOOKS, 348
HOOPER, 32
HOOVER, 339 347 355 358
HOPE, 55
HOPKINS, 337
HOTCHKIP, 343 345
HOTCHKISS, 352
HOUSE, 54
HOUSTON, 34 54 57 133 229 293 335 348 350 425
HOVIS, 341 347 351 358
HOWARD, 11 54 56 335 341 354
HOWELL, 266 334 338 339 356 357
HOWEY, 335
HOWIE, 56 270 292 306 346 348 350 355 358
HOYLE, 339
HUBBARD, 416
HUCKS, 348 350
HUDSON, 337 354
HUMBLE, 338
HUMPHREY, 344
HUMPHREYS, 244
HUNSUCKER, 351 356
HUNT, 340

HUNTER, 39 40 42 56 106-113 176 234-236 273 304 330 334 337 339 341 342 348 350-352 357 358 367 383 415 421 (bio) 107-114 234-236
HURSTON, 337
HUTCHISON, 19 53 55 59 72 124 192 205 246 300 325 335 336 341 347 348 358
HUTSPETH, 341
HUX, 352
HYMANS, 335
ICEHOUR, 54
ICEHOWER, 335 341
ICENHOUR, 338 350
INGLE, 344
INGOLD, 335
INGRAHAM, 250
INGRIM, 340
IREDELL, 146
IRKPATRICK, 358
IRWIN, 16 26 32 34 54 56 58 61 78 81 241 246 271 287 333 348 379 404 405 413 418 (bio) 404 405
ISEMAN, 197
ISREAL, 335
IVEY, 56
J, 174
JACCOUR, 54
JACK, 11 32 33 40 51 424-426 428 (bio) 425 426
JACKSON, 45 46 51 52 55 62 88 188 252 338 352 426
JACOBS, 334
JAMERSON, 338 342
JAMES I, King of England 386
JAMESON, 342

SURNAME INDEX.

JAMISON, 306 337 345 350 354 358
JANNISON, 338
JARRETT, 347
JARVIS, 146
JASWA, 334
JEFFERSON, 34 39 44 47
JENKINS, 179 340 341 350
JENNINGS, 14 337 346 358
JETTON, 83 134 349 (bio) 134
JIMISON, 52
JOHN, 53 192 340
JOHNATHAN, 267
JOHNSON, 335-338 340 341 344 388 393 395
JOHNSTON, 19 53-55 65 126 132 133 147 148 152 161 172 189 237 253 293 300 325 330 342 345-354 356 357 379 (bio) 132-134 147 148 188-190
JONES, 13 55 60 180 229 235 247 300 306 334 338 352 376 389 416
JORDAN, 16 305 337 348 352
JULIN, 55
JUNDERBUSK, 56
KAISER, 351
KALORAM, 340
KANAPUM, 338
KANIP, 339
KARR, 56
KARY, 52
KASCIUS, 393
KATZ, 335 355
KEELOUGH, 54
KEENAN, 335 344 348 353
KELL, 345
KELLEY, 54 338 350
KENAN, 354
KENEDY, 341
KENIER, 354
KENNEDY, 42 338
KENNERLY, 352
KENNON, 30 32 33 416 417 (bio) 417
KENTY, 54
KERNS, 239 341 348-350 352
KERR, 55 65 195 269 275 334 337 340 342 344 345 354 358 363
KESIAH, 334
KESTLER, 342
KETCHIE, 352
KEY, 344
KILOUGH, 348
KILPATRICK, 344
KIMBALL, 345
KIMMONS, 54 356
KING, 56 307 337 341 344 347 351 355 401
KINNEV, 341
KINSEY, 335
KIRBY, 237 337 338
KIRK, 59 348
KIRKLEY, 351
KIRKPATRICK, 345 346 354 355 357 358
KISER, 54 356
KISLER, 338
KISSIAH, 351
KISTLER, 335 351
KIZZIAH, 336
KLUTS, 356
KNIGHT, 357
KNIPPER, 341
KNOX, 96 235 244 335 343-345 350 355 387

SURNAME INDEX.

KNUIPE, 340
KUCK, 300
KURTZ, 338
KUSTLER, 358
KYLE, 342
KYLES, 342
LACY, 357
LAFAYETTE, 45 186
LAFFERTY, 258 (bio) 258
LAMB, 340
LAMBERT, 56 343
LANCEY, 53
LANDLER, 334
LANE, 20 53 338 340
LATTA, 76
LATTIMER, 340
LAUGHLIN, 340
LAWING, 340 347
LAWLER, 340
LAWRING, 351
LAWSON, 343
LAWYER, 54
LAY, 356
LEACH, 350
LEADWELL, 14
LEAVENWORTH, 325
LEDFORD, 340 356
LEDWELL, 342
LEE, 20 39 103 112 139 201 203 269 270 299 334 345 346
LEEPER, 358
LEFTER, 356
LEGGETT, 293
LELAIN, 337
LEMMON, 53
LEMMONS, 59
LENTZ, 350 358
LEON, 335 355
LEOPOLD, 335
LEVENWORTH, 13
LEVEY, 54
LEVI, 335
LEVINSTEIN, 198
LEWELLYN, 336
LEWING, 55
LEWIS, 337 339 341 343 346
LIBERMAN, 345
LIGHT, 54
LILLINGTON, 390
LINCOLN, 148 203 424
LINDSAY, 105 358
LINDSEY, 340
LINEBERGER, 343
LINEBURGER, 340
LINKER, 54 356
LINN, 293
LINTZ, 357
LITTLE, 307 350 357
LIVINGSTON, 48 352
LOCKE, 70 86 199
LOFTEN, 343
LONERGAN, 271
LONG, 54 207 430
LONGSTREET, 187
LOOKER, 351
LOSSING, 392 424
LOURIE, 351
LOVE, 52 55 355 358
LOWRANCE, 352
LOWRIE, 51 58 91 132 133 135-137 160 177 179 305 334 339 343 344 (bio) 91 135-137
LUCAS, 53 119 347
LUCKEY, 350
LUDWICK, 358
LUTHER, 54

LYNCH, 347
LYONS, 339
M'CAULAY, (bio) 245
M'COMBS, (bio) 190 191
M(?)ERS, 346
MACILWAINE, 16
MADDEN, 343 344
MADISON, 29 34
MAGLAUCHLIN, 56
MAHONY, 340
MAKALER, 353
MANESS, 345
MANNING, 351
MANNIS, 357
MANSION, 268
MAPE, 53
MARKCUS, 339
MARKS, 345 355
MARRABLE, 340
MARSHAL, 340
MARSHBURN, 344
MARTIN, 28 29 34 54 220 246 337 343 352 389 391 408 424
MASON, 53 338 348 351 354
MASSEY, 59
MASSINGALE, 346
MATHISON, 343
MATTHEWS, 56 142 292 354
MAXWELL, 64 152-155 280 306 333 336 339 348 349 351 355 (bio) 152 153
MAYBEN, 109
MAYGEEHEE, 56
MAYS, 54
MCADEN, 25 286 301 379
MCALEXANDER, 341
MCALISTER, 354
MCALLISTER, 350

MCALROY, 56
MCAULAY, 226
MCAULEY, 314 350 352
MCBEAN, 338
MCCAFFRY, 340
MCCAIN, 54
MCCALL, 56 337 341 347 348 351 358
MCCALLOK, 53
MCCARVER, 337
MCCAUGHNEYHEY, 62
MCCAULAY, 96 245
MCCAUSLAND, 340
MCCEWON, 349
MCCLELLAN, 187 228
MCCLINTOCK, 63
MCCLURE, 32 414 430 (bio) 414
MCCOFFIN, 101
MCCOMBS, 55 59 190 191 306 348 355 429
MCCONNELL, 338 341 345 349 352
MCCORCLE, 54
MCCORD, 192 347 351
MCCORKLE, 334 335 340 341 343 349
MCCOY, 56 83 299 350 351 356
MCCRACKEN, 55
MCCRARY, 355
MCCRUM, 355
MCCULLOCK, 56 292
MCCULLOUGH, 139
MCCURRY, 346
MCDANIEL, 356
MCDILL, 235
MCDONALD, 64 306 334 335 342 358

SURNAME INDEX.

MCDOWELL, 55 60 175 201 224
MCDUFFIE, 340
MCDUFFY, 340
MCELHANY, 358
MCELROY, 335 341 355
MCENTIRE, 356
MCFADDEN, 350
MCGAHEY, 347 352
MCGARAR, 338
MCGEE, 347
MCGHEE, 347 351
MCGILBRY, 340
MCGINN, 193 269 335 341 345 351 355
MCGINNESS, 357
MCGINNIS, 334 338 341 348
MCGRAW, 54
MCGUIRE, 338
MCGWIRT, 357
MCILWAIN, 191
MCINTIRE, 428 429
MCINTOSH, 150
MCINTYRE, 116 131
MCKAMIE, 149
MCKAY, 348
MCKEAN, 48
MCKEE, 58 142 291 292
MCKEEVER, 335
MCKELLERAND, 55
MCKELVIA, 55
MCKENZIE, 15 71
MCKINLEY, 335
MCKINNEY, 340 346 355
MCKINZIE, 358
MCKNIGHT, 55 272 273
MCKNITT, 26 116 160 399 405
MCLAUGHLIN, 274 348
MCLEAN, 76 86 104 136 150 339 344-346 348
MCLEARY, 59
MCLELLAN, 338
MCLEOD, 336 337
MCLILIE, 53
MCLOYD, 53
MCLURE, 53 337 343 348
MCMALLEN, 346
MCMANUS, 306
MCMILLAN, 289 344
MCMORDIE, 286
MCNEELEY, 352
MCNEELY, 287 337 352
MCNEIL, 228 395
MCNINCH, 299
MCQUAIG, 344 346
MCQUAISE, 344
MCQUAY, 343
MCRANEY, 354
MCRAVEN, 243
MCREA, 52 242 346
MCREE, 225 288
MCRELEY, 53
MCRUMB, 345
MCWHIRTER, 22 25 76 82 89 109 341 399
MCWHITE, 357
MCWHORTER, 408
MEAGHIM, 340
MEANS, 55 200 334 342 347 358 404
MEDLIN, 306
MEEK, 55 261
MEHOLERS, 334
MENTITH, 55
MEREDITH, 338
MERRIMON, 146
MERRITT, 355

MICHAEL, 55
MILES, 55 245 246
MILLEN, 358
MILLER, 49 54 153 191 258
    306 336 343 346 348 350
    352 354 358 (bio) 258-260
MILLS, 267 347
MILTON, 286 346 353
MINCEL, 344
MINOR, 353
MINUS, 358
MIRABEAU, 220
MISENHEIMER, 356
MISENHEMIER, 356
MITCHA, 343
MITCHELL, 58 353 355
MOAD, 340
MOBLE, 352
MOCHA, 363
MOCK, 359
MOFFITT, 340
MOLLAY, 337
MONROE, 267
MONSON, 42
MONTEETH, 176
MONTEITH, 335 341 350
MONTGOMERY, 56 265 266
    341 349 351 358
MOODY, 351
MOONEY, 351
MOORE, 52 53 56 60 194 225
    226 268 280 289 336 350
    352 354 356-358 390
MOOSE, 242
MOREHEAD, 169
MORETON, 356
MORGAN, 352 406 410 411
    421 422

MORRIS, 53 152 172-174 280
    337 340 346 349 354 (bio)
    172-175
MORRISON, 13 32 54-57 59
    69 75 142 188 207 253 294
    344 345 349 350 355 411
    412 (bio) 411 412
MORROW, 59 65 322 336 345
MOSER, 53 345
MOSLEY, 334
MOSS, 237 246 248
MOSTERS, 351
MOTZ, 340
MOWERY, 352
MOYLE, 335
MUIRHEAD, 385
MULLIS, 351 357
MULSON, 338
MULWEE, 345
MUNDAY, 343
MUNSEY, 338
MUNTEETH, 53
MUNY, 334
MURDOCK, 343
MURPHY, 19 340
MURRY, 339
MYERS, 60 106 205 347
NAIL, 338
NANCE, 352 358
NANTZ, 338 340 350
NARSON, 343
NASH, 116 391 393
NEAGLE, 345 358
NEAL, 175 181 336 341 343
    349 353 (bio) 175 176
NEALY, 123
NEEDHAM, 340
NEEL, 57 105 306 354

NEELE, 54
NEELS, 54
NEELY, 55 336 341 344 354
NELSON, 346 349 352 358
NESBITT, 343
NEVINS, 345
NEWELL, 342 349 354
NEWITT, 54
NEWTON, 338 340
NICHOLS, 334 342 346
NICHOLSON, 345 347 351 410
NOLAND, 271
NOLES, 337 349
NONE, 53
NORFLEET, 91 136
NORMAN, 99 194
NORMENT, 334 335 341 347 353 355
NORWOOD, 358
NULL, 343
O'CONNELL, 271
O'DONIHO, 340
OATE, 351
OATES, 64 136 137 177 178 248 265 307 334 355 379 (bio) 177 178
OATS, 350
OCHILTREE, 80 81 406 424
ODELL, 347
OKLEY, 345
OLIPHANT, 352
OLIVER, 338
OPPENHEIM, 336
ORMAN, 336 342
ORMAND, 54
ORMSBY, 340
ORR, 59 168 194 250 306 334 336 337 342 345 346 349

ORR (continued)
351 363 364 (bio) 250 251
ORRELL, 353
OSBORN, 352
OSBORNE, 55 60 65 76 82 86 89 93 137 184 204 223 231-233 243 300 304 306 336 349 352 354 356 399 (bio) 93 231-234
OSTWALD, 343
OTTERS, 355
OVERSHINE, 198
OWEN, 270
OWENS, 246 334 355
PACE, 356
PACKARD, 338
PAGE, 337 350
PALMER, 357
PAREDOE, 334
PARISH, 52 55
PARKER, 52 55 340 345
PARKES, 55
PARKS, 13 17 56 150 240 258 287 337 345 347 355 379
PARSONS, 357
PATTERSON, 133 268 269 292 338 346 351 354 355 359
PATTON, 32 78
PATTS, 336
PAUL, 337 353
PAXTON, 354 357
PAYNE, 352
PAYSOUR, 342 351
PEACH, 337
PEARSON, 55 147 201
PEELER, 339
PEGRAM, 301 351
PELT, 55

SURNAME INDEX.

PENDER, 356
PENMAN, 120 121
PENNIX, 343
PENWORTHY, 121
PEOPLES, 56 175 235 294 339
PEPPEN, 344
PERKINS, 356
PERRY, 55 353
PETIT, 338
PETRE, 349
PETTUS, 336 342 349
PHARR, 106 175 181 182 239 240 253 255 325 349 (bio) 180-182
PHELPS, 334
PHIFER, 32 34 58 78 81 82 86 168-172 198 334 354 405 406 423 (bio) 168-172
PHILLIPS, 52 56 336 347 351 353 357
PHOLAN, 337
PICKENS, 91
PICKERELL, 347
PIERCE, 346 354
PIRANT, 53
PITT, 52
PLYLER, 338 356
POLK, 10 30 32 34 41 42 45 46 51 58 62 73 78 79 82 89 90 95 96 98 104 108 199 250 353 380 385-396 398 400 403 409 416 419 420 422-425 (bio) 95 96 385-396 424 425
POLLOCK, 385-387
POOL, 54 333 340 343
PORTER, 18 55 268 344 345 354 387
POTTER, 13 79
POTTS, 59 62 183 185 292 334 336 337 340 349 353 355
POWELL, 342 345
PRAG, 345
PRATHER, 345 354 358
PRESLEY, 344 357
PRESSON, 357
PRESTON, 158
PREVITT, 354
PRICE, 55 166 272 334 344 350 353 357 412
PRIFLEY, 53
PRIM, 55 342
PRINGLE, 289
PRITCHARD, 13 158 267 277 299 (bio) 157-159
PRIVETTE, 353
PROCTOR, 347
PUCKETT, 343 347 349 350
PUGH, 336
PULLOAK, 385 386
PURSER, 56
PURVIS, 53
QUEARY, 32 293 294 414 (bio) 414 415
QUEEN, 340
QUEERY, 239 280
QUENY, 336
QUERY, 334 342 349
QUIN, 340
QUINN, 172 338
QUIRY, 358
RABB, 280
RABON, 342
RACHELLE, 344
RAFFERTY, 338
RAMSAY, 45 73 80 161 292 293 397 399-401 407 422

RAMSEUR, 224
RAMSEY, 349 395
RAMSOUR, 415 418
RANDALL, 353
RANKIN, 239 249 349 359
RANSOM, 201 221
RANSON, 273 274
RAPE, 56
RAREFIELD, 351
RATCHFORD, 342
RATERREE, 354
RAWLINSON, 72
RAY, 59 346 356
RAYNER, 346
REA, 54 172 292 334 336 337 349 354 357 358
READ, 401
REAH, 293
REAK, 56
REAMS, 357
REAVES, 356
REDFORD, 53
REDING, 339
REED, 55 56 152 345 347 350 358
REENHARDT, 337
REESE, 17 32 46 61 249 352 399 418 419 421 (bio) 418 419
REGLER, 358
REID, 60 64 307 343 344 347 350 351 354 355
RENER, 56
REYNOLDS, 338
RHEA, 59 142
RHETT, 247
RHINE, 344
RHODES, 338
RHVNE, 343
RHYNE, 350 353 356
RICE, 53 344 349 356
RICH, 56
RICHARDS, 340 356
RICHARDSON, 270 346 354 390
RICHLEY, 343
RIDDICK, 338
RIELER, 334
RIGGINS, 338
RIGHT, 54
RIGLER, 350
RINDAL, 353
RINEHART, 54 356
RINGSTAFF, 357
RIVAFINOLI, 199
RIVES, 343
ROBBINSON, 186
ROBERT, 192 410
ROBERTS, 340 342 349
ROBERTSON, 53 56 83
ROBINSON, 59 70 99 136 148 176 238 253 254 261 268 344 346 350 351 355 357 430 (bio) 253 254
ROBSON, 337
RODAY, 349
RODDEN, 340 347 355
RODE, 143
RODEN, 52
RODGERS, 192 280 349 350
ROGERS, 56 338 349
ROLMER, 338
RONE, 56 269 270
ROPER, 358
ROSE, 334
ROSICK, 347

SURNAME INDEX.

ROSS, 54 59 64 105 108 153 154 167 307 335 341 342 344 346 354 410
ROSZZELL, 342
ROUCHE, 271
ROUSE, 288
ROWDON, 394
ROWE, 54
ROWLAND, 203
ROZZELL, 334 343
RUDDOCK, 336 341 342
RUDISILL, 306 351
RUGEBY, 425
RUGELEY, 394
RUIS, 343
RUMAGE, 351
RUMELL, 344
RUNFELT, 339
RUPEL, 350 351
RUPERT, 387
RUSKIN, 207
RUSS, 349
RUSSEL, 65
RUSSELL, 344 346 355 358
RUTHERFORD, 78 86 105 109 110 395 403 404 412 418 423-425
RUTLIDGE, 241
SADDLER, 334
SADLER, 55 194 195 334
SAMMOND, 350
SAMPLE, 142 239 346 350 355
SANDERS, 337 338 344 356
SANFORD, 347
SANRING, 353
SAUNDERS, 95
SAVILLE, 336 343 346
SCALES, 223
SCHENCK, 146 229
SCHNEIDER, 337
SCONNEL, 408
SCOTT, 53 289 340 344 347 353
SEAGLE, 340
SEAGRAVES, 338
SECREST, 357
SEIGLE, 339
SELLERS, 350
SEVERS, 271 353
SEYMOUR, 233
SHAFFER, 349
SHANK, 54
SHANNONHOUSE, 225
SHANON, 53
SHARP, 53 78 81-83 86 351 358
SHARPE, 334 353 405
SHARPLY, 53
SHAVER, 350
SHAW, 57 105 228 300 334 340 346 350 351 354
SHEFFIELD, 345
SHEHORN, 56
SHELBEY, 56
SHELBY, 104 237 339 340 346 347 401
SHELVEY, 55
SHEPARD, 352
SHEPHERD, 53
SHEPPARD, 16 334
SHERIDAN, 338
SHERILL, 338
SHERMAN, 147 211
SHERRELL, 343
SHERRILL, 357
SHEVER, 53
SHIELDS, 352

SHINES, 155
SHIPLEY, 430
SHIPP, 145 146 300 (bio) 145 146
SHOE, 351
SHOEMAKER, 353
SHORE, 356
SHUMAN, 358
SIKES, 357
SIMMERELL, 241
SIMMON, 54
SIMMONS, 346
SIMPSON, 336 342 346 351 357
SIMS, 54 306 336 341
SINGLETON, 353 357
SIZER, 336
SKINNER, 338
SLADE, 55
SLAVE, Blind Dick 124 Cato 81 82 Lige 126 Ruth 81 82 Venus 81
SLOAN, 53 55 62 194 195 340 345 350 352 358
SLOOP, 344
SMART, 41 50 51 56 95 96
SMITH, 13 53 54 62 167 169 237 300 334 336 337 339 340 342-346 351-356 358 426
SMTH, 343
SNEAD, 105 344
SNEED, 54
SNIDER, 344
SOLOMON, 53 349 350
SOLON, 52
SOSAMAN, 352
SOSSAMAN, 356 376
SOULE, 268

SPARROW, 337 374
SPAWL, 338
SPEARS, 338 351
SPENCER, 105 286 345 352
SPRATT, 10 50 51 178 247 248 354 387 388 (bio) 247 248
SPRAVEY, 56
SPRINGS, 16 106 164 248 305 306 336 354 355 363 379 403
SQUIRE, 344
SQUIRES, 269 334 346 354
STACKS, 357
STALEY, 335 338
STALY, 338
STAMIE, 340
STAMY, 340
STANCEL, 357
STANCIL, 346
STANER, 353
STANFORD, 346 354
STANIS, 337
STANNING, 338
STARNES, 356
STARNS, 53 56 337 356
STATEN, 353
STEARNS, 336 350-352 357
STEDMAN, 393
STEEL, 55 56 334 336 346
STEELE, 336 337 342 357
STEGALL, 357
STEPHENS, 338 347
STEPHENSON, 346 354
STERLING, 345 397
STEVENSON, 53
STEWART, 53 56 239 293 338 351 355
STILL, 357

SURNAME INDEX.

STILLWELL, 340
STILWELL, 56
STINSON, 343 349 351 407
STITT, 250 268 292 294 350 354
STOKES, 55 353
STONE, 47 336 343 353 355
STORY, 56 57
STOUGH, 277 353
STOUT, 340 357
STOWE, 246 334 336 342 345 356
STRANTER, 356
STRONG, 144 145 (bio) 144 145
STROUP, 350
STROUPS, 338
STUART, 349 350
STUCKER, 337
STUNFORD, 53
STURGAN, 345
STUTTS, 340
SULIVAN, 355
SULLEVAN, 102
SULLIVAN, 53 338
SUMMERVILLE, 340
SUMMIMER, 53
SUMNEY, 344
SUMTER, 413
SURVIS, 358
SWAIN, 210
SWAN, 354
SWANN, 287 344
SWEAT, 355
SWIFT, 357
SYKES, 299
TAGGART, 344
TALLENT, 340
TALLY, 351
TALTON, 353
TARGART, 351
TARLETON, 86 110
TARLTON, 291 349
TART, 346
TASKER, 387
TATE, 119 335 336 358
TATUM, 299
TAYLOR, 56 157 158 168 228 237 238 273 306 334 335 337 341 342 345 349-351 354 355 358
TAYLOUS, 54
TEATE, 293
TEDDER, 346
TELL, 216
TEMPLETON, 353
TEPLETON, 353
TEREPAUGH, 340
TERRES, 347
TERRIS, 335 358
TEVEPAUGH, 354
THACKSTON, 78
THESTON, 430
THOMAS, 20 346 355 356
THOMASON, 342
THOMASSON, 346
THOMBURG, 345
THOMPSON, 10 53 54 56 272 335 337 344-346 349 428-430
THORNBURG, 357
THORNTON, 47
THUNER, 344
TICER, 345
TIDDY, 299 334
TIDWELL, 354
TIFFINS, 350
TISER, 358

TODD, 52 62 192 193 336 340 344 345 347 350 351 355 (bio) 192 193
TOMBERLEN, 337
TOMBERLIN, 56
TOMLIN, 337
TOMPKINS, 376
TORRANCE, 117 134 135 185 272 349 350 (bio) 134 135
TORRENCE, 13 334 337 345 358
TOVAM, 334
TOWERY, 340
TOWEY, 338
TOWRY, 340
TOWY, 340
TRADEWICE, 345
TRAIN, 56
TREDERMICK, 336
TRELOAN, 336
TRELOAR, 306
TRENHOLM, 171
TRIPLETTE, 353
TROTTER, 299 335 355
TROUTMAN, 356
TROWER, 346
TRYON, 26 75 105 199 401 402
TUCKER, 270
TUMMICE, 350
TURBIFIELD, 344
TURNER, 342 343 352 354 356
TURRENTINE, 159
TUTER, 56
TUTTS, 340
TYE, 337 353
UALLE, 337
UNDERWOOD, 337 340

VAIL, 307
VAKER, 338
VANCE, 98 147 203 209-213 215 216 220 221 295 300 337 338 353 381 (bio) 209-221
VANLANDINGHAM, 178
VANPELT, 337
VAUGHN, 338
VENO, 340
VICK, 56
VICKERS, 355 356
VICTOR, 267
VINCENT, 338
VINSENT, 56
WADDELL, 105 284 401 402
WAGNER, 335
WAGSTAFF, 350
WALKER, 52 53 55 59 60 63 137-139 190 337 343-345 350 352 354 (bio) 137-139
WALKUP, 250
WALL, 132
WALLACE, 52 101-103 121 123 225 226 241 291 292 337 340 342 349 350 356 358 408 (bio) 101-103 225 226
WALLIS, 55 56 62 82 168 254 255 258 281 282 293 407 (bio) 258
WALLS, 340 353
WALSH, 353
WALSTON, 347
WALTER, 54
WARING, 60 162 163 300 306 357 (bio) 162-164
WARREN, 340 344
WARSHAM, 350

SURNAME INDEX.

WARWICK, 354
WASHAM, 339
WASHINGTON, 44 45 73 79 89 169 391 403
WATSON, 53 156 157 173 290 337 354 392 395 (bio) 156 157
WATT, 175 288 336 340 344 345
WATTERS, 344 347
WATTS, 340 353 354
WEARING, 376
WEAVER, 338 345 358
WEBB, 57 347
WEDDINGTON, 350
WEDLOCK, 337
WEEKS, 347 354
WEIR, 53
WERNER, 337
WESLEY, 264 265
WEST, 55 340 342 347
WHALEN, 340
WHALON, 338
WHEELER, 83 106 392 405
WHITAKER, 337
WHITE, 55 61 62 139 169 171 172 234 289 307 337 340 345 349 350 354 355 358
WHITESIDES, 55 354
WHITLEY, 352 353
WIATT, 53
WIER, 83
WILEY, 52-54 335 336 345 350 357
WILKENSON, 355
WILKERSON, 338 344 355
WILKES, 299
WILKINSON, 56
WILL, 340
WILLIAM, 340
WILLIAM OF ORANGE, 216
WILLIAMS, 17 55 56 59 119 194 294 321 334 335 337 339 342 347 350 352 353 355 368 378 379
WILLIAMSON, 29 115 175 256 257 335 337 338 343 352 355-357 (bio) 256 257
WILLIFORD, 337
WILSON, 10 11 32 52 53 55-57 59 60-62 74 76 78 83 91-95 115 117 120 133 149-152 167 197 241 252-254 280 287 299 300 304 337-340 342 343 345 349 350 352 353 355-358 409-411 422 424 (bio) 91-94 149-152 252 253 409-411
WINDERS, 355
WINDLE, 335
WINECOFF, 339
WINENS, 55
WINES, 54
WINGATE, 336 342-345 354
WINSLOW, 10 82 83 86
WINSTON, 348
WINTHROP, 415
WITHERS, 342
WITHERSPOON, 345 347 400
WOLF, 347 352 354
WOLFE, 269 335 336 355
WOLFER, 345
WOMACK, 357
WOOD, 53 91
WOODALL, 16 56 349 352
WOODARD, 338
WORSHAM, 53 353
WORTHEN, 355

WRIGHT, 342 358
WRYFIELD, 345 358
WYATT, 334
WYNNS, 55
YANCY, 339
YANDLE, 337 349 350 352
YANDLES, 54 56
YATES, 120 142 172 306 376 391 (bio) 142 143
YAUNT, 339
YEARGAN, 347
YERBY, 56
YONT, 339
YORK, 343
YOUNG, 60 203 225 226 306 344 347 352 358 379
YOUNGBLOOD, 344
YOUNTS, 269 343 358
YOUTH, 347